Mathematical Land Use
Theory

Mathematical Land Use Theory

Edited by

George J. Papageorgiou
McMaster University

Lexington Books
D.C. Heath and Company
Lexington, Massachusetts
Toronto   London

Library of Congress Cataloging in Publication Data

Main entry under title:

Mathematical land use theory.

"A coded bibliography of the new urban economics, compiled by
A. Anas and D.S. Dendrinos": p. 293
1. Urban economics—Mathematical models—Addresses, essays, lectures. 2. Land—Mathematical models—Addresses, essays,
lectures. 3. Regional planning—Mathematical models—Addresses,
essays, lectures. I. Papageorgiou, George J.
HT321.M27   333.7'01'82   75-21303
ISBN 0-669-00164-3

Published simultaneously in Canada

Printed in the United States of America

International Standard Book Number: 0-669-00164-3

Library of Congress Catalog Card Number: 75-21303

To the Memory of ΙΓΠ

v

Contents

List of Figures

List of Tables

Preface

This volume grew out of a symposium on mathematical land use theory held at McMaster University during Spring 1975. The symposium became reality through the generous support of the Canada Council and McMaster University.

The idea was first raised by John Amson and Emilio Casetti. The underlying rationale was an urge to increase interaction between the different groups operating within this rich, ever-increasing, interdisciplinary field. As a result, scholars from the areas of business administration, economics, geography, mathematics, planning, and regional science are contributors to this volume. Nevertheless, it is significant to note that occupational differences do not imply differences in methodology: although interdisciplinary, the field is dominated by what is commonly referred to as "the new urban economics." Only three of the chapters do not fall within this category. Of course this reflects the background of the participants. However, in terms of current output of theoretical work, the proportions do not seem to be exceedingly misleading.

The structuring of references reflects the overwhelming dominance of the new urban economics. The bibliography at the end of this volume is an expansion of that by Anas and Dendrinos [1975]. Additional works have been inserted and noted with an asterisk. The result is an homogeneous, almost comprehensive bibliography of the new urban economics. At the end of each chapter, the dated references refer to this bibliography—for example, Strotz [1965]—while other references are given in full.

Introduction

The text is in two parts. The first part contains three general statements related to mathematical land use theory. The second contains fifteen chapters related to specific problems in the field.

Two of the general statements, by Harris and by Richardson, were prepared as position papers for a discussion that took place during the symposium. The discussion concerned the relevance of mathematical land use theory to applications. Both statements refer to mathematical land use theory in general. Quite naturally, Richardson focusses on the new urban economics. The new urban economics is the exclusive subject of the third general statement by Anas and Dendrinos. This review of the new urban economics was not prepared in conjunction with the symposium. It is however an integral part of this volume because, together with the other general statements, it provides a perspective of the field and a frame of reference within which the papers of the second part are organized. Indeed, the general statements and the bibliography on the new urban economics provide a foundation for the synthesis of the ideas, problems, and issues raised within this volume.

Operationality and policy relevance are the fundamental issues raised by Harris and Richardson. The same issues concerned Mills and Mackinnon [1973]. In relation to operationality, the consensus is that there must be an alternative to the simple, continuous, closed form paradigm of the new urban economics. Proposed alternatives range from discrete equivalents to computer simulation. There is general discontent on the issues of policy relevance. Harris states that probably ". . . normative applications arouse the widest dispute and distrust among decision makers. . . ." Richardson states that ". . . the new urban economics have already attracted some urban economists away from the policy end of the spectrum toward the theory end" and that he sees ". . . little prospect of (the new urban economics) being applied in the sense of offering direct insights into the solution of urban problems or of being much help to planners". Now these are hard criticisms and they may be true—for the time being. Nevertheless, to project them into the future, as Richardson does, constitutes an article of faith—faith that we are not ready to share. Instead, we choose to believe that these difficulties reflect the state of the art rather than inherent shortcomings in philosophy and direction.

Such an aura of guarded optimism can be supported by the existing accomplishments, problems, and issues surrounding the normative models of the new urban economics as described in the chapter by Anas and Dendrinos. This detailed report on the state of the art makes a clear distinction between positive and normative models of the new urban economics. The former are labelled first generation, the latter second generation models. There is also a statement on third generation developments, mostly projecting into the future and partially overlapping with the second generation. One third generation area is that of urban dynamics.

The chapters of the second part follow roughly this order suggested by Anas and Dendrinos: positive, normative, dynamic. Several issues discussed in the general statements appear in the chapters. For example, positive models raise issues of spatial income distribution and of locational interdependence among different land uses; normative models raise issues of policy relevance and of congestion. Finally, both types raise the issue of public goods. Such issues provide an adequate link between the general statements of the first part and the chapters of the second part. Furthermore, such issues provide the background upon which the ensuing discussion is organized.

The first two chapters of the second part, can be viewed as related to Wheaton's [1974a] recent comparative static analysis of the monocentric city. Like Wheaton, both papers adopt the standard long-run equilibrium model as a basis for comparative statics of a closed city. The contribution by Hartwick, Schweizer, and Varaiya complements Wheaton's analysis by extending it to the case of several classes of residential locators. These classes have such preference structures that they would be located away from the center in the order of increasing income and that higher income households would consume more land than lower income households. Naturally, the most interesting issue concerns the impact of changes within one class upon the welfare and locational extent of the other classes. The authors derived the counterintuitive result that increases in the income or size of a richer class have opposing effects on a poorer class. In particular, increasing the income of a class increases the utilities of the poorer classes while it decreases the utilities of the richer classes, whereas increasing the size of a class decreases the utility of all classes. This result, which has unexpected social welfare implications, loses some of its surprise value when the authors continue to show, through numerical calculations, that the positive effect on the poor due to the income increase of the richer class is far smaller than the negative effect due to the size increase of the richer class. The chapter demonstrates the ability of mathematical land use theory to uncover counterintuitive truths through what Solow [1973a] has called "pencil and paper analysis," yet at the same time show that numerical verification of these truths is necessary before any policy implications can be drawn. Large-scale modeling with its cumbersome empirical requirements has failed all too often in demonstrating this flexibility of discovery and verification.

In the second chapter, Miron obtains a specific approximate relationship between land rents and city size. He tests the validity of the approximate relation by comparing its predictive ability to that of the more cumbersome exact relation arising out of the Cobb-Douglas model. This too is an example of the use of numerical analysis in operationalizing the results of the new urban economics. Miron's approach can be used in narrowing down a set of arbitrarily postulated descriptive models to a theoretically meaningful few which can be used in empirical analysis.

The next four contributions share the ambition of examining urban structure patterns that provide an alternative to the standard monocentric model with the sharply segregated and noninteracting sets of locators. Amson's chapter stands separately within this group in that concepts from physics are used to develop a model of phenomena that are given an urban locational interpretation. These phenomena involve interactions among types of "populations" and, thus, bear resemblence to locational patterns in a multisectoral urban economy. Smith's commentary focuses on this generality, characteristic to the Amson chapter. It correctly implies that Amson has developed a model of models, a construct abstracting from the context-specific nature of particular problems to concentrate upon their underlying, fundamental structure. Without explaining urban microeconomic behavior, Amson succeeds in creating a picture reminiscent of urban structure and urban interactions.

Beckmann's contribution is a pleasant departure from the strictly radial commuting pattern that forms the basis of the standard model. We are instead invited to think of a linear city in which each household makes the same number of trips to every other point within the city for purposes such as shopping, recreation, and social visits. Beckmann compares the structure of this dispersed city with that of the centralized monocentric city which has the same population and physical extent. His main conclusions are that densities at the center of the dispersed city form a smooth peak and that they are lower than the corresponding densities of the centralized city. Comparing transport costs in his dispersed city with those generated by a dispersed city of uniform population density, Beckmann finds that aggregate transport costs are substantially lower in the former.

Capozza's amendment of the standard monocentric model is of a different nature. He aims at deriving an outcome in which two land uses are integrated in at least part of a circular city. The single center plays a major role in Capozza's model: firms are attracted to it because of agglomeration economies and are repelled from it since at more peripheral locations they could pay lower wages because of their higher proximity to commuting workers. Neither of these forces are derived through an explicit analysis of shipment and commuting patterns, but rather, exogenous agglomeration savings and wage-distance schedules are specified. There are three assumptions in the chapter that determine an integrated employment-population ring between the two segregated rings. These are that firms operate according to a fixed coefficient technology, that there is a uniform distribution of firms classified according to the slopes of their bid rent functions, and, most crucially, that the residential bid rent structure is exogenously given as a determinant of the opportunity cost of land for nonresidential use. This last idea is particularly interesting and may be closer to realism than the standard profit maximizing specification of firm behavior. As there is no factor substitution, if the number of firms cannot exhaust the entire land in a residential ring, a mixture of industry and residence results. Capozza's chapter relates to the attempts by Mills [1970] and Goldstein and Moses [1975]. The former derived the conditions under which integration of population with cost minimizing fixed coefficient technology is efficient. Travel and shipment patterns were explicitly analyzed. The latter, quite recent contribution encroaches upon urban agglomeration—a new urban economist's nightmare—by explicitly analyzing the location of interdependent land uses and intermediate goods shipments within a monocentric context.

A quest for realism characterizes the chapter by Papageorgiou. As a variant to the monocentric form, ideas of central place theory are introduced leading to a multinuclear structure similar to the one discussed in Mills and Mackinnon [1973] and in Richardson's chapter. An exogenous externality reflecting either amenity resources, public goods, or both is also introduced. Consumer behavior is more sophisticated than is traditional and the society is represented by a continuum of incomes. The city is open. The deep impact of the externality upon the spatial range of individuals is emphasized in a section related to a given price system. In the special case of a price system that leads to a state of spatial equilibrium the results depart from the standard paradigm. The spatial distribution of incomes is more flexible than the usual rigid concentric arrangement. The form of the rent gradients contains many peaks. The externality may cause a reversal of the rent gradient discussed in Richardson's chapter. It is significant that positively sloped rent gradients can also be observed and explained within the entirely different dynamic frameworks of Muth, Pines, and Anas.

In the next chapter, Fisch examines what may be the most important urban policy issue: the provision and financing of public goods. The Anas-Dendrinos survey provides a discussion of this issue based upon the work of Barr [1972, 1973] which addresses both the intraurban and the interurban (Tiebout) aspects of public goods provision. The aim of Fisch is to reconsider the Tiebout hypotheses by deriving the spatial equilibrium conditions for such a market of public goods. He analyzes the spatial dimensions of public goods, their degree of "localness," and their impact on land values. He shows that Tiebout's optimal community size hypothesis is implicit in the equilibrium outcome and that land rent is a poor indicator of Tiebout's equilibrium conditions.

The chapters by Alao and Livesey emerge as a justifiable reaction to the cursory attention the CBD has received in both equilibrium and optimum models, particularly those second generation developments that have so exhaustively examined the traffic congestion issue. This neglect has manifested itself in two striking inconsistencies. The first of these appears in the Dixit [1973] paper where a macro CBD model is combined with the micro residential ring model. Such a combination is quite unsatisfactory since Dixit has to argue that increasing returns in the CBD are due to economies external to the firms. The model implies that the CBD is one huge plant operating at increasing returns to scale. The second inconsistency appears in the papers of Sheshinski [1973] and Livesey [1973] who, in amending the Mills-deFerranti [1971] cost-minimizing analysis of the residential sector, assumed the mathematically natural, but quite unrealistic, travel behavior implying that all workers converge at the edge of the CBD simultaneously. This might be acceptable in relation to the Dixit conception of the one-factory CBD but less so in the Sheshinski-Livesey models where there is further travel within the CBD. Alao is concerned with the first inconsistency. He argues that transport economics and central port facilities are sufficient justification of CBD existence despite constant returns to scale in production. This is reminiscent of Mills [1967] and provides a consistent micro model of the CBD, though does not explicitly show how the agglomeration arguments imply increasing returns in production. Apart from his concern with CBD texture, Alao provides a useful review of optimum versus equilibrium analysis in the presence of externalities. Livesey is concerned with both conceptual inconsistencies. He constructs several models of the CBD with an aggregated (à la Dixit) production function and with disaggregated, location specific production functions. He also analyzes aggregate social profit maximization vis-à-vis aggregate social cost minimization.

The next group of chapters constitutes a departure from static analysis. Although developed completely independently, all three papers show agreement in basic premises and results. This is true despite substantial differences in formulation and in the specific problems examined. For example, Pines develops an optimum analysis, while both Muth and Anas focus on models of the urban housing market. While Muth considers space only implicitly, Anas considers both time and space explicitly. Both Pines and Anas derive recursive results and difference equations by focusing on a two-stage analysis of urban growth, whereas Muth capitalizes on his suppression of space and performs an analysis that relies solely on differential calculus. All three authors would seem to agree that dynamic urban analyses are not possible without treating housing capital as durable. This forms the common basis of the three chapters. Pines assumes infinite capital adjustment costs (or perfect durability) and a myopic behavior on the part of the planner. Within the market context, Anas also postulates myopic households and housing developers but, later, relaxes both the perfect durability and the myopic assumptions by introducing finite demolition costs and expectations. Muth's analysis involves foresight from the very beginning and accounts for expenditures on the durable as well as the variable components of housing. A result derived by both Pines and Anas is that the discontinuous nature of stage by stage growth implies jumps in the relevant spatial distribution profiles. All three authors find that densities need not always rise with accessibility but could decline as well. (In Muth's chapter, age of housing is a proxy of accessibility.) Anas shows the particular conditions that lead to this and to positively sloped rent gradients for open and closed cities. In his model, housing abandonment is also discussed and shown to be a possible symptom of rising household welfare.

It is quite clear from these chapters that the standard static modeling framework is at a serious disadvantage compared to the dynamic framework which recognizes the aspects of capital durability and the intertemporal nature of private investment and planning decisions. It seems that some progress has been made since Mills and Mackinnon [1973] were emphasizing the difficulty of constructing dynamic models.

Within the context of this volume, the last chapter by Webber stands by itself. The frame of reference is entropy, to many an alien, an easily misunderstood, yet evergrowing field that transcends diverse disciplines and classes of phenomena, a credible manifestation of the program and principles set forth by general systems theory. The main result of this chapter is the demonstration that the entropy paradigm may be interpreted as emerging from consistent and general logical principles. This interpretation resolves several raging controversies at once: the views that entropy models are merely analogies drawn from statistical mechanics, that they are based on the assumption of random behavior, that they only describe systems at equilibrium, that they are predicated on equal a priori probabilities, and that they can emcompass only independent events, seem to be views of the past.

G.J. Papageorgiou
A. Anas

Part I

1

Notes on the Relation Between Mathematical Land Use Theory and Public Policy Applications

Britton Harris

In the field of land use planning, and urban policy in general, there are two or three principal types of applications for which we judge mathematical models to be of some considerable interest. The first of these areas has to do with public and private urban capital investment and with the reservation of land for later uses or for open space. These decisions are important because urban capital has a long life and the decisions become irreversible. Decisions of this type are, by their nature, particularistic and detailed. A slightly different use of models has to do with overall policy decisions that influence the location of capital investments and activities within the metropolitan region. A special case of such models may be the dynamic models that are used to identify or predict catastrophic situations such as large-scale urban blight and abandonment, hopeless transportation congestion, or disastrous pollution. These broad-brush models may also have more direct and simple uses dealing with such things as land use controls and the pricing of government services. Finally, there are spatial models of system function, which may be useful in planning operating systems such as health, education, welfare, and public protection.

The practitioner who is interested in these application-oriented problems is not concerned with theory per se, but makes use of models and other operational instruments for dealing with his problems. The academic researcher, on the other hand, is interested in exploring the structure of reality and the appropriate forms of abstract definition of that reality. In the experimental sense, one of the best means available for testing hypotheses is also models. Therefore, models play an intermediate role between theory and application, and, as a matter of convenience in discourse, the relation between theory and practice is clarified and well mediated by constant reference to the intervening activity of modeling.

The concerns of the practitioner in urban management and planning introduce two confusing elements with respect to these relationships. The concern with quick results and a "practical" approach has led to the widespread development of purely descriptive models whose supposed validity is tested in a very pragmatic and simplistic way. Such purely descriptive models are excluded by definition from considerations of the

Britton Harris is a member of the Department of City and Regional Planning, University of Pennsylvania.

relevance of land use theory. In the second place, despite the long-run consequences of urban investment and its environmental impacts, many policymakers profess to be concerned only with short-run and incremental decision making. The assessment of long-term impacts of present and planned actions is certainly a proper intellectual concern for academic investigators, as well as for any citizen who believes such matters to be important. The long-run impact of long-run investigations on policymaking may be indirect, but we are not obligated to accept the view of present bureaucrats and officials as to what aspects of theory are important.

We now have to look at the nature of "mathematical land use theory." For the present discussion, mathematical land use models can be divided into four groups by taking two different cuts at the problem. First, models are either positive or normative, although every normative model contains a (possibly truncated) positive model. Some models can play a dual role in this context. In the second place, models can be abstract or detailed. The accompanying diagram gives some examples of how existing models and theories might be placed in this four-way classification.

	Positive	Normative
Abstract	Forrester[2]	Mills[4]
Detailed	Ingram, et al.[3]	Schlager[5]

Theories and models represent successive abstractions from the real world. These abstractions are intended to capture the essential nature of the phenomena with which they deal, but such abstractions may once again be at different levels of detail. In scientific work, the essential function of these abstractions is to generate hypotheses about previously unobserved phenomena. In practical applications, the essential purpose is similar—to make predictions about what will happen under previously unobserved circumstances. The core question with respect to relevance thus becomes how accurately theories and models are able to cope with new circumstances. This requirement demands a "correct" specification of the theory, a proper measurement of its relation to unobserved hypothetical phenomena.

The question arises as to whether land use theories developed in this context might need to be mathematical. Viewing this from a purely operational point of view, we can see three different levels at which mathematics is relevant to land use theories and models.

First, at a purely observational level, mathematics is needed to interpret the complex reality with which social science is concerned. There are many sciences—such as sociology, psychology, biology, and geology—in which theories of measurement and statistical analysis have proved to be essential mathematical tools in the development of disciplinary theory. This situation has obtained even though the latter theories themselves have been systematic and logical. For those experienced with statistical investigations, it is quite clear that there is a strong interaction between statistical analysis and theory building. Given a set of data, many investigators look for ways of presenting the data that will embody linear or clearly understandable relationships. Contrariwise, what to look for and how to organize and interpret the data is strongly influenced by theory even though the theory may not be mathematical. In a certain sense, since a a statistical test cannot be made without a model, the necessity for statistical interpretation enforces at a simple level the mathematization of verbal theories.

At a second level, the interrelationship among phenomena of interest and between them and their environment may be systematized and formulated mathematically in such a way as to withstand more rigorous analysis and to sustain more precise predictions. Models in economics, mathematical ecology, chemistry, and physics, for example, are usually of this type. Disciplinary paradigms of many of the social sciences are not as rigorous or as quantitative as those of the physical sciences. Some would maintain that sociology, anthropology, and political science are in the ''preparadigmatic'' phase of disciplinary development. For this reason, the formulation of mathematical theories is constantly involved, even if only peripherally, with the most basic paradigmatic disputes within the disciplines. In particular reference to the issues for which public policymakers need predictions, it is still too early to say that these disciplines have thoroughly and conscientiously investigated whether such predictions are indeed possible.

At a third level, normative models require optimization procedures that cannot be systematically and rigorously undertaken unless the second level of theory formulation has been achieved. These normative models require in addition optimization procedures that may be formally based on mathematical programming. This difficult area is complicated by the intricate and extended nature of land use systems and by the fact that optimization is over discrete space in a situation which is likely to yield many local optima.

Perhaps the application of normative models arouses the widest dispute and distrust amongst decision makers and some social scientists. The optimization of these models may fail, in the broader sense, for a number of reasons. The predictive models on which they rely may be too weak, especially in the face of major uncertainties. Such uncertainty suggests incremental decision making which is normative only in a very narrow sense and which leaves unanswered questions about major investments and large-scale policies with long-term effects. In order to develop a normative model, a social objective function must be formulated. This obviously introduces problems of ethics, politics, and special interest that may be mathematically intractable or unapproachable. Finally, a systematic normative model assumes that the available measures constitute a well-defined decision space. In the actual process of planning, new measures may be discovered or invented, and this assumption of mathematical optimization is violated.

Both mathematics and computer science may make an independent contribution, in that new discoveries in these fields may facilitate the solution of more and more difficult problems in the fields of statistical estimation, simulation, and optimization. It is also true that the discovery of any given mathematical method—such as linear programming or the multinomial logit model—may have widespread applications in a number of fields. Thus, the knowledge of mathematical methods is cumulative and may be transferable. This is not to say, however, that the correct approach to problems is most often, or even frequently, to design theories and models to fit existing mathematics. Quite frequently the mathematics must be invented to be in proper conformity with the presumed models.

Until very recently, trends in modeling urban development have had two principal sources. The particularistic urban descriptive models arising out of the transportation studies of the fifties provide many interesting insights and are somewhat attuned to the needs of public decision making, but they do not meet the standards of rigor which have been implicitly set forth above. On the other hand, the models of the new urban economics attempt to combine the insights of Alonso[1] and Wingo[6] with respect to urban location with the elegance and compactness of general equilibrium theory and economic growth theory. The new urban economics approach is very well represented in the papers at this conference, and this whole body of work demonstrates both the strength and the weakness of its method. There is a strong tendency to prefer closed-form solutions to the models developed in urban economics. Such a preference is based not only on a psychological need for closure, but more significantly on the rigorous nature of such solutions. On the other hand, this approach requires an extraordinary number of simplifying assumptions as to the structure of the metropolitan area, as to socioeconomic and behavioral differentiation, as to social objectives, and as to political feasibility. From the point of view of the decision maker, these somewhat arbitrary assumptions render the conclusions of modeling suspect. Clearly for large complex systems, for complex objectives, and for particularistic decisions, there must be a new synthesis of simplified mathematical modeling of the new urban economics variety and of descriptive computer-based modeling of the transportation study variety. The difficult problem is to avoid brute-force solutions and to achieve some degree of mathematical elegance and originality without a sacrifice of realism and relevance.

Notes

1. W. Alonso [1964].

2. J.W. Forrester, 1969, *Urban Dynamics*. Cambridge: MIT Press.

3. Ingram, G., et al., 1972, *The Detroit Prototype of the NBER Urban Simulation Model*. New York: National Bureau of Economic Research.

4. E.S. Mills [1972b].

5. Schlager, K., 1968, "Construction of Models," *Urban Development Models, Special Report 97*. Washington, D.C.: Highway Research Board.

6. L. Wingo, Jr. [1961b].

2

Relevance of Mathematical Land Use Theory to Applications

Harry W. Richardson

The following comments are limited to one branch of mathematical land use theory—the area of urban economics that has been labeled "the new urban economics," NUE,[a] by Mills and MacKinnon.[28] This field is, of course, rather broader than economics, since many with disciplinary bases outside economics have made notable contributions. We have fewer reservations about the practicality of other branches of mathematical land use analysis, e.g., the planning models area covered by Wilson,[46] and the reservations we do have are somewhat different. However, the narrower focus of these comments is not inappropriate since most of the chapters in this volume fall within the NUE classification.

"Applications" are defined here as referring to both empirical testing and to urban policy and planning applications. The criticisms discussed here are directed to the questions of operationality, utility, and policy relevance, and there is no intention to downgrade the intrinsic intellectual interest, elegance, and theoretical contributions of work in this area.

Unlike most contributions to this volume, the perspective here is that of an (academic) consumer rather than that of a producer. This means that this author's judgment of the value of this field is colored by his assessment of its help in providing answers to, or at least aiding understanding of, those problems within urban economics considered by him to be important. Many of these problems are assumed away by the initial assumptions of NUE models.

Theoretical Framework

There would be no value in a theory that closely represented reality in detail. The essence of theory is simplicity, and economists tend to judge the quality of a theory by its simplicity and elegance. If theory is studied for its own sake, this criterion makes sense. An economic model—like a master game of chess—may be admired for its beauty. But if theories are also to be

Harry W. Richardson is a member of the Department of Economics, University of Southern California, Los Angeles.

[a] Opinions disagree on the seminal origins of NUE. The slate of chief candidates might include Alonso,[2] Beckmann,[8] Mills,[25] Muth,[31] and Strotz.[45]

9

judged by their operational potential and by their value to planners and policymakers, the criteria have to be broader. In particular, the overlap between simplicity and relevance may be very small. NUE models are undoubtedly a radical simplication of that complex phenomenon—the modern city. The assumptions common to most of the models are rather drastic: a monocentric city; rigid segregation of land uses with production in the CBD and residences in the surrounding rings; the ubiquity of transportation routes; the absence of locational interdependence; the continuity and smoothness of rent and density gradients; and the underlying reliance on competitive forces, marginal adjustments, and, at best, a passive role for a planning authority.[b]

These simplifications would have been acceptable if they had been a prerequisite for the formulation of a testable model, and if the tests carried out had yielded sound predictions. There have been no such tests. The closest approximation has been simple numerical solutions which have, in the opinion of the designers of the model, generated plausible findings compatible with the predictions of the older, partial, and less mathematical theories and with available empirical evidence. However, these predictions tend to be too general, e.g., a negative rent gradient or the poor living closer in than the rich. Moreover, as pointed out below, some of these general predictions are not as universally applicable as is sometimes thought. To this extent, the capacity to generate the standard predictions is a weakness and an indication of the theory's restrictiveness or the theorists' blinkered outlook, rather than testimony to its soundness.

A related problem is that if a theoretical framework is being judged for policy relevance, assumptions that oversimplify—a plus point for neat and elegant theory—may be unhelpful. First, policy is concerned inter alia with identifying strategic levers for bringing about change, and it is necessary to quantify the impacts that follow from exerting specific degrees of pressure to these levers. The qualitative results so highly prized by pure theorists are insufficiently precise for the policymaker. Second, urban policy has always to keep locational interdependencies at the forefront. The more important of these are assumed away in NUE. Third, policy is applied in a particular institutional context. NUE either ignores this or makes implicit institutional assumptions that frequently conflict with reality.

An interesting analogy has been drawn between NUE and macroeconomics. This is that the abstract models of NUE may eventually be justified because they will lead to practical, useful policy models, in the same way as basic macroeconomic theory has led to the development of national short-run forecasting models. Solow notes that "The relation seems closely analogous to that in macroeconomics, between the large

[b] A passive role is assumed, at least, in the sense of zoning, lot size restrictions, acquisition of land for public uses, and so on. Some of the models do allow for a transportation authority with the power to levy congestion tolls on roads.

econometric models on the one hand and the tradition of small-scale macroeconomic theory—whether mathematical, graphical, or verbal—on the other'' (Solow,[44] p. 267).

This argument relies more on fond hope than on reasoned logic. First, there are big differences between macroeconomic and urban (especially NUE) models that make the transition to applications much more problematic in the latter case. The macroeconomic models (i) are linear; (ii) use more easily measurable variables; (iii) include simple, key control variables (e.g., the level of government expenditures, the tax rate) that have no direct parallel in NUE; and (iv) are nonspatial and, hence, are much easier both to model and to calibrate.

Second, there is another theoretical subfield in macroeconomics that is even less encouraging to the ''progress to applications'' thesis. This is, of course, aggregate growth theory. Is NUE closer to the simple Keynesian macroeconomic model or to the aggregate growth models? The parallels between NUE and aggregate growth theory are very close: a standard model where slight changes in the assumptions yield marginally differentiated results; the same mathematical tools (calculus of variations, optimal control theory); a similar degree of abstraction with models that are notable, above all, for the stark—though attractive—simplicity of their assumptions; and the two games even share some of the same players. Aggregate growth theory has not led to applications, and it has not been helpful to policymakers. Its main output has been displays of ''neoclassical pyrotechnics,''—an observed feature of the early NUE models.[28]

Some Problems of NUE Models

Though we cannot expect a general theoretical framework to be directly useful for the analysis of detailed planning problems, it would be helpful if the theory could be expressed in terms (level of disaggregation, treatment of time dimension, etc.) within which these problems could, at least, be discussed. Many major planning problems fall into two categories: (i) predictions of overall urban change using a forecasting model and (ii) studies of changes in the spatial structure at the intraurban level (e.g., the dynamics of land use competition between residences and nonresidences; neighborhood upgrading and blight; the design of transportation systems, capacities, and networks; the growth and planning of secondary subcenters within metropolitan areas).

NUE has no insights—however broad—to offer on these questions, primarily because the models do not include time and they trivialize space (one dimension rather than two or, better still, three). Despite the limitations of simple models, such as the Lowry model,[24] they have provided planners with approximate forecasts of the spatial allocative changes consequent upon given increments of overall urban growth, even if they have failed to say very much about the nature of the adjustment paths. The closest that NUE models can come to forecasting is by exploring parameter changes in a sensitivity analysis using numerical methods.

The value of NUE for intraurban analysis is severely restricted by its one-dimensional linear ray assumption and hence its inability to deal with intraurban zones. In fact, zones would not have much of a role in NUE models because of its rigid land use segregation. It is difficult to justify its claimed virtue as a *competitive* model of land use because it rules out, by assumption, the more important aspects of this competition—namely, the competition between residential and commercial use. Competition for land in the NUE model is between housing and roads. However, this is a distorted competitive market because road development is a public sector function wherein land is frequently acquired compulsorily at purchase prices that are not "true" market prices.

A satisfactory competitive model of land use would require, in our view:

1. Two-dimensional zones permitting analysis of neighborhood change and the growth of subcenters via nonresidential takeovers or expansion of noncentral sites
2. Different types of nonresidential land use with varying site and accessibility requirements
   a. large commercial and office establishments mainly in the CBD
   b. Large-scale retail establishments, either in the CBD or at suburban agglomerations
   c. manufacturing, competing with housing and agriculture on the urban fringe
   d. small retail establishments interspersed with residences at varying distances from the CBD
3. Due allowance for the constraints on the operation of market forces
   a. occupation of most sites, sluggishness of change due to long leases and locational inertia, etc.
   b. the degree of control exerted over the urban land market by the planning authority (zoning, lot size standards, building codes, planning permits
   c. imperfections in competition for other economic and social reasons such as residential segregation theory, dual housing and labor markets for blacks and whites, environmental quality differences in neighborhoods which affect property values irregularly with dis-

tance, heterogeneity of housing (ignored because housing demand is usually treated as the demand for land),[c] and locational interdependence.

The argument, of course, is not that all these considerations should be taken into account in detail, for that would be to expect theory to replicate reality, but rather that urban models should focus on the key elements of land use competition and that they should recognize the existence of constraints on competitition (inertia constraints, adjustments lags, etc.). These features can probably be handled much more easily with, say, a system simulation model than with a neoclassical competitive equilibrium model.

Monocentricity

A major weakness of the standard NUE model is its monocentricity and the corollary assumption of a single CBD workplace.

The assumption of a single employment center has been maintained by the urban economists in the face of increasing decentralization, and a decline of the role of the CBD as the single focus of productive activity. It has survived despite its increasing irrelevance because it produces simplifications in the analysis and permits important results to be derived which would be difficult to obtain otherwise . . . this assumption leads to unrealistic conclusions about the spatial structure of cities. Ultimately, it must be rejected in order to remove inconsistencies from the theory (p. 105).[4]

The few empirical studies that have been carried out tend to reinforce this conclusion. For instance, Angel and Hyman themselves found that the transport expenditures incurred by households at different residential locations were very different from those to be expected if all jobs were centralized, with transport costs incurred by households close to the CBD much higher than those in the monocentric model, while households living at distances far from the city center incurred, on an average, much lower transport expenditures than predicted by the monocentric model. These findings imply that many workplaces are decentralized. The "exclusive zoning hypothesis,"—that workplaces are confined to a central core surrounded by a residential ring—was found deficient, in both nineteenth-century Chicago[15] and a sample of modern American cities.[12] Empirical

[c] Introducing housing would raise serious difficulties. If the housing sector is treated properly, housing supply must be considered as well as housing demand. Unless the housing stock is constant, this implies at least one type of decentralized workplaces so that one class of workers—construction workers—do not have to commute to the CBD. Solving NUE models becomes very difficult if the single CBD workplace assumption is dropped.

estimates of employment density gradients confirm the existence of decentralized workplaces and of increasing decentralization over time.[20,27] These empirical findings have yet to have much of an impact on the reformulation of NUE theories.

There are two somewhat different approaches to relaxing the assumption of the monocentric city. One is to develop a multicentric locational framework; the other is to construct a model of a more general decentralized city where workplaces are located outside the CBD though not necessarily clustering to form subcenters. The complications introduced with multicentricity are severe, particularly from the point of view of mathematical tractability. The single workplace is a key assumption for compressing two dimensions into one, unless jobs are equally distributed radially—an implausible case. If multiple centers are permitted, an early extension is to permit specialization of function among an intraurban hierarchy of centers, which means abandoning the analytical convenience of the composite consumption good assumption. With multiple goods and specialization among centers, a satisfactory model would need to accommodate intrametropolitan freight shipments as well as coping with more complex commuting patterns. It consequently becomes much more difficult to obtain determinate solutions, and rent and density surfaces may no longer be smooth and differentiable.

Papageorgiou and Casetti[37] and Papageorgiou[36] have carried out some preliminary work on residential spatial structure in a multicentric system, in the latter study for a continuous income distribution. Hartwick and Hartwick generalized a Mills-type linear programming model to deal with multiple centers and intermediate goods.[18] Lave showed that decentralization becomes efficient when freight and commuting costs and rent savings outweigh agglomeration economies.[22] Interestingly, his model suggests that once the monopoly of the CBD breaks up, several centers rather than merely two develop. This is consistent with what happens in the real world. The model tends to overproduce centers, but this is due to its simplified treatment of the city as a workplace, production locus, and shopping center rather than as a complex system for economic and social interaction. The failure hitherto to develop a fully satisfactory subcentering model is probably due to an incomplete understanding of the agglomeration process. To explain the decline of the CBD it is important to know why it grew in the first place. Although there has been much diffuse analysis of agglomeration economies and a few interesting insights into the ''public goods'' aspects of city centers (see Artle[5], for example) most NUE modelers—with a few exceptions[1,13,23]—have treated the CBD as having no intrinsic interest, but as being merely a dumping ground for commuters. Since the growth of secondary centers in a metropolitan area is part of a dynamic process, the deficiencies of static models are quite glaring on this point.

More general decentralized land use models have not generated much attention. Niedercorn showed how the nonresidential demand for land may generate a negative exponential rental gradient, so that allowing for mixed land uses need not destroy the basic findings of the standard model.[33] Beckmann allows jobs to be distributed in the same way as population and demonstrates that introducing a substitute agglomerating factor (the need for social interaction, c.f. Artle's "Agora model"[5] still leads to a negative density gradient, though the "peaking" at the center is much less pronounced than in the single CBD workplace model.[9] There remains much work to be done in this area. These observations suggest that there is still much to be achieved by extensions of the theory; one justification for the slow pace of applications so far is that testing incomplete models would be premature.

Residential Rent Gradient

One advantage of NUE models is that they produce results consistent with data from real cities and with the findings of earlier urban theory. An example worth examining is that of the negative residential rent gradient, accepted by NUE (and most other urban) modelers as beyond dispute, apart from minor quibbles as to whether the rent function is exponential or not.[19]

In fact, there are several reasons why the residential rent function may be positive, or at least much more irregular than is usually implied. First, although the origins of the negative rent function derive from the Von Thünen model, it has recently been shown that this does not follow from Von Thünen's own assumptions.[6] Rents (profits) may increase with distance if money wages decline with distance faster than transport costs. Von Thünen assumed that real wages are constant everywhere, and it is this assumption that opens the door to positively inclined sections on the rent gradient (money wages fall with distance because food is more expensive close to city center).

Second, some empirical research has shown that residential property values and rents may increase with distance.[41,42,47] In one study, for instance, a quadratic distance function yielded the best fit.[41] One explanation of the predominance of negative rent gradients is the competition of nonresidential land uses which boosts the demand for land close to the city center. This competition is expressly ruled out in NUE models. Another important factor is that NUE, in particular, and urban land rent theory, in general, treat urban rent solely as location rent with increasing distance from the CBD being associated with reductions in accessibility and hence with lower rents.

Thus, a third objection to the negative rent gradient prediction is that it is derived from a very narrow view of the determinants of urban residential rents. There may be other influences on residential property values and rents that tend to make them increase with distance.[d] One of these is environmental and neighborhood quality characteristics. For operational purposes, these may be represented by the surrogate measure of low density.[29,46] The evidence for a negative density gradient is very strong. Theoretically, therefore, declining location rent with increasing distance is associated with rising "externality rent".[40] In other words, a fall in accessibility to the CBD is accompanied by the countervailing advantage of improvement in neighborhood and environmental quality. Total rents may decline or increase with distance according to the relative weight of the two effects, which depends on the values of the parameters. It is possible to introduce externality rent and environmental quality variables into NUE models, and there have been a few hints of how this might be done.[36,40] However, the fact that such models have not yet been fully analyzed suggests that the theory is still in an underdeveloped state and not yet ripe for empirical testing.

Alternatives

This writer's prejudice is that urban economics should be primarily a policy-oriented field, and we are not convinced that NUE has much to offer as a guide to policymakers. Indeed, NUE has already attracted some urban economists away from the policy end of the spectrum towards the theory end. That would be all right if the theories developed had important policy variables in them. Apart from transportation policy instruments dealing with a very abstract model of the transportation system, pollution and congestion levies, and a few other pricing strategies there are few signs of this type of theory in NUE. On the contrary, the choice of structure of NUE models appears to have been determined by what is mathematically manipulable rather than by what would aid policymakers the most. When NUE models contain policy instruments these are almost always the pricing tools and the user charges that betray their neoclassical origins.

A similar problem is that in order to obtain solutions to the differential equations of NUE models, the theorists often have to assume tha particular functions are of a very simple and highly specific form (e.g., the logarithmic utility function). The simulation models, on the other hand, allow considerable experimentation with the parameters and form of functional relationships once the basic model has been set up. Examples include the elas-

---

[d] Apart from the factors discussed here, Rose-Ackerman has shown how racial residential preferences may lead to a positive section on the rent gradient.[43] More generally, "group" rather than "individual household" residential location decisions may yield different results from those of the standard model.[21]

ticities of demand for housing, technology (in housing, production, or transportation), and the structure of the transportation system. These specifics determine the outcome when a policy instrument is introduced. The kind of prediction possible with NUE models—e.g., a congestion toll on road use will result in a smaller city—is too general to be of practical help. The real question is how the spatial structure of the city would change, over what time period, and in what particular ways.

Pessimism about the operational potential of NUE is reinforced by the belief that some of the other mathematical approaches to urban analysis offer much more scope for applications. These alternative approaches are frequently denigrated by economic theorists because they are "inelegant" and "empirical." That may be so, but they have the offsetting advantages that they can be, and in many cases have been, applied, and that they are useful to planners and urban policymakers. Examples include the linear programming models suggested by Mills,[26] the Lowry model and its descendants,[17] Wilson's "comprehensive" models,[48] and Baumol's dynamic cumulative deterioration model.[7,34]

Mills' approach has several advantages: (i) division of the city into zones (square grids), which deals with two-dimensional space in a non-trivial way; (ii) capital-land substitution is allowed so that the city can grow upwards as well as outwards; (iii) production is endogenous; and (iv) institutional constraints can be accommodated. These benefits offset the loss of theoretical purity, the need for real data, and the reliance on linear approximations to changes in cost functions.

The simplicity of the Lowry model has not prevented interesting and useful applications. Although the model has been refined and disaggregated since it was first introduced in 1962-1963 its essential characteristics remain: (i) the generation of total employment and its spatial distribution from exogenously determined basic employment; (ii) the generation of residential locations from the work-to-residence trip using a gravity model; and (iii) constraints on these allocations in the form of maximum zonal residential density constraints and minimum threshold sizes for service employment clusters at the neighborhood, local, and metropolitan levels.

The Wilson "comprehensive" approach is cumbersome but effective. The analysis is based on the assumption that urban modeling requires the specification of interrelated submodels referring to population, economic activity, transportation, and location. Particular emphasis is placed on residential-workplace interdependencies. The models are intended to be heavily spatially disaggregated and to deal with urban change over a single discrete time period. For practical planning purposes Wilson stresses the importance of keeping models relatively simple "to match data availability."

Baumol's cumulative deterioration models have rarely been applied (an exception is simple econometric testing[10]), yet their emphasis on positive feedback loops suggests a ready use in system simulation models of the Forrester type. Conceptually, the models are attractive because their emphasis on dynamic disequilibrium processes (with a low-level equilibrium trap) contrasts strikingly with the competitive equilibrium of NUE models. Also, they can be used to focus either on individual neighborhood change or on central city-suburban relations. Moreover, they concentrate attention on policy variables and on the differential effects of various kinds of policies. The rationale of the models, according to Oates, is

the dynamic, cumulative nature of the forces which appear to compound the difficulties of the cities from period to period. One finds in a variety of elements of urban life that the process of change involves obvious feedback relationships which reinforce one another and are likely to generate cumulative movements over time (p. 142).[34]

With refinement, such approaches have considerable potential as a framework for applied urban policy models, especially for declining or rapidly expanding cities.

Many of the alternatives to NUE fall within the classification of simulation models. The simulation approach has received a bad press among economists. There are several reasons for this. Economists are traditionally more familiar with, and have a strong preference for, econometric models. One example from the simulation model group—Jay Forrester's *Urban Dynamics*—has tarnished the reputation of simulation models.[16] Some economists have criticized simulation models because "no one can fully understand what is happening in the bowels of the machine" (p. 267).[44] This argument is weak since the models are built from individual blocks, the structural equations of which have to be very specific. Similarly, the related argument that it is difficult to know what is going on if simultaneous changes are introduced is also overstated, since tests can be controlled by varying parameters sequentially and in combination. A further misplaced argument is that major modifications to simple assumptions should not be made simultaneously but should be introduced one by one, even on an ad hoc basis. However, interdependencies in urban economies are so great that fewer mistakes may be made if major problems are handled simultaneously, as they can easily be in a simulation model. The behavior of NUE models is very sensitive to their assumptions, so that the ad hoc handling of one problem may solve one difficulty, but at the same time create another.

It may be arguable that NUE theory and simulation models are complementary:

The building blocks of the big models come from the theory, and from single-equation testing. When they are put together in a bid model, anomalies sometimes appear which pose new theoretical questions. Tentative theoretical answers to back into the big models, because pencil-and-paper ones are inadequate for direct application" (p. 267).[44]

There is some value in this argument, but NUE models may not provide the most appropriate theory. The reason is that they assume narrowly economic rational responses, whereas complex behavioral responses are more relevant and can be simulated relatively easily in a computer model. NUE theories abstract from adjustment lags, constraints on competition, and locational inertia. These made a difference to the predictions and can be handled without trouble within the framework of a simulation model.

On the other hand, the difficulties of simulation models should not be underestimated. The experience with them has hardly been a series of undiluted successes. For example, not too much confidence should be attached to a model simply because it satisfactorily replicates reality in the test city. A test of the model in other cities may quickly reveal misspecifications.

The Future of NUE

To clarify the stand taken here, NUE models are being judged solely on the criterion of whether they will be applied and shown to be relevant to planners and policymakers. Some NUE theorists would argue that this was never their intention. We have no quarrel with this position. Although still sceptical of a theory based on assumptions that seem more relevant to an analysis of the nineteenth century rather than the modern city (though even in the nineteenth-century case, the standard model may work poorly,[15] we respect the right to play this particular game. Moreover, our ciritcisms,[39] of some years ago now seem too harsh, and the recent progress in NUE has been quite remarkable.

For instance, there have been some attempts to remedy the restrictiveness of static analysis. Although these attempts have not been conspicuously successful, at least the problems of confronting dynamics have been recognized. In this volume, for example, Anas[3] identifies the critical questions of durability (the constraints upon factor substitution) and the influence of future expectations on current housing (and other urban) expenditure decisions, while Pines[38] indicates how the apparently insuperable problem of handling time and space simultaneously in a continuous model may be made a little more tractable by treating one dimension continuously and the other discretely. Muth's paper,[32] and a not dissimilar earlier study by Evans,[14] illustrate a different approach: the development of nonspatial models of urban growth similar in structure to the much more familiar aggregate growth models. These models are then used to draw inferences about the dynamics of urban spatial structure. Building upon work by Bussière,[11] Mogridge[30] has shown how a simple concept, such as the density gradient, may be made dynamic by allowing its main parameters to be functionally related to population and income growth. All of this work is very preliminary, but already it suggests that dynamic models will yield different qualitative results than do the standard static models. However, it hardly needs stressing that the extension of the theory into dynamics—desirable and necessary as it is—is likely to postpone the prospect of applications even further into the future.

Thus, there seems little prospect of NUE being applied in the sense of offering direct insights into the solution of urban problems or of being much help to planners. The analogy with growth theory comes to mind again. This prestigious field of economic theory did not help to explain why some countries grew faster than others, what the underlying determinants of growth were, or how policymakers could raise a country's rate of growth. This is not a pejorative statement; we are not implying that it was meant to do these things, but merely stating the fact that it never did. Indeed, we would argue that it could not. Just as with NUE, the straightjacket of the model's assumptions—needed to obtain determinate solutions—rules out the possibility of applications. NUE will undoubtedly flourish and encompass interesting new theoretical discoveries. But it is unlikely to have increasing contact with operational models or disseminate among planners and urban policymakers. Although NUE and applied urban analysis will probably advance in parallel rather than converge, progress in urban economics will be much stronger if the theorists and policymakers maintain contact and try to learn from each other.

Notes

1. N. Alao [1974].

2. W. Alonso [1964].

3. A. Anas [1975b].

4. S. Angel and G.F. Hyman, 1972, "Urban Transport Expenditures," *Papers and Proceedings, Regional Science Association,* vol. 29, 105-123.

5. R.A. Artle [1973].

6. R.A. Artle and P. Varaiya [1974].

7. W.J. Baumol, 1963, "Interactions of Public and Private Decisions," in H.G. Schaller (ed.), *Public Expenditure Decisions in the Urban Community* (Baltimore: Johns Hopkins Press), pp. 1-18.

8. M.J. Beckmann [1969].

9. M.J. Beckmann [1975].

10. D.F. Bradford and H. Kelejian, 1973, "An Econometric Model of the Flight to the Suburbs," *Journal of Political Economy*, vol. 81, 566-589.

11. R. Bussière, 1972, *Modèle Urbain de Localization Résidentielle*. Paris: Centre de Recherche d'Urbanisme.

12. D. Cappozza [1975].

13. A. Dixit [1973].

14. A.W. Evans [1974].

15. R. Fales and L.N. Moses [1972].

16. J. Forrester, 1969, *Urban Dynamics*, Cambridge: MIT Press.

17. W. Goldner, 1971, "The Lowry Model Heritage," *Journal of the American Institute of Planners*, vol. 37, 100-110.

18. P.G. Hartwick and J.M. Hartwick [1974].

19. O. Hochman and D. Pines [1971].

20. P. Kemper and R. Schmenner, 1974, "The Density Gradient for Manufacturing Industry," *Journal of Urban Economics*, vol. 1, 410-427.

21. R.S. Kirwan and M.J. Ball [1974].

22. L. Lave [1974].

23. D.A. Livesey [1975].

24. I.S. Lowry, 1964, *A Model of Metropolis*. Santa Monica: RAND Corporation.

25. E.S. Mills [1967].

26. E.S. Mills [1972a].

27. E.S. Mills [1972b].

28. E.S. Mills and J. Mackinnon [1973].

29. J.A. Mirrlees [1972].

30. M.J.H. Mogridge [1974].

31. R.F. Muth [1969].

32. R.F. Muth [1975b].

33. J.H. Niedercorn [1971].

34. W.E. Oates, et al. [1971].

35. G.J. Papageorgiou [1973b].

36. G.J. Papageorgiou [1975].

37. G.J. Papageorgiou and E. Casetti [1971].

38. D. Pines [1975a].

39. H.W. Richardson [1973].

40. H.W. Richardson [1975a].

22

41. H.W. Richardson, et al. [1974].

42. R.G. Ridker and J.A. Henning [1967].

43. S. Rose-Ackerman [1975].

44. R.M. Solow [1973c].

45. R.H. Strotz [1965].

46. J.S. Wabe [1971].

47. R.K. Wilkinson [1972].

48. A.G. Wilson, 1974, *Urban and Regional Models in Geography and Planning*. London: Wiley.

3

The New Urban Economics: A Brief Survey

Alex Anas
Dimitrios S. Dendrinos

The aim of this brief survey is to present a thematic exposition of the various issues examined during the past two decades, now comprising a specialized area within the literature of theoretical economics and referred to as "the new urban economics." The survey focuses on recent contributions and identifies the streams of ongoing and some forthcoming research. A predecessor to this work, the Goldstein and Moses survey of urban economics published in the *Journal of Economic Literature* in 1973 was much broader in scope and drew from earlier work. The numerous new developments, we feel, warrant a fresh look at the field. This survey was completed in December 1974 and revised in March 1975. The bibliography compiled by the authors and associated with this survey appears at the end of this volume, and is referred to throughout the chapter notes.

Development of the NUE

It has been argued, that the field of NUE holds within the mainstream of theoretical economics a place similar to that of the neoclassical growth theory. While growth theorists are concerned with the behavior "over time" of an economic system, urban economists deal, instead, with the allocation of activities, people, and capital "over space."

Up to the late 1950s, those concerned with urban problems (geographers, regional scientists, city planners, and economists) had at their disposal two significant theoretical paradigms: (i) the location rent theory of Von Thünen developed within the context of the location of agricultural activity[77] and (ii) the central place theory of Lösch.[31] The sixties witnessed an extension of the Von Thünen model to the urban context. One can

Alex Anas is a member of the Department of Civil Engineering, The Technological Institute, Northwestern University.

Dimitrios S. Dendrinos is a member of the Institute for Social and Environmental Studies, The University of Kansas.

The authors would like to thank Professors M.J. Bechmann, D. Pines, A. Dixit, J. Barr, and J. Riley for their specific comments on a first draft of this chapter.

discern three independent efforts that followed the Von Thünen approach. A paper presented by Beckmann arrived at a market determination of land rents and residential densities with the conclusion that higher income families will locate at the outskirts of the city.[7] These results were based on several restrictive assumptions about the relationship between household income and locational expenditures (rent plus commuting costs), as well as the consumption and commuting costs functions. Specifically, it was assumed that households maximize the size of the lot for a given level of expenditures on housing, and that the mean expenditure on residence plus commuting of a household is a well-defined function of household income. Wingo, in a book that investigated the relationship between traffic flow and land values, presented an explicit mathematical model of the residential land market.[82] In Wingo's model, preferences for accessibility and for land were separated. Prices and quantities were related by postulating demand functions and the equilibrium relation for the urban land market hinged on assuming the complementarity of rent and transport costs. Both Beckmann and Wingo focused on the importance of the size of residential lot and cleared the market by equating supply and demand. In this respect their work was more sophisticated than preceeding theories of urban land values developed by Wendt[79] and Haig.[16] Mohring and Harwitz put forth another model in which employment took place in the CBD and identical families consumed fixed-size lots located around this center.[42] In this simple model, land rents declined linearly from the edge of the CBD to zero at the edge of the city. Rents and transport costs were fully complementary to assure equilibrium. The Mohring-Harwitz model was aimed at measuring the effects in terms of land values of introducing improvements in transport technology.

The pioneering work of Alonso was a generalization of Beckmann's model, but based on far less restrictive assumptions.[1] Specifically, Alonso came up with a theory of locational rent based on the microeconomic theory of the firm and of consumer behavior. The isotropic transport plane with the centrally located CBD and the surrounding residential suburbs, proved a remarkably useful and powerful simplification that has aided in answering fundamental questions, and, there is good reason to believe, without much loss of generality. Contemporary to Alonso's work was the linear programming model of Herbert and Stevens.[21]

Further contributions to Alonso's model were made by Muth[44,45] and Beckmann.[9] These constituted the major first generation contributions or "standard models"—a term later coined by Solow.

R.H. Strotz developed several simple models of welfare optimal urban form and discussed the corrective pricing of the congestion externality.[73] Unfortunately, Strotz's work remained apparently unread until it was brought to readers' attention in a recent paper by Riley.[61] Had the Strotz paper become known earlier, it would have surely made its mark by preempting some of Mirrlees's[40] much later work. If we cannot refer here to the Strotz piece as one that led to major second generation developments it is simply because it went unnoticed.

The Mills model can be viewed as a springboard for a good deal of the second generation work, since he introduced several issues of significance transcending the previous analyses and opening the way to a general equilibrium approach by jointly modeling the supply and demand for transportation, housing, and production.[35]

Landmarks in second generation developments were the three papers by Mills,[36] Solow,[65] and Mirrlees[40] published in the *Swedish Journal of Economics* and the three-paper symposium by Solow,[66] Oron et al.,[52] and Dixit[14] that appeared in the *Bell Journal of Economics and Management Science*, together with a brief survey of the field by Mills and MacKinnon.[39]

The growth of publications within the new urban economics is significant. A total of thirty publications in some way related to the field can be found in the period 1960-1970. In 1971 alone, there were fifteen, in 1972 there were twenty-three, and in 1973 there were thirty. In 1974 there were twenty-six publications and the *Journal of Urban Economics* appeared in response to the growing interest in urban problems by economists and the plethora of uninvestigated theoretical issues.

It is perhaps still early to detect whether the field is exhibiting real growth or just inflating. There is skepticism among some insiders that, perhaps, the point of diminishing returns has already been reached. This thought is clearly stated by Mills and MacKinnon:

The analogy with growth theory is irresistible. Many economists feel that some of the neoclassical growth theory in the sixties consisted of technical pyrotechnics that added neither insight nor realism to previous work (p. 597).[39]

Whether the field can meaningfully contribute to urban public policy formation is an issue of controversy. In particular, the simplifying assumptions made in order to derive closed form solutions have come under heavy fire from other researchers involved in urban economics and planning.[a] These critics often fail to appreciate the fact that despite the complexity of urban systems these models have produced—with very few inputs, for a high level of aggregation, and within a short period of time—consistent results that are of significant interest, insight, and realism. It is perhaps unfair to expect more. After all, the best way to play chess is on an eight by eight chessboard and with the sixteen chess pieces on each side.

[a] See, for example, the criticism of Solow and Mirrlees by Richardson,[58] as well as the rejoinders by the former.[41,68]

First- and Second-Generation Models

Surveying the new urban economics at this date is not a very difficult task. This is partly due to the small number of publications but more significantly due to the fact that the research effort has been centered around a set of well-defined problems and the investigation of tangential and secondary issues has been properly restrained. In this survey, we shall provide a brief overview of the field emphasizing the thematic developments.

The bulk of what we have grouped as first-generation models is from work completed in the sixties. Several issues tie these models together. First, these are partial equilibrium models in which one sector (usually the residential) is represented. Second, most of the work is centered around the issue of locational equilibrium with nonuniform tastes and/or incomes. Third, there is no consideration of any kind of urban externality. Fourth, partly due to the strictly positive nature of the models and partly due to the absence of externalities, important policy issues do not arise.

With the exception of the early work of Strotz, and the 1967 Mills model, all of the second-generation models appeared in the seventies. The break between these models and the first-generation work can be characterized by the following features. First, in second-generation models of the market equilibrium kind there is (i) an explicit concern with a major urban externality (usually traffic congestion) and the policy issues associated with it and/or (ii) concern with the interaction of several sectors such as households, housing, production, and transportation. Second, as another manifestation of the concern with public policy many of these models are optimum formulations, i.e., they admit explicitly or implicitly the existence of a public sector, which through policies of income distribution, external- ity pricing, and zoning, leads the market to realize a "superior" equilib- rium. The optimum models are of two kinds: (i) those that aim at minimiz- ing aggregate social costs and (ii) those that maximize a Bergsonian welfare function. Finally, second-generation models display a higher level of math- ematical sophistication and rigor, which appears in the use of the calculus of variations, control theory, and differential equations in solving optimum and market equilibrium problems with externalities. As it often proves difficult to get full closed-form results through these methods, second- generation models are often solved by resorting to numerical simulation techniques.

To summarize, our first/second generation dichotomy seems to best capture the distinctions expressed in the following seven dimensions along which models can be discerned:

1. partial vs. general equilibrium models
2. positive models (no public sector) vs. policy-oriented models (implicit public sector) and normative models (explicit public sector)

3. utility maximization with flexible demands for space and the composite commodity vs. cost minimization and infinitely inelastic demand for space

4. heterogeneous vs. homogeneous incomes and tastes among locators

5. monocentric vs. policentric urban form

6. continuous vs. discrete representation of space

7. absence vs. presence of externalities

The contrast is sharpest along the first two of these dimensions, since all first-generation models are positive partial equilibrium models and perhaps along the fourth dimension since all second-generation models assume completely homogeneous locators.

In this survey four attempts are made at synthesizing the findings reported in the literature. These attempts are centered around the following issues:

1. income distribution and locational choices in first-generation models

2. congestion externality and the allocation of urban land between housing and roads in second-generation models

3. comparison of various welfare criteria in second-generation models

4. the measurement of benefits from land improvement projects

As the number of contributions to each of these issues is significant, comparison of results and synthesis is possible and called for. The policy issues of zoning—Ohls, Weisberg, and White[49]; the issues of segregation and discrimination in the spatial context—Rose-Ackerman[62]; and the issues of income and property taxation—Ohls[48]—have, so far, received isolated attention from researchers within the field. These attempts can be characterized as extensions of either first- or second-generation models, and their proximity to the main paradigm does not, in our view, justify the title "third generation."

Our closing remarks about third-generation developments is the expression of some bias. We feel the title should be reserved for developments that Mirrlees[40] has called "optimum geography" and the development of dynamic models, considered a difficult task by Mills and MacKinnon.[39]

First-Generation Models

The important issue dealt with in first-generation models was the effect of income on the locational equilibrium of households.

The analysis has followed two paths. One stream of research has taken up the case of a quasi-concave general utility function (assumed the same for each locating household) with a nonspecific income distribution. Such are the models of Alonso[1] and Muth.[45] The second stream of research has assumed a specific utility function, normally of a Cobb-Douglas form (identical for all households), with a prespecified income distribution. The first such model has been proposed by Beckmann[9] corrected by Delson,[12] and restated by Montesano,[43] followed by the models developed by Casetti[10] and Papageorgiou.[53]

Recently, Pines provided an excellent discussion of the differences between these two streams of research.[55] Pines shows that when all households have the same utility function and differ only by income, the effect on the bid rent function of income changes can be seen through the sign of the right side of the following expression:

$$\frac{\partial \dot{B}}{\partial Y} = \frac{1}{H} \left\{ P \left[\frac{d(U_X/U_Z)}{dY} - \frac{\eta}{Y} \cdot \frac{U_X}{U_Z} \right] - t_{XY} + \frac{\eta}{Y} t_X \right\} \tag{3.1}$$

where X = distance from the center

   B = the bid rent function

   Y = household income

   H = amount of land

   P = the price of the composite commodity

   η = the income elasticity of the demand for land

   Z = the amount of composite commodity

   t = the transport costs (as a function of distance and income) and the dot signifies a partial derivative with respect to distance.

Both Alonso and Muth make further assumptions regarding the income and distance effect on transport costs, distance as an argument of the utility function, and the composition of money income, in order to analytically derive conclusions regarding the relative location of higher income households. In Alonso, distance is an explicit argument of the utility function ($U_X \neq 0$) and transport costs are a general function of distance with $t_X \neq 0$ but $t_{XY} = 0$ (that is, transport costs are invariant by income); while in Muth, $U_X = 0$, t_X is constant, and $t_{XY} \neq 0$ (that is, transport costs are a linear function of distance and vary by income). Under different assumptions, the higher income households may or may not be located farther out from the center than lower income households. In particular, in the Alonso model, the wealthy will always settle at the periphery; while in Muth's model, the magnitude of t_{XY} could make the slope of the bid rent steeper for the rich, causing them to locate centrally.

In the case of specific utility function and income distribution models with $t_x \neq 0$ and $t_{XY} = 0$, higher income households are located further away from the center, and utility increases with distance. Beckmann worked out analytically the case of a Pareto income distribution and a Cobb-Douglas utility function with distance as an argument. Montesano has drawn attention to two pathological cases.[43] One stems from assuming that the transport rate is equal to zero in Beckmann's model, with the result that residential density and land rent are increasing functions of distance tending to infinity. In the second, that again in the Beckmann model, income decreases with distance only when the income at the edge of the center is infinitely large.

No strong conclusions can be drawn—for the case of arbitrarily distributed tastes and incomes—about the order in which various household types locate relative to the central workplace. However, Alonso[1] and Herbert and Stevens[21] have proposed two specific algorithms for the solution of this general problem. The original Herbert-Stevens model was a linear programming algorithm based on Alonso's bid rent concept. Given the bid rents of household types (implied by prespecified utility levels) for discrete zone/house type combinations of fixed characteristics, the model produced an "equilibrium" outcome that did not satisfy the usual Pareto efficiency conditions and had to be supported by a set of tax/subsidy dual variables for each household type. Wheaton has shown how the original formulation can be converted to a "pure transportation problem" in linear programming, which if used in a scheme of two nested iterations can produce a market equilibrium solution that satisfies the Pareto efficiency conditions and produces a set of tax/subsidy dual variables equal to zero.[81] Wheaton's work is partly based on a decade of research at the University of Pennsylvania under the direction of Britton Harris.[17] Part of Wheaton's doctoral dissertation involves the empirical estimation of locational utility functions (Cobb-Douglas and C.E.S.) for stratifications of households by income and social characteristics.

The case of market equilibrium with arbitrary distribution of tastes and incomes is thus capable of solution—in the continuous case through the iterative Alonso algorithm and in the discrete case with housing through Wheaton's version of the Herbert-Stevens model. Incidentally, the latter method can also be used for an arbitrary arrangement of a number of workplaces as long as households are stratified by workplace as well as by other characteristics.

In a recent paper, Wheaton performs a rigorous comparative statics analysis of the standard model with a nonspecific utility function defined over the amounts of land and the composite good.[80] The analysis is performed for both a closed city and an open city. The former refers to a city in which population is exogenous while the utility level is endogenous; the latter refers to a city imbedded into a larger interurban market (or urban-rural market) which has attained a uniform utility level. Thus, for the open city, the welfare level is exogenous while the population is endogenous. The open city model was previously used by Barr in the quite different context of exploring the provision of public goods within the spatial context.[5]

Wheaton's comparative static results confirmed well-established intuition: For a closed city, an increase in population expands the city, lowers the welfare, and increases rents and densities throughout the city. An increase in the opportunity cost of land compacts the urban area and again increases rents and densities throughout the city while lowering the welfare. An increase in income or a reduction in the marginal costs of travel expands the city, increases welfare, while lower rents and densities close to the center raise rents and densities away from the center. For an open city, an increase in the opportunity cost of land or the welfare level leads to a decline in the population size and a contraction of the city. The former leaves rents and densities unchanged, while the latter causes them to decline at all points. In sharp contrast to a closed city, an increase in income or a decline in the marginal costs of transport leads to higher densities and rents throughout the open city. As in the closed city, both an income rise and a decline in the costs of transport expand the city (by inducing inmigration).

No discussion of first-generation models can be complete without special reference to the work of Richard Muth.[45] His main concern was the locational aspects of the urban housing market. Under the specific assumptions of real-income constant price elasticity for housing equal to minus one and a constant transport rate, Muth derived a negative exponential housing price gradient. Further, under a Cobb-Douglas production function for housing services with land and labor as input factors, he showed that the density gradient is also a negative exponential. It is only fair to note that the in-depth analysis carried out by Muth exhibited a particular economic elegance, contributing significantly to the attraction of economists to the new field. Muth also put forth hypotheses based on his analysis and tested them empirically. The results were not always satisfactory but identified variables, such as the age of dwelling units, as significant factors in explaining locational decisions. In a recent paper, Muth has introduced dynamic elements into the supply and demand sides of the housing market.[46]

The research by Casetti and Papageorgiou[11] and Papageorgiou[53] deserves special mention. Through their research, the monocentric model of land use has been extended to a policentric context in which the centers belong to a Löschian central place type hierarchy. A center belonging to a particular level in the hierarchy provides those goods and services to be found in each lower level as well. To acquire goods of a given level the consumer has to travel to the nearest center of that level. Papageorgiou proves several general theorems about the distribution of rents and densities and the structure of the rent surface within such a setting.[53]

Of secondary importance are some extensions of first-generation models that deal with the issues of environmental quality and leisure time. Examples are the work of Nelson[47] and Yamada.[83]

Whether the chapter of first-generation models has been closed remains to be seen. Solow, for one, in "On Equilibrium Models of Urban Location," examined the problem of diffused local employment outside the central core.[67] This, and other forms of employment decentralization, such as the suburbanization of the centrally located production sector, may prove to be promising areas of future research.

Second-Generation Models

There are four seminal contributions in second-generation models: Mills,[33] Mills and DeFerranti,[38] Solow and Vickrey,[69] and Mirrlees.[40]

These four papers introduced the major concepts that transcended earlier work, in terms of complexity and policy content, and formed the major preoccupation of later second-generation models.

Mills' contribution was the first general equilibrium model that was cognizant of the economic reasons for the existence of cities. Explaining how constant returns to scale in production could be used in a transport savings way, eliminating the need to agglomerate economic activity in a city, Mills focused on two reasons for city existence: (i) the effect of land productivity differences on the coefficients of production functions and (ii) an increase in returns to scale in production. Mills drew attention to the trade-off between diseconomies in transportation and economies in city size that resulted from increasing returns in production—an issue later investigated by Dixit. He assumed a constant returns to scale Cobb-Douglas function in the production of housing services. Commodities with nonconstant returns to scale production were aggregated into a composite good produced in the CBD by another Cobb-Douglas function. Factor use was determined according to marginal profibability conditions and the demand for land in roads was endogenous. Mills arrived at key differential equations, solved these explicitly, and reduced the problem to a two-equation nonlinear system in which the CBD and city boundaries were the unknowns.

The paper by Mills and DeFerranti[38] was one of the three papers that appeared in 1971 addressing the problem of traffic congestion. The reason for counting this paper as a seminal contribution, however, is not its concern with congestion as much as its more general concern with the efficient pricing of urban externalities. An efficient land use pattern was defined as that which can be achieved when the public sector minimizes the aggregate of urban travel costs and the costs of purchasing the urban land from its alternate use. By simplifying the private sector substantially, the authors formulated and solved analytically, a calculus of variations problem.

Another pioneering paper in which a cost minimizing solution to efficient urban form is provided is that of Solow and Vickrey.[69] In "Land Use in a Long Narrow City," these authors provided a study of congestion in a rectangular business district within which a known total amount of land was devoted to production and the rest to transportation. Under simple traffic generation assumptions—namely the uniform distribution of an amount of traffic originating in any unit of the business area over the entire business district—the problem was to derive the aggregate travel cost minimizing the amount-of-land-in-roads profile for the city. Some of the basic results of congestion analyses, such as overinvestment near the center in the absence of congestion tolls, were derived within this simple model. In an unpublished paper, Dixit attempted to extend the analysis to a similar but circular city.[13] Kraus has also worked on this problem.[24]

In "The Optimum Town," Mirrlees formulated the problem of maximizing a simple sum of household utilities and proved that such an optimum solution has a competitive realization provided that prices are set so as to satisfy marginal utility conditions, and income is appropriately redistributed.[40] Mirrlees also analyzed the cases of uniform traffic congestion and of density externalities, as well as the competitive realization of the optimum for these cases.

Back in 1965, Strotz[73] put forth his seven parables which remained unnoticed until recently. In this early work, the concepts of welfare optimum and its competitive realization, congestion and its efficient pricing, optimum expenditures on roads under variable and constant returns to scale, and increasing returns in the production of the composite good were examined. In the first four parables, Strotz took up the simple cases of congestion and allocation of trips in one and two roads and under peak and off-peak travel conditions, deriving explicit solutions for tolls and optimum road expenditures. In the more sophisticated last three, Strotz introduced a fixed radius discrete model of a monocentric city divided into rings. The household's utility function depended explicitly on the level of total congestion experienced from the place of residence to the center, the number of trips to the center, the distance to the center, and the amounts of land and composite good consumed. In the sixth parable Strotz allowed land to be used for transportation as well as for residences. The level of congestion was a general function of traffic volume, expenditures in roads, and land in roads. An explicit relationship among the amount of road expenditures, land in roads, and the degree of increasing or decreasing returns in road production was derived.

Maximum Welfare Models, the Treatment of Equals, and the Distribution of Utility and Income. An issue of concern in welfare optimum models is the form of the Bergsonian welfare function used, involving an ethical decision about the equal versus unequal treatment of identical households.

In Strotz's parables, households are not assumed identical in tastes.[73] The welfare function is a weighted sum of household utilities. These weights are either exogenously fixed and the optimum utility levels are determined, or the utility levels are fixed and the weights are treated as variables. All later work has assumed households to be identical in tastes. Mirrlees[40] uses a simple sum of household utilities, while Dixit[14] and Riley[60] use functions that penalize inequality. Specifically, in the Dixit model, the negative sum of household utilities raised to an exponent is maximized. As the value of the exponent approaches negative infinity, inequality of optimum utility levels disappears and the objective becomes equivalent to the Rawlsian criterion of maximizing lim inf $U(X)$, where $U(X)$ is the utility level at distance X. Riley maximizes the sum of the logarithms of household utilities—a welfare function that is more egalitarian than a simple sum. Oron et al. impose absolute equality of optimum utility levels by introducing a constraint and maximizing the utility level thus equalized.[51]

In an unpublished paper, Levhari, Oron, and Pines discuss the different treatment of equals under Von Neumann-Morgenstern expected utility conditions.[28] These are realized by institutionalizing a fair lottery system, in which entrepreneurs can purchase housing bundles and distribute them by lottery. They show that competitive equilibrium with lottery is preferred by each and every household to a competitive equilibrium without lottery, and that there exist some unfair lotteries as well—preferred to market equilibrium. Under expected utility assumptions, and only then, social welfare functions which penalize inequality are shown to be Pareto inferior. Levhari et al. depict this in Figure 3-1 for the case of two individuals with identical preference functions and initial holdings and the case of two goods, one a perfectly indivisible good (that is, location in urban space) and the other a perfectly divisible good (for example, the composite commodity). In the Mirrlees model, the socially expected utility level is at point M_0, although the individual assignments can be either at point M_1 or M_2. In this case, the elasticity of substitution of utilities is unity. In the case of Riley, for an elasticity of substitution less than unity, the possible individual outcomes are at R_1 and R_2 while the socially expected indifference level is at R_0, dominated by M_0. The welfare function used by Dixit in its extreme case (of zero elasticity of substitution) provides the solution D_0, dominated

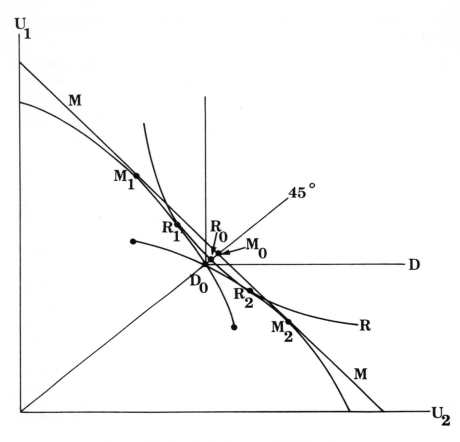

Figure 3-1. Socially Expected Utility Levels

by both R_0 and M_0. Thus, Mirrlees' welfare function dominates both Riley's and Dixit's in the Pareto sense when expected utility assumptions hold.

Mirrlees himself hinted at an expected utility interpretation of his model when he wrote

One may feel that inequality is not necessary for optimality in our model, since no harm is done by frequently changing the treatment of individuals while keeping the overall distribution of incomes constant. After all, it does not matter who receives a high income, only that some people should receive relatively high incomes. But there is no consideration in the model to show that such a constant permutation of incomes would yield an improvement in social welfare (p. 123).[40]

In models that are indifferent to inequality, an interesting result is the manner in which utilities and income should be distributed over space.

Mirrlees has examined this issue at some length. He cites several utility functions for which utility is uniform over distance. One of them is the case of a utility function homogeneous in composite good and land. Stern has investigated this case in more detail.[72]

Mirrlees proceeds to consider the more general case of nonuniform distribution of utilities. His discussion is in terms of the following special-case utility function, in which the enjoyment of consumption c, is separated from the enjoyment of space and location, a and r:

$$u = v(c - tr) + w(a, r) \qquad (3.2)$$

where t is the cost of traveling a unit distance. From this he derives that

$$\frac{du}{dr} = \frac{w_r^2}{aw_{aa}} \left[\frac{\partial}{\partial a} \left(\frac{aw_a}{w_r} \right) - \frac{w_a}{w_r^2} v't \right] \qquad (3.3)$$

His results are that utility will usually increase with distance and more so the greater the transport costs. On the other hand, it could decrease with distance if preferences are such that an increase in income would make people want to move inward. Furthermore, if transport costs are large enough near the center of the town, utility might be an increasing function of r near the center but a decreasing function after a certain point.

Riley produced, for a Cobb-Douglas utility function—with composite commodity, land, leisure and distance as arguments—the results that utility will increase exponentially with distance despite his somewhat egalitarian welfare function and regardless of the sign of the elasticity of utility with respect to distance from the center.[60]

Unequal distribution of utilities, of course, implies that nonwage income subsidies will be unequally distributed. In Gammaville, this turns out to be a truncated gamma distribution.

The models of Oron et al. and Dixit, unlike those of Mirrlees and Riley, derive the uniform income subsidy for the case of uniform utility endogenously as the average of all profits in the economy including the aggregate rents on land, taxed away, and all other tolls collected by the central government. Also, unlike Mirrlees and Riley and because of the multisectoral nature of their models, they rely on numerical simulation, as opposed to deriving complete analytical solutions.

Urban Externalities. The major urban externality examined in the second-generation literature is that of traffic congestion. As early as 1961, Wingo had discussed the problem of congestion and its effect on urban land use.[82] Beckmann, in 1968,[8] had argued in favor of maintaining the same level of congestion everywhere—what was later shown to be a second best solution. The measurement of private and social costs of highway congestion and the marginal cost pricing of roads were the important policy issues associated with traffic congestion. These have received ample attention from economists in the past decade and a half; for two examples see Walters[78] and Vickrey.[76]

It wasn't until 1971 when three papers, one by Mills and DeFerranti, another by Hockman and Pines, and the third by Solow and Vickrey, provided, within three substantially different models of urban spatial structure, the first careful expositions of the congestion problem.

The version taken up by Mills and DeFerranti was posed, we pointed out earlier, as the minimization of aggregate travel costs and the costs of purchasing the urban land from agricultural landlords. In the analysis it was assumed that each house requires a fixed amount of land. The aggregate amount of land in transportation and residential use, the level of congestion as functions of distance, and the city boundary were all endogenously derived. The effect on these of varying the number of households was examined. The authors succeeded in deriving a major result about the allocation of land to roads, a result that was later generalized by Livesey[30] and Sheshinski[64] and verified by Oron et al.[51] and Dixit[14] in more complex and substantially different models.

This result hinges on the following form of congestion cost per traveler, suggested by Vickrey:

$$p(x) = \bar{p} + \delta[T(x)/G(x)]^\gamma \qquad (3.4)$$

where $T(x) = $ the volume of traffic passing distance x

$G(x) = $ the amount of land in transportation at x

$\bar{p} = $ the congestion-free cost of traveling a unit distance (assumed to be zero for convenience)

and δ and γ are parameters. The boundary of the CBD was $\underline{x}$ and exogeneous, while the city boundary was $\bar{x}$ and endogenous (see figure 3-2). The total amount of land available at distance x is θx where $0 < \theta \leqslant 2\pi$. Analysis has shown that $G(x)$ is always concave. For the number of households N sufficiently small, $G(x)$ is continuously decreasing as in curve 1. For N sufficiently large, there is a saturated annulus of width $\Delta = x^* - \underline{x}$ surrounding the CBD, and beyond which $G(x)$ first increases and then decreases (curve 3). For some intermediate N, with no saturation of the land around the CBD, $G(x)$ attains a maximum at its intersection with the ray of slope $\gamma/(\gamma + 1)$.

The paper by Legey et al.[27] verifies the above result in a context slightly more general than that of Mills and DeFerranti. The authors maintain the fixed lot size assumption but introduce capital into the production of transportation and housing. They minimize the aggregate of the interest on capital, transportation costs, and the opportunity cost of land. In addition,

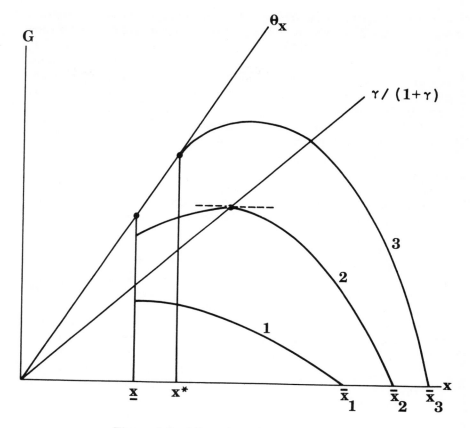

Figure 3-2. Allocation of Land to Roads

the authors derive the market solution assuming that landlords adjust housing capital to maximize profits, while the public sector adjusts land and capital inputs into transportation to minimize social costs. They show that the city will be more suburbanized if no congestion toll is levied and indicate that without corrective pricing there will be overinvestment in the transportation facilities around the CBD.

Livesey[30] and Sheshinski[64] generalized the result depicted in Figure 3-2 by reformulating the Mills-Deferranti model, with transport costs within the CBD as well as in the suburban ring. In their models, the city and CBD boundaries and the function $G(x)$ are all endogenously derived. Both authors show that the maximum amount of land used for transportation occurs at the CBD boundary, that there is never saturation, and that the amount of land in roads is a convex function within the CBD and concave inside the suburban ring. Their models, independently worked out as a result of Artle's discussion[3] of the Mills-DeFerranti model, conclude that the ratio of the CBD boundary to the city boundary is independent of the number of households in the urban area. Livesey further indicates, through sensitivity analysis on the opportunity cost of land, that there exists, for each level of population, a finite maximum and a finite minimum for the city and CBD boundaries.

Hochmann and Pines developed a market equilibrium model with interesting features.[22] The demand for transportation was assumed to be sensitive to prices, and transportation costs as a function of distance were endogenously determined. Cobb-Douglas production of housing and transportation with land and other inputs into both was assumed. With flexible demand for transportation, the household's utility maximization was formulated as a calculus of variations problem, and the model was solved analytically for the land, housing, and transportation price gradients, as well as for the density gradient. The authors showed that, for certain values of the production function coefficients, the land rent, the price of transportation, and the density gradients can be concave while the housing price gradient is always convex. They also examined the rent and density gradients under the assumption of unitary real-income-constant-price elasticity for the case of congested travel, thus extending some of Muth's results. Finally, the efficiency implications of the model were that greater congestion could be tolerated in the vicinity of the CBD, relative to more outlying areas of the city. Hockman and Pines did not elaborate on the amount of land in transportation as a function of distance from the center. This is especially unfortunate since their model has certain results— namely the concavity of the land rent and density gradients—not encountered in other studies.

Another study of traffic congestion within a market equilibrium context was that of Solow.[65,66] In the second paper, Solow performs numerical simulation by varying an exogenously specified function $G(x)$. He concludes that congestion makes the rent gradient more convex and the city more compact. He shows that benefit cost analysis will lead to excessive road building around the CBD, a result also derived by Legey et al. as pointed out above. Another result characterized as "mildly counterintuitive" by Solow is that upon fixing the city boundary and increasing the amount of land in housing, average commuting costs per household fall, apparently due to the sufficiently large inward movement of households to overcome the increase in congestion costs.

Oron et al.[51] and Dixit[14] looked at traffic congestion in social welfare maximizing models. In both of these models, which have realistic demand sides and no transport costs within the CBD, the result depicted in Figure 3-2 was verified and the corrective toll that should be levied upon road users was derived. The Dixit model also addressed the trade-off between diseconomies in congestion and increasing returns in production with land and labor hours as inputs. Through numerical simulation, it was shown that there is an optimum city size for each degree of increasing returns.

The case of second best allocation of land to roads—uniform speed of travel—has been examined by Mirrlees, who proves competitive realization of the optimum under the assumptions of both constant returns to scale and decreasing costs in the provision of roads.[40] In another optimum town model, Riley introduces a general construction cost function for roads and examines the effect of a road technology parameter.[61] Both the Mirrlees and Riley analyses deserve special attention, since they do not rely on specific forms of utility or congestion cost functions and are concerned with establishing results of general validity. Riley's general utility function, for example, is defined over the consumption of composite good, amount of land, and leisure time. In addition he distinguishes between private and public transportation costs. He assumes that for a given road technology M, maintenance and operating costs are proportional to road use $T(X)$, the volume of traffic, but are independent of traffic density, i.e.:

$$ H = T(X) \cdot g[M(X)] \qquad g_M > 0, \; g_{MM} \geq 0 \qquad (3.5) $$

In addition, travel time per mile, t, is a function of road width per car, $K(X)$, and road technology, $M(X)$, that is,

$$ t = t[K(X), M(X)] \qquad (3.6) $$

This is assumed to be a convex function (not just convex in each variable). These assumptions yield that $\dot{K}(X) > 0$ and $\dot{M}(X) < 0$. The latter result implies that road technology improves steadily as the center of the city is approached. The former result is utilized to show that the percentage of aggregate land in roads is *not* monotonic. This is seen as follows: Let $S(X) = K(X) \cdot T(X)/\theta X$ be the percentage of land in roads, where θ radians of land are available. Then:

$$ \dot{S}(X) = \left[\frac{\dot{K}(X)}{K(X)} + \frac{\dot{T}(X)}{T(X)} - \frac{1}{X} \right] S(X) \qquad (3.7) $$

Since $\dot{K}(X) > 0$ it is seen that $S(X)$ is *not* in general monotonic. Thus the result depicted in curve 2 of Figure 3-2 is a special case since with the specific congestion function as in equation (3.4), the proportion $G(X)/\theta X$ is always monotonic. Riley's result, of course, it not merely due to the nonspecificity of his functions but also due to his assumptions about travel time and public transportation expenditures.

In the sixth parable of Strotz,[73] an equation was derived relating for every ring at distance r^j, road expenditures, amount of land in roads to tolls charged at that distance, and the degree of decreasing or increasing returns:

$$E_r + q_r L_r = \tau'(r) \sum_{j:r(j)>r} t^j + \frac{S_r}{D_E^r} \qquad (3.8)$$

where E_r = expenditures on roads in ring r

q_r = the land rent at r

L_r = the amount of land in roads

$\tau'(r)$ = the toll charge at r.

t^j = the number of trips generated by a household at distance r^j

The congestion experienced by a household at i is a general function:

$$D^i = \sum_{r=1}^{r(i)-1} f^r \left(\sum_{j:r(j)>r} t^j, E_r, L_r \right) \qquad (3.9)$$

S_r, the degree of increasing or decreasing returns is measured as

$$S_{r(i)} = \frac{D^{r(i)}}{\Sigma t} \sum_{j:r(j)>r} t^j + D_E^{r(i)} E_{r(i)} + D_L^{r(i)} L_{r(i)} \qquad (3.10)$$

Solving equation (3.8) for L_r one can see that the amount of land in roads is, in general, nonmonotonic.

Both Strotz and Riley obtain the result that the public budget will show a surplus or deficit depending on whether there are decreasing or increasing returns to scale in road production. It will break even with constant returns to scale.

Very recently, Henderson provided the first analysis of the congestion problem for an open city.[20] The problem was formulated as the minimization of total transport costs subject to the exogenously given utility level and the profit maximizing provision of housing. In this model, equilibrium is characterized by average costs plus gasoline tax pricing of travel, while optimum involves the usual marginal cost pricing assured by congestion tolls. Revenues from tolls and taxes are used to cover increasing returns-to-scale road construction costs. Two noteworthy results are obtained. First, due to the openness of the model, the optimum city is more suburbanized than the equilibrium city. Second, it is found that speeds at the outskirts of the city can increase before starting their decline as one moves toward the center. This is due, in part, to the increasing-returns assumption and in part to the increase in land rents. As the latter inevitably overtakes the former, road costs increase and speeds start declining.

We think it is fair to say that the congestion problem has been quite extensively studied within the new urban economics. There are several isolated treatments of other externalities. Oron and Pines[50] examine pollution from a source fixed at the center, while Oron et al.[52] discuss automobile pollution in a model in which there is no congestion. Riley discusses automobile pollution in conjunction with traffic congestion.[61]

The only analysis of the residential density externality is to be found in Mirrlees' "The Optimum Town."[40] Mirrlees introduces a general utility function concave for a given distance from the center and a given level of residential density. He proceeds to show that the maximization of the sum of household utilities produces an optimum that can be realized under either one of two kinds of policies. One involves the introduction of a commuter tax or subsidy to correct the distortion; the other internalizes the externality by setting prices that make consumers indifferent to lot size given their choice of distance from the center and an assurance that the local density will be of a particular level. This level of density could be achieved by profit-maximizing housing estate developers, as Mirrlees suggests, or instituted through a form of externality zoning.

Public goods, Land Improvements, and the Measurement of Benefits. A policy issue in second-generation models is the provision and financing of public goods, i.e., goods the consumption of which by one individual does not diminish the consumption of them by another, at least when there are no external effects arising from their consumption. Strotz drew attention to roads as pure public goods in the above sense, when congestion could be assumed away, and as sources of externalities, when congestion effects were significant.[73]

Although of primary importance, the supply of public goods attracted little attention within the urban spatial structure context. There are two papers by Barr addressing the intraurban and interurban aspects of the issue respectively.[5,6] In the first paper, Barr introduces a public good, provided at the center of an open city, into the locating household's utility function. He discusses three different schemes for financing the aggregate outlays undertaken by the government in supplying the public good. These are: (i) land value taxation—under which each household pays an amount equal to the price of providing a unit of the public good, times the proportion of that household's expenditures on land to aggregate expenditures on land; (ii) site value taxation—under which each household pays a sum equal to the price of a unit amount of public good times the proportion of that household's expenditure on its housing bundle to the aggregate of such expenditures; and (iii) head taxation—under which each household meets the average cost of providing the public good.

The important conclusions are that:

1. Land value taxation is Pareto superior to site value taxation in the sense that it leads to higher profits on the part of the monopsonist (producer of the consumption good) and higher land rents everywhere in the city, while it does not affect the fixed open city utility level.

2. Land value taxation and head tax financing could each be superior to the other under different conditions.

Barr also shows how a rich class of households could exploit a poor class by "forcing" it to finance the public good and how, in the absence of a public good, a numerous rich class could altogether drive out the poor, a result that again hinges on the openness of the city.

In his second paper, Barr introduces a public-goods provision within the Tiebout[75] context of several urban communities competing for constituent households by providing packages of public goods under conditions of competitive bidding by the households for sites in these communities. The main concern is to derive the basic relationships of an inter-community equilibrium, labeled STE (Simple Tiebout Equilibrium), by ignoring land rent (transport cost) variations within each community and focusing instead on the relationships among average community rent and income, community population, fraction of community land in residential use, and the tax rate for financing of the public goods. The approach has interesting connections with the theory of clubs, and Barr himself provides an interpretation along these lines.

A recent article by Lind has spurred a controversy on the subject of the measurement of land improvement benefits.[29] Since the late 1950s, transportation economists and urban planners have been concerned with the extent to which land values could be taken to reflect the benefits resulting from public investments. (See, for example, Zettel,[84] Lang and Wohl,[26] Mohring and Harwitz.[42]

The Lind criterion was that, in the measurement of benefits, only the changes in land values where an improvement project is implemented are relevant, and that they provide an upper bound for the benefit. In an unpublished note, Pines discussed the difficulty of employing a Koopmans-Beckmann algorithm used by Lind in order to derive equilibrium land rents.[54] Using a simple Von Thünen model, Pines shows that sometimes positive benefits can even be associated with a negative effect on land values.

In a forthcoming paper, Pines and Weiss discuss several approaches to the problem.[56] According to them the approach of Bailey,[4] Rothenberg,[63] and Mills[34] claims that the benefit of an improvement in a part of the city can be measured by the net change in land values over the entire city; whereas in Strotz's[74] general equilibrium model, the benefit equals the change in the value of land where the improvement takes place less the change in land values in the rest of the urban area. In an empirical study, Ridker and Henning assume that a change in the total value of land is related to net benefit from pollution abatement.[59] Anderson and Crocker use an assignment model to show that the change in the total value of land provides a lower bound to the benefit.[2]

Pines and Weiss develop a model of a city with two subareas. A number of identical households are allocated to the subareas and a known amount of composite commodity is distributed among them, so that a uniform utility level is achieved. The households derive utility from land, composite good, and a quality variable related to the public investment. The social benefit is defined as

$$B = m \frac{dw}{d\alpha} \tag{3.11}$$

where m is the number of households, w the common utility level, and α the quality variable. They show that this benefit is related to land value changes as follows:

$$B = U_x^2 \left[\frac{dR_1}{d\alpha_1} - \frac{m_1}{m_2} \cdot \frac{dR_2}{d\alpha_1} \right] \tag{3.12}$$

where $R_1, R_2 =$ aggregate land rents in the two subareas

$\quad m_1, m_2 =$ the equilibrium allocation of households

$\quad\quad \alpha_1 =$ the quality level in area 1 where an improvement is introduced

$\quad\quad U_x^2 =$ the level of marginal utility with respect to the composite good in area 2 ($U_x^1 \neq U_x^2$)

According to this result the sum of changes in land values is a misleading criterion and does not satisfy the sign test; the change in land values where the improvement takes place is also misleading and may fail the sign test. Strotz's criterion ignores the correction factor U_x^2, although it satisfies the sign test. This is due to the fact that Strotz allows households to locate in both areas simultaneously.

Finally:

$$\begin{array}{cccc} \text{(Strotz)} & \text{(Lind)} & \text{(Rothenberg)} \end{array}$$

$$B = \frac{dR_1}{d\alpha_1} - \frac{m_1}{m_2} \frac{dR_2}{d\alpha_1} > \frac{dR_1}{d\alpha_1} > \frac{dR_1}{d\alpha_1} + \frac{dR_2}{d\alpha_1} \gtrless 0 \tag{3.13}$$

In another optimum versus equilibrium study by Oron et al., where the effect of automobile pollution in a monocentric city is examined and where the level of air quality is an argument in the utility function, it is shown that in the short run (land consumption pattern unchanged), the change in the aggregate value of land underestimates the social benefit accruing from pollution abatement.[52]

In an analysis of a general market equilibrium model with a fixed schedule of air quality, Polinsky and Shavell examine the effect of air quality on the rent and density functions of both an open and a closed city.[57] For the latter case, the rent of land at any location depends only on the level of air quality at that location. In the former case, property values at any point within the city depend on the air quality index in all locations, and land values understate the total willingness to pay.

Discrete Models.

There are several features special to an urban economy that can be more suitably dealt with through discrete, as opposed to continuous, methods of analysis.

In continuous models, all production is concentrated in a central core, under the assumptions that either firms operate at the level of minimum average costs, where the Euler equation is stationary (i.e., there are constant returns to scale), or that a single firm operates at regions of nonconvexity (i.e., there are increasing returns to scale).[b] Continuous models can be criticized for assuming concentration under constant returns to scale. As we shall see below, Mills has shown, for both the discrete and the continuous cases, the additional conditions that ought to hold for the concentration of production under constant returns to be possible. A problem of interest is to examine the geographical dispersion of productive activity relating to several commodities that can be exported, locally consumed, or used as intermediate goods in production, that could take place under several different activities characterized by distinct capital to land ratios. The assignment of production activities over space under such conditions is most efficiently analyzed through linear programming. Considering the case of increasing returns, Hartwick and Hartwick have commented on incorporating scale effects into a linear programming model (i.e., providing lower bounds for the production of different commodities in different locations).[19] They point out the difficulty with price sustainability of nonlinear programming location assignments of the Koopmans and Beckmann kind.[23] Hartwick has addressed this problem of market sustainability in a recent paper.[18]

Another vulnerability of continuous models is their monocentricity and the associated unidimensional representation of space. The existence of more than one center complicates the continuous representation of space and makes resorting to discrete techniques necessary. Without explaining the reasons for the existence of centers, discrete models can examine the effect of several centers on the urban form and the intraurban distribution

---

[b] Solow[67] introduces a local service sector dispersed throughout the urban area. We are here referring to the deconcentration of manufacturing activity.

of activities. In the Hartwick and Hartwick paper the "centers" represent nodes from which exports are shipped. In the work of Casetti and Papageorgiou, the Löschian approach of hierarchical distribution of production centers is taken up and general theorems of (uniform), and rent, and density distributions are proved for a specific utility function.[11] In this model, households are employed in the nearest production center and make trips to the higher order centers.

Finally, in discrete models, the isotropic transport-plane assumption can be relaxed. It is possible to introduce travel in several directions, with our without choice of route, on a transport network of given geometry the links of which may or may not occupy land.

The move from continuous to discrete methods of analysis can be viewed as a response to the need for more realism. Large-scale urban simulation models used for policymaking did not have a satisfactory base in economic theory. As Mills put it:

Whereas the optimization models have no market interpretation, the market-oriented models contain no optimality criteria. Most are either too complex or inadequately articulated to permit determination of whether market solutions are efficient and, if not, what kind of intervention would be best to ensure efficiency. The situation is paradoxical because most of the market-oriented models are formulated to guide public sector planning for future urban growth (p. 101).[36]

The discrete models developed in the early seventies by Mills,[36] Hartwick and Hartwick,[19] and MacKinnon[32] focused mainly on policy issues, such as the provision of transportation services and the efficient pricing of congestion. Mills introduced the aggregate transport cost minimizing definition of efficiency.[35] Assuming fixed coefficients of land consumption for a unit of labor and a unit of productive activity, with different transport rates for workers and goods, he showed that outward commuting by workers is inefficient. The result of the model was an integrated or a segregated allocation depending on the values of the two land consumption coefficients and the transport rates. Under an integrated outcome, workers did not commute and goods were shipped to the center. Under a segregated outcome, production was concentrated around the centers with workers commuting to jobs, and products being shipped to the center. Mills also showed the competitive market realization of both the segregated and integrated outcomes. Integration of two land uses has also been derived in the recent contribution of Goldstein and Moses who explicitly recognize the interdependence among the locating activities.[15] In their model there are two goods, each of which is used in its own and the other good's production, along with land. It is shown that integrated solutions can be obtained. One of these, for example, occurs when good one is grown in an inner ring while both goods are grown in a surrounding ring with good one in this ring grown strictly as an intermediate product. The authors show that a decentralized price system will sustain an optimal integrated allocation, and that nonoptimal allocations will not be sustained.

In his pioneering paper, Mills developed a discrete linear programming model of a monocentric urban area in which land was divided into a grid.[36] In each of the squares several goods could be produced. Each household consumed one unit of the "housing good," which was assumed to include consumption goods and services. All other goods were export goods and had to be shipped to the central port or railhead. One of several possible activities could be used in the production of each good, each activity corresponding to production in a building of a certain height (capital-land ratio). Labor, land, and capital were employed in each activity according to a fixed Leontieff input coefficients technology. Aggregate production of each export good satisfied exogenous production targets. The price of capital and labor and the opportunity cost of land were exogenous constants. Transportation services were produced utilizing land and capital inputs, and several discrete congestion levels were assumed. Transportation was possible in two directions only, both towards the center.

In the model, the optimum production level for each good by each activity in each square is solved by minimizing aggregate production and transport costs. The model produced the integrated and segregated allocations encountered in the above mentioned simpler model. The solution switched from one of these outcomes to the other, again depending on the values of the transport rates and the input output coefficients. Market rental rates for land were obtained as dual variables. Mills showed how, through an iterative procedure, the model could be used to calculate the welfare loss resulting from average cost pricing of the transport network. In a later paper, Mills' model was modified to allow for intermediate goods in production, the local consumption of export goods, and the possibility of exporting goods through peripheral transportation interchanges as well as the central point.[37]

The Mills model was later extended by Hartwick and Hartwick.[19] The two important modifications were (i) the allowance for multiple "nuclei," that is, centers from where the export goods were shipped; (ii) the possibility of using any of the produced goods as intermediate inputs in the production of a good. Furthermore, (iii) no congestion costs were assumed and, (iv) transportation was allowed in four directions (toward and away from the center). Hartwick and Hartwick discussed the interpretations of the dual constraints that imply nonpositive profits in each production activity operating at equilibrium. They also showed that real income and the consumptions of the composite good and of housing were uniform. Numerical solutions were obtained for a city. The authors indicate that the primal problem was consistently solved with nonunique solutions that resulted in a symmetrical land rent distribution around the two centers but a nonsymmetrical allocation of activities.

As we pointed out earlier, the Herbert-Stevens algorithm[21] and the version of it recently developed by Wheaton[81] provide a discrete method for solving the market equilibrium problem for a set of household strata with nonuniform tastes and incomes.

MacKinnon[32] has shown how a particular version of simplicial search algorithms called the "sandwich method" (developed by Kuhn and Mac-Kinnon[25]) can be used to solve similar market equilibrium problems by deriving the solution rent vector. MacKinnon has also applied the sandwich method to market equilibrium problems with externalities.

Optimum Geography and Dynamic Aspects of Urban Form

Drawing from topics that have been touched upon in published articles, as well as yet unpublished work, we feel that one could safely point to two forthcoming third-generation developments. We will refer to these as *optimum geography* and *dynamic aspects of urban form*.

Optimum geography, a term used by Mirrlees, is meant here to refer to the problem of maximizing a given social welfare function for the total population of a country, subject to production, input factor, and land area constraints. The outcome of such a formulation is the optimum number of urban areas in the country and their respective market area with their surrounding agricultural hinterland and population size. This problem was independently addressed by Mirrlees[40] and by Starrett.[70,71]

Mirrlees examined a simple case in which labor was the only factor of production and in which part of the population could be allocated to cities and the remaining to rural areas. The welfare objective was the maximization of the simple sum of household utilities subject to a production and to a total land area constraint. In accordance with the optimum town analysis, the utility of each urban household was defined over the amount of consumption, land per household, distance from the city center, and the local residential density externality; while rural consumption of goods and land were uniform. Mirrlees derived the amount of goods (possibly negative) that should be transferred to the rural households.[40] As there were no features that could differentiate towns, they were all of equal size, although there could be more than one optimal size due to the allowance for nonconvexities in the production technology. It was also implied that the total land area constraint was not binding, justifying the assumption that each town was circular in shape.

Starrett, concerned with the applicability of standard propositions of classical price theory to cases where transport costs and other locational considerations are introduced, argues that it is, in general, optimal to have firms operate in regions of increasing returns in a spatial context.[70] Under a general production function for all output commodities, with land as a factor, and transportation services produced in each urban area under constant returns, also with land an input factor, Starrett (like Mirrlees) further assumes no interurban trade and identical urban areas. Unlike Mirrlees, who incorporates into his analysis the microeconomic behavior of the urban households, Starett emphasizes the macroeconomic aspects of the problem. He shows that, with no externalities, there is an optimum degree of increasing returns under which firms should operate. He explicitly derives the relationship among the average degree of increasing returns in an urban area, the ratios of total transport costs to value of total output, and the total differential rents to the value of output. Under further assumptions of land homogeneity and self-sufficiency of rural life, Starrett shows that in such a case, the optimum degree of increasing returns in an urban area is equal to the ratio of the total differential rents to the value of total output. Starrett discusses decentralized decision making through the possibility of rationing on outputs by a process of setting and readjusting production targets.

The second area where research potential seems promising involves the relaxation of the static nature of the models. Such attempts would be a pronounced departure from the present modeling tradition. Dynamic models of urban spatial structure could be positive or normative in nature. In either case, the crucial concept is the indivisibility and durability of urban capital (housing, streets, etc.) and the associated fact that investment decisions pertaining to urban goods have to be made intertemporally, whether by individual utility, profit maximizing agents, or a welfare maximizing or cost minimizing society. Further, introducing the element of time in the spatial context of the new urban economics, the growth paths of an urban economy can be studied under alternative investment behavior at the production side. Questions of steady state growth or urban decay can be analyzed under market equilibrium or optimum urban growth context.

Notes

1. W. Alonso [1964].

2. R.J. Anderson, Jr., and T.D. Crocker, 1971, "Air Pollution and Residential Property Values," *Urban Studies*, vol. 8, 171-180.

3. R. Artle [1971].

4. M.J. Bailey, 1959, "Notes on the Economics of Residential Zoning and Urban Renewal," *Land Economics*, vol. 35, 288-292.

5. J.L. Barr [1972].

6. J.L. Barr [1973].

7. M.J. Beckmann [1957].

8. M.J. Beckmann, 1968, *Location Theory*. New York: Random House.

9. M.J. Beckmann [1969].

10. E. Casetti [1972].

11. E. Casetti and G.J. Papageorgiou [1971].

12. J.K. Delson [1970].

13. A. Dixit [1971].

14. A. Dixit [1973].

15. G.S. Goldstein and L.N. Moses [1975].

16. R.M. Haig, 1926, "Toward an Understanding of the Metropolis," *Quarterly Journal of Economics*, vol. 40, 179-208.

17. B. Harris, et al. [1966].

18. J.M. Hartwick [1974].

19. P.G. Hartwick and J.M. Hartwick [1974].

20. J.V. Henderson [1975].

21. J. Herbert and B. Stevens [1960].

22. O. Hochman and D. Pines [1971].

23. T. Koopmans and M.J. Beckmann, 1957, "Assignment Problems in the Location of Economic Activities," *Econometrica*, vol. 25, 53-76.

24. M. Kraus [1974].

25. H.W. Kuhn and J. Mackinnon, "The Sandwich Method for Finding Fixed Points," manuscript.

26. A.S. Lang and M. Wohl, 1961, "Influence of Transportation Changes on Urban Land Uses and Values," Bulletin No. 268, NAS-NRC *Some Evaluations of Highway Improvement Impacts*.

27. L. Legey, et al. [1973].

28. D. Levhari, et al. [1972].

29. R.C. Lind [1973].

30. D.A. Livesey [1973].

31. A. Lösch, 1954, *The Economics of Location*. New Haven: Yale University Press.

32. J. Mackinnon [1974].

33. E.S. Mills [1967].

34. E.S. Mills [1969].

35. E.S. Mills [1970].

36. E.S. Mills [1972a].

37. E.S. Mills [1974].

38. E.S. Mills and D.M. deFerranti [1971].

39. E.S. Mills and J. Mackinnon [1973].

40. J.A. Mirrlees [1972].

41. J.A. Mirrlees [1973].

42. H. Mohring and M. Harwitz, 1962, *Highway Benefits: An Analytical Framework*. Evanston: Northwestern University Press.

43. A. Montesano [1972].

44. R.F. Muth [1961a].

45. R.F. Muth [1969].

46. R.F. Muth [1974].

47. R.H. Nelson [1973].

48. J.C. Ohls [1974].

49. J.C. Ohls, et al. [1974].

50. Y. Oron and D. Pines [1972].

51. Y. Oron, et al. [1973].

52. Y. Oron, et al. [1974].

53. G.J. Papageorgiou [1973b].

54. D. Pines [1974].

55. D. Pines [1975b].

56. D. Pines and Y. Weiss [1975].

57. A.M. Polinski and S. Shavell [1972].

58. H.W. Richardson [1973].

59. R.G. Ridker and H.A. Henning, 1967, "The Determinants of Residential Property Values with Special References to Air Pollution," *Review of Economics and Statistics*, vol. 49, 246-267.

60. J.G. Riley [1973].

61. J.G. Riley [1974].

62. S. Rose-Ackerman [1975].

63. J. Rothenberg, 1965, "Urban Renewal Programs," in R. Dorfman (ed.), *Measuring Benefits of Government Investment*. Washington, D.C.: The Brookings Institution.

64. E. Sheshinski [1973].

65. R.M. Solow [1972].

66. R.M. Solow [1973a].

67. R.M. Solow [1973b].

68. R.M. Solow [1973c].

69. R.M. Solow and W.S. Vickrey [1971].

70. D.A. Starrett [1972].

71. D.A. Starrett [1974].

72. N.H. Stern [1973].

73. R.H. Strotz [1965].

74. R.H. Strotz [1968].

75. C. Tiebout, 1956, "A Pure Theory of Local Expenditures," *The Journal of Political Economy*, vol. 64, 416-425.

76. W. Vickrey, 1965, "Pricing as a Tool in Coordination of Local Transportation," in J. Meyer (ed.), *Transportation Economics*. New York: National Bureau of Economic Research.

77. J.H. Von Thünen, 1826, *Der Isolierte Staat in Beziehung auf Landwirtschaft und Nationalökonomie*. Hamburg.

78. A.A. Walters, 1961, "The Theory and Measurement of Private and Social Cost of Highway Congestion," *Econometrica*, vol. 29, 676-699.

79. P. Wendt, 1957, "Theory of Urban Land Values," *Journal of Land Economics*, vol. 33, 228-240.

80. W.C. Wheaton [1974a].

81. W.C. Wheaton [1974b].

82. L. Wingo, Jr. [1961b].

83. H. Yamada [1972].

84. R.M. Zettel, 1959, *Notes on the Incidence of Highway Benefits*. Berkeley: University of California, Institute of Transportation and Traffic Engineering.

Part II

4

Comparative Statics of a Residential Economy with Several Classes

John Hartwick
Urs Schweizer
Pravin Varaiya

The geography and economic structure of the city model under consideration are orthodox. The city is circular and its center is the CBD with radius ρ. People live at distances $x \geq \rho$ and they commute to work in the CBD. Commuting cost is solely a money cost and depends only upon the distance of the residences from the CBD. Individuals have fixed money wages and use them to occupy land (housing) and to consume other commodities. These latter are available at fixed prices which are constant throughout the city. The land market is competitive, so land rents, in equilibrium, coincide with the maximum of individual bid rents and an exogenously specified agricultural rent r_A. Land is owned by absentee landlords.

There are n classes of people. Class i is characterized by the number of people in the class N_i; and, for each individual in the class, there is his wage w_i and utility function U_i. It is assumed that U_i is smooth, strictly quasi-concave, and such that housing is a normal good. Furthermore, it is assumed that preferences between classes are related in such a way that a richer individual will occupy more land than a poorer one.

Under these assumptions, in equilibrium, people in different classes reside in characteristic concentric rings around the CBD with poorer classes living closer to the CBD. Suppose $w_1 > w_2 \ldots > w_n$; and suppose class i occupies the ring $J_i = (x_{i+1}, x_i)$ where $x_1 > \ldots > x_{n+1} = \rho$, the CBD radius. Let $u_1, \ldots, u_n$ denote the equilibrium utility levels. The dependence

John Hartwick is associated with Department of Economics, Queen's University.

Urs Schweizer is associated with Department of Economics, Massachusetts Institute of Technology.

Pravin Varaiya is associated with Decision and Control Sciences Group, Electronic Systems Laboratory, Department of Electrical Engineering and Computer Science, Massachusetts Institute of Technology.

Research was partially supported by the National Science Foundation under Grant GK-41647, by the Swiss National Science Foundation, and by the Canada Council. The authors are grateful for helpful comments from members of the Urban Workship, Department of Economics, Massachusetts Institute of Technology.

of these equilibrium values on the exogenous parameters can be expressed in a functional form.

$$x_i = x_i(N_1, \ldots, N_n, w_1, \ldots, w_n) \qquad i = 1, \ldots, n$$

$$u_i = u_i(N_1, \ldots, N_n, w_1, \ldots, w_n) \qquad i = 1, \ldots, n$$

Our first set of results shows that the signs of the various partial derivatives are unambiguous. The specific statements are these:

$$\frac{\partial x_j}{\partial N_i} > 0 \text{ if } j \le i, \qquad \frac{\partial x_j}{\partial N_i} < 0 \text{ if } j > i; \quad \text{and} \quad \frac{\partial u_j}{\partial N_i} < 0 \text{ all } j \qquad (4.1)$$

That is, if the ith class increases in size, then the richer classes are pushed away from the CBD whereas the poorer ones are squeezed towards it, and everyone's real income is reduced. This is not at all surprising. Further:

$$\frac{\partial x_j}{\partial w_i} > 0 \text{ all } j; \quad \text{and} \quad \frac{\partial u_j}{\partial w_i} > 0 \text{ if } j \ge i, \qquad \frac{\partial u_j}{\partial w_i} < 0 \text{ if } j < i \qquad (4.2)$$

That is, if the ith class's income rises, then all classes are more suburbanized, and the richer classes suffer a reduction in their real income whereas the poorer classes enjoy an increase. The total assummetry of (4.1) and (4.2) is of a striking simplicity. Many people may find (4.2) counterintuitive since it would appear at first sight that, since increases in N_i or w_i both create increased demand pressures in the land market, they would have the same impact on the real income of the other classes.

These qualitative results, while telling us that increases in the income or size of a richer class have opposing impacts on a poorer class, do not provide any clue to the relative magnitudes of these two effects. Our second set of results is the outcome of some numerical exercises designed to reveal what magnitudes of these effects might plausibly be expected. Choosing $n = 2$ and the same Cobb-Douglas utility function for both classes, we show that the negative effect on the poor due to an increase in the size of the richer class is far greater than the positive effect due to an increase in the latter's income.

To our knowledge the only other work relating to ours is the extensive comparative static analysis carried out by Wheaton for the case of a single class, $n = 1.$[2] Since our interest is solely to understand interclass effects, his results and ours are complementary.

The Model and Its Equilibrium

Aside from the notation introduced already, we need the following.

ASSUMPTION 4.1: The money cost of commuting from x is $t(x)$ and is such that

$$t_x = \frac{dt}{dx} > 0$$

Rent of land is denoted by r and the amount of land available for housing at x is exogenously given to be $\theta(x)x$ (for a circular city we have $\theta(x)x = 2\pi x$). The amount of land occupied by an individual is denoted h and the bundle of other goods he consumes is the (column) vector c. The exogenously fixed prices of these other goods is the (row) vector p.

The *expenditure function* for an individual of class i can then be defined in the usual way as

$$E^i(r, u) = \min\{pc + rh \mid u^i(c, h) = u\}$$

and this is related to his *compensated demand functions* C^i and H^i by

$$E^i(r, u) = pC^i(r, u) + rH^i(r, u) \qquad U^i(C^i(r, u), H^i(r, u)) = u \quad (4.3)$$

E^i has the following well-known properties:

$$E^i_u = \frac{\partial E^i}{\partial u} > 0 \qquad E^i_r = \frac{\partial E^i}{\partial r} = H^i > 0 \qquad E^i_{rr} = \frac{\partial^2 E^i}{\partial r^2} = H^i_r < 0 \quad (4.4)$$

Let $r^i(u, I)$ be the function that gives the maximum rent the individual can offer and still achieve a utility level u when his disposable income (net of commuting costs) is I:

$$r^i(u, I) = \max\{h^{-1}(I - pc) \mid U^i(c, h) = u\}$$

From this definition it follows that

$$E^i(r^i(u, I), u) = I \tag{4.5}$$

Define the demand for land, when $r^i(u, I)$ is the rent, by

$$h^i(u, I) = H^i(r^i(u, I), u) \tag{4.6}$$

ASSUMPTION 4.2: We assume that housing is a normal good. More precisely, if two individuals face the same rent r, the one with the higher income demands more land.

$$\bar{I} = E^i(r, \bar{u}) > I = E^j(r, u) \quad \text{implies } H^i(r, \bar{u}) > H^j(r, u)$$

For the case $i = j$, this reduces to

$$H^i_u = \frac{\partial H^i}{\partial u} > 0 \tag{4.7}$$

and so, together with (4.4), this yields

$$E_{ru}^i = E_{ur}^i = \frac{\partial^2 E^i}{\partial_u \partial_r} > 0 \tag{4.8}$$

Next, from (4.4) and (4.5), we have

$$r_I^i = (E_r^i)^{-1} > 0 \qquad r_u^i = -E_u^i(E_r^i)^{-1} < 0 \tag{4.9}$$

while, from (4.4), (4.6), (4.7), and (4.9), we have

$$h_I^i = H_r^i r_I^i < 0 \qquad h_u^i = H_r^i r_u^i + H_u^i > 0 \tag{4.10}$$

Finally, since the wage of an individual of class i is w_i, and since $t(x)$ is his commuting cost, his *bid rent* function is $r^i(u, w_i - t(x))$, considered as a function of w and x. From Assumption 4.1 and equation (4.9) we find

$$\dot{r}_x^i = \frac{\partial r^i}{\partial x} = -t_x r_I^i < 0 \tag{4.11}$$

The next result, which is used repeatedly, shows that the difference in two bid rent functions varies strictly monotonically in x.

LEMMA 4.1: Suppose

$$\bar{r} = r^i(\bar{u}, \bar{w} - t(\bar{x})) = r^j(u, w - t(\bar{x})) \qquad \text{and} \qquad \bar{w} > w$$

Then

$$r_x^j(u, w - t(x)) < r_x^i(\bar{u}, \bar{w} - t(\bar{x})) < 0 \quad \text{for } x \le \bar{x} \tag{4.12}$$

Proof: $\qquad E^i(\bar{r}, \bar{u}) = \bar{w} - t(\bar{x}) > w - t(\bar{x}) = E^j(\bar{r}, u)$

by (4.5) and so, by Assumption 4.2,

$$H^i(\bar{r}, \bar{u}) > H^j(\bar{r}, u) \tag{4.13}$$

From (4.5), $E^i[r^i(\bar{u}, \bar{w} - t(x)), u] = \bar{w} - t(x)$, and if we differentiate this with respect to x and then use (4.4), we obtain

$$H^i[r^i(\bar{u}, \bar{w} - t(x)), \bar{u}]r_x^i(\bar{u}, \bar{w} - t(x)) = -t_x \tag{4.14}$$

and, similarly,

$$H^j[r^j(u, w - t(x)) u]r_x^j(u, w - t(x)) = -t_x \tag{4.15}$$

From (4.13)-(4.15) we conclude that (4.12) holds for $x = \bar{x}$.

Next, as long as both $x < \bar{x}$ and $r^i(\bar{u}, \bar{w} - t(x)) < r^j(u, w - t(x))$, we can show, using (4.4), Assumption 4.2, and (4.7), that

$$H^i[r^i(\bar{u}, \bar{w} - t(x)), \bar{u}] > H^i[r^j(u, w - t(x)), \bar{u}] > H^j[r^j(u, w - t(x)), u]$$

and so, using (4.14) and (4.15) we can again conclude that (4.12) holds.

Using this fact and knowing that (4.12) holds at least for $x = \bar{x}$, the assertion follows quite readily.

COROLLARY 4.1:   Under the assumptions of Lemma 4.1,

$$r^i(\bar{u}, \bar{w} - t(x)) \gtreqless r^j(u, w - t(x)) \qquad (4.16)$$

according as $x \gtreqless \bar{x}$.

Next we define the envelope of the individual bid rent functions as

$$R(u_1, \ldots, u_n, w_1 - t(x), \ldots, w_n - t(x))$$
$$= \max \{r^1(u_1, w_1 - t(x)), \ldots, r^n(u_n, w_n - t(x)), r_A\}$$

Recall that $\theta(x)x \, dx$ is the amount of land available for residences in the ring $[x, x+dx]$. We can now define the notion of an equilibrium.

Definition   An *equilibrium* consists of a set of utility levels $u_1, \ldots, u_n$ and a set of residence rings $J_1, \ldots, J_n$ contained in $[\rho, \infty]$ such that $x \, \varepsilon \, J_i$ if and only if

$$r^i(u_i, w_i - t(x))$$
$$= R(u_1, \ldots, u_n, w_1 - t(x), \ldots, w_n - t(x)) \qquad i = 1, \ldots, n \qquad (4.17)$$

where

$$R(u_1, \ldots, u_n, w_1 - t(x), \ldots, w_n - t(x)) \quad \text{is continuous in } x \qquad (4.18)$$

and, also,

$$N_i = \int_{J_i} \frac{\theta(x)x}{h^i(u_i, w_i - t(x))} \, dx \qquad i = 1, \ldots, n \qquad (4.19)$$

Condition (4.17) ensures that land is occupied by the highest bidder; (4.18) says that the equilibrium rent must be continuous across the boundary between land occupied by adjacent classes—that is, no individual pays more than he has to; and (4.19) is simply the land market clearing condition.

We now derive some properties of an equilibrium. First of all, from (4.16) and (4.17) we see that poorer individuals live closer to the CBD. Hence the rings must have the form

$$J_i = [x_{i+1}, x_i] \qquad x_1 > x_2 > \ldots > x_{n+1} = \rho \qquad (4.20)$$

so that (4.18) can be rewritten more directly as

$$r^1(u_1, w_1 - t(x_1)) = r_A \qquad (4.21a)$$
$$r^i(u_i, w_i - t(x_i)) = r^{i-1}(u_{i-1}, w_{i-1} - t(x_i)) \qquad i = 2, \ldots, n \qquad (4.21b)$$

From (4.21) we can solve for u_1 as a function of x_1 and w_1. Then, by induction, we can solve for u_i as a function of $x_i, \ldots, x_1$ and $w_i, \ldots, w_1$. The signs of the partial derivatives of these functions can be determined as follows:

LEMMA 4.2: $\qquad \dfrac{\partial u_i}{\partial x_j} < 0 \quad$ and $\quad \dfrac{\partial u_i}{\partial w_j} > 0 \qquad j \le i \qquad\qquad$ (4.22)

Proof: We proceed by induction. Differentiating (4.21a) gives

$$r_u^1 \frac{\partial u_1}{\partial w_1} + r_l^1 = 0 \qquad r_l^1 \frac{\partial u_1}{\partial x_1} - t_x r_l^1 = 0$$

and so, together with (4.9) and (4.11) this yields

$$\frac{\partial u_1}{\partial w_1} > 0 \qquad \frac{\partial u_1}{\partial x_1} < 0$$

Hence, (4.22) is true for $i = 1$.

Now suppose (4.22) holds for $i - 1$. Just as before, we still have, after differentiating (4.21b) with respect to w_i, that

$$r_u^i(u_i, w_i - t(x_i)) \frac{\partial u_i}{\partial w_i} + r_l^i(u_i, w_i - t(x_i)) = 0 \qquad\qquad (4.23)$$

so that again $\partial u_i / \partial w_i > 0$; whereas differentiation with respect to x_i gives us

$$r_u^i(u_i, w_i - t(x_i)) \frac{\partial u_i}{\partial x_i} + r_x^i(u_i, w_i - t(x_i)) = r_x^{i-1}(u_{i-1}, w_{i-1} - t(x_i)) \qquad (4.24)$$

From (4.24), (4.9), (4.12), and the fact that $w_i < w_{i-1}$, we conclude that $\partial u_i / \partial x_i < 0$. Let us also note from (4.9) and (4.23) that

$$\frac{\partial u_i}{\partial w_i} = -\frac{r_l^i(u_i, w_i - t(x_i))}{r_u^i(u_i, w_i - t(x_i))} = \frac{1}{E_u^i[r^i(u_i, w_i - t(x_i)), u_i]} > 0 \qquad (4.25)$$

To evaluate the derivative for $j < i$, we again differentiate (4.21b). Thus, we have,

$$r_u^i(u_i, w_i - t(x_i)) \frac{\partial u_i}{\partial w_{i-1}}$$

$$= r_u^{i-1}(u_{i-1}, w_{i-1} - t(x_i)) \frac{\partial u_{i-1}}{\partial w_{i-1}} + r_l^{i-1}(u_{i-1}, w_{i-1} - t(x_i))$$

$$= r_l^{i-1}(u_{i-1}, w_{i-1} - t(x_i)) \left\{ 1 + E_u^{i-1}[r^{i-1}(u_{i-1}, w_{i-1} - t(x_i)), u_{i-1}] \frac{\partial u_{i-1}}{\partial w_{i-1}} \right\}$$

and

$$= r_I^{i-1} \left\{ 1 - \frac{E_u^{i-1}[r^{i-1}(u_{i-1}, w_{i-1}-t(x_i)), u_{i-1}]}{E_u^{i-1}[r^{i-1}(u_{i-1}, w_{i-1}-t(x_{i-1})), u_{i-1}]} \right\}$$

using (4.23) and (4.25).

The expression in brackets is negative because of (4.8) and so using (4.9) we get $\partial u_i / \partial w_{i-1} > 0$. Now, from (4.21),

$$r_u^i \frac{\partial u_i}{\partial u_{i-1}} = r_u^{i-1}$$

so that $\partial u_i / \partial u_{i-1} > 0$. Hence, using the induction hypothesis, we get

$$\frac{\partial u_i}{\partial x_j} = \frac{\partial u_i}{\partial u_{i-1}} \frac{\partial u_{i-1}}{\partial x_j} < 0 \qquad j < i$$

and

$$\frac{\partial u_i}{\partial w_j} = \frac{\partial u_i}{\partial u_{i-1}} \frac{\partial u_{i-1}}{\partial w_j} > 0 \qquad j < i - 1$$

Hence, (4.22) holds for i, and Lemma 4.2 is proved.

From (4.19) and the remark preceding Lemma 4.2 we note that N_i is determined by $x_{i+1}, \ldots, x_1$ and $w_i, \ldots, w_1$. The derivatives in the next lemma are with respect to this functional dependence.

LEMMA 4.3:
$$\frac{\partial N_i}{\partial x_j} > 0 \qquad j \leq i$$

$$\frac{\partial N_i}{\partial x_{i+1}} < 0 \qquad \frac{\partial N_i}{\partial w_j} < 0 \qquad j \leq i$$

Proof: From (4.19) and (4.20), we obtain

$$\frac{\partial N_i}{\partial x_{i+1}} = - \frac{\theta(x_{i+1})x_{i+1}}{h^i(u_i, w_i - t(x_{i+1}))} < 0$$

and by (4.10) and (4.22)

$$\frac{\partial N_i}{\partial x_i} =$$

$$- \int_{x_{i+1}}^{x_i} \frac{\theta(x)x}{[h^i(u_i, w_i - t(x))]^2} h_u^i(u_i, w_i - t(x)) \frac{\partial u_i}{\partial x_i} \, dx + \frac{\theta(x_i)x_i}{h^i(u_i, w_i - t(x_i))} > 0$$

Furthermore, using (4.19) and (4.22), we get for $j < i$,

$$\frac{\partial N_i}{\partial x_j} = -\int_{x_{i+1}}^{x_i} \frac{\theta(x)x}{[h^i(u_i,\ w_i-t(x))]^2} h_u^i(u_i,\ w_i-t(x)) \frac{\partial u_i}{\partial x_j}\ dx > 0$$

It only remains to prove the last assertion, which, for $j < i$, follows in the same way as above from (4.19) and (4.22). Finally, for $j = i$, we get

$$\frac{\partial N_i}{\partial w_i} = -\int_{x_{i+1}}^{x_i} \frac{\theta(x)x}{[h^i(u_i,\ w_i-t(x))]^2}\left[h_u^i \frac{\partial u_i}{\partial w_i} + h_i^i\right]dx \qquad (4.26)$$

Now, from (4.4), (4.6), and (4.10), we have

$$h_u^i \frac{\partial u_i}{\partial w_i} + h_i^i = \frac{E_{ru}^i[r^i(u_i,\ w_i-t(x)),\ u_i]}{E_u^i[r^i(u_i,\ w_i-t(x_i)),\ u_i]}$$

$$+ \frac{E_{rr}^i[\ldots x \ldots]}{E_r^i[\ldots x \ldots]}\left\{1 - \frac{E_u^i[\ldots x \ldots]}{E_u^i[\ldots x_i \ldots]}\right\}$$

which is positive, since each of the terms on the right is positive. Hence, from (4.26), $\partial N_i/\partial w_i > 0$ also.

Comparative Statics

If we express the functional dependence of N_i on $x_{i+1}, \ldots, x_1$ and $w_i, \ldots, w_1$ in differential form we get

$$dN_i = \sum_{j=1}^{i+1} \frac{\partial N_i}{\partial x_j}\ dx_j + \sum_{j=1}^{i} \frac{\partial N_i}{\partial w_j}\ dw_j \qquad i = 1, \ldots, n$$

or in matrix notation

$$dN = A\,dx + a\,dx_{n+1} - B\,dw \qquad (4.27)$$

By Lemma 4.3, the vector a and the $n \times n$ matrices A and B, we have the sign pattern shown below.

$$a = \begin{bmatrix} 0 \\ \cdot \\ \cdot \\ \cdot \\ 0 \\ - \end{bmatrix} \qquad A = \begin{bmatrix} + & - & 0 & \cdot & \cdot & \cdot & 0 \\ \cdot & \cdot & \cdot & \cdot & & & \cdot \\ \cdot & & \cdot & \cdot & \cdot & & \cdot \\ \cdot & & & \cdot & \cdot & \cdot & \cdot \\ \cdot & & & & \cdot & \cdot & 0 \\ \cdot & & & & & \cdot & - \\ + & \cdot & \cdot & \cdot & \cdot & \cdot & + \end{bmatrix} \qquad (4.28)$$

$$
B = \begin{bmatrix} + & 0 & \cdot & \cdot & \cdot & 0 \\ & \cdot & & & & \\ \cdot & & \cdot & & & \cdot \\ & & & \cdot & \cdot & \\ \cdot & & \cdot & \cdot & & \cdot \\ & & & \cdot & \cdot & \\ \cdot & & & & \cdot & 0 \\ & & & & \cdot & \\ + & \cdot & & \cdot & \cdot & + \end{bmatrix} \qquad \text{(4.28, cont.)}
$$

Here $dx = (dx_1, \ldots, dx_n)'$ and $dw = (dw_1, \ldots, dw_n)'$.

Now, to obtain the results announced in the introduction, we will first obtain the sign pattern of A^{-1}, as well as some information about the relative magnitudes of some of its coefficients. With this knowledge and the results obtained so far, we will be able to reach the desired conclusion.

A portion of the sign pattern of A^{-1} can already be determined from (4.28).

LEMMA 4.4: If A has the pattern of (4.28), then $\det A > 0$, and A^{-1} has the pattern shown below.

$$
A^{-1} = \begin{bmatrix} + & \cdot & \cdot & \cdot & + \\ - & \cdot & & & \cdot \\ ? & \cdot & \cdot & & \cdot \\ \cdot & \cdot & \cdot & \cdot & \cdot \\ \cdot & & \cdot & \cdot & \cdot \\ \cdot & & \cdot & \cdot & \cdot \\ ? & \cdot & \cdot & ? & - & + \end{bmatrix} \qquad \text{(4.29)}
$$

where ? means the sign is unknown.

Proof: See Appendix 4A.

As a corollary, we can see the effect of a change in the size of the poorest class, N_n:

COROLLARY 4.2:
$$\frac{\partial x_j}{\partial N_n} > 0 \quad \text{all } j$$

$$\frac{\partial u_j}{\partial N_n} < 0 \quad \text{all } j$$

Proof: From (4.27) and (4.29), we can see that the vector $dx = A^{-1}(dN_n)e_n > 0$, if $dN_n > 0$, where $e_n = (0, \ldots, 0, 1)'$, thus giving the first result. The second assertion follows from the first one and Lemma 2.

To determine the effects of a change in N_i, $i < n$, it is necessary to proceed somewhat circuitously. Instead of considering an exogenously fixed agricultural rent r_A, as in (4.21), we consider the outer radius of the city, x_1, as exogenously given. This will cause some simple changes in the various functional dependencies. Specifically, u_1 is no longer determined by x_1 and w_1 via (4.21). As a consequence, u_i becomes a function of x_i, $\ldots$, x_2 and u_1 via (4.21). (In the following argument, w_1, $\ldots$, w_n are fixed throughout.) Hence, N_i is a function of x_{i+1}, $\ldots$, x_1 and u_1, so that

$$\sum_{j=2}^{i+1} \frac{\partial N_i}{\partial x_j} dx_j + \frac{\partial N_i}{\partial u_1} du_1 = -\frac{\partial N_i}{\partial x_1} dx_1$$

After dividing both sides by $\partial N_i / \partial x_1$, which is positive by Lemma 4.3, we can express this in matrix form.

$$\tilde{A} \begin{bmatrix} du_1 \\ dx_2 \\ \vdots \\ dx_n \end{bmatrix} = \begin{bmatrix} -dx_1 \\ 0 \\ \vdots \\ 0 \end{bmatrix} \tag{4.30}$$

The sign pattern of $\tilde{A}$ can be shown, in a way similar to the proof of Lemma 4.3, to be of this form:

$$\tilde{A} = \begin{bmatrix} - & - & 0 & \cdot & \cdot & \cdot & 0 \\ \cdot & + & \cdot & \cdot & \cdot & & \cdot \\ \cdot & & \cdot & \cdot & \cdot & & \cdot \\ \cdot & & & \cdot & \cdot & & \cdot \\ \cdot & & & & \cdot & \cdot & 0 \\ \cdot & \cdot & & & & \cdot & - \\ - & + & \cdot & & \cdot & & + \end{bmatrix}$$

and applying Cramer's rule to (4.30), as in the proof of Lemma 4.24, we get

$$\begin{bmatrix} du_1 \\ dx_2 \end{bmatrix} = \begin{bmatrix} + \\ + \end{bmatrix} dx_1 \qquad (4.31)$$

Next, we observe that if we fix x_2 and consider only classes $2, \ldots, n$, we are in the same situation as the one considered above (where we fixed x_1 and considered classes $1, \ldots, n$). Thus, (4.31) stated for this situation is of the form

$$\begin{bmatrix} du_2 \\ dx_3 \end{bmatrix} = \begin{bmatrix} + \\ + \end{bmatrix} dx_2 = \begin{bmatrix} + \\ + \end{bmatrix} dx_1$$

where the last equality follows from (4.31). Proceeding inductively we obtain

$$\begin{bmatrix} du_1 \\ \vdots \\ du_n \end{bmatrix} = \begin{bmatrix} + \\ \vdots \\ + \end{bmatrix} dx_1 \quad \text{and} \quad \begin{bmatrix} dx_2 \\ \vdots \\ dx_n \end{bmatrix} = \begin{bmatrix} + \\ \vdots \\ + \end{bmatrix} dx_1 \qquad (4.32)$$

an intuitive result, since it states that if the city boundary is shifted outwards, then all classes get more suburbanized and everyone's welfare improves. We can now prove (4.1).

THEOREM 4.1: Under Assumptions 4.1 and 4.2

$$\frac{\partial x_j}{\partial N_i} > 0 \qquad j \le i$$

$$\frac{\partial x_j}{\partial N_i} < 0 \qquad j > i$$

$$\frac{\partial u_j}{\partial N_i} < 0 \qquad \text{all } j$$

66

Proof: Suppose $dN_j = 0$ $(j \neq i)$ and $dw_j = 0$ (all j). Then (4.27) reads

$$Adx = \begin{bmatrix} 0 \\ \vdots \\ dN_i \\ \vdots \\ 0 \end{bmatrix}$$

By Lemma 4.4 and then by Lemma 4.2 we get

$$\begin{bmatrix} dx_1 \\ \vdots \\ dx_i \\ dx_{i+1} \end{bmatrix} = \begin{bmatrix} + \\ \vdots \\ + \\ - \end{bmatrix} dN_i \begin{bmatrix} du_1 \\ \vdots \\ du_i \end{bmatrix} = \begin{bmatrix} - \\ \vdots \\ - \end{bmatrix} dN_i \qquad (4.33)$$

The behavior of the remaining classes, $i+1, \ldots, n$, is the same as if they lived in a city of radius x_{i+1} which changed by dx_{i+1}. Hence, from (4.32), and (4.33),

$$\begin{bmatrix} du_{i+1} \\ \vdots \\ du_n \end{bmatrix} = \begin{bmatrix} + \\ \vdots \\ + \end{bmatrix} dx_{i+1} = \begin{bmatrix} - \\ \vdots \\ - \end{bmatrix} dN_i \qquad (4.34)$$

The result follows from (4.33) and (4.32).

We now evaluate the effects of income changes. Once again this is easy to see when only the poorest class's income, w_n, changes. From (4.27), (4.28), Lemma 4.4 and Lemma 4.2, it is easy to show that

$$\begin{bmatrix} dx_1 \\ \vdots \\ dx_n \end{bmatrix} = \begin{bmatrix} + \\ \vdots \\ + \end{bmatrix} dw_n \begin{bmatrix} du_1 \\ \vdots \\ du_{n-1} \end{bmatrix} = \begin{bmatrix} - \\ \vdots \\ - \end{bmatrix} dw_n \qquad (4.35)$$

Let us show that $\partial u_n / \partial w_n > 0$, that is,

$$du_n = [+]dw_n \qquad (4.36)$$

From (4.19) we get

$$0 = \frac{dN_n}{dw_n} = -\int_{x_{n+1}}^{x_n} \frac{\theta(x)x}{[h^n]^2}\left(h^n_u\frac{\partial u_n}{\partial w_n} + h^n_l\right)dx + \frac{\theta(x_n)x_n}{h^n}\frac{\partial x_n}{\partial w_n}$$

since $dN_n = dx_{n+1} = 0$. Since the second term on the right is positive by (4.35) this relation can hold only if there exists $x \, \varepsilon \, (x_{n+1}, \, x_n)$ where

$$h^n_u\frac{\partial u_n}{\partial w_n} + h^n_l > 0$$

which implies (4.36) because of (4.10). Thus, the case where only w_n changes is completely settled. For later purposes, however, we need to determine how the rent at the CBD changes with w_n, that is, we need the sign of $\partial r_{n+1} / \partial w_n$ where $r_{n+1} = r^n(u_n, \, w_n - t(x_{n+1}))$. We will show that

$$\frac{\partial r_{n+1}}{\partial w_n} < 0$$

provided that the following assumption holds,

ASSUMPTION 4.3:

$$[\theta(x)x]^{-1}\frac{d}{dx}(\theta(x)x) > [t_x(x)]^{-1}\frac{d}{dx}(t_x(x)) \quad \text{all } x$$

We will discuss this condition later, but note here that if $\theta(x) = 2\pi$, Assumption 4.3 reads

$$1 > \frac{x}{t(x)}\frac{d}{dx}t_x(x)$$

which is the condition imposed by Wheaton;[2] whereas, if t_x is constant, then Assumption 3 requires only that $\theta(x)x$ is increasing in x. We also define

$$r_1 = r_A, \qquad r_{i+1} = r^i(u_i, \, w_i - t(x_{i+1})) \qquad i = 1, \ldots, n \qquad (4.37)$$

These rents are interrelated by

$$N_i = \frac{\theta(x_{i+1})x_{i+1}}{t_x(x_{i+1})}r_{i+1} - \frac{\theta(x_i)x_i}{t_x(x_i)}r_i$$

$$+ \int_{x_{i+1}}^{x_i} \frac{d}{dx}\left[\frac{\theta(x)x}{t_x(x)}\right]r^i(u_i, \, w_i - t(x))\,dx \qquad (4.38)$$

The formula is obtained by differentiating the identity

$$E^i[r^i(u_i, w_i-t(x)), u_i] = w_i-t(x)$$

to obtain $h^i r_x^i = -t_x$, so that

$$N_i = \int_{x_{i+1}}^{x_i} \frac{\theta(x)x}{h^i(x)}\, dx = -\int_{x_{i+1}}^{x_i} \frac{\theta(x)x}{t_x(x)} r_x^i(x)\, dx$$

which, upon integration by parts, yields (4.38).[a] Now differentiate (4.38):

$$0 = \frac{dN_i}{dw_n} = \frac{\theta(x_{i+1})x_{i+1}}{t_x'(x_{i+1})}\frac{\partial r_{i+1}}{\partial w_n} - \frac{\theta(x_i)x_i}{t_x(x_i)}\frac{\partial r_i}{\partial w_n}$$

$$+ \int_{x_{i+1}}^{x_i} \frac{d}{dx}\left[\frac{\theta(x)x}{t_x(x)}\right]\frac{\partial}{\partial w_n} r^i(u_i, w_i-t(x))\, dx \tag{4.39}$$

$$x_{i+1}$$

In this relation, by Assumption 4.3;

$$\frac{d}{dx}\left[\frac{\theta(x)x}{t_x(x)}\right] > 0$$

and, by (4.35),

$$\frac{\partial}{\partial w_n} r^i(u_i, w_i-t(x)) = r_u^i \frac{\partial u_i}{\partial w_n} < 0 \qquad \text{for } i < n$$

so that

$$\frac{\theta(x_{i+1})x_{i+1}}{t_x(x_{i+1})}\frac{\partial r_{i+1}}{\partial w_n} < \frac{\theta(x_i)x_i}{t_x(x_i)}\frac{\partial r_i}{\partial w_n} \qquad i < n \tag{4.40}$$

Starting with the fact that $\partial r_1/\partial w_n = 0$, we can proceed recursively, using (4.40) to conclude that $\partial r_2/\partial w_n < 0, \ldots, \partial r_n/\partial w_n < 0$. An argument similar to the one used in Lemma 4.3 shows that

$$\frac{\partial}{\partial w_n} r^n(u_n, w_n-t(x)) = r_u^n \frac{\partial u_n}{\partial w_n} + r_I^n$$

$$= \frac{E_u^n(\ldots x \ldots)}{h^n(u_n, w_n-t(x))}\left[\frac{1}{E_u^n(\ldots x \ldots)} - \frac{\partial u_r}{\partial w_n}\right]$$

where the term in square brackets is increasing in x by virtue of (4.8), in which case if $(\partial/\partial w_n) r^n(u_n, w_n-t(x_{n+1})) = (\partial r_{n+1}/\partial w_n) \geq 0$, then we must have $(\partial/\partial w_n) r^n(u_n, w_n-t(x)) > 0$ for $x > x_{n+1}$, which contradicts (4.39). Thus we have proved that

---

[a] This formula is interesting in its own right, since it directly relates the population to the rent function and transportation cost.

$$\frac{\partial r_{n+1}}{\partial w_n} < 0 \qquad (4.41)$$

as desired. Inequality (4.41) implies that the rent at the CBD decreases as the income of the poorest class increases. While it is obvious that the density at the CBD must decrease with increases in w_n, since people in class n will demand more land, it does not follow that the reduction in density will be so large that rents will decrease also. To reach this conclusion, Assumption 4.3 is crucial.

We will make critical use of (4.41) to study the effects of a change in w_i, $i < n$. But first let us note that if $dN = 0$, $dw = 0$; but $dx_{n+1} \neq 0$ in (4.27), then we have $A\,dx = -a\,dx_{n+1}$ so that from (4.28) and (4.29) we get

$$\begin{bmatrix} dx_1 \\ \cdot \\ \cdot \\ \cdot \\ dx_n \end{bmatrix} = \begin{bmatrix} + \\ \cdot \\ \cdot \\ \cdot \\ + \end{bmatrix} dx_{n+1} \qquad (4.42a)$$

and, using Lemma 4.2,

$$\begin{bmatrix} du_1 \\ \cdot \\ \cdot \\ \cdot \\ du_n \end{bmatrix} = \begin{bmatrix} - \\ \cdot \\ \cdot \\ \cdot \\ - \end{bmatrix} dx_{n+1} \qquad (4.42b)$$

This last equation is obvious; it asserts that everyone will be worse off (due to increased transport cost) if the CBD grows. Equation (4.42a) is perhaps less obvious; it asserts that all classes will be more suburbanized (even without any increase in income) if the CBD grows.

Now, consider a change in w_i, for some $i < n$. Setting $dx_{n+1} = 0$, $dN = 0$, and $dw_j = 0$ $(j \neq 1)$ in (4.27), we see, using (4.28), that

$$A \begin{bmatrix} dx_1 \\ \cdot \\ \cdot \\ \cdot \\ \cdot \\ dx_n \end{bmatrix} = \begin{bmatrix} 0 \\ \cdot \\ \cdot \\ 0 \\ + \\ \cdot \\ \cdot \\ + \end{bmatrix} dw_i \qquad (4.43)$$

where exactly the first $i - 1$ components are zero. From (4.43) and (4.29), and then from Lemma 4.2, we can deduce that

$$\begin{bmatrix} dx_1 \\ \vdots \\ dx_i \end{bmatrix} = \begin{bmatrix} + \\ \vdots \\ + \end{bmatrix} dw_i \quad \text{and} \quad \begin{bmatrix} du_1 \\ \vdots \\ du_{i-1} \end{bmatrix} = \begin{bmatrix} - \\ \vdots \\ - \end{bmatrix} dw_i \qquad (4.44)$$

Thus, the classes richer than i get more suburbanized and suffer a loss in real income when the income of class i increases.

Regarding the poorer classes $i+1, \ldots, n$, their allocation is the same as if they lived in a city of radius x_{i+1} and the other classes did not exist at all. Since class $i+1$ is the richest among these classes we can use (4.32) to conclude that

$$\begin{bmatrix} du_{i+1} \\ \vdots \\ du_n \end{bmatrix} = \begin{bmatrix} + \\ \vdots \\ + \end{bmatrix} dx_{i+1} \qquad \begin{bmatrix} dx_{i+2} \\ \vdots \\ dx_n \end{bmatrix} = \begin{bmatrix} + \\ \vdots \\ + \end{bmatrix} dx_{i+1} \qquad (4.45)$$

so that we must determine the sign of dx_{i+1}.

But before we do this, let us note that the richer classes $1, \ldots, i$ receive the same allocation as if they alone lived in a city whose CBD radius was x_{i+1}. In this sense u_i is determined by x_{i+1} and w_i, and we may express this as $u_i = F(x_{i+1}, w_i)$. Since class i is the poorest among these classes, we can use (4.42) and (4.36) respectively to conclude that

$$\frac{\partial F}{\partial x_{i+1}} < 0 \qquad \frac{\partial F}{\partial w_i} > 0 \qquad (4.46)$$

To determine the sign of dx_{i+1}, we differentiate the equilibrium condition (4.21),

$$r^{i+1}(u_{i+1}, w_{i+1} - t(x_{i+1})) = r^i(u_i, w_i - t(x_{i+1}))$$

to obtain

$$r_u^{i+1} \frac{du_{i+1}}{dx_{i+1}} dx_{i+1} + r_x^{i+1} dx_{i+1} = r_u^i \left[\frac{\partial F}{\partial x_{i+1}} dx_{i+1} + \frac{\partial F}{\partial w_i} dw_i \right]$$
$$+ r_I^i dw_i + r_x^i dx_{i+1} \qquad (4.47)$$

which can be rearranged as

$$\left[r_u^i \frac{\partial F}{\partial w_i} + r_I^i\right] dw_i = \left[r_u^{i+1} \frac{du_{i+1}}{dx_{i+1}} + (r_x^{i+1} - r_x^i) - r_u^i \frac{\partial F}{\partial x_{i+1}}\right] dx_{i+1}$$

Now, $r_u^{i+1} < 0$ by (4.9); $du_{i+1}/dx_{i+1} < 0$ by (4.45); $(r_x^{i+1} - r_x^i) < 0$ by Lemma 4.1; and $-r_u^i (\partial F/\partial x_{i+1}) < 0$ by (4.9) and (4.46). Thus, the coefficient multiplying dx_{i+1} is negative. On the other hand, by (4.41), we know that

$$\frac{\partial r_{i+1}}{\partial w_i} = \left[r_u^i \frac{\partial F}{\partial w_i} + r_I^i\right] < 0 \tag{4.48}$$

Thus, we have shown that

$$dx_{i+1} = [+] dw_i \tag{4.49}$$

Only the sign of du_i remains. From (4.47), we note that

$$r_u^i \frac{\partial u_i}{\partial w_i} dw_i = r_n^i \left[\frac{\partial F}{\partial w_i} dw_i + \frac{\partial F}{\partial w_{i+1}} dx_{i+1}\right]$$

$$= r_u^{i+1} \frac{du_{i+1}}{dx_{i+1}} dx_{i+1} + (r_x^{i+1} - r_x^i) dx_{i+1}$$

$$= r_u^{i+1} \frac{du_{i+1}}{dx_{i+1}} dx_{i+1} + (r_x^{i+1} - r_x^i) dx_{i+1} - r_I^i dw_i$$

$$= [-] dw_i$$

Whence, since $r_u^i < 0$ by (4.9), we get

$$du_i = [+] dw_i \tag{4.50}$$

THEOREM 4.2 Under Assumptions 4.1, 4.2, and 4.3,

$$\frac{\partial x_j}{\partial w_i} > 0 \quad \text{all } j$$

$$\frac{\partial u_j}{\partial w_i} > 0 \quad \text{if } j \geq i$$

$$\frac{\partial u_j}{\partial w_i} < 0 \quad \text{if } j < i$$

Proof: The first assertion follows from (4.43), (4.44), and (4.49); whereas (4.45), (4.49), and (4.50) imply that $\partial u_j/\partial w_i > 0$ if $j \geq i$. The remaining assertion has already been proved in (4.44).

The critical step in proving Theorem 4.2 was the establishment of (4.49), or (4.48) which assert that an increase in w_i causes, not only a suburbanization of the ith class, but a reduction in the rent faced by the $(i+1)$th class. To reach this conclusion, Assumption 4.3 is imposed. Indeed, if Assumption

72

4.3 is violated—which can happen if, at some distance x, transportation costs increase very rapidly or land available for housing increases very slowly—then it is always possible to choose a set of parameters $N_1, \ldots, N_n$ and $w_1, \ldots, w_n$ at which the signs in (4.48) and (4.49) are reversed so that Theorem 4.2 no longer holds.

In the course of deriving Theorems 4.1 and 4.2, we have had to determine how the equilibrium rent function shifts due to changes in the N_i and w_i. Since these comparative statics results have some independent interest, we state it separately here.

THEOREM 4.3: Let $r(x) = r(x, N_1, \ldots, N_n, w_1, \ldots, w_n)$ denote the equilibrium rent function. Under Assumptions 4.1 and 4.2,

$$\frac{\partial r}{\partial N_i}(x) > 0 \qquad x_{n+1} \leq x \leq x_1 \quad \text{all } i$$

Under Assumptions 4.1, 4.2, and 4.3,

$$\frac{\partial r}{\partial w_i}(x) > 0 \qquad x_i \leq x \leq x_1 \quad \text{all } i$$

$$\frac{\partial r}{\partial w_i}(x) < 0 \qquad x_{n+1} \leq x \leq x_{i+1} \quad \text{all } i$$

A Numerical Example

We consider here a city model with two population classes. The parameter values chosen are adapted from Solow.[1] There is only one other good besides land. Every individual has the same utility function,

$$U(c, h) = c^{.75} h^{.25}$$

The population of the poor class is fixed at $N_2 = 135,000$; and their annual income is fixed at $w_2 = \$5,000$. The unit of distance (corresponding roughly to 2 miles) is such that the radius of the CBD is $x_3 = 1$. The price of the other good is \$1. Transportation cost per annum per individual is linear in distance and is given by $t(x) = \$1,200x$. Agricultural rent per annum per unit area is \$20,000. A constant proportion of the area of each circular ring is available for housing and it is given by $\theta(x) = 0.4\pi$ radians.

Table 4-1 shows how various equilibrium values change as the population of the rich class, N_1, grows from 79,000 to 246,000. Table 4-2 shows how various equilibrium values change as the income of the rich class, w_1, grows from \$6,000 to \$97,000. The same notation as before is maintained

Table 4-1
Impact of Population Changes of the Rich Class
($w_1 = \$12,000$)

N_1	79,000	97,000	116,000	149,000	171,000	207,000	246,000
x_1	2.46	2.57	2.68	2.85	2.95	3.10	3.25
x_2	1.60	1.58	1.55	1.53	1.50	1.48	1.45
u_2	58.1	57.6	57.1	56.2	55.7	54.9	54.1
u_1	153.2	151.2	149.2	146.2	144.4	141.7	139.1
r_2	29,400	31,300	33,300	36,600	38,800	42,300	46,000
r_3	54,700	56,700	58,700	62,700	64,700	68,700	72,700
$C_2(x_3)$	0.00	45	89	174	214	293	368
$C_2(x_2)$	0.00	39	77	152	189	260	329
$C_1(x_2)$	0.00	152	302	547	693	930	1,161
$C_1(x_1)$	0.00	135	265	470	587	770	942

Table 4-2
Impact of Income Changes of the Rich Class
($N_1 = 200,000$)

w_1	97,000	65,000	25,000	11,500	6,000
x_1	8.95	7.21	4.43	3.02	2.30
x_2	1.60	1.58	1.53	1.48	1.45
u_2	58.1	57.6	56.2	54.9	54.1
u_1	1,308	853	320	136	66
r_2	29,400	31,300	36,600	42,300	46,000
r_3	54,700	56,700	62,700	68,700	72,700
$C_2(x_3)$	0.00	45	174	293	368
$C_2(x_2)$	0.00	39	152	260	329

with the exception of the row labels $C_1(x)$ and $C_2(x)$. Here, $C_1(x)$ is the compensation in dollars per annum necessary for one rich individual at x to achieve the utility level $u_1 = 153.2$; whereas $C_2(x)$ is the corresponding compensation for a poor individual at x to maintain the utility land $u_2 = 58.1$. Thus the $C_i(x)$ is a simple measure of welfare loss.

A comparison of these two tables reveals that the loss incurred by a poor individual due to a threefold increase in the population of the rich from 79,000 to 246,000 is the same as a sixteenfold decrease in their income from $97,000 to $6,000.

Appendix 4A:
Proof of Lemma 4.4

Suppose

$$
A = \begin{bmatrix}
\alpha_{11} & \beta_2 & 0 & \cdot & \cdot & \cdot & 0 \\
\cdot & \cdot & \cdot & \cdot & \cdot & & \cdot \\
& & \cdot & \cdot & \cdot & & \\
& & & \cdot & \cdot & \cdot & \cdot \\
& & & & \cdot & \cdot & 0 \\
\cdot & & & & & \cdot & \beta_2 \\
\alpha_{n1} & \cdot & & \cdot & & \cdot & \alpha_{nn}
\end{bmatrix}
$$

where $\alpha_{ij} > 0$, $\beta_j > 0$. By an elementary column operation we see that

$$
\det A = \det \hat{A} = \det \begin{bmatrix}
\hat{\alpha}_{11} & 0 & \cdot & & \cdot & & 0 \\
\cdot & \cdot & \cdot & \cdot & & & \cdot \\
& & \cdot & \cdot & \cdot & & \\
\cdot & & & \cdot & \cdot & \cdot & \\
& & & & \cdot & \cdot & 0 \\
\cdot & & & & & \cdot & \\
\hat{\alpha}_{n1} & \cdot & & \cdot & & \cdot & \hat{\alpha}_{nn}+
\end{bmatrix}
$$

$$
= \hat{\alpha}_{11} \ldots \hat{\alpha}_{nn}
$$

where

$$
\hat{\alpha}_{i1} = \alpha_{ij} \quad \text{and} \quad \hat{\alpha}_{ij} = \alpha_{ij} + \hat{\alpha}_{i,j-1} \frac{\beta_j}{\alpha_{j-1,j-1}}.
$$

75

This implies $\hat{\alpha}_{jj} > 0$, and so $\det A > 0$. Let $A^{-1} = (\beta_{ij})$. Then, by Cramer's rule:

$$\beta_{ij} = \frac{\det A^{i,j}}{\det A}$$

where $A^{i,j}$ is obtained from A by replacing ith column by a vector whose only nonzero component is 1, which appears in the jth row. For $j > i$ we then have

$$\det A^{i,j} = \det \begin{bmatrix} + & - & \cdot & \cdot & \cdot & 0 & \vdots & & & & \\ \cdot & \cdot & \cdot & & & \cdot & \vdots & & & 0 & \\ \cdot & & \cdot & \cdot & & \cdot & \vdots & & & & \\ \cdot & & & \cdot & \cdot & - & \vdots & & & & \\ + & \cdot & \cdot & \cdot & \cdot & + & \vdots & & & & \\ \hline + & \cdot & \cdot & \cdot & \cdot & + & \vdots & 0 & - & & & 0 \\ \cdot & & & & & \cdot & \vdots & & \cdot & + & & \cdot \\ \cdot & & & & & \cdot & \vdots & & 1 & & & - \\ + & \cdot & \cdot & \cdot & \cdot & + & \vdots & 0 & + & \cdot & \cdot & + \end{bmatrix}$$

$$= \det \begin{bmatrix} + & - & \cdot & \cdot & \cdot & 0 \\ \cdot & \cdot & \cdot & & & \cdot \\ \cdot & & \cdot & \cdot & & \cdot \\ \cdot & & & \cdot & & - \\ + & \cdot & \cdot & \cdot & \cdot & + \end{bmatrix} \det \begin{bmatrix} 0 & - & \cdot & \cdot & 0 \\ \cdot & \cdot & \cdot & & \cdot \\ \cdot & + & & & \cdot \\ 1 & \cdot & & & - \\ 0 & + & \cdot & \cdot & + \end{bmatrix}$$

where the first matrix is of dimensions $(i-1) \times (i-1)$. Evidently, just as before, its determination is positive; whereas, by an elementary row operation,

$$\det \begin{bmatrix} 0 & - & \cdot & \cdot & 0 \\ \cdot & \cdot & \cdot & & \cdot \\ \cdot & + & & & \cdot \\ 1 & \cdot & & & - \\ \cdot & \cdot & & \cdot & \cdot \\ 0 & + & \cdot & \cdot & + \end{bmatrix} = \det \begin{bmatrix} + & 0 & \cdot & \cdot & \cdot & 0 \\ \cdot & \cdot & \cdot & & & \cdot \\ \cdot & & \cdot & \cdot & & \cdot \\ + & & & \cdot & \cdot & \cdot \\ 0 & & & & \cdot & 0 \\ 0 & + & \cdot & \cdot & \cdot & + \end{bmatrix} > 0$$

Thus $\det A^{i,j} > 0 \qquad$ for $j \geq i$.

For $j = i - 1$, we get,

$$
\det A^{i,j} = \det
\left[
\begin{array}{ccccc|cccc}
+ & - & \cdot & \cdot & 0 & & & & 0 \\
\cdot & \cdot & \cdot & & \cdot & & & \cdot & \\
\cdot & & \cdot & & \cdot & & \cdot & & \\
\cdot & & & \cdot & \cdot & & \cdot & & \\
+ & \cdot & \cdot & \cdot & + & 1 & & & \\
\hline
+ & \cdot & \cdot & \cdot & + & 0 & - & \cdot & 0 \\
\cdot & & & & \cdot & \cdot & \cdot & & \cdot \\
\cdot & & & & \cdot & \cdot & + & \cdot & \\
\cdot & & & & \cdot & \cdot & \cdot & & - \\
+ & \cdot & \cdot & \cdot & + & 0 & + & \cdot & +
\end{array}
\right]
$$

$$
= \det
\left[
\begin{array}{ccccc|cccc}
+ & & \cdot & \cdot & 0 & & & & 0 \\
\cdot & \cdot & & & \cdot & & & \cdot & \\
\cdot & & \cdot & & \cdot & & \cdot & & \\
\cdot & & & \cdot & \cdot & & \cdot & & \\
+ & \cdot & \cdot & \cdot & + & 1 & & & \\
\hline
+ & \cdot & \cdot & \cdot & + & 0 & 0 & \cdot & 0 \\
\cdot & & & & \cdot & \cdot & \cdot & & \cdot \\
\cdot & & & & \cdot & \cdot & + & \cdot & 0 \\
\cdot & & & & \cdot & \cdot & \cdot & & 0 \\
+ & \cdot & \cdot & \cdot & + & 0 & + & \cdot & +
\end{array}
\right]
$$

$$
= \det
\left[
\begin{array}{ccccc|ccccc}
+ & & & & & & & & & \\
\cdot & \cdot & & & & & & & & \\
\cdot & & \cdot & & & & & & & \\
\cdot & & & \cdot & & & & & & \\
+ & \cdot & \cdot & \cdot & + & & & & & \\
\hline
+ & \cdot & \cdot & \cdot & + & - & & & & \\
\cdot & & & & \cdot & \cdot & + & & & \\
\cdot & & & & \cdot & \cdot & \cdot & \cdot & & \\
\cdot & & & & \cdot & \cdot & \cdot & & \cdot & \\
+ & \cdot & \cdot & \cdot & + & - & + & \cdot & \cdot & +
\end{array}
\right]
$$

$$= \det \begin{bmatrix} + \\ \cdot & \cdot \\ \cdot & & \cdot \\ \cdot & & & \cdot \\ + & \cdot & \cdot & \cdot & + \end{bmatrix} \det \begin{bmatrix} - \\ & \cdot & + \\ & \cdot & & \cdot \\ & \cdot & & & \cdot \\ - & + & \cdot & \cdot & + \end{bmatrix}$$

$$= (+)(-1) \det \begin{bmatrix} + \\ \cdot & \cdot \\ \cdot & & \cdot \\ \cdot & & & \cdot \\ + & \cdot & \cdot & \cdot & + \end{bmatrix} < 0$$

and Lemma 4.4 follows.

Notes

1. R.M. Solow [1973a].
2. W.C. Wheaton [1947a], p. 232.

5 City Size and Land Rents in a Closed Model of Urban Spatial Structure

John Robert Miron

Theories of equilibrium in city sizes rest upon a notion common to all equilibrium constructs. There must exist forces which (i) act both to increase city size and to deter such growth, (ii) are in balance at an equilibrium city size, and (iii) act to define the dynamic nature of city size away from the equilibrium. In this chapter, consideration will be given to some forces that act to deter such growth. The role of rents and of access to the city center will be explored as particular forces.

Some attention has been given to the relationship between city size and either land rents or access. Borukhov has attempted to define a relationship between city size and CBD-bound trip costs.[1] It is argued in this paper that his approach is inadequate because (i) he is restricted to an invalid approximate solution and (ii) he uses an awkward notion about the consumption of residential housing. Wheaton develops a general comparative static analysis to explore the relationship between city size and land rents where city size is an exogenous variable.[3] He found that land rents increase with city size, but the general nature of his model makes it impossible to specify a particular form for this relationship.

In the first section of this chapter, we reintroduce a commonly used model of spatial structure in a monocentric city. From this model are derived relationships between city size and a number of variables (land rent at any distance, average land rent, the city boundary, and average distance to the CBD). An approximate form is derived in the second section, and some mathematical and numerical properties of this solution are described.

The Basic Model

Following Mills,[2] we assume a reason for the existence of a point in space to which the location of a set of P residences can be related. Each residence, which is identical in nature to every other, has to bear constant distance-marginal transportation costs in going from the residential site selected to the central point. Each residence has a utility level, U, defined by the amounts of land, L, and other goods, N, consumed:

$$U = L^\alpha N^{1-\alpha} \qquad 0 < \alpha < 1 \qquad (5.1)$$

John Robert Miron is a member of the Department of Geography, Queen's University.

Each residence maximizes utility subject to a budget constraint, Y, involving land and other goods prices, $R(s)$ and n, and the marginal cost of commuting, c.

$$Y = R(s)L + nN + cs \qquad n, c > 0 \qquad (5.2)$$

Land rents vary with distance s from the center but n is constant everywhere. The usual first-order conditions follow:

$$L = \frac{\alpha(Y - cs)}{R(s)} \qquad (5.3)$$

$$L\frac{\partial R(s)}{\partial s} + c = 0 \qquad (5.4)$$

This individual maximization is carried out subject to two constraints. First, all P residences must be accounted for in this city. Given a circular city of radius $\bar{s}$, this means that

$$P = 2\pi \int_0^{\bar{s}} \frac{s}{L} ds \qquad (5.5)$$

Secondly, at the boundary, the rent on land is equal to its nonzero nonurban opportunity cost R_a.

$$R(\bar{s}) = R_a > 0 \qquad (5.6)$$

Rents and Land Use as Functions of City Size and Distance from Center

Explicit expressions can now be derived for the Ricardian rent at any distance from the city center. From (5.3) and (5.4), we derive

$$R(s) = R_a g^{-1/\alpha}[1 - (c/Y)s]^{1/\alpha} \qquad 0 \leq g \leq 1 \qquad (5.7)$$

$$L(s) = \alpha(Y/R_a)g^{1/\alpha}[1 - (c/Y)s]^{(\alpha-1)/\alpha} \qquad (5.8)$$

where g is a constant definable, using (5.5) and (5.6). Using these and integrating by parts, the following nonlinear condition is obtained:

$$f(g) = \alpha g^{-1/\alpha} + g - (1 + \alpha) - \frac{(1 + \alpha)(c/Y)(c/R_a)P}{2\pi} = 0 \qquad (5.9)$$

It is evident that g takes its value in part from P and this provides the means by which city size affects land rents and use intensity. That an explicit solution for (5.9) is possible only for a few special values of α (namely, 1, ½, and ⅓) is, therefore, discouraging.

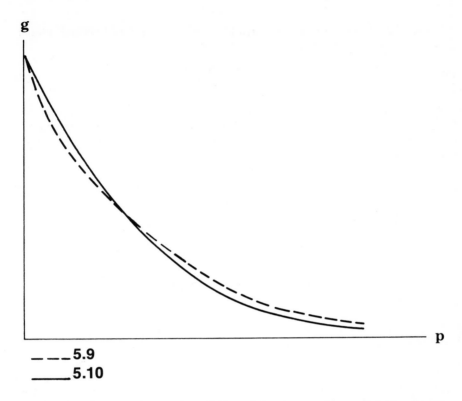

Figure 5-1. Graph of Equation (5.9) and the Approximate Solution (5.10)

Approximate solutions to (5.9) are possible. From Appendix 5A, it is seen that $f(g) = 0$ has a unique solution in the interval $0 \leq g \leq 1$. As illustrated in Figure 5-1, it can also be shown that the slope of g approaches $-\infty$ at $(0, 1)$ and approaches $g = 0$ asymptotically for large values of P. One approximation is the negative exponential model:

$$g = e^{-b_1 P} \qquad b_1 > 0 \tag{5.10}$$

It differs in that, for low values of P, the derivative of (5.10) is greater than that for (5.9), while the opposite is true for larger values of P.

There are at least two difficulties in using approximations such as (5.10). First, the significance of the discrepancy from (5.9) is unknown. Secondly, the new parameter, b_1 is somehow related to α, c/R_a, and c/Y. It would be useful to understand how these parameters interact within the rent-city size relationship.

We may measure how city size affects g and therefore land use intensity. By implicit differentiation of (5.9), one obtains

$$\frac{\partial g}{\partial P} = -\frac{(1 + \alpha)(1/2\pi)(c/R_a)(c/Y)}{g^{-(1+\alpha)/\alpha} - 1} < 0 \qquad (5.11)$$

Thus, as Wheaton established, an increase in city size leads to an increase in rent levels and decreases in lot size at every distance from the center.[3] This can be seen here, in the case of rents for instance, by substitution (5.11) into the population derivative of (5.7):

$$\frac{\partial R(s)}{\partial P} = \frac{(1 + \alpha)c^2}{2\alpha\pi Y}\left(1 - \frac{c}{Y}s\right)^{1/\alpha}(1 - g^{(1+\alpha)/\alpha})^{-1} > 0 \qquad (5.12)$$

The elasticity, ϵ, of distance-specific rent with respect to city size is thus

$$\epsilon = \frac{1}{\alpha}\left[\frac{\alpha + g^{(1+\alpha)/\alpha} - (1 + \alpha)g^{1/\alpha}}{1 - g^{(1+\alpha)/\alpha}}\right] \qquad (5.13)$$

From Appendix 4B, it is established that ϵ increases from zero to unity as P increases from zero to some infinitely large value.

Average Rents and Access as Functions of City Size

We are interested in evaluating how the typical rent paid by a new arrival changes as city size increases. It is not enough to say that rents everywhere increase with city size because changes in the relative spatial distribution of population may tend to ameliorate the increase in distance-specific rent (even while, of course, increasing the average commuting distance). There are several methods of defining an average rent level. The most direct would be a simple average of the rents paid for each unit of land in the city. This average, R_1, is defined by

$$R_1 = \frac{2\pi}{\pi(\bar{s})^2}\int_0^{\bar{s}} sR(s)\,ds \qquad (5.14a)$$

from which we may derive

$$R_1 = \frac{2\alpha R_a}{1 + 2\alpha} + \frac{\alpha c^2}{\pi(1 + 2\alpha)Y} \cdot \frac{P}{(1 - g)^2} \qquad (5.14b)$$

A judicious application of L'Hôpitals Rule leads to

$$\lim_{P\to 0} R_1 = R_a \quad \text{and} \quad \lim_{P\to\infty} R_1 \to \infty \qquad (5.14c)$$

In Appendix 4C, we show that R_1 is a monotonically increasing function of city size.

An alternative would be to consider the average rent paid by a household for each unit of land used. This quantity, R_2, is defined by

$$R_2 = \frac{2\pi}{P} \int_0^{\bar{s}} \frac{sR(s)}{L(s)} ds \qquad (5.15a)$$

After some manipulation we may derive

$$R_2 = \frac{R_a}{\alpha(2 + \alpha)c^2}$$

$$\times \left[\pi R_a Y \frac{(1-g)^2}{P} + (1+\alpha)^2 c^2 - (1+\alpha)c^2 g + \frac{(1+\alpha)^2 c^4}{4\pi R_a Y} P \right] (5.15b)$$

As in the case of R_1, the expected limiting values for R_2 can again be found:

$$\lim_{P \to 0} R_2 = R_a \quad \text{and} \quad \lim_{P \to \infty} R_2 \to \infty \qquad (5.15c)$$

An average commuting distance can be calculated in a similar manner. We may define an S_2 in an analagous manner to R_2:

$$S_2 = \frac{2\pi}{P} \int_0^{\bar{s}} \frac{sR(s)}{L(s)} ds \qquad (5.16a)$$

This yields

$$S_2 = \frac{2\pi(R_a/Y)(Y/c)^3}{(1+\alpha)(1+2\alpha)}$$

$$\left[(1+3\alpha)(1-g)^2 + 2\alpha(1+2\alpha)(1-g) + \frac{\alpha(1+\alpha)c^2}{\pi R_a Y} P \right] \qquad (5.16b)$$

for which it is evident that S_2 is an increasing monotonic function limited by

$$\lim_{P \to 0} S_2 = 0 \qquad (5.16c)$$

We are now faced with a certain problem. All of our measures rest on complicated relationships with respect to g, which in turn rests on a nonintuitive relationship to city size and various parameters. It would be advantageous if we could approximate g by some simple function whose validity could be ascertained.

We turn to this problem later.

A Comparison with Borukhov

First, however, it is instructive to examine the solution of Borukhov.[1] Since he derived a simple relationship between city size and access to the

CBD, it is important to understand why the present solution diverges and why it is superior.

Borukhov defines his model in terms of "housing" production. He assumes that there exist housing producers operating with the same Cobb-Douglas production function. These firms operate in a competitive land market. Nonland inputs are purchasable at a spatially uniform price. Finally, the amount of land in any ring of distance s from the CBD is given. Letting $h(s)$, r, $K(s)$, $\pi(s)$, and $p(s)$ denote housing production, nonland inputs price, nonland inputs, profits, and housing prices at distance s, these conditions imply that

$$h(s) = L(s)^\gamma K(s)^{1-\gamma} \quad 0 < \gamma < 1$$

$$\pi(s) = p(s)h(s) - R(s)L(s) - rK(s)$$

$$dL(s)/ds = 2\pi s$$

Profit maximizing behavior under these conditions implies a simple link between housing prices and Ricardian land rents.

$$p(s) = BR(s)^\gamma \quad \text{where} \quad B = \frac{r^{1-\gamma}}{\gamma^\gamma(1-\gamma)^{1-\gamma}} \quad (5.17)$$

Each household in Borukhov's model consumes exactly one unit of housing and this has several implications. First, the price bid for housing is tied directly to commuting costs.

$$\frac{dP(s)}{ds} = -c \quad (5.18)$$

Using (5.17), this implies a differential land rent condition whose solution is

$$R(s) = \left[\frac{c}{B}(\bar{s} - s) + R_a^\gamma \right]^{1/\gamma} \quad (5.19)$$

when the boundary rent condition, $R(\bar{s}) = R_a$, is applied. For the efficient housing producer, the amount of housing produced at distance s, is therefore

$$h(s) = \frac{2\pi s}{\alpha B} \left[\frac{c}{B}(\bar{s} - s) + R_a^\gamma \right]^{(1-\gamma)/\gamma} \quad (5.20)$$

The second main implication is that since each household occupies one unit of housing, $h(s)$ gives the number of households at distance s. Therefore there is a relationship between city size P and the city boundary $\bar{s}$.

$$P = \int_0^{\bar{s}} h(s) \, ds$$

$$= -\frac{2\pi R_a}{c}\left[\frac{\gamma}{1 + \gamma} \cdot \frac{BR_a}{c} + \bar{s}\right]$$

$$+ \frac{\alpha}{1 + \alpha} \cdot \frac{2\pi B}{c^2}\left[\frac{c\bar{s}}{B} + R_a^{\gamma}\right]^{(1+\gamma)/\gamma} \tag{5.21}$$

Since, in the earlier model, $\bar{s} = (Y/c) \cdot (1 - g)$, (5.21) would appear to express as complicated a relationship as found in (5.9). However, Borukhov notes that when $R_a = 0$, (5.21) and (5.19) reduce to

$$\bar{s} = \frac{B}{c}\left[\frac{c^2(1 + \alpha)}{2\pi\alpha B}\right]^{\gamma/(1+\gamma)} P^{\gamma/(1+\gamma)} \tag{5.22}$$

and

$$R(s) = \left\{\left[\frac{c^2(1 + \alpha)}{2B\pi\alpha}\right]^{\gamma/(1+\gamma)} P^{\gamma/(1+\gamma)} - \frac{c}{B}s\right\}^{1/\gamma} \tag{5.23}$$

Thus, Borukhov would assert that (5.22) and (5.23) provide approximate solutions of a particularly simple nature when R_a is near but not exactly zero.

One may, at this point, take exception to Borukhov's result on two grounds. First, not only are his equations merely approximations, but they are also wrong in the case when $R_a = 0$. To see this, we note that in deriving (5.19) one must solve a differential equation of the form

$$\frac{\alpha B}{c R(s)^{1-\alpha}} \, dR = ds \tag{5.24}$$

A solution is possible only when $R(s)$ is everywhere nonzero, and $R_a = 0$ evidently violates this assumption. R_a must be strictly positive for (5.19) to hold.

The second exception is seen when we ask ourselves how the two models differ. Because, in Borukhov's model, each household consumes exactly one unit of housing, commuting costs affect housing prices but not the individually consumed quantity. Housing producers respond to land rent variations by changing land use intensity, but the household still consumes just one unit. In the present model, households consume land directly, presumably using land to consume other goods (such as dwellings and autos). They have a distinct preference for land itself and react to land price variations by directly varying land consumption. In Borukhov's model, the amount of housing consumed is always the same even though

Table 5-1
Minimum, Maximum, and Increment Values for Parameters

Parameter	Minimum	Maximum	Increment
P	0.05	1.00	0.05
α	0.08	0.12	0.01
c/R_a	0.80	1.20	0.10
c/Y	0.002	0.018	0.004

the price of housing varies spatially. It is this perfectly inelastic demand for housing that makes Borukhov's model less than satisfactory.

An Approximate Solution

It is possible, in numerical terms, to solve (5.9) for g given any values for α, c/R_a, c/Y, and P. It is useful, however, for our discussion of average rents and access to have an explicit, if approximate, functional form linking g to these values.

A Sampling Experiment to Find an Approximate Form

The kind of approximation that is most appropriate will depend in part on the relevant parameter ranges chosen. We choose, for instance, to examine g and P ranges from zero to unity. This is a relevant range for P in cases where we want to think of P as a city's proportion of a region's population. Relevent values for α, the land preference parameters, were assumed to lie between 0.008 and 0.012. The ratio of c to R_a is assumed to lie between 0.8 and 1.2. Finally, the ratio of c to Y is assumed to be between 0.002 and 0.018. A set of 2,400 combinations of these parameters was generated by having each parameter incremented, from its minimum to its maximum, at the rates given in Table 5-1.

We wished, at this stage, to develop a workable sample of these parameter combinations for which g values could be numerically estimated. Pure random sampling was used, with each ($P, \alpha, c/R_a, c/Y$) combination being given a 4 percent chance of inclusion. A sample of 107 combinations was so generated; and, for each, (5.9) was solved numerically to find the exact corresponding value of g.

A structural form was then needed to relate g to the parameters. Since P is always less than or equal to one, one approximation is

$$\hat{g} = 1 - A\sqrt{P} \tag{5.25}$$

where A is a constant related to α, c/R_a, and C/Y. This approximation shares some features with (5.9) since it satisfies

$$\hat{g}(P{=}0) = 1 \qquad \lim_{P \to 0} \frac{\partial \hat{g}}{\partial P} \to -\infty$$

$$\frac{\partial \hat{g}}{\partial P} \leq 0 \qquad \frac{\partial^2 \hat{g}}{\partial P^2} \geq 0$$

The approximation (5.25) is also attractive because it postulates a simple role for P whose effect is of primary interest here.

To develop a clear understanding of this model, we need to identify the effects of α, c/R_a, and c/Y on A. To do this, we observe that (5.25) can be rewritten as

$$\left\{ \frac{1 - \hat{g}}{\sqrt{P}} \right\} = \delta_0 \alpha^{\delta_1} \left(\frac{c}{R_a} \right)^{\delta_2} \left(\frac{c}{Y} \right)^{\delta_3} \tag{5.26a}$$

where it is assumed that A is log-linearly related to these other parameters. This model was estimated using OLS:[a]

$$\left\{ \frac{1 - \hat{g}}{\sqrt{P}} \right\} = -0.5991 + 0.51509\alpha^*$$
$$(0.00502)$$

$$+ \; 0.49913(c/R_a)^* + \; 0.49240(c/Y)^* + u$$
$$(0.00509) \qquad\qquad (0.00096) \tag{5.26b}$$

A very close approximation is afforded by (5.26b). A comparison among the exact g values, the best fitting approximation of the types (5.10) and (5.26b) for one particular parameter combination, is shown in Figure 5-2.

Use of the Approximation

The approximation (5.25) can be used with varying degrees of ease to derive relationships between city size and other variables.[b] A particularly easy application involves the city boundary, $\bar{s}$. Using $\hat{g}$ and $\bar{s} = (1 - g)Y/c$, we have the following:

$$\bar{s} = \sqrt{\frac{\alpha YP}{\pi R_a}} \tag{5.27}$$

Thus, the city boundary increases proportionately to the square root of city

---

[a] In equation (5.26b), $R^2 = 0.9996$; the asterisk denotes a natural logarithm; standard errors appear in parentheses, and u is an error term.

[b] Note that the empirical form (5.26b) reduces to $g = 1 - \sqrt{\alpha c^2 P/\pi R_a Y}$ when only one significant decimal place is used.

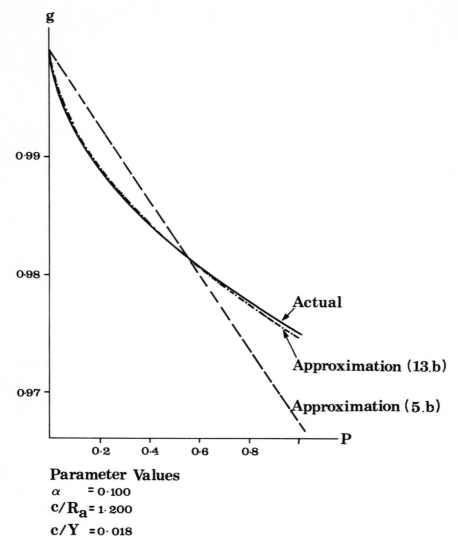

Figure 5-2. The g-P Relationship and Two Approximations: An Example

size. The proportioning factor varies directly with the land preference parameter and income. It varies inversely with the rural land rent but is independent of the marginal commuting cost.

Most of the remaining approximations are slightly more cumbersome:

$$\hat{R}(s) = R_a\left[1 + \sqrt{\frac{c^2 P}{\pi \alpha R_a Y}} + \frac{(1 + \alpha)}{2} \frac{c^2 P}{\pi R_a \alpha Y}\right]\left(1 - \frac{c}{Y}s\right)^{1/\alpha}$$

$$\hat{R}_1 = R_a$$

$$\hat{R}_2 = \frac{1 + \alpha}{2 + \alpha} R_a + \frac{R_a}{2 + \alpha}\left[1 + \frac{(1 + \alpha)c\sqrt{P}}{2\sqrt{\pi \alpha R_a Y}}\right]^2$$

$$\hat{S}_2 = \frac{4\alpha}{1 + \alpha} \frac{Y}{c} \sqrt{\pi \alpha \frac{R_a}{c} \frac{Y}{c} P} + \frac{4\alpha}{1 + \alpha} \frac{Y}{c} P$$

These approximations are useful for numerical work but lack the simplicity of (5.27).[c]

Conclusions

The purpose of this chapter has been to identify relationships between city size and both rent levels and access to the city center. Using a simple model of urban spatial structure, a consistent set of such relationships has been developed. These relationships link city size to rents and access in an indirect, complex manner. An approximation that affords a direct linkage has been identified and its validity tested over a range of parameter values. Where the approximation is appropriate, we can state a direct relationship between rents or access and city size. Further, the effect of changes in land preferences, marginal commuting costs, incomes, and rural land rents on these relationships can be identified.

Finally, the method used by Borukhov in approximating city size relationships has been discussed. It has been shown to be inferior in both theoretical and operational terms.

---

[c] We note that $\hat{R}_1$ is a constant here, although R_1 is not. This difference is apparently due to the restricted range of P values over which the approximation is valid.

Appendix 5A:
On the Shape of $f(g)$ from (5.9)

Consider the expression

$$f(g) = \alpha g^{-1/\alpha} + g - (1 + \alpha) - \frac{(1 + \alpha)(c/R_a)(c/Y)}{2\pi} P$$

We note that

$$\frac{\partial f(g)}{\partial g} = -g^{-(1+\alpha)/\alpha} + 1 \leq 0 \quad \text{when} \quad g \leq 1$$

and that

$$\frac{\partial f(g)}{\partial g} = 0 \quad \text{implies} \quad g = 1$$

Since we observe that, at the limiting values of g,

$$f(g=1) = -\frac{(1 + \alpha)(c/R_a)(c/Y)}{2\pi} P \leq 0$$

$$\lim_{g \to 0} f(g) \to +\infty \geq 0$$

the expression $f(g)$ has the shape shown in Figure 5A-1. The expression therefore has a unique solution for which $f(g) = 0$ and $0 \leq g \leq 1$.

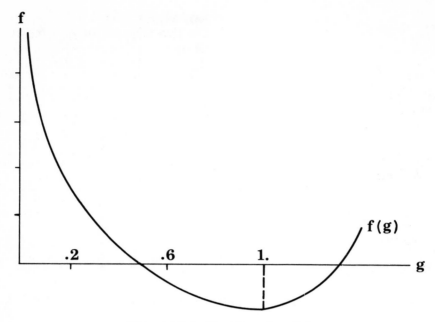

Figure 5A-1. The Function $f(g)$

Appendix 5B:
On the Elasticity of Distance-Specific Rent with Respect to City Size

From (5.13), we observe that

$$\epsilon = \frac{1}{\alpha}\left[\frac{\alpha + g^{(1+\alpha)/\alpha} - (1 + \alpha)g^{1/\alpha}}{1 - g^{(1+\alpha)/\alpha}}\right]$$

We note that

$$\lim_{P\to 0} \epsilon \to \frac{0}{0}$$

Using L'Hôpital's Rule, however, it can be shown that

$$\lim_{P\to 0} \epsilon = \lim_{P\to 0} \frac{g^{(1-\alpha)/\alpha} - g^{1/\alpha}}{g^{1/\alpha}} = 0$$

We also observe that

$$\lim_{P\to\infty} \epsilon = 1$$

Between these two extremes, the nature of ϵ is found by estimating its slope:

$$\frac{\partial\epsilon}{\partial P} = \frac{1 + \alpha}{\alpha^2} \frac{g^{(1-\alpha)/\alpha}}{(1 - g^{(1+\alpha)/\alpha})^2} h(g)\frac{\partial g}{\partial P}$$

where $h(g) = (1 + \alpha)g - 1 - \alpha g^{(1+\alpha)/\alpha}$

We note that $h(0) = -1$, $h(1) = 0$, and $\partial h/\partial g \geq 0$ when $g \leq 1$. Therefore h is nonpositive so that ϵ is a monotonically increasing function of city size. Thus, ϵ is nonnegative and increases from zero to unity with increasing city size.

Appendix 5C:
R_1 as a Function of City Size

We can derive an expression for R_1:

$$R_1 = \frac{2R_a\alpha^2}{(1 + \alpha)(1 + 2\alpha)} \cdot \frac{g^{-1/\alpha}w}{(1 - g)^2}$$

where

$$w = 1 - \frac{1 + 2\alpha}{\alpha} g^{-(1+\alpha)/\alpha} + \frac{1 + \alpha}{\alpha} g^{(1+2\alpha)/\alpha}$$

and

$$\frac{\partial R_1}{\partial P} = \frac{2R_a}{(1 + 2\alpha)(1 + \alpha)} \cdot \frac{g^{-(1+\alpha)/\alpha}}{(1 - g)^3} h(g) \frac{\partial g}{\partial P}$$

where $h(g) = -\alpha[1 - (1 + 2\alpha)g](1 - g^{1/\alpha}) - \alpha(1 - g^2)g^{1/\alpha}$.

We note that $h(g=0) = -\alpha \leq 0$ and $h(g=1) = 0$. It is also seen that

$$\frac{\partial h}{\partial g} = (1 + 2\alpha)[\alpha - (1 + \alpha - g)g^{1/\alpha}]$$

Since

$$\frac{\partial h}{\partial g}(g=0) > 0, \quad \frac{\partial h}{\partial g}(g=1) = 0, \quad \text{and} \quad \frac{\partial^2 h}{\partial g^2} \leq 0$$

it is seen that $\partial h/\partial g$ is nonnegative, and that h is, therefore, nonpositive. This implies that $\partial R_1/\partial P$ is nonnegative.

Notes

1. E. Borukhov [1973].
2. E.S. Mills [1972c], chap. 4.
3. W.C. Wheaton [1974a].

6

Introductory Remarks on "Plasma" Models

Tony E. Smith

In the following paper, John Amson presents a fresh approach to the study of land use. On first glance, this "plasma" viewpoint appears to be simply another effort to resurrect the social physics approach to spatial interaction, and, as such, is of course subject to all of the familiar behavioral criticisms. But Amson has added several new twists to this old approach which, in my view, place his work in the vanguard of urban modeling. In particular, he presents for the first time a general analytical framework within which global interactions between continuously dispersed populations can be studied explicitly.

To see the relevance of this contribution, one need only consider the other papers presented at this conference. A major shortcoming of the bulk of these models is their strict segregation of land use by sector. Such CBD models assume that production and retail alike are confined to a small island in the midst of a sea of residential land use. While certain relaxations of this assumption have been attempted by a number of authors, such attempts have not yet begun to capture the rich mixture of land uses we observe in modern cities. What seems to be needed is a new approach in which large numbers of competing land uses are allowed to interact at each point in space. Amson's model of interacting densities, or "plasmas," provides us with one possible framework for doing so.

A second major contribution of Amson's approach is the general perspective that it provides for synthesizing spatial interaction phenomena of many types. In particular, his plasmas of the second kind suggest a general paradigm of spatial equilibrium that unifies a remarkable number of spatial theories. Here he envisages spatial equilibrium as an interplay between global *attraction* effects and local *repulsion* effects. This interplay is seen, for example, in literally all equilibrium models of the urban housing market, where locational equilibrium for each household is characterized as a balance between the global attraction of employment and shopping opportunities and the local competition for space consumption reflected in rent. Similarly, the interplay between global network accessibility and local route congestion effects provides the basis for most equilibrium models of urban traffic flows. Moreover, these same elements are found in many of

Tony E. Smith is a member of the Department of Regional Science, University of Pennsylvania.

the sociological models of urban spatial competition between different social and ethnic groups. Hence by modeling the central elements common to all these theories, Amson provides us with a framework within which they might be combined.

As one illustration of this framework, it is of interest to consider a possible extension of the papers presented by Beckmann and Capozza (Chapters 8 and 9). Like Amson, Beckmann calls for a more explicit consideration of dispersed spatial activity. To do so, he focuses on a simple model of spatial interactions within a continuously dispersed household sector, thereby abstracting from any interactions with other sectors (such as work trips and shopping trips). In this context he characterizes spatial equilibrium for the housing sector as a balance between global within-sector interactions and local space consumption. In a similar vein, Capozza sketches a simple model of "agglomeration economies" in which he abstracts from the housing sector and focuses on the interactions within a continuously dispersed business sector.

Given these two within-sector models, Amson's framework suggests how they might be combined to include between-sector interactions as well. In particular, we might consider the simultaneous interactions between a continuously dispersed housing density $h(x)$ and business density $b(x)$ over all locations x. In this context, we might define a spatial utility function $u(x)$ for households as an extension of Beckmann's utility function, which includes not only within-sector interaction costs depending on the housing density $h(x)$, but also between-sector interaction costs of commuting and shopping which depend on the business density $b(x)$. Similarly, we might imagine a spatial profit function $\pi(x)$ for businesses that involves not only Capozza's within-sector agglomeration economies in terms of business density $b(x)$, but also the between-sector revenues generated by spatial demand in terms of the housing density $h(x)$. In this way, the usual equilibrium conditions of constant utility and constant profits over space might be combined to determine densities $h^*(x)$ and $b^*(x)$ of housing and businesses that are in equilibrium with one another at each point of space.

Amson's "plasma" approach to spatial interaction thus suggests the possibility of studying multisector spatial equilibria within a dispersed urban context. An explicit two-sector model of the case outlined above will be presented in a subsequent paper.

7

A Regional Plasma Theory of Land Use

John Amson

The Present Theory and Some Sketches for Its Later Development.

By a *regional plasma* we mean a system of distinct populations distributed throughout a region in which each population interacts not only with itself but with each other population. Each population has associated with it a spatial density distribution, and it is the relative proportion of the different densities at any location that determines the land use at that location. The population interactions we envisage arise through two effects: gravity attractions (coercions) and density-dependent location costs. Two kinds of plasmas will be considered: those in which interactions of the gravity type alone are present ("first" kind) and those in which both types of interactions are present ("second" kind).

While the particular natures of the populations in our plasma need not be specified at this stage, it is perhaps helpful to think of them as being populations of, say, different socioeconomic classes, or job places, workers' residences, traffic flow rates, and so on. We shall restrict ourselves in this essay to plasmas having at most three populations in order not to obscure the main ideas.

Each population in the plasma is distributed as a spatial measure or "charge" throughout the region. For analytical tractability alone, we restrict the present study to central regions in a Euclidean plane and require the populations distributions to have circular symmetry. However, spatial densities need not always be positive quantities; for instance, traffic flow rates can be negative (egress) as well as positive (ingress), and rural populations could be assigned negative densities to distinguish between them and urban populations at positive densities. The distributions of the spatial measures and their spatial densities are, of course, functionally related (see Figure 7-1). And all the density functions, etc. employed in the present examples are assumed to be continuous and smooth enough to permit us to use standard analytical methods, though computer-based

John Amson is a member of the Department of Pure Mathematics, The Mathematical Institute, University of St. Andrews.

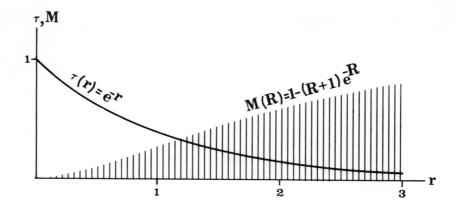

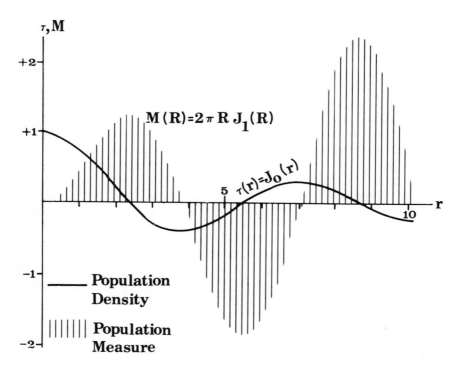

Figure 7-1. Illustrations of the Functional Relation Between a Population Measure and Its Density. J_0, J_1 are Bessel functions of order 0, 1, respectively. In the second example, multiply by 2π for the $M(R)$ scale.

methods could obviously be developed to handle examples under less idealistic assumptions.

While the theory in the form outlined here will be seen to draw heavily on other studies of equilibrium models of cities[1,2]—indeed, the examples illustrated are for the most part taken from work in progress in that area—there are a number of ways in which it is capable of significant generalization. We sketch just a few possibilities.

1. Instead of just two or three populations, plasmas that are comprised of very many populations might be studied. Such systems would benefit from a statistical mechanics approach, and the studies of interacting biological species by, for example, Kerner[14,15,16,17] and Goel et al.,[7] might be relevant here.

2. Instead of demanding just local equilibrium at each location in the region, we could impose the global condition that the net sum, throughout the region, of the local imbalance (''dissatisfaction'' or lack of equilibrium) be minimized. The familiar equilibrium models would then be regarded as ideal limiting cases.

3. Instead of imposing circular symmetry on the population distributions, we could take a first step towards more realistic assumptions by requiring elliptical symmetries. In such a theory a long narrow city could be approximated by elliptical distributions with high eccentricity, and the all too familiar circular models would arise as the limiting cases as the eccentricity tended to zero. Their analysis would be that much more cumbersome, but not excessively so (see Kellogg[12] and Ramsey[21] for standard accounts of the general theory of Newtonian attractions). It would, however, force the theoretician to face up to the fact that urban and regional forces cannot be expected to obey the vector law of addition. The latter is an absolutely basic assumption in the theory of physical attractions, and while it is possible to evade this issue in the case of circular distributions, some tentative explorations of elliptical distributions have shown that happy circumstance might no longer apply when forces are no longer directed to or from the region's center.

4. Instead of treating the gravity type of interaction between populations in a plasma in such metaphorical terms as *attraction* and *coercion*, we could emphasize instead the potential theoretic approach (see, e.g., Stewart,[24] Stewart and Warntz,[25] Carrothers,[5] Isard,[8] and Olsson.[20] Mechanical potentials, through their spatial gradients, correspond to gravitational attractions and conversely, as is well understood. But what is perhaps less familiar is the connection, established comparatively recently, between the theory of potentials and the theory of Brownian motions (limits of random walks) (see Spitzer[23] and Kemeny et al.[13]). Its implications for a regional plasma theory of land use are perhaps considerable. We

have a shift of approach from a concept of force—an elusive one at best, even in physics—to that of the much more empirically discernible and, above all, measurable one of potential and then on again to the concept of a probability distribution of population members performing Brownian motions about their base locations in the region (cf. the characteristic "oscillations" of people in terms of their hourly/daily/weekly/monthly/annual journeys within their terrestial spaces as well as their information spaces, as noted by Meier,[19] Doxiadis,[6] and Young and Ziman.[27] Such a shift of approach is more likely to shed light on the underlying mechanisms in a regional population plasma than a protracted discussion as to whether gravitational type forces really exist. The basic connection referred to is the fact that the potential of a particle at a given place, due to the presence of a body occupying a given zone, has precisely the same value as the probability that a particle performing a Brownian motion about that place will eventually hit that zone (see Kemeny et al.,[13] ch. 7). Given the probability distribution, one can construct the potential distribution, and conversely. The connection exists only under specified assumptions, of course, and much more work needs to be done before it might become possible to measure the attraction of a big city in terms of the probability of a member of the population encountering the city in the course of the prevailing regional activities.

5. Instead of equating the attraction coercions and other relocation inducements at each individual place in the region (a barely tenable assumption) or of minimizing their net imbalance as in (2) above, we might elaborate on the potential theoretic approaches outlined above and develop the notion of a potential wealth or "opulence"[3] akin to an "energy of interchange"[24] or a "social energy."[9] The strategy then would be to seek those distributions of populations that cause a minimal potential opulence. The theory, involving as it does a variational principle would initially possess analogies with Lagrangian dynamics (see, e.g., Lanczos,[18] ch. 5). In this context, a regional plasma would likely have some features quite similar to those of the social system of Isard and Liossatos—regulated as the latter is by a version of Hamilton's principle of least action. However, the full implication of this suggested development might best be appreciated if the concept of "function" that dominates physics were to be replaced by the more general one of "relation." (A function maps points to points; a relation maps subsets of points to subsets of points; every function is a relation, but there are many more relations that are not functions, e.g., "fuzzy maps.") Rashevsky's extensive explorations along these lines, published in a series of papers between 1967 and 1971, have already given some qualitative indication of the suitability of this approach in his chosen area, the attempt to unify physics, biology, and sociology.[22] It would seem to be equally relevant for the future of regional science. Both these areas have in common the feature that an adequate progress has been delayed too

long by too strict an adherence (albeit from erstwhile necessity) to a kind of mathematics that has its origins in and was expressly invented to deal with the problems of the physical sciences. These problems (witness the failure of even the vector law of addition of "forces") are not really those of the urban and regional sciences. Progress, however tentative, along the lines outlined in this last paragraph, could benefit both the social sciences and the mathematical sciences equally.

Regional Plasmas of the First Kind

Consider a regional plasma (P_1, P_2, P_3) having three populations, P_1, P_2, P_3, whose measures, M_1, M_2, M_3, are distributed in the plane at densities τ_1, τ_2, τ_3.[a] The assumption of circular symmetry means that each measure and density is a function of the radial distance $r \geq 0$ from the center of the plane and has the following functional relationships (see Figure 7-1):

$$dM_i(r) = \tau_i(r) \cdot 2\pi r \, dr \qquad r \geq 0, \, i = 1, 2, 3 \qquad (7.1a)$$

$$M_i(R) = \int_0^R dM_i(r)$$

$$= \int_0^R \tau_i(r) \cdot 2\pi r \, dr \qquad R \geq 0, \, i = 1, 2, 3 \qquad (7.1b)$$

We are assuming a gravitational interaction of two-dimensional Newtonian form. Thus, there is coercion on each unit of the population P_i due to the presence of the population P_j ($i, j = 1, 2, 3$). If $i = j$, then the coercion arises through the self-interaction in the ith population, and if $i \neq j$, then the coercion arises through the mutual interaction between the ith population and the jth population (which need not, of course, be symmetrical). And the values of these coercions at a distance r depend only on that distance r and the total population measure $M(r)$ occupying the central disc of radius r (Newton's theorem), that is, it is proportional to $M(r)/r$. The constants of proportionality (coercion coefficients) are denoted by k_{ij}; there are nine of these and they form a matrix $k = [k_{ij}]$. There values need not be equal, nor symmetric.

The amount of the population P_i occupying a small area dA at radial distance r in the region has the measure $\tau_i(r) \, dA$. It experiences three coercions in response to each of the three populations; their magnitudes are

$$k_{ij} \, \tau_i(r) \, dA \frac{M_j(r)}{r} \qquad j = 1, 2, 3$$

and they are radially directed.

---

[a] The notations used in this chapter are, for the most part, similar to those used in Amson.[1,2,]

Since we are assuming that there is local equilibrium within each population at every location in the region, the population measures and densities have to satisfy three basic equilibrium equations of the form

$$\sum_{j=1}^{3} k_{ij}\tau_i(r)\, dA \frac{M_j(r)}{r} = 0 \qquad i = 1, 2, 3 \tag{7.2}$$

Since the factor $\tau_i(r)\, dA/r$ is common to all three terms in the ith equation, we may cancel it and so obtain a simpler equation system:

$$\sum_{j=1}^{3} k_{ij}M_j(r) = 0 \qquad i = 1, 2, 3 \tag{7.3}$$

For each $r \geq 0$, this system is simply a matrix-vector equation $[k_{ij}][M_j(r)] = 0$ and it has nontrivial solutions $[M_j(r)]$ if and only if the coercion matrix $k = [k_{ij}]$ is singular, that is, has rank $r(k) = 0, 1, 2$, but not 3. That is the case if and only if the coercion coefficient vectors $k_1 = (k_{11}, k_{12}, k_{13})$, $k_2 = (k_{21}, k_{22}, k_{23})$, and $k_3 = (k_{31}, k_{32}, k_{33})$ happen to be linearly dependent. Whether such a restrictive condition could be satisfied in "reality" is a matter for speculation.

If the matrix k has rank 2, then one of the measures M_i can have its values assigned arbitrarily throughout the region, and the other two are then everywhere simply proportional to it. If k has rank 1 then two of the measures can be assigned arbitrary values throughout the region, and those of the third are given as a linear combination of them. If k has rank 0, the result is trivial since every coefficient k_{ij} is then zero, and the three measures are wholly arbitrary.

Since the densities τ_i are assumed to be continuous functions it follows at once that they must then obey the same relationships as do their integrals M_i.

$$\textbf{EXAMPLE 1:} \quad \text{Let } k = \begin{bmatrix} 3 & -1 & 0 \\ 4 & 1 & 1 \\ -1 & -2 & -1 \end{bmatrix}$$

Here, k is of rank 2 and the following interactions between the populations are indicated: P_1 is strongly self-attractive ($k_{11} = 3$) but is repelled by P_2 ($k_{12} = -1$) and is indifferent to P_3 ($k_{13} = 0$); P_2 is even more strongly attracted to P_1 ($k_{21} = 4$), is self-attractive ($k_{22} = 1$), and is attracted to P_3 ($k_{23} = 1$); and P_3 is equally repelled by both P_1 and itself—more so by P_2. Solving the equilibrium equation shows that we must have $M_3(r) = 7M_1(r)$, $M_2(r) = 3M_1(r)$, and $M_1(r)$ arbitrary, for each $r \geq 0$; and then the same relations hold between the densities τ_1, τ_2, and τ_3. (See Figure 7-2.)

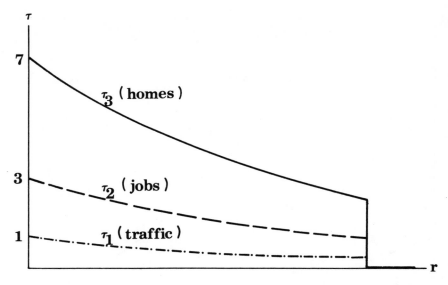

Figure 7-2. Some Density Distributions in a Three-Population Regional Plasma of First Kind, with a Rank 2 Coercion Matrix k.

$$\text{EXAMPLE 2:} \quad \text{Let } k = \begin{bmatrix} 4 & 4 & -2 \\ -2 & -2 & 1 \\ 2 & 2 & -1 \end{bmatrix}$$

Here, k is of rank 1; the population interactions may be interpreted as they were in Example 1. Equilibrium solutions are given, in terms of the density functions, by $\tau_1(r)$ and $\tau_2(r)$—both arbitrary—and $\tau_3(r) = 2\tau_1(r) + 2\tau_2(r)$, for all $r \geq 0$. (See Figure 7-3.)

Regional Plasmas of the Second Kind

Since the analysis of second-kind plasmas is much more complicated than that of first kind, we shall, for clarity, consider regional plasmas (P_1, P_2) with merely two distinct populations P_1 and P_2.

In addition to the gravitational interactions, we now have to admit new interactions of the location cost gradient type. Thus the populations P_1 and P_2 also experience a location cost p_1 and p_2, respectively. It may be helpful to think of these costs as land rental prices, say; but alternatively they could

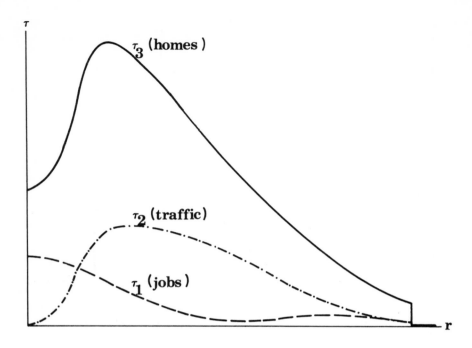

Figure 7-3. Density Distributions in a Three-Population Regional Plasma of First Kind, with a Rank 1 Coercion Matrix k.

of course be evaluations of environmental stress or lack of accessibility, etc.

In the presence of circular symmetry the gradients of the cost functions $p_i (i = 1, 2)$ are directed radially, and their magnitudes at distance r from the center are their radial derivatives $p_i'(r)$ with respect to r. By hypothesis, the greater the absolute magnitude $|p_i'(r)|$, the more inducement there is on the ith population to relocate itself at less costly places. Following the kind of analysis developed in detail in the single population studies[1,2] we may establish similar fundamental equilibrium equations (one for each population):

$$\sum_{j=1}^{2} k_{ij}\tau_i(r) \; \frac{M_j(r)}{r} + p_i'(r) = 0 \qquad i = 1, 2 \qquad (7.4)$$

Since, from (7.1), the radial derivative of $M_j(r)$ is just $\tau_j(r) \cdot 2\pi r$, we can manipulate this equation system into the following one involving the density functions but not the measures:

$$\sum_{j=1}^{2} k_{ij}\tau_j(r) + \frac{1}{2\pi r}\left[\frac{rp'_i(r)}{\tau_i(r)}\right]' = 0 \qquad i = 1, 2 \qquad (7.5)$$

Our problem now is to find solution functions τ_1 and τ_2 for this differential equation system. But first we must decide how the cost functions p_i are to be determined. We have two alternatives: either their values are given exogenously or they are functionally related to the population densities. The first alternative, though valid, is of less technical interest; we shall not stop to consider it here but choose instead the second one. For lack of any detailed information as to what the functional relationship should be, we shall assume one having the form

$$p_i = K_i \, \tau_1^{\gamma_{i1}}\tau_2^{\gamma_{i2}} \qquad i = 1, 2 \qquad (7.6)$$

This form implies that the relative increment dp_i/p_i in the cost p_i is proportional to the linear combination $\gamma_{i1}(d\tau_1/\tau_1) + \gamma_{i2}(d\tau_2/\tau_2)$ of those in the densities τ_1 and τ_2. The proportionality constants K_1 and K_2 are called the *rental coefficients*. The constants γ_{ij} are called the *rental exponents*; they determine the relative extent of the dependence of the ith cost on the jth density. We call their matrix, $\gamma = [\gamma_{ij}]$, the *rental exponent matrix* for the given plasma. Substituting for the derivatives $p'_i(r)$ in (7.5) gives us this second-order differential equation system for the densities:

$$\sum_{j=1}^{2} g_{ij}\tau_j(r) + \frac{1}{r}\left[\frac{r}{\tau_i(r)}(\tau_1^{\gamma_{i1}}\tau_2^{\gamma_{i2}})'\right]' = 0 \qquad i = 1, 2 \qquad (7.7)$$

where the new coefficients g_{ij} have the values $2\pi k_{ij}/K_i$ and form a matrix $g = [g_{ij}]$ which we call the *coercion matrix*.

It is now evident that each regional plasma (P_1, P_2) is characterized by these two coefficient matrices $g = [g_{ij}]$ and $\gamma = [\gamma_{ij}]$. And it transpires, just as in the single population theory, that the mode of analysis to be utilized in solving (7.7) depends heavily on what values we assign to the eight matrix coefficients g_{ij} and γ_{ij}. A general analysis being out of the question for the time being, let us instead analyze just two regional plasmas of the second kind. The first will be a "doubly Bessel plasma" and the second will be a "doubly Mesotropic plasma"[2] having, respectively,

$$\gamma = \begin{bmatrix} 2 & 0 \\ 0 & 2 \end{bmatrix}$$

and

$$\gamma = \begin{bmatrix} 1 & 0 \\ 0 & 1 \end{bmatrix}$$

A Doubly Bessel Plasma

Here, $p_1 = K_1\tau_1^2$ and $p_2 = K_2\tau_2^2$, that is, the exponent matrix is diagonal—each cost depends on the square of the density of its own population but not of the other. (With a simultaneous dependence on both densities, the analysis unfortunately becomes disproportionately complicated.) Equation (7.7) can then be reduced and simplified to read

$$\tau_1'' + \frac{1}{r}\tau_1' + g_{11}\tau_1 + g_{12}\tau_2 = 0$$

$$\tau_2'' + \frac{1}{r}\tau_2 + g_{21}\tau_1 + g_{22}\tau_2 = 0$$

$$(7.8)$$

These can be solved numerically for a wide variety of coercion matrix coefficients g_{ij}. Analytical solutions are more difficult to arrive at unless we make some further simplifying assumptions. First we assume that the matrix g is singular, i.e., that its determinant $g_{11}g_{22} - g_{12}g_{21} = 0$. Then, in (7.8), multiplying the first equation by g_{22}, the second by g_{12}, and subtracting one from another reveals that the function $f(r) = g_{22}\tau_1(r) - g_{12}\tau_2(r)$ has to satisfy Laplace's differential equation $f'' + f'/r = 0$ whose general solution is $f(r) = B \log(r) + C$ (B and C are integration constants). This implies that any solutions τ_1 and τ_2 of (7.8) have to be functionally related:

$$g_{12}\tau_2 = g_{22}\tau_1 + B \log(r) + C \qquad r > 0 \qquad (7.9)$$

If population densities must remain finite everywhere, then we must take $B = 0$, so that the two solutions τ_1 and τ_2 have to be simply proportional to each other to within a constant term C. Hence, substituting for τ_2 from (7.9) into (7.8) gives us a linear equation for τ_1:

$$\tau_1'' + \frac{1}{r}\tau_1' + \tau_1(g_{11} + g_{22}) + C = 0 \qquad (7.10)$$

Solutions are easily found if we assume that $g_{11} + g_{22} = 0$; they are then simple quadratic functions of distance:

$$\tau_1(r) = C_1 - (1/4)Cr^2$$

$$(7.11)$$

$$\tau_2(r) = \frac{1}{g_{12}}[(g_{22}C_1 + C) - (1/4)g_{22}Cr^2]$$

where C_1 is another arbitrary constant. The examples of Figure 7-4 relate to a coercion matrix g such that $g_{11} + g_{22} = 0$ and rank $(g) = 1$. In particular (Figure 7-4), the coercion matrices are

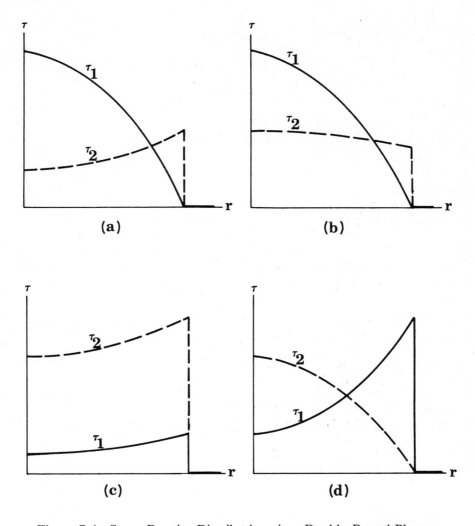

Figure 7-4. Some Density Distributions in a Doubly Bessel Plasma

(a) $g = \begin{bmatrix} 2 & 8 \\ -1/2 & -2 \end{bmatrix} \equiv \begin{bmatrix} + & + \\ - & - \end{bmatrix}$

(b) $g = \begin{bmatrix} -1 & 10 \\ -1/10 & 1 \end{bmatrix} \equiv \begin{bmatrix} - & + \\ - & + \end{bmatrix}$

(c) $g = \begin{bmatrix} 2 & -1 \\ 4 & -2 \end{bmatrix} \equiv \begin{bmatrix} + & - \\ + & - \end{bmatrix}$

(d) $g = \begin{bmatrix} -1 & -1 \\ 1 & 1 \end{bmatrix} \equiv \begin{bmatrix} - & - \\ + & + \end{bmatrix}$

The integration constant $C \neq 0$. In examples (a) and (b) $C = 4$, while in examples (c) and (d) $C = -4$.

For more generality, we suppose $g_{11} + g_{22} \neq 0$. Then, if $C = 0$, (7.10) is a Bessel equation and the solutions τ_1 and τ_2 are found to be a pair of proportional Bessel functions, one of them being everywhere increased by a constant amount—a result which is not without interest.

If $C \neq 0$, (7.10) is a nonhomogeneous Bessel equation whose solutions are given [Kamke,[11] p. 442; Watson,[26] p. 345; and equations (7.4) and (7.5)]—after making yet another simplification, namely $g_{11} + g_{22} = 1$, and assigning the central density $\tau_1(0)$ the value 1—by using

$$\tau_1(r) = J_0(r) - C \cdot S(r) \qquad r \geq 0 \qquad (7.12)$$

Here $J_0(r)$ is a tabulated Bessel function[10] and $S(r)$ (a Lommel function) is given by the everywhere-convergent power series

$S(r) =$

$$\left(\frac{r}{2}\right)^2 \left[1 - r^2 \frac{1}{16} + r^4 \frac{1}{576} + \ldots + (-1)^m \left(\frac{r}{2}\right)^{2m} \left(\frac{1}{(m+1)!}\right)^2 + \ldots\right]$$

The corresponding values of the other population density are then

$$\tau_2(r) = \frac{g_{22}}{g_{12}}[J_0(r) - C \cdot S(r)] + \frac{C}{g_{12}} \qquad r \geq 0 \qquad (7.13)$$

Some representative solutions are illustrated in Figure 7-5, where the examples relate to a coercion matrix g such that $g_{11} + g_{22} = 1$ and rank $(g) = 1$. In particular:

(a) $\quad g = \begin{bmatrix} 8 & -32 \\ -3 & 12 \end{bmatrix} \div 20 \equiv \begin{bmatrix} + & - \\ - & + \end{bmatrix}$

$\tau_1(r) = J_0(r) + S(r)$

$\tau_2(r) = \dfrac{5}{8} - \dfrac{3}{8}\tau_1(r)$

$C = -1$

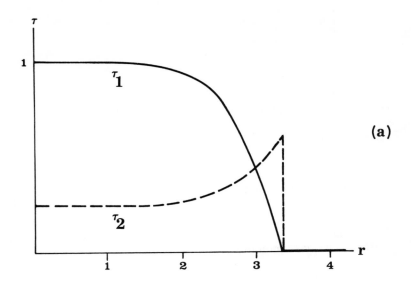

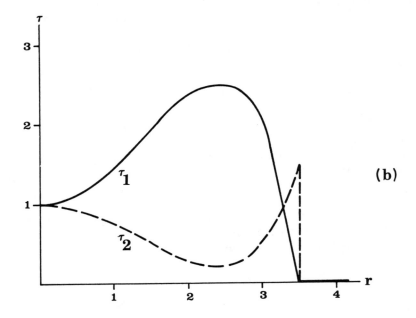

Figure 7-5. More Density Distributions in a Doubly Bessel Plasma

(b) $\quad g = \begin{bmatrix} 0 & -2 \\ 0 & 1 \end{bmatrix} \equiv \begin{bmatrix} 0 & - \\ 0 & + \end{bmatrix}$

$$\tau_1(r) = J_0(r) + 3S(r)$$

$$\tau_2(r) = \frac{3}{2} - \frac{1}{2}\tau_1(r)$$

$$C = -3$$

A Doubly Mesotropic Plasma

Here, $p_1 = K_1\tau_1$; $p_2 = K_2\tau_2$; again, the exponent matrix is diagonal, each cost depending directly on the density of its own population but not on that of the other. The basic equation (10.7) becomes

$$\sum_{j=1}^{2} g_{ij}\tau_j(r) + \frac{1}{r}\left[r\frac{\tau_i'(r)}{\tau_i(r)}\right] = 0 \qquad i = 1, 2 \qquad (7.14)$$

These differential equations can be solved if we introduce new functions $u_i = \log(\tau_i)$, that is, $\tau_i = \exp(u_i)$, $(i = 1, 2)$, which transforms (7.14) into

$$u_1'' + \frac{1}{r}u_1' + g_{11}\exp(u_1) + g_{12}\exp(u_2) = 0 \qquad (7.15a)$$

$$u_2'' + \frac{1}{r}u_2' + g_{21}\exp(u_1) + g_{22}\exp(u_2) = 0 \qquad (7.15b)$$

As with the Bessel plasma, we shall again treat only the case with a singular coercion matrix g, that is, with $g_{11}g_{22} - g_{12}g_{21} = 0$, whereby a similar argument shows again that any solutions u_1 and u_2 to (7.15) must be functionally related by

$$g_{12}u_2 = g_{22}u_1 + B \cdot \log(r) + C \qquad (7.16)$$

where B and C are arbitrary constants. Substituting for u_2 from (7.16) into (7.15) gives us a nonlinear equation for u_1, which, on making the simplifying assumption that $g_{22} = g_{12}$, and rewriting, becomes

$$u_1'' + \frac{1}{r}u_1' + (g_{11} + D \cdot r^E)\exp(u_1) = 0 \qquad (7.17)$$

where $D = g_{12}\exp(C/g_{12})$ and $E = B/g_{12}$ are arbitrary constants.

If u_1 is a solution of (7.17), it follows from (7.16) that its mate solution u_2 is then

$$u_2 = u_1 + E \cdot \log(r) + \log(D/g_{12})$$

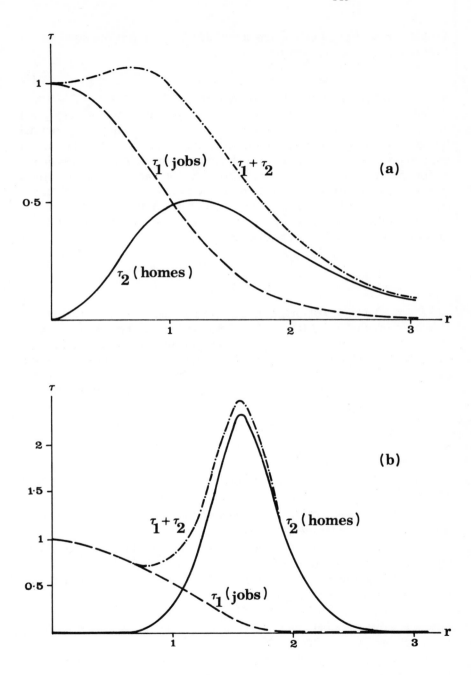

Figure 7-6. Some Density Distributions in a Doubly Mesotropic Plasma

so that, on reverting to the original variables, if τ_1 and τ_2 are solutions of (7.14) then they are related by

$$\tau_2 = \tau_1 r^E(D/g_{12}) \tag{7.18}$$

Since central densities have to be finite we must choose $E \geq 0$. If $E = 0$ then τ_1 and τ_2 are merely proportional—a solution that is not of very great interest. But if $E > 0$ and $\tau_1(r)$ behaves rather like the negative exponential function $\exp(-r)$—as numerical solutions reveal it can do—then the second population's density function $\tau_2(r)$ behaves very much like a gamma distribution. Such solution systems are of considerable interest in view of their similarity with observed distributions of, for example, workers' residences (τ_2) and associated job places (τ_1) in the Greater Manchester Region.[4]

Some solutions of the system (7.14) obtained by numerical methods are illustrated in Figure 7-6. In both cases,

$$g = \begin{bmatrix} 1 & 1 \\ 1 & 1 \end{bmatrix}$$

and $E > 0$. The values of integration constants in equation (7.16) are $B = 2$, $C = 0$ for graph (a) and $B = 8$, $C = 0$ for graph (b). These can hardly be thought to be representative of the full range of solutions of what appears to be a particularly interesting system—especially since they arise under the very restrictive assumptions that the coercion matrix g was singular and the rental exponent matrix γ was diagonal. More general solutions will be sought in due course.

Notes

1. J.C. Amson, 1972, "Equilibrium Models of Cities: 1. An Axiomatic Theory," *Environment & Planning*, vol. 4, 429-444.

2. J.C. Amson, 1973, "Equilibrium Models of Cities: 2. Single-Species Cities," *Environment & Planning*, vol. 5, 295-338.

3. J.C. Amson, 1974, "Equilibrium and Catastrophic Modes of Urban Growth," *London Papers in Regional Science*, vol. 4, 108-128.

4. S. Angel and G.F. Hyman, 1972, "Urban Spatial Interaction," *Environment & Planning*, vol. 4, 99-118.

5. G.A.P. Carrothers, 1956, "An Historical Review of the Gravity and Potential Concepts of Human Interaction," *Journal of the American Institute of Planners*, vol. 22, 94-102.

6. C.A. Doxiadis, 1970, "Man's Movements and His Settlements," *Ekistics*, vol. 29, 291-321.

7. N.S. Goel, et al., 1971, "On the Volterra and Other Non-Linear Models of Interacting Populations," *Reviews of Modern Physics*, vol. 43, 231-276.

8. W. Isard, 1960, *Methods of Regional Science*. Cambridge: MIT Press.

9. W. Isard and P. Liossatos, 1972, "Social Energy: A Relevant New Concept for Regional Science," *London Papers in Regional Science*, vol. 3, 1-30.

10. E. Jahnke and F. Emde, 1945, *Tables of Function*. New York: Dover.

11. E. Kamke, 1944, *Differentialgleichungen Lösungmethoden und Lösungen, Band*. New York: Chelsea.

12. O.D. Kellogg, 1929, *Foundations of Potential Theory*. Berlin: Springer-Verlag.

13. J.C. Kemeny, J.L. Snell, and A.W. Knapp, 1966, *Denumerable Markov Chains*. Princeton: Van Nostrand.

14. E.H. Kerner, 1957, "A Statistical Mechanics of Interacting Biological Species," *Bulletin of Mathematical Biophysics*, vol. 19, 121-146.

15. E.H. Kerner, 1959, "Further Considerations on the Statistical Mechanics of Biological Associations," *Bulletin of Mathematical Biophysics*, vol. 21, 217-255.

16. E.H. Kerner, 1964, "Dynamical Aspects of Kinetics," *Bulletin of Mathematical Biophysics*, vol. 26, 333-349.

17. E.H. Kerner, 1969, "Gibbs Ensemble and Biological Ensemble," in C.H. Waddington (ed.), *Towards a Theoretical Biology: 2. Sketches*. Edinburgh: Edinburgh University Press.

18. C. Lanczos, 1949, *The Variational Principles of Mechanics*. Toronto: Toronto University Press.

19. R. Meier, 1962, *A Communications Theory of Urban Growth*. Princeton: MIT Press.

20. G. Olsson, 1965, *Distance and Human Interaction: A Review and Bibliography*. Philadelphia: Regional Science Research Institute.

21. A.S. Ramsey, 1940, *An Introduction to the Theory of Newtonian Attraction*. Cambridge: Cambridge University Press.

22. N. Rashevsky, 1970, "A Remark on the Course of Development of Organismic Sets," *Bulletin of Mathematical Biophysics*, vol. 32, 79-81.

23. F. Spitzer, 1964, *Principles of Random Walk*. Princeton: Van Nostrand.

24. J.Q. Stewart, 1947, "Empirical and Mathematical Rules Concern-

ing the Distribution and Equilibrium of Population," *Geographical Review*, vol. 37, 461-481.

25. J.Q. Stewart and W. Warntz, 1958, "Physics of Population Distribution," *Journal of Regional Science*, vol. 1, 99-123.

26. G.N. Watson, 1974, *Theory of Bessel Functions*. Cambridge: Cambridge University Press.

27. M. Young and J. Ziman, 1971, "Cycles in Social Behaviour," *Nature*, vol. 229, 91-95.

8

Spatial Equilibrium in the Dispersed City

Martin J. Beckmann

The standard model of residential land use in a city as treated in "Notes on the New Urban Economics"[1] assumes that all working and shopping opportunities are concentrated in the center of the city, the CBD, and that a definite orientation with respect to the center is introduced into residential land use. The effect of any other interactions over distance is overlooked. To put it bluntly, work and consumption (shopping) dominate all trip-making behavior; the interaction with other residents through social and recreational contacts is completely ignored.

In this chapter, we will focus instead on interaction among households, on the utility of this interaction to the individual household and on the role of this interaction in shaping equilibrium patterns of residential living. For simplicity and transparency, we shall ignore work and shopping trips completely. An alternative interpretation would be to assume that work and shopping have the same areal distribution as population.

In order to keep things mathematically simple we assume a one-dimensional—a long narrow city—in the sense of Solow and Vickrey.[2] The amount of land allocated to transportation is not treated explicitly. It is assumed that transportation cost, or more precisely the time cost of interaction for any pair of households, is proportional to their distance. The utility function for a household is assumed to depend on two variables: the cost of interaction with others as measured by the average distance of this household from all other households in the city, and the amount of space occupied. In addition, there may be a utility of consumption, but this turns out to have no effect on spatial behavior if the utility function is separable with respect to the three variables. Specifically, utility is treated as logarithmic with respect to space and linear with respect to average distance and other consumption:

$$u = a \log s - \bar{r} + c \qquad (8.1)$$

Martin J. Beckmann is a member of the Department of Economics, Brown University, and Institute für Angewandte Mathematik, Technische Universität München.

The assistance of Mr. J. Fischer in the calculations and drawing of figures is gratefully acknowledged.

where u = utility

s = space

$\bar{r}$ = average distance

c = consumption

a = a parameter

Let x denote the location of a household.

We assume free mobility—that is, each household is free to choose among locations it desires. We observe first that at given prices $p(x)$ a household will choose the same amount of space regardless of income. For given income y and price $p(x)$, the household's utility becomes

$$u(x) = a \log s - \bar{r}(x) + y - p(x)s \qquad (8.2)$$

Maximization of (8.2) with respect to s yields

$$\frac{a}{s} - p(x) = 0 \qquad \text{or} \qquad s = \frac{a}{p(x)} \qquad (8.3)$$

Expenditure on living space is thus constant, $p(x)s = a$, and utility becomes

$$u(x) = a \log s(x) - \bar{r}(x) + y - a \qquad (8.4)$$

where $s(x)$ is determined by (8.3) from the given $p(x)$. Utility is thus a linear function of income y.

While this is a special property of the logarithmic utility function, the same result would apply if we assume that all households pay the same rent (possibly zero) and that the amount of space $s(x)$ allocated to every household must be such that everybody is satisfied, i.e., indifferent among locations.

A necessary condition for equilibrium is therefore that utility, given y, is constant:

$$a \log s(x) - \bar{r}(x) = \text{constant} \qquad (8.5)$$

In terms of density m,

$$m = 1/s$$

the condition is

$$a \log m(x) + \bar{r}(x) = \text{constant} = u_0 \qquad (8.6)$$

Population Distribution in a Dispersed City

We shall now establish a relationship between the density distribution $m(x)$

and the average distance function $\bar{r}(x)$. Assume that the city extends between points $-R$ and R along the x axis. By definition:

$$\bar{r}(x) = \int_{-R}^{x} m(r)(x - r)\,dr + \int_{x}^{R} m(r)(r - x)\,dr \qquad (8.7)$$

Differentiation yields

$$\frac{d^2\bar{r}(x)}{dx^2} = 2m(x) \qquad (8.8)$$

Although we are mainly interested in $m(x)$, it will be convenient to consider $\bar{r}$ first:

$$a \log \frac{1}{2}\bar{r} = u_0$$

$$\bar{r} = 2e^{\,u_0/a - \bar{r}/a}$$

By a suitable choice of units for time and distance,

$$v = \frac{\bar{r}}{a} \qquad \xi = \frac{2x}{\sqrt{a^{-1}\,e^{u_0/a}}}$$

the equation may be standardized:

$$v'' = \frac{1}{2}e^{-v} \qquad (8.9)$$

Its range of definition is the positive axis $\xi \geq 0$.

A solution to (8.9) in closed form may be found as follows: Multiply (8.9) by $2v'$ and integrate $\int 2v'v''\,dx = \int e^{-v}v'\,dx$, where we have written x again for ξ.

$$(v')^2 = -e^{-v} + c_1 \quad \text{or} \quad \frac{dv}{\sqrt{c_1 - e^{-v}}} = dx \qquad (8.10)$$

Let

$$c_1 - e^{-v} = z^2, \qquad e^{-v}\,dv = 2z\,dz, \quad \text{or} \quad dv = \frac{2z\,dz}{c_1 - z^2} \qquad (8.11)$$

Substituting in (8.10) gives

$$\frac{2\,dz}{c_1 - z^2} = dx$$

Let

$$c_1 = k^2 \qquad (8.12)$$

and observe that

$$\frac{2}{k^2 - z^2} = \frac{1}{k}\frac{1}{k+z} + \frac{1}{k}\frac{1}{k-z}$$

Substituting and integrating, we have

$$\int \frac{1}{k}\frac{dz}{k+z} + \int \frac{1}{k}\frac{dz}{k-z} = \int dx$$

$$\frac{1}{k}\log\frac{k+z}{k-z} = x + c_2$$

$$z = k\frac{e^{k(x+c_2)} - 1}{e^{k(x+c_2)} + 1} \qquad (8.13)$$

Recall the definitions (8.11) of z and (8.12) of k. Thus,

$$k^2 - e^{-v} = k^2 \left(\frac{e^{k(x+c_2)} - 1}{e^{k(x+c_2)} + 1}\right)^2$$

and from this,

$$v = -\log k^2 \left[1 - \left(\frac{e^{k(x+c_2)} - 1}{e^{k(x+c_2)} + 1}\right)^2\right]$$

In order that the solution be valid on the negative axis, we must set

$$v = -\log k^2 \left[1 - \left(\frac{e^{k(|x|+c_2)} - 1}{e^{k(|x|+c_2)} + 1}\right)^2\right]$$

In order to determine c_2, observe that average transportation time has a minimum at $|x| = 0$. For this it is necessary and sufficient that $c_2 = 0$. Thus, finally, we have

$$v(x) = -\log k^2 \frac{4e^{k|x|}}{(1 + e^{k|x|})^2} \qquad (8.14)$$

The function of interest, housing density $m(x)$, may now be found by substituting (8.14) in the differential equation (8.9):

$$m(x) = (1/2)v''$$

$$= (1/4)e^{-v}$$

$$= k^2 \frac{e^{k|x|}}{(1 + e^{k|x|})^2} \qquad (8.15)$$

The unknown coefficient k is to be determined by the condition that a given number of households N be housed in the given space $2R$:

$$N = 2\int_0^R \frac{1}{m}\, dx$$

$$= \frac{2}{k^2}\int_0^R \frac{(1 + e^{kx})^2}{e^{kx}}\, dx$$

$$= \frac{2}{k^3} e^{kR} + \frac{4R}{k^2} - \frac{2}{k^3} e^{-kR} \tag{8.16}$$

Figure 8-1 shows how k depends on N for given $R = 1$. The function (8.15) which, except for a factor k, may be interpreted as the derivative of the logistic function $1/(1 + e^{-kx})$ is decreasing from $m(0) = k^2/4$ to arbitrarily small values as $|x|$ is increased. The function has been graphed in Figure 8-2 for various values of k.

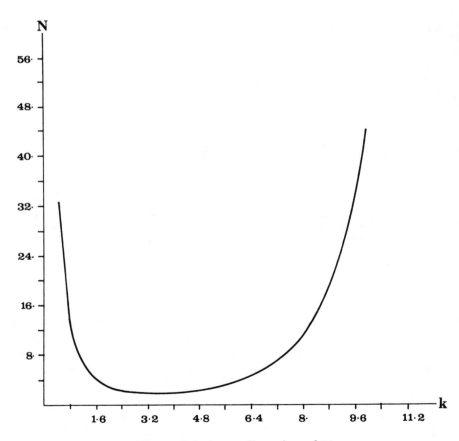

Figure 8-1. k as a Function of N

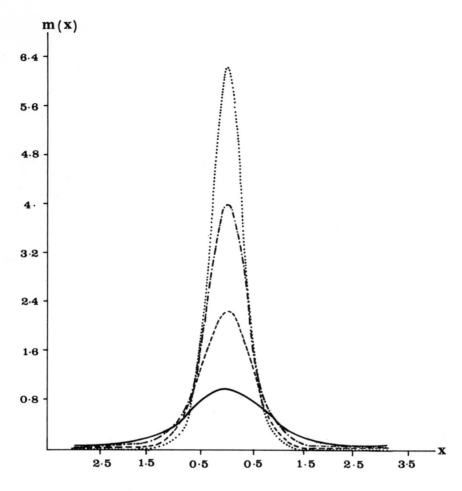

Figure 8-2. Impact of k upon $m(x)$

   The conclusions to be drawn from the solution (8.15) are as follows. In the dispersed city, locations continue to differ with respect to centrality. More central locations enjoy greater proximity and hence better opportunities for contacts with others. To compensate for this, households are squeezed into more compressed quarters.
   The competitive equilibrium of this market is Pareto optimal. The greatest utility sum is squeezed out of a given amount $2R$ of space for a given number N of households by inducing a density distribution that is symmetric and decreasing from the center. The distribution is such that

every individual is indifferent among locations, space being traded for proximity to others at rates that are equally acceptable to all. General economic principles suggest that this also yields the greatest sum of utility. (A formal proof in terms of a calculus of variations problem is not difficult.)

Population Distribution a Centralized City

Compare now the dispersed equilibrium with that of a city with a dominant CBD. In the latter case, in equation (8.5):

$$a \log s(x) = \text{constant} + |x|$$

$$s(x) = e^{c_3 + |x|/a} \tag{8.17}$$

Since we have standardized $a = 1$, the density distribution is

$$\tilde{m}(x) = m(0)e^{-|x|} \tag{8.18}$$

For comparable boundary conditions in (8.15), a k value must be found that results from the same area $2R$ and the same population N. As an example, consider $R = 1$ and $k = 1$. The corresponding N value may be calculated as

$$N^* = 4 + 2e - e^{-2} = 8.700805\ldots \tag{8.19}$$

The value of $m(0)$ is then obtained from

$$N^* = \int_{-R}^{R} m(x)\, dx = 2m(0) \int_{0}^{1} e^{-x}\, dx \tag{8.20}$$

or

$$m(0) = \frac{N^*}{2(1 - e^{-1})} = 1.850918 \tag{8.21}$$

The graphs of (8.15) and (8.18) for this special case have been plotted in Figure 8-3. It is interesting that, in the case of the dispersed city, the density graph is smooth at the center, whereas, in the concentrated case, it has a sharp peak.

Transportation Costs and Density Distribution

It is also of interest to study the savings in transportation costs that are achieved by the relative compressions of density in the central parts of the city in the decentralized case. If N families are housed at a uniform density δ in the space $2R$, then the resulting uniform density is $N/2R$ and the resulting total time cost of transportation is

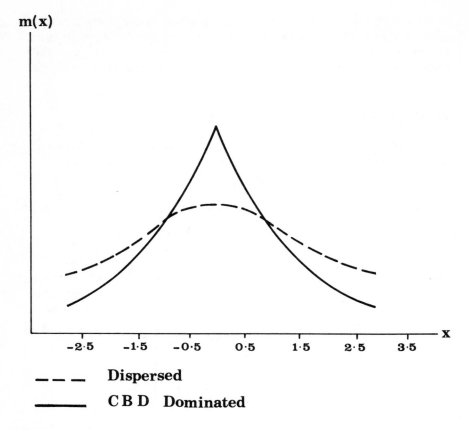

Figure 8-3. Population Distribution in a Dispersed City and in a City with Dominant CBD

$$\bar{\bar{r}} = \delta \int_{-R}^{R} \bar{r}(x)\, dx = 2\delta \int_{0}^{R} \bar{r}(x)\, dx$$

$$= 2\delta \int_{0}^{R} \left[\int_{-R}^{x} m(r)(x - r)\, dr + \int_{x}^{R} m(r)(r - x)\, dr \right] dx$$

$$= \frac{N}{R} \int_{0}^{R} \left[\int_{-R}^{x} (x - r)\, dr + \int_{x}^{R} (r - x)\, dr \right] dx$$

and

$$\bar{\bar{r}} = \frac{1}{3}\, NR^{2} \tag{8.22}$$

In the case where $R = 1$, $k = 1$, and $N = N^{*}$, one has

$$\bar{\bar{r}} = \frac{1}{3}\,N^* \approx 2.900268 \tag{8.23}$$

$$\bar{\bar{r}} = 2\int_0^1 \left[\int_{-1}^x \frac{e^r\,(x - r)}{(1 + e^r)^2}\,dr\right.$$

$$\left. + \int_x^1 \frac{e^r\,(r - x)}{(1 + e^r)^2}\,dr\right]dx \approx 0.85 \tag{8.24}$$

Thus, the density distribution in the dispersed case achieves a savings of 71 percent in the example considered.

Notes

1. E.S. Mills and J. MacKinnon [1973].
2. R.M. Solow and W.S. Vickrey [1971].

9

Employment/Population Ratios in Urban Areas: A Model of The Urban Land, Labor, and Goods Markets

Dennis R. Capozza

In recent years, many writers have explored the theory of urban structure and have greatly increased our understanding of urbanization and suburbanization. In modeling urban structure, most writers have looked at some combination of the urban goods, transportation, land, housing, and labor markets. Generally, these models are based on von Thünen's theory of land rent with modern extensions. However, despite considerable sophistication and elaboration, these models are still open to the criticism that they are only vaguely representative of actual cities. Fales and Moses present extensive criticism of this type.[3]

Of course, no model of as complex a system as the modern city can ever hope to accurately represent all the intricacies. However, a simplified model can focus on one or more aspects of cities and provide insights. Many efforts have analyzed congestion,[7,9] others have looked at the distribution of population by income,[1] while others have examined the effects of multiple modes of transportation.[2]

This chapter attempts to analyze the interaction between the distribution of employment and population in urban areas in three parts. In the first section, the Fales and Moses[3] criticisms are evaluated and, some empirical evidence on the employment/population gradients in cities is presented. The second section reviews the nature of central attraction for firms. The third section presents the model of the land, labor, and goods markets.

The empirical evidence indicates that employment has suburbanized and suburbanized faster than population. Several questions can be raised. Is employment suburbanization the result of population suburbanization or are other, independent forces responsible? Could the observed suburbanization of population be the result of employment shifts rather than income or population increases? Why do we observe an intermingling of population and employment rather than exclusive zones? An attempt is made to answer these questions by introducing heterogeneity of goods producers into a model of urban structure. One conclusion is that it appears that employment suburbanization should not be attributed to population suburbanization, but rather to independent forces.

Dennis R. Capozza is a member of the Department of Finance and Business Economics, University of Southern California, Los Angeles.

Some Empirical Evidence on the Urban
Employment/Population Relationship

Two previous studies provide evidence relevant to the issues considered here—Fales' and Moses'[3] study of land use in Chicago after the great fire of 1871 and Mills'[7] study of density functions for employment and population in U.S. cities. The Fales' and Moses' study contains an evaluation of von Thünen-type models and an empirical analysis of employment and population in Chicago by city quadrant and by annular ring. Fales and Moses considered three implications of von Thünen-type models. First, the intensity of land use declines with distance from the center of the city. For the most part, this is supported by the evidence they present; however, the decline is not monotonic. There is evidence of minor subcenters even in the last century.

Secondly, the decline in intensity is uniform in all radial directions. The evidence is less supportive of this implication. There was considerable variation between quadrants in Chicago at that time.

The third implication of von Thünen models is the exclusive zone concept—that each industry or land use will occupy one concentric zone exclusively. This implication is of most interest here. Fales and Moses tested this implication by dividing the city into nine half-mile rings. Employment in each of thirteen industries is then allocated to each ring and tabulated. Fales and Moses interpreted the results as suggesting that "land use tended to be quite mixed rather than exclusive in nineteenth century Chicago, and that linkages between firms may have been very important."[3] The basis for this interpretation is the fact that for nine of the industries, employment is spread across five or more rings. This is perhaps a bit unsympathetic to the von Thünen approach. The same data can be read as being quite supportive of von Thünen models. That is, for eleven of the thirteen industries, 70 percent or more of the employment was concentrated in two adjacent rings. The exceptions are intermediate goods (planning mills and millwork), which probably sold output to several other industries.

Somewhat more damaging to the exclusive zone concept is the data Fales and Moses presented on the distribution of population and employment. In von Thünen models population is spatially separated from employment and generally located in the outlying rings, e.g. Mills.[6] In nineteenth-century Chicago, there was considerable mixing of population and employment in every ring, as there is today in all large U.S. cities. However, industry was most heavily concentrated in the first two rings (68 percent of total employment in the thirteen industries), while population peaked in the fifth ring.

Mills' study is primarily concerned with the estimation of density functions for population and employment for eighteen U.S. metropolitan areas.[7] The estimates then make it possible to compare density functions across both space and time.

Mills assumed that the density functions are negative exponential:[a]

$$D_i(u) = A_i e^{-B_i u} \tag{9.1}$$

where $D_i(u)$ = the density for the ith category

u = distance from the center of the city

A_i, B_i = parameters to be estimated

He then uses the central city-suburb data to estimate the parameters, using an iterative procedure to fit the density function to the two data points.

The resulting density functions reveal several trends. First, during the postwar period from 1948-1963, for a sample of eighteen metropolitan areas, all sectors showed a consistent movement towards more suburbanization (falling B_i's). Secondly, the most suburbanized sector is population, followed by employment in manufacturing, retailing, services, and wholesaling respectively. Thirdly, in a smaller sample of six cities going back to 1920, the same suburbanization trend appears for all sectors. That is, suburbanization is not a postwar phenomenon; it dates back to at least 1920. Virtually the same pattern among sectors remains. Fourthly, in a still smaller sample of four cities, suburbanization of population appears to have continued uninterrupted since 1880. Fifthly, the rate of suburbanization is fastest in prosperous periods (1920s and 1950s), and somewhat slower during recession (1930s).

In attempting to find causes for the suburbanization trend, Mills considered size of SMSA, income, time, (dummy for transportation prices), and the lagged dependent variable. The regression results are disappointing statistically with few significant coefficients except on the lagged dependent variable. Mills points out that the regressions "do not quite rule out the possibility that the entire process of flattening of urban density functions is a first-order Markov process in which B responds to a once-for-all change in its equilibrium values."[7] That is, the causal variables may be irrelevant.

Mills' data on density functions make it possible to consider the relative trends in employment and population densities. The questions that we wish to raise concern the mechanism by which the change in the internal structure of the city takes place. It is clear that there is considerable intermingling of population and employment in the annular rings of any city. The empirical point to be established in this section is whether the employment sectors have suburbanized more or less rapidly than population.

---

[a]There is much support, both empirical and theoretical, for this functional form.

If we accept the premise that employment and population density functions are negative exponential, then the ratio of employment to population will be negative exponential, as well. The employment to population ratio will be

$$\frac{E}{P} = \frac{A_w e^{-B_w u}}{A_p e^{-B_p u}} = \frac{A_w}{A_p} e^{-(B_w - B_p)u} \tag{9.2}$$

where subscript w denotes the appropriate employment category, and subscript p distinguishes the parameters of the population density function. Provided $B_w > B_p$, (9.2) is negative exponential.

In Table 9-1 the average E/P ratios have been tabulated for eighteen metropolitan areas in the postwar period. The values are based on the data for density gradients presented by Mills. Notice that for every employment category the gradient of E/P falls in each period. The implication is that throughout the period employment in all categories was suburbanizing more rapidly than population. Retailing suburbanized particularly fast. The average gradient for E/P in retailing fell by 80 percent from 1948-1963.

In Table 9-2 the gradients of E/P are tabulated for the smaller sample of six metropolitan areas, but going back as far as 1920. The same general pattern is apparent, however, three of the four categories show increasing

Table 9-1

Employment/Population Gradients by Sector and Year: Eighteen Metropolitan Areas $(B_w - B_p)$

	1948	1954	1958	1963
Manufacturing	.1	.08	.06	.04
Retailing	.3	.28	.17	.06
Services	.39	.34	.24	.15
Wholesaling	.42	.39	.28	.18

Table 9-2

Employment/Population Gradients for Six Metropolitan Areas $(B_w - B_p)$

	1920	1929	1939	1948	1954	1958	1963
Manufacturing	.09	.09	.10	.19	.21	.19	.12
Retailing	—	.29	.23	.19	.27	.17	.05
Services	—	—	.45	.31	.35	.29	.19
Wholesaling	—	.70	.57	.44	.43	.36	.33

gradients of E/P for 1954. Population suburbanized more rapidly than employment in these cities from 1948-1954. Also the gradient of E/P for manufacturing shows an irregular pattern for the longer time interval. Population suburbanized more rapidly than manufacturing employment through 1954, but less rapidly afterwards.

Since most of the increase in the gradient of E/P for manufacturing took place in the immediate postwar period, one possible interpretation would be that the movement of people to the suburbs occurred first and attracted manufacturing employment to the suburbs rather than vice versa.[b] However, in most models of urban structure, employment and population interact only at the boundary of exclusive zones. Suburbanization of population would not be an important cause of employment suburbanization in such a model.

The Nature of Central Attraction in Cities

In any city, a wide variety of factors influence the optimal (profit-maximizing) locations for firms. A common classification of costs consists of procurement, production, and distribution costs (e.g., Hoover[5]). In the context of intraurban location, there is a symmetry in procurement and distribution that should permit a unified treatment of both as transportation costs. Production cost can be separated into agglomeration economies and the costs associated with each factor of production, land, labor, and capital.

Each of these costs vary in importance for individual firms. As a result we should expect central attraction to vary widely for firms in any city. A discussion of each follows.

Transportation Costs

The typical von Thünen model of intraurban location is based on the assumption that goods must be shipped to some specified location either for sale at that point (a central marketplace) or for export out of the city (a port or rail terminal). The simplest case occurs when all firms must ship output to the same location. In this case, the most desirable locations are near the central market or transhipment point (CBD), and these locations command the highest rents. The resulting rent gradient declines monotonically from the CBD. Such a model gives rise to the objection that in modern U.S. cities there is no one location that is a dominant attraction. Subcenters are now a feature of cities that cannot be ignored. However, a generalization of the

[b] Mills gives this interpretation to the data (p. 47).[7]

basic von Thünen model in which more than one location is attractive to firms is possible (e.g., Hartwick and Hartwick[4]).

There is a second type of procurement and/or distribution cost that is not explicitly treated in von Thünen models. There are many firms that must transport inputs or outputs not to just one location, but rather to a large number of locations. To take an extreme example, consider a diaper service. Here the inputs, soiled diapers, must be gathered from customers distributed over the entire city. The output, clean diapers, must then be returned to the same customers. In less extreme cases a firm might be drawing inputs alone from the whole city—for example, its labor force; alternatively, output might only be shipped to dispersed locations in the entire city. This would be the case for many wholesaling operations and local manufacturers.

Two questions can be raised. First, what locations are attractive to firms with transport costs of the second type? It is easily shown that central locations minimize transport costs for these firms as well. Secondly, if central locations are still desirable, is the nature of the attraction similar for both types of transport cost? A simplified model will provide answers.

Consider two firms in a square city with a rectangular grid of streets.[c] For the first firm, let the only transportation expense be the cost of delivering output to the central market. If transport cost is proportional to distance, this firm's transportation cost per unit will vary with its location according to

$$T(u) = t(|x_0| + |y_0|) = tu \qquad (9.3)$$

where $t =$ transport cost

$u = |x_0| + |y_0|$ the distance to the city center

Thus, transport cost is linear in distance.

The second firm delivers output to customers evenly distributed over the entire city. Its transport cost will be

$$T(x_0, y_0) = t \int_{-k}^{+k} \int_{-(k-x)}^{k-x} (|x - x_0| + |y - y_0|)\, dy\, dx \qquad (9.4)$$

where k is the radius of the city. Taking advantage of the symmetry of the problem, we have

$$T(u) = 2t\{2k^3 + k^2u + ku^2 - 1/3\, u^3\} \qquad (9.5)$$

which is a cubic in distance to the center.

Two items are worth noting. First, the minimum transport cost location

---

[c] This city is homeomorphic to the usual circular city. Thus, qualitative results apply equally well to the circular city.

is still at the center of the city (at $u = 0$).[d] Secondly, the rate at which transport costs increase is given by

$$\frac{\partial T}{\partial u} = 2t\{k^2 + 2ku - u^2\} > 0 \tag{9.6}$$

That is, transport cost in this case is not proportional to distance. It increases nonlinearly with both distance and the radius of the city. Also notice that as the radius of the city increases, the slope of the transport cost function increases. This would tend to cause firms to centralize if city size increases, ceteris paribus.[e] A centralization of firms as city size (population) increases is consistent with what Mills observes to be happening for retailing, wholesaling, and services (p. 55).[7]

The two firms, therefore, differ considerably in terms of the value of central location to each. In general, firms will have transport costs that are a combination of the two types discussed above. As a result, we might expect the value of accessibility to central locations for a large number of heterogeneous firms to have a continuous and wide range of values.

Agglomeration Economies

Agglomeration economies are often cited as one of the main reasons for the existence of city, but no formal model of urban structure considers these economies explicitly. Since agglomeration economies are analogous to the second type of transport cost, it can be argued that explicit treatment would be unnecessary.

Suppose that a firm is able to reduce costs through interaction with other firms. Further assume that the benefits it receives from proximity to other firms are proportional to the distance to the other firms and that firms are evenly distributed throughout the city. Then by analogy to (9.4) the value of proximity will be

$$A(u) = A_0 - 2a \int_{-k}^{+k} \int_{0}^{k-x} \{y + (x - u)\}\, dy\, dx \tag{9.6}$$

where $A_0 =$ the value of agglomeration economies at the city center

$a =$ rate of decline of the external effect for a unit increase in distance

---

[d] For all $0 < u \le k$, $k^2u + ku^2 > 1/3\, u^3$. Since $k^2u + ku^2 = 0$ at $u = 0$, $T(u)$ is smallest at the center.

[e] If land rents are negative exponential and only transport costs vary with location, then it can be shown that the least cost location is at that distance from the CBD for which the slope of the rent gradient and the slope of the transport cost function are equal in absolute value. Thus, an increase in city size accompanied by a parallel outward shift in the rent gradient would result in a centralization of firms of this type.

The maximum benefit from agglomeration economies is obtained by locating at the center of the city. This represents an additional force attracting firms to the CBD. As with transport costs, we might expect the benefit from agglomeration economies to vary considerably between firms. Large firms could internalize more of the economies and might be less attracted than small firms.

Capital Costs

Capital is generally taken to be perfectly mobile within cities. As a result the price of capital should not influence location decisions, except indirectly. The interest rate gradient is a horizontal line, i.e., the interest rate is constant everywhere in the city.

Labor and Land Costs

The two remaining factors, labor and land, both provide firms with an incentive to locate away from the city center. That is, we expect the cost of both of these factors to decline with distance.

Moses has made the argument that when the intraurban labor market is in equilibrium, workers must be paid a lower wage for employment close to residences.[8] The money cost of commuting and the value of lost leisure encourage workers to accept the lower wage. That is, a worker can maintain the same level of satisfaction by accepting less money income in exchange for a shorter commute. In equilibrium, wages will fall with distance from the city center at a rate equal to the value that workers place on the cost of commuting an extra mile. This decline in wage rates will attract activities to suburban locations. The greatest attraction should be for labor intensive industries.

Land costs are also observed to decline with distance. Often, in urban models, this decline is a result of the profit maximizing behavior of firms. Land rents effectively become the difference between revenues and non-land costs and absorb all possible profits. An implicit assumption is that all the land within a given radius is demanded by firms. There is no competition between alternative uses for land within any annular ring.

If the number of firms willing to rent the land within an annular ring is insufficient to exhaust the available land, the rent on all the land in the ring will be determined by the amount that the competing use is able to pay. The competing use in cities is residential. Firms can acquire or rent as much of the land as desired by offering a rent slightly greater than the rent on residential land.

In the model that follows, firms compete for land with housing consumers. The rents firms pay are determined by residential land rents. An exception is land inside the CBD, where only firms are competing for land.

In sum, firms are influenced by a variety of factors in making intraurban location decisions. These forces both attract and repel firms to and from central locations. Because of the diversity of influencing factors and the diversity of firms, the degree of attraction will vary greatly. The model explores the implications of diversity for urban structure and analyzes the factors that effect the employment/population gradient in cities.

A Model of the Urban Land, Labor, and Goods Markets

This model is an equilibrium model of the land, labor, and goods markets as opposed to an optimization model. There are two sectors—households and businesses. Households are assumed to be homogeneous in all respects; but businesses are heterogeneous.

The Consumer

The model begins with the theory of consumer behavior. We assume households have identical tastes for two available goods, land, and a composite of "other" goods. Each household contains one worker supplying his services to the goods producers.

The household utility function is log-linear

$$V(l, X) = Al^\alpha X^\beta \tag{9.7}$$

where l = space consumed per household

X = other goods consumed per household.

A worker employed at distance u_w from the center of the city receives wage

$$y(u) = y(k) + t_w(k - u_w) \tag{9.8}$$

where $y(k)$ = the wage received by someone employed at the edge of the city

t_w = transport cost per mile per worker

That is, for the labor market to be in equilibrium between all locations, employers must absorb commuting costs. Notice that as the city expands wages rise as in Figure 9-1.

The budget constraint then is

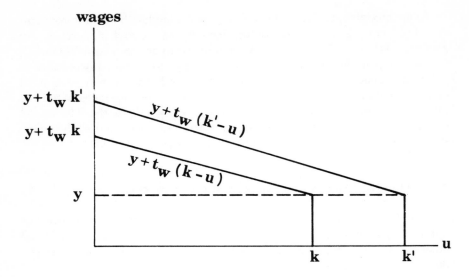

Figure 9-1. Wages over Space

$$\{y + t_w(k - u_w)\} - t_w(u_r - u_w) - R(u)l - pX = 0 \qquad (9.9)$$

where $u_r - u_w =$ the distance between residence and work

$$p = \text{ the price of the composite good}$$

$$R(u) = \text{ the rent or land at } u$$

Using the first order condition, a unitary elastic demand for space is obtained:

$$l = \frac{\alpha}{\alpha + \beta} \; \frac{\{y + t_w(k - u_r)\}}{R(u)} \qquad (9.10)$$

Again, from the first order conditions, the rent gradient in residential areas is

$$R(u) = R_0\{y + t_w(k - u_r)\}^\gamma \qquad (9.11)$$

where R_0 is a constant of integration, and $\gamma = (\alpha + \beta)/\alpha$. If land must be bid away from agriculture at the edge of the city, k, then

$$R_0 = \gamma R_a/y \qquad (9.12)$$

where R_a is the value of land in agricultural uses.

The Labor Market

The labor market is assumed to be perfectly competitive. Labor is perfectly mobile both within the city and among cities. One consequence of these assumptions has already been noted. The wage rate necessary to attract labor will be the greatest at the center of the city and will fall with distance at a rate equal to the cost of commuting. In addition, the mobile labor force will equalize real incomes among cities. In this model, equal real incomes mean equal utility levels. Since the composite good has price p in all cities and since only the composite and land enter the utility function, it is sufficient that among cities any two locations with equal land rents have equal net wages (net of commuting costs). In particular, since every city must bid land away from agriculture, land rent at the edge of each city will be R_a; therefore, wages will be equal at the city edge in all cities:

$$y_i = y^* \qquad \text{all } i \text{ indexing cities}$$

where y^* is the national net wage (net of transport cost).

The Goods Sector

In the goods sector, firms produce output according to the fixed coefficients production function:

$$X = \min\left(L, \frac{K}{k}, \frac{N}{n}\right) \tag{9.13}$$

where $K =$ capital

$N =$ labor

$k =$ the capital/output ratio

$n =$ the labor/output ratio

The production function is normalized around a unitary land/output ratio.

For a variety of reasons discussed above, each firm is attracted to central locations. This attraction is proportional in distance from the center of the city. The per mile attraction is t_a. Therefore, the cost of production at loaction u will be the sum of factor payments and the cost of noncentral location.

$$C = R(u) + kr + n\{y + t_w(k - u)\} + t_a u \tag{9.14}$$

If the firm minimizes costs, we have

$$\frac{dC}{du} = R'(u) + t_a - nt_w = 0 \qquad (9.15)$$

The firms bid rent function then has slope

$$R'(u) = -(t_a - nt_w) = -t \qquad (9.16)$$

Four factors determine the slope of this bid rent function. The greater the central attraction, the steeper is the slope of the bid rent function. The more labor the firm uses per unit output, the flatter the slope. The greater the cost of commuting, the flatter the slope; and, implicitly, the more land required per unit output, the flatter the slope.

Combining (9.11) and (9.16), we get

$$t(u) = R'(u) = \frac{R_a t_w^\gamma}{y}\left\{1 + \frac{t_w}{y}(k - u)\right\}^{\gamma-1} \qquad (9.17)$$

Since the bid rent curves differ among firms, we can define the associated rate of change of slopes by

$$dt = R''(u)\,du = \gamma(\gamma - 1)\frac{R_a t_w^2}{y^2}\left\{1 + \frac{t_w}{y}(k - u)\right\}^{\gamma-2}du \qquad (9.18)$$

If we know how much output of each good is produced, it is possible to determine the amount of land required for goods production. Suppose the types of goods produced are a continuous variable indexed by the slope of the bid rent function. Further, let the slopes range over values between t_0 and t_1 with a uniform distribution:

$$F'(t) = f(t) = \delta \qquad (9.19)$$

and

$$F(t) = \delta(t - t_0) \qquad (9.20)$$

The amount of land required by firms in an annulus of width du will be $\delta\, dt$.

From (9.18) and (9.19), the amount of land required at u for goods production is

$$L_G(u) = \delta\gamma(\gamma - 1)\frac{R_a t_w^2}{y^2}\left\{1 + \frac{t_w}{y}(k - u)\right\}^{\gamma-2}du \qquad (9.21)$$

An essential restriction is that less than 100 percent of the land at each u goes to goods production. Thus the amount of land specified in (9.18) must be less than $2\pi u\, du$. The residual is available for residential purposes:

$$L_r(u) = 2\pi u - L_G(u) \qquad (9.22)$$

In those areas of the city where goods production and residences coexist, goods production must bid land away from residences. Close to the center of city, only a small amount of land is available. If goods producers require all the land, then rents will be determined by competitive bidding of goods producers against one another.

Goods producers will in fact bid for all the land at some small u if the maximum slope of their bid rent function is greater than the bid rent function of households for residential land at the center of the city. That is, if

$$t_0 > R_a\left(1 + \frac{t_w k}{y}\right)^{\gamma} \tag{9.23}$$

If we define the radius of the CBD to be the radius of the area inside which all land goes to goods producers, then this radius is that u satisfying

$$\delta\, dt = 2\pi u\, du \tag{9.24}$$

From (9.24) and (9.16) we have

$$R''(u) = \frac{2\pi u}{\delta} \tag{9.25}$$

Integrating twice, we obtain

$$R(u) = C_1 + C_2 u - \frac{\pi u^3}{3\delta} \tag{9.26}$$

where C_1, C_2 are constants of integration. The initial conditions defining the constants are

$$R(\hat{u}) = R_a\left\{1 + \frac{t_w}{y}(k - \hat{u})\right\}^{\gamma} \tag{9.27}$$

and

$$R'(\hat{u}) = -R_a\frac{t_w}{y}\left\{1 + \frac{t_w}{y}(k - \hat{u})\right\}^{\gamma-1} \tag{9.28}$$

At some distance, goods producers will cease to demand any land. This distance, $\bar{u}$, is defined by that u satisfying

$$t_1 = R'(u) \tag{9.29}$$

The city, therefore, is divided into three rings as shown in Figure 9-2. In the first ring at the center, all land is devoted to goods production; this ring

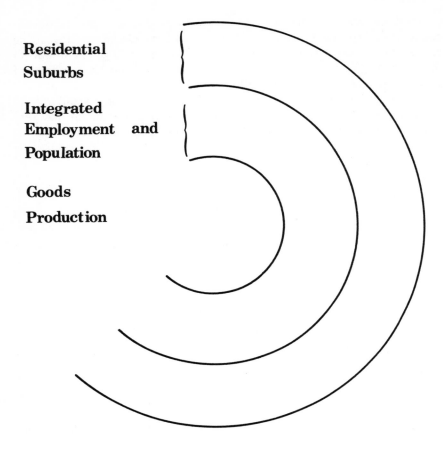

Residential
Suburbs

Integrated
Employment and
Population

Goods
Production

Figure 9-2. Employment and Population

is commonly called the CBD. In the second ring, goods production and residences coexist. In many cities it is this ring that has increased in relative importance. The manifestation of this is the rise of non-CBD employment centers. In the third ring, the suburbs, land is entirely residential.

The Employment/Population Ratio

A characteristic of most cities is an employment/population ratio that declines with distance from the CBD. This model conforms to this characteristic. The amount of space demanded per household at u is given by (9.10). The amount of land devoted to residences is given by (9.22). The ratio of these is population at u:

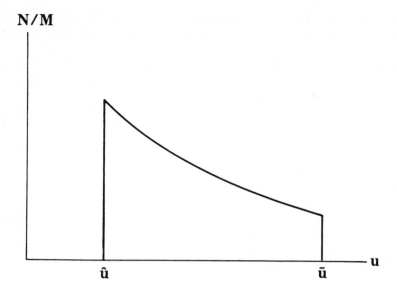

Figure 9-3. Employment/Population Ratio

$$M(u) = \frac{\gamma L_r(u)R(u)}{y + t_w(k - u)} \tag{9.30}$$

The employment at u is given by the labor/output ratio times output:

$$N(u) = \frac{L_G}{n} \tag{9.31}$$

The ratio is

$$\frac{N(u)}{M(u)} = \frac{\delta R''\{y - t_w(k - u)\}}{\gamma n\{2\pi u - \delta R''\}R(u)} \tag{9.32}$$

The properties of this function are such that the employment/population ratio declines with distance, as shown in Figure 9-3, on the interval $\hat{u} < u < \tilde{u}$. The ratio is undefined for $u < \hat{u}$.[f]

Equation (9.32) is sufficiently complicated to rule out analytical solution of the comparative statics. Further results await a numerical analysis. However, the model does provide some insight into the response of city structure to exogenous changes.

---

[f]Under the assumptions here, this function is convex to the origin and, therefore, has the appearance of a negative exponential.

Consider the effect of a nationwide increase in income. The equilibrium location for firms occurs when (9.17) is met—that is, when the slope of the rent gradient $R(u, y_0)$ equals the slope of the firm's bid rent function (see Figure 9-4). An increase in income will suburbanize the population and reduce the slope of the rent gradient at every distance. The new rent gradient $R(u, y_1)$ will no longer be tangent to the firm's bid rent function. In the long run, the firm will relocate at $u_2 < u_1$. Thus, the effect of an increase in income is to suburbanize population, centralize firms, and centralize the employment to population ratio. A similar argument can be made concerning the effect of a fall in transport costs.[g]

Since suburbanization of population has been attributed, in a large extent, to rising income and falling transport costs and since both of these changes tend to centralize production, it does not seem plausible to attribute suburbanization of employment to suburbanization of population. One must look elsewhere, perhaps to technological changes or to a more sophisticated treatment of agglomeration economies, for an explanation of the simultaneous suburbanization of employment and population.

Summary and Conclusions

This chapter has studied the relationship between employment and population in urban areas. The empirical evidence of the first section indicated that employment and population are quite mixed. That is, there is no evidence of exclusive zones (annular rings) for population and employment. In addition, both employment and population have suburbanized during the last fifty years but employment has tended to suburbanize faster. The result has been declining gradients of the employment/population function. The remaining sections of the chapter are a first attempt at explaining this phenomenon.

The basic tenet of the model is that in any city there is a wide variety of industries and types of firms. The cost structure of each firm varies considerably depending upon (a) the strength of central attraction arising from the cost of transportation and from agglomeration economies and (b) the factor intensities of production technology. Because firms differ in these respects, the profit-maximizing locations for each firm will differ as well.

The model developed in the final section incorporates heterogeneity of firms into a model of urban structure. The nature of interaction between employment and population in this model is such that a suburbanization of population will tend to cause a centralization of employment. Thus, it

[g] A fall in transport costs causes the slope of the firm's bid rent function to fall as well as the slope of the rent gradient. For the centralization result to obtain, the slope of the rent gradient must respond more than the slope of the bid rent function.

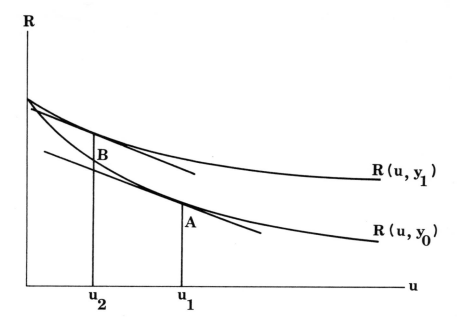

Figure 9-4. Equilibrium Location as Incomes Rise

appears that employment suburbanization cannot be attributed to the suburbanization of population.

Notes

1. M.J. Beckmann [1969].
2. D. Capozza [1973].
3. R. Fales and L.N. Moses [1972].
4. P.G. Hartwick and J.M. Hartwick [1974].
5. E. Hoover, 1948, *The Location of Economic Activity*. New York: McGraw-Hill.
6. E.S. Mills [1967].
7. E.S. Mills [1972b].
8. L.N. Moses [1962].
9. R.M. Solow [1973a].

10 Spatial Consumer Equilibrium

G.J. Papageorgiou

This account reports without proof on some results of long-run, ongoing investigations about urban equilibrium structure. The basic model stems from neoclassical consumer equilibrium: with the exception of land values, the price system is exogenous. Thus, the model falls within the ever increasing set of studies inspired by William Alonso.

The exposition relates to three main themes. The first two are general as they correspond to any given price system. The third corresponds to an important special case: a price system that leads to spatial consumer equilibrium. The first theme is a description and analysis of the elements that are taken to constitute an urban spatial structure. The impact of this urban spatial structure upon the spatial choice of individuals and upon the structure of the urban society itself constitutes the second theme. The third theme is a description of residential values and land use under conditions of spatial consumer equilibrium.

The model differs in several respects from the "typical" paradigm.

The treatment is general, not limited to specific forms of the postulated functional relationships.

The world of the model seems closer to reality. The urban environment allows for any spatial distribution of any number of centers. Consumer behavior allows for decisions affected by, among other things, environmental quality, time, and subsistence constraints. The society is represented by a continuum of incomes.

The model is analytically tractable in the sense that, given a particular utility structure, the spatial distribution of population and land values can be analytically determined. For example, results associated with a Cobb-Douglas model are available. These results probably represent the only solved case of a model related to a hierarchy of centers and to a continuous distribution of incomes over a continuous space.

G.J. Papageorgiou is a member of the Department of Geography, McMaster University.

The support of Canada Council is gratefully acknowledged. Some of the results in the section on Spatial Consumer Equilibrium represent work with H. Mullally.

Urban Structure

Environment

The physical space $\mathfrak{S}$ is the set containing all locations $\mathfrak{s}$.

ASSUMPTION 10.1 $\mathfrak{S}$ is closed and connected.

Since $\mathfrak{S}$ is connected, distance between locations could be measured everywhere along paths that belong to $\mathfrak{S}$. The physical space is related to a distance function $\mathcal{D}$.

ASSUMPTION 10.2: $\mathcal{D}: \mathfrak{S} \times \mathfrak{S} \to \mathcal{R}_+$ is differentiable on $\mathfrak{S} \times \mathfrak{S}$.

The physical space is also related to an externality $\mathcal{E}: \mathfrak{S} \to \mathcal{R}_+$. Intuitively, $\mathcal{E}$ may be interpreted as residential attractiveness, being a composite index that reflects a variety of natural factors such as topography, manmade factors such as condition of housing, and social factors such as prestige of the neighborhood. Thus, $\mathcal{E}$ may imply the existence of amenity resources, public goods, or both.

Centers

The urban structure adopted reflects some ideas of Christaller[4] and Lösch[6] extended within the realm of the city. The city is viewed as a highly dense concentration of centers associated with the distribution of goods and services and with the provision of employment opportunities. From a spatial point of view, a center $\mathcal{C}$ is a subset of $\mathfrak{S}$.

ASSUMPTION 10.3: $\mathcal{C} \subset \mathfrak{S}$ is simply connected.

Locations in $\mathcal{C}$ are called central locations. Otherwise, they are called residential locations.

It is assumed that commodities can be partitioned into groups homogeneous in respect to a certain criterion. It is also assumed that the centers constitute a hierarchy in the following manner. Every center is associated with a nonempty set with different groups as elements. For any two centers, the associated sets are such that one is a subset of the other. If the two sets are identical, the centers are of the same order. If one is a proper subset of the other, the center associated with the larger set is of higher order than the center associated with the smaller set. A center of order i is called a $\mathcal{C}_i$. Of course, the highest order centers contain all groups. Otherwise, there must be centers of still higher order outside the realm and, therefore, irrelevant. The highest order centers are of order n.

It is possible to identify a group by the corresponding order in the following manner.

ASSUMPTION 10.4:   A $\mathscr{C}_i$ is related to all lower order $(i-1, \ldots, 1)$ groups in addition to the group or groups of order i.

Intuitively, the centers are scattered within the physical space.

ASSUMPTION 10.5:   The number of centers is finite and the distances among them are finite.

Spatial Structure

A particular urban spatial structure corresponds to a particular spatial distribution of centers with known hierarchical properties.

Definition 10.1: $\mathscr{L}$ is the set of centers.

Given the urban spatial structure, every location $\mathfrak{z}^1 \in \mathfrak{S}$ can be related to vector $\mathscr{C}^1$ of the closest centers that contain group or groups of order $1, 2, \ldots, n$.[a] If $\mathfrak{z}^1$ is equidistant to more than one center related to group or groups of order i, then $\mathscr{C}^1$ is not unique. This particular assignment of centers to every $\mathfrak{z}^1 \in \mathfrak{S}$ can be represented by a function $\delta: \mathfrak{S} \to \mathscr{L} \times \mathfrak{S}$. An element of the range contains the closest centers and, in addition, $\mathfrak{z}^1$.

Consider now the spatial distribution of centers related to the group or groups of order i. Using Assumption 10.4, these are centers of order i.

Definition 10.2: $\mathscr{B}_i \subset \mathfrak{S}$ consists of the boundaries of the Dirichlet regions corresponding to centers that contain group or groups of order i.

LEMMA 10.1: $\delta: \mathfrak{S} \to \mathscr{L} \times \mathfrak{S}$ is differentiable on $\mathfrak{S} - \cup_{i=1}^{n} \mathscr{B}_i$.

Intuitively, since every $\mathfrak{z}^1 \in \mathfrak{S}$ can be related to a set of closest centers $\mathscr{C}^1$, it is possible to characterize the position of $\mathfrak{z}^1$ relative to the spatial economy by a vector $\mathbf{s} \in S$ with elements s_i representing the shortest distance between this location and the boundary of the closest center or centers that contain the group or groups of order i. Such a unique shortest distance exists by Assumptions 10.2 and 10.3. Therefore, $\mathbf{s}$ is unique for every location related to a given urban spatial structure, and $\mathbf{s} \in \mathscr{R}_+^n$. In order to compute $\mathbf{s}$, a vector function $\mathscr{D}^n$ is defined as follows.

---

[a] All vectors are column vectors. Transportation is denoted with a prime.

Definition 10.3: $\mathscr{D}^n$: $\mathscr{L} \times \mathfrak{S} \rightarrow S$ has components $\mathscr{D}$.

LEMMA 10.2: $\mathscr{D}^n$ is differentiable on $\mathscr{L} \times$ int $\mathfrak{S}$ and continuous on $\mathscr{L} \times \mathfrak{S}$.

The vector s, characterizing the position of $\mathfrak{s}$ relative to the spatial economy, can now be estimated through the composite function $\mathscr{D}^n \cdot \delta$: $\mathfrak{S} \rightarrow S$. The range of this function is a convex subset of $\mathscr{R}_+^n$.

LEMMA 10.3: $s \in S$; $S \subset \mathscr{R}_+^n$ such that $s_1 \leq s_2 \leq \ldots \leq s_n$.

Lemma 10.3 suggests that the criterion of classification into groups can be $s_1 \leq s_2 \leq \ldots \leq s_n$. In this case, groups of the same order are combined without loss of generality, so that immediately lower order centers contain all groups but one, and so on, to the lowest order centers that contain one group; if there are n orders of centers, there are n groups. Moreover, if commodities can be partitioned according to the relation $s_1 \leq s_2 \leq \ldots \leq s_n$, then higher order centers must contain all lower order groups. Otherwise, there is a location with s such that a lower order distance is greater than a higher order distance.

The set $\mathfrak{S}$ is interpreted as the landscape. Therefore, $\mathfrak{s}$ represents a physical location. In contrast, as already stated, s represents the position of $\mathfrak{s}$ relative to the spatial economy. This distinction between $\mathfrak{S}$ and S must remain explicit.

THEOREM 10.1: $\mathscr{D}^n \cdot \delta$ is differentiable on $\mathfrak{S} - \cup_i \mathscr{B}_i$ and continuous on $\mathfrak{S}$.

Theorem 10.1 establishes the main connection between $\mathfrak{S}$ and S.[b] The immediately following results are based upon this theorem and are useful in examining spatial phenomena (on $\mathfrak{S}$) through results obtained on S.

THEOREM 10.2: If the function f: $S \rightarrow \mathscr{R}^m$ is differentiable int S and continuous on S, then $f \cdot \mathscr{D}^n \cdot \delta$ is differentiable on $\mathfrak{S} - \cup_i \mathscr{B}_i$ and continuous on $\mathfrak{S}$.

THEOREM 10.3: Let $\mathscr{F}$: $X \rightarrow \mathfrak{S}$ be a correspondence and F: $X \rightarrow S$ be its representation on S. Then, if F is upper (lower) semicontinuous on X, $\mathscr{F}$ is upper (lower) semicontinuous on X.

THEOREM 10.4: Let $\mathscr{A} \subset \mathfrak{S}$ and its representation $A \subset S$. Then, A is compact if and only if $\mathscr{A}$ is compact; A is connected if $\mathscr{A}$ is connected.

[b] I am grateful to Tony Smith for pointing out the nondifferentiability of $\mathscr{D}^n \cdot \delta$ at the boundaries.

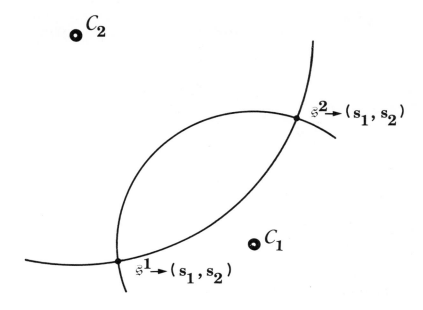

Figure 10-1. (s_1, s_2) Corresponds to Both $\mathfrak{s}^1$ and $\mathfrak{s}^2$

Theorem 10.4 indicates an important lack of symmetry between $\mathfrak{S}$ and S: any connected subset of S does not necessarily correspond to a connected area in $\mathfrak{S}$. For example, to every $\mathfrak{s}$ there corresponds a single s but not necessarily vice versa (see Figure 10-1). Every urban spatial structure is represented in S. Furthermore, every s can be related to an urban spatial structure. For example, arbitrarily locate $\mathfrak{s}$ on $\mathfrak{S}$, arbitrarily determine a shortest path with origin at $\mathfrak{s}$, and locate a $\mathscr{C}_i$ such that a given s_i represents the shortest distance between $\mathfrak{s}$ and the boundary of $\mathscr{C}_i$ located along this path.

It is useful to view S independently of a particular urban structure. Changes within S refer to changes in position relative to the spatial economy. Such changes are represented by the corresponding gradient $\nabla .^c$ For S treated independently of a particular urban structure, ∇ has a natural, abstract interpretation. Since, however, the objective is spatial analysis on $\mathfrak{S}$, ∇ must be spatially meaningful. A mapping from $\mathfrak{S}$ to S is in effect a mapping from $\mathscr{R}^2$ to $\mathscr{R}^n_+$. In consequence, $\partial / \partial s_i$ in ∇ corresponds to spatial shifts represented by $d\mathfrak{s}$ only in the case of one- or two-order hierarchies (see Figure 10-2). In the case of higher order urban systems this correspondence does not exist because a shift in location cannot be related to change in a single component of s; compare for example $\mathfrak{s}^1$ and $\mathfrak{s}^3$ (see Figure 10-3).

$^c\nabla$ denotes the vector $(\partial / \partial S_1, \partial / \partial S_2, \ldots, \partial / \partial S_n)$.

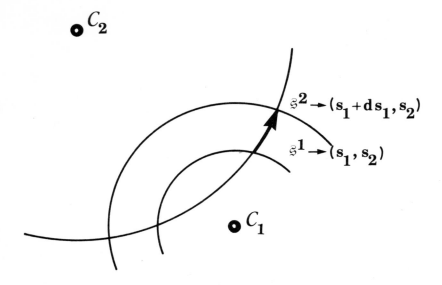

Figure 10-2. $\partial/\partial s_1$ Corresponds to a Small Shift in Location

One can always construct examples of distant locations related by $\partial/\partial s_i$; compare for example $\mathfrak{s}^1$ and $\mathfrak{s}^2$ (Figure 10-3). Nevertheless, there is a more general relationship among spatial shifts and changes in position relative to the spatial economy. This relationship is represented by the directional derivative

$$\frac{d}{d\mathfrak{s}} = \nabla' \frac{ds}{d\mathfrak{s}}$$

which, according to Theorem 10.2 exists on $\mathfrak{S} - \cup_i \mathscr{B}_i$ for functions differentiable on S.

The ensuing analysis refers primarily to S. Of course, spatial analysis on $\mathfrak{S}$ is the main objective. Results obtained on S can be applied to $\mathfrak{S}$ through the four theorems of this section.

Although the lack of symmetry between $\mathfrak{S}$ and S may seem awkward, we believe that it represents the deepest advantage of the model. Cities appear messy, yet we search for order. We maintain that order exists in the form of an abstract urban structure. Then, it must be that the spatial manifestation of urban structure blurs this order. S represents the abstract urban structure; $\mathfrak{S}$ represents the spatial manifestation of urban structure. Assumptions are made on $\mathfrak{S}$; search for order is conducted on S. Results on S are general, while the corresponding results on $\mathfrak{S}$ must be related to a

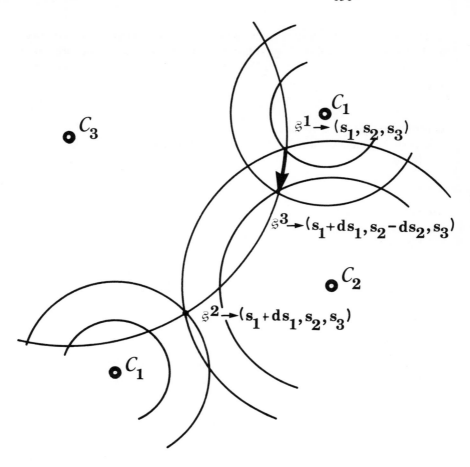

Figure 10-3. $\partial/\partial s_1$ Does Not Correspond to a Small Shift in Location

particular urban structure. Order on S may appear as disorder on $\mathfrak{S}$ due to the lack of symmetry between $\mathfrak{S}$ and S.

In addition to $\mathcal{D}$, $\mathfrak{S}$ has also been related to the externality $\mathcal{E}$. The representation of $\mathcal{E}$ in S is E.

ASSUMPTION 10.6 $E: S \to \mathcal{R}_+$ is differentiable on int S and continuous on S.

Of course, $\mathcal{E} = E \cdot \mathcal{D}^n \cdot \delta$. Thus, according to Theorem 10.2, $\mathcal{E}$ is differentiable on $\mathfrak{S} - \cup_i \mathcal{B}_i$ and continuous on $\mathfrak{S}$.

Due to the lack of symmetry between $\widetilde{\mathfrak{S}}$ and S, $E[\mathbf{s}]$ poses a difficulty: locations with identical position relative to the spatial economy correspond to identical $\mathscr{E}$. This is restrictive. However, S can be written more generally as $\{\mathbf{s}, \mathbf{x}\}$ where $\mathbf{x}$ is a vector of distances from a number of fixed poles necessary and sufficient to describe other exogenous types of environmental variation. There is no difficulty in considering $\mathbf{x}$. Very few results require convexity of S. In such cases, convexity of the redefined set could be imposed as an assumption. With this understanding, $\mathbf{x}$ is not included for simplicity.

Commodities and Prices

ASSUMPTION 10.7:   No inferior commodities.

It is not difficult to consider every commodity separately. However, the next assumption is introduced for notational simplicity.

ASSUMPTION 10.8:   All mill price changes for the commodities belonging to the group of order i are proportional.

Therefore, commodities belonging to the group of order i can be represented by a composite commodity of order i. The corresponding prices vary over space because they are weighted by transportation costs. If mill prices and the structure of transportation costs are known, then prices for the composite goods are also known. Of course, if it is natural to assume that the price for the composite good of order i may be written as $p_i[s_i]$. Nevertheless, prices that depend upon location rather than upon a single component of $\mathbf{s}$ also exist. One such is price for housing. For convenience, all known prices are assumed to depend upon location. The following assumption refers to every known price structure, including the prices for the composite goods of the hierarchy.

ASSUMPTION 10.9: $p: S \to \mathscr{R}_+$ is differentiable on int S and continuous on S; $p > 0$.

Households

The archetype of household behavior for this and other related models is provided by the consumer optimization problem:

PROBLEM:

$$\max u[\mathbf{z}] \quad \text{subject to} \quad \mathbf{p}'\mathbf{z} - y \leq 0 \qquad (10.1)$$

where u = the utility index

$\mathbf{p}$ = the known vector of prices

$\mathbf{z}$ = unknown vector of commodities

y = the household's income

Subsequent works discussed here are generalizations of problem (10.1) to account for spatial effects. The list is by no means exhaustive: a few equilibrium models have been selected among many and arranged as examples that characterize a particular theoretical trend. They are presented as a sequence leading from general to more specific descriptions and, consequently, from abstract to more realistic representations of consumer behavior. Intuitively, more realistic representations of consumer behavior should result in better descriptions of urban residential structure.

An elegant transition from neoclassical consumer behavior to spatial consumer behavior is provided by

PROBLEM:

$$\max u[\mathbf{z}] \quad \text{subject to} \quad \mathbf{p}'[\mathfrak{s}]\mathbf{z} - y \leq 0 \qquad (10.2)$$

due to Long.[5] Prices now depend upon location.[d] For any fixed location $\mathbf{p}'[\mathfrak{s}]\mathbf{z} - y$ is convex so that if $u[\mathbf{z}]$ is strictly concave, there is a unique solution $\mathbf{z}[\mathfrak{s}, y]$ which clearly indicates the dependence of consumption upon spatial arrangement. Thus, spatial consumer behavior is a generalization of neoclassical consumer behavior, since, for any fixed location, the former reduces to the latter.

A comment about the budget constraint of problem (10.2) is now in order. Almost every spatial generalization of (10.1) assumes a budget constraint of the form

$$\mathbf{p}'\mathbf{z} + T[\mathfrak{s}] - y \leq 0$$

where T is a transportation cost function. Thus, transportation costs are considered to be independent of consumption and are treated as invariant over space. In Long's model, the two types of cost are combined as

$$p_i[\mathfrak{s}] = p_i^0 + c_i[\mathfrak{s}]$$

---

[d] The form of all the models discussed here has been slightly altered. The intent was to achieve comparability without significant distortion of the consumer behavior postulated in these models. Since a distinction among single and multiple center models is emphasized, $p[\mathfrak{s}] = p \cdot \mathscr{D}^n \cdot \delta$ is used instead of $p: S \rightarrow R_+$ as being more neutral in this respect.

where p_i^0 is the mill price and $c_i[\hat{s}]$ is transportation costs per unit of z_i at location $\hat{s}$. In consequence, the budget constraint of problem (10.2) may be written as

$$(\mathbf{p}^0)'\mathbf{z} + \mathbf{c}'[\hat{s}]\mathbf{z} - y \le 0$$

where $\mathbf{c}'[\hat{s}]\mathbf{z} = T[\hat{s}, \mathbf{z}]$ represents a transportation function more reasonable than the usual $T[\hat{s}]$ in many respects.

Although very general and formally corresponding to the neoclassical framework, the power of Long's work is somewhat limited precisely because of these attractive characteristics. The gist of the problem is that, for generality, there is no differentiation among commodities and that, for consistency with the neoclassical framework, all prices are assumed known. Experience, however, suggests that at least one commodity, residential land, and its price are of crucial importance to understanding urban spatial structure. The inverse of the demand function for land describes the spatial distribution of population density, while land values in the form of bid rents provide an important mechanism for the analysis of land use patterns in cities. Clearly then, since the study of land values is interesting and since their structure is complex, it is appropriate to derive the corresponding spatial distribution using first principles rather than to assume it.

Abstracting residential land q and its price r from $\mathbf{z}$ and $\mathbf{p}$ respectively leads to the new optimization problem:

PROBLEM:

$$\max u[\mathbf{z}, q] \quad \text{subject to} \quad \mathbf{p}'[\hat{s}]\mathbf{z} + rq - y \le 0 \qquad (10.3)$$

with $\mathbf{z}$ and $\mathbf{p}$ obviously redefined.[e] This form was first proposed and analyzed for a particular utility function by Muth.[7] A variant of problem (10.3) was studied by Solow who introduced congestion effects.[9] Congestion effects are important and have generated considerable interest. Their study, however, leads to such analytical difficulties that either numerical methods or conceptual compromise is required.

Muth's formulation implies that people do not have explicit spatial preferences. If people have explicit spatial preferences then problem (10.3) becomes

PROBLEM:

$$\max u[\mathbf{z}, q, \hat{s}] \quad \text{subject to} \quad \mathbf{p}'[\hat{s}]\mathbf{z} + rq - y \le 0 \qquad (10.4)$$

[e] The interpretation of q and r varies. For example, q may represent quantity of housing, an aggregate that contains both land and structure. Also, with the exception of Long, transportation costs are separated from the vector of prices. In this case, even with $\hat{s}$ treated as an endogenous variable, the constant remains linear so that a unique solution exists for u strictly concave. Of course, if transportation costs are included in the price vector and if $\hat{s}$ is treated as an endogenous variable then the existence of a unique solution must be assumed.

Chronologically, this form preceded problems (10.2) and (10.3) and represents the original work of Alonso.[1] The emphasis in Alonso's work is on household behavior, so that different households can be associated with different preference structures. In contrast, many equilibrium models of the type discussed here emphasize the implications of household behavior on spatial patterns. The related aggregation problem requires operational comparability of bid rents: the highest bidder captures the land and this, in turn, associates residential location to known population density and land value. Therefore, in order to determine the implications of household behavior on spatial patterns, a postulate imposing identical preference structures seems inevitable.[f] The simplest possible case of such an aggregation procedure stemming from Alonso's framework is represented by the model of Casetti where a number of identical households locate around a single center.[3] In this world, bid rents and the composite rent surface are identical. Generalizations involve either households with different incomes located around a single center or identical households located within a multicenter environment of the type already discussed. The model by Beckmann[2] provides an example of the first type, while the model by Papageorgiou and Casetti[8] provides an example of the second.

Apart from the differences already stated, models of urban residential structure also differ in terms of (1) additional assumptions required and (2) maximization strategy adopted.

1. It should be noted that the problems (10.3) and (10.4), which represent two distinct classes of models, are not closed. This happens because, in contrast to problems (10.1) and (10.2), where every price is assumed known, problems (10.3) and (10.4) assume that one price, r, is unknown. Thus, at least one additional assumption is necessary. Models of urban residential structure differ in terms of these additional assumptions. Typically, there are two alternatives. First, supply equals demand for land at every location—an assumption adopted, for example, by Beckmann.[2] Second, the spatial equilibrium condition requiring explicitly, for every household, indifference among locations—an assumption adopted, for example, by Casetti.[3]

2. Differences in maximization strategy reduce to differences in the treatment of location. Again, there are two alternatives. First, location is treated as a decision variable—a strategy adopted, for example, by Beckmann.[2] Second, location is treated as a parameter—a strategy adopted, for example, by Casetti.[3]

To summarize, equilibrium models of urban residential structure extending from neoclassical demand theory differ in terms of income distribution, the urban environment, the additional assumptions used, and maximization strategy. This classification of alternatives will now be fol-

[f]This also applies to the work of Muth[7] and Solow.[9]

lowed in the discussion of the proposed model. It will be seen that decisions among these alternatives are to a certain extent interrelated.

In general, households are distinguished by preference structure and by income. Whenever the analysis is at the level of the household, preference structure may indeed vary between households. Whenever the analysis is at the aggregate level, households are distinguished only by income.

ASSUMPTION 10.10: $y \in Y$; $Y \subset \mathscr{R}_+$ is compact.

The set Y will be further constrained later.

Composite goods relate to the preference structure. Composite goods also relate the household to the hierarchical urban structure through s. The intuition behind s is that, if there is no variation in quality and if mill prices are such that there is no advantage in visiting more distant centers, a rational household is expected to interact with the closest center or centers that provide the required commodities. Since, by Assumption 10.3, every center is simply connected and, if travel costs within centers are neglected, the definition of s is intuitively unambiguous. Thus, s reflects the pattern of interaction between a household at ŝ and the city. It is assumed that work trips are covered by this pattern of interaction. Social trips however are omitted.

The proposed model is based upon a more explicit consideration of housing characteristics. It is recognized that, in addition to the hierarchical composite goods, the physical structure of the house, the lot size, its location, and the residential attractiveness of the neighborhood influence household decisions.

The physical structure of the house may be treated as a component of z. This component, quantity of physical structure, is an aggregate measure reflecting simultaneously size, construction type, and condition. Its related prices is assumed to be known. It could for example be spatially invariant, but this is not necessary. Lot size is treated as before.

In the models that correspond to problem (10.4), location is introduced directly as distance from the center or centers of the city. Other things being equal, more distant locations correspond to less satisfaction. This is an abstract treatment and, certainly, distance is not a commodity in the usual, intuitive sense. On the other hand, it seems that purely spatial preferences reflect the relationship between location and free time available to the consumer. Since commuting takes time, other things being equal, more distant locations correspond to less time available for consumption. Time available for consumption is called t. If time requirements for working and sleeping purposes are treated as institutional constants and if frequency of purchasing a good is independent of the quantity purchased, then time available for consumption will depend upon location and upon speed of travel. Of course, speed of travel depends upon congestion. For tractability, it is assumed that congestion is not a factor within the world described by this model.[g]

ASSUMPTION 10.11: $t: S \to \mathcal{R}_+$ is differentiable on int S and continuous on S; t is strictly decreasing on S and, for any nondecreasing unbounded sequence $\{s^k\} \subset S$, there is a finite $s \in \{s^k\}$ such that $t[s] = 0$.

Time considerations relate to time constraints. The role of t in the time constraint is similar to the role of y in the income constraint. This symmetry extends to the qualitative similarities between consumption rates and prices. A consumption rate τ_i describes the time necessary to consume one unit of the composite good of order i. Consumption rates are assumed to be constant.

ASSUMPTION 10.12: $\tau \in \mathcal{R}_+^{n+1}$; $\tau > 0$.

The reason for $\tau > 0$ instead of $\tau \geqslant 0$ is because the consumption rate that corresponds to the physical structure of the house must equal zero.

Residential attractiveness is the last housing characteristic to be taken into account by the model. Residential attractiveness is peculiar because it constrains spatial choice in a way related to the socioeconomic status of the household. Minimum requirements for residential attractiveness seem to exist and these requirements increase with income. From this point of view, spatial choice decreases as income increases. The minimum requirements for residential attractiveness are represented by $\hat{\mathcal{E}}$.

ASSUMPTION 10.13: $\hat{\mathcal{E}}: Y \to \mathcal{R}_+$ is continuous, strictly increasing on Y.

The same idea may be extended to commodities in general. Thus, it is assumed that consumption is at least equal to certain subsistence quantities—manifestations of the truth that substitution does not make sense below certain levels. Of course, the subsistence quantity of a good may be zero, and these quantities may or may not be determined by income. For example, they may reflect physiological rather than socioeconomic needs. The second, and simpler, alternative has been adopted. The subsistence level of a commodity z_i is called $\hat{z}_i$.

ASSUMPTION 10.14: $z \in Z, Z \subset \mathcal{R}_+^{n+1}$; $q \in Q, Q \subset \mathcal{R}_+$.

The preference structure of a household is associated with a utility function u defined over z, q, t, and E.

[g]This also explains the exogenous form of E in Assumption (10.6).

ASSUMPTION 10.15: $u:Z \times Q \times \mathcal{R}_+ \times \mathcal{R}_+ \to \mathcal{R}_+$ is differentiable strictly increasing, and strictly concave on $Z \times Q \times \mathcal{R}_+ \times \mathcal{R}_+$.

The decision to adopt a multicenter environment constrains the choice of the additional assumptions required and of the maximization strategy.

There are two alternative assumptions. (i) supply equals demand for land and (ii) spatial indifference. The first alternative requires an ability to estimate the population that corresponds to a particular area. Given the lack of symmetry between $\mathfrak{S}$ and S, this is a difficult task at the multicenter case. Furthermore, spatial equilibrium and spatial indifference are conceptually associated in a natural, simple manner. Therefore, the second alternative has been adopted. Spatial indifference implies the same utility level for different locations. The next assumption refers to the level of utility attained under conditions of spatial equilibrium.

ASSUMPTION 10.16 $\bar{u}: Y \to \mathcal{R}_+$ is differentiable on int Y, and continuous, strictly increasing on Y.

There are two alternative maximization strategies—namely, treatment of $\mathfrak{s}$ as either a decision variable or as a parameter. In the single center case, the first alternative leads to a differential equation which, in the multicenter case, corresponds to an intractable system of partial differential equations. Thus, the second alternative has been adopted. The treatment of $\mathfrak{s}$ as a parameter is also natural from a different viewpoint. It seems awkward to consider location as a decision variable once spatial indifference has been imposed.

In consequence, consumer behavior is represented by the following:

PROBLEM:

$$\max u[\mathbf{z}, q, t[\mathbf{s}], E[\mathbf{s}]]$$

$$\text{subject to} \qquad \mathbf{p}'[\mathbf{s}]\mathbf{z} + rq - y \le 0$$

$$\boldsymbol{\tau}'\mathbf{z} - t[\mathbf{s}] \le 0$$

$$\mathbf{z} - \hat{\mathbf{z}} \ge \mathbf{0}$$

$$q = \hat{q} \ge 0$$

$$E[\mathbf{s}] - \hat{\mathscr{E}}[y] \ge 0 \qquad\qquad (10.5)$$

and

$$u = \bar{u}[y] \qquad\qquad (10.6)$$

The material preceding the final section of this chapter deals with some ideas that are general in that they do not require a condition of spatial equilibrium. They simply relate to any known price system. Thus, for the next four sections, the price system is assumed to be known. In other words, imagine that the bidding process has been concluded and a composite rent surface R has been determined. It should be noted that differentiality of $\mathcal{D}$, E, p, t, and u (Assumptions 10.2, 10.6, 10.9, 10.11, and 10.15 respectively) is not required until the final section. Results before this section depent only upon continuity. It follows that these general results are applicable for any continuous spatial distribution of land values.

For a known price system, residential land and its price are included within z and p respectively because of notational simplicity. This affects Assumptions 10.12, 10.14, and 10.15:

ASSUMPTION 10.12': $\tau \in \mathcal{R}_+^{n+2}$, $\tau > 0$.

ASSUMPTION 10.14': $z \in Z$, $Z \subset \mathcal{R}_+^{n+2}$.

ASSUMPTION 10.15': $u: Z \times \mathcal{R}_+ \times \mathcal{R}_+ \to \mathcal{R}_+$ is differentiable, strictly increasing, and strictly concave on $Z \times \mathcal{R}_+ \times \mathcal{R}_+$.

Therefore, problem (10.5) now becomes

PROBLEM:

$$\max u[z, t[s], E[s]]$$
$$\text{subject to} \qquad p'[s]z - y \leq 0$$
$$\tau'z - t[s] \leq 0$$
$$z - \hat{z} \geq 0$$
$$E[s] = \hat{\mathcal{E}}[y] \geq 0 \qquad\qquad (10.5')$$

This more general problem provides the basis for the ensuing analysis until the concept of spatial equilibrium is formally introduced.

Kuhn-Tucker Conditions

Problem (10.5') is now considered in the context of a particular individual at a particular location. This treatment agrees with the treatment of y and s as parameters.

LEMMA 10.4: Given y and s, if the related feasible set of the problem (10.5') is nonempty, then problem (10.5') has a unique solution corresponding to y and s.

LEMMA 10.5:   Given y and s, if the related feasible set of the problem (10.5') is nonempty, then the income constraint is effective.

The intuition behind Lemma 10.5 is that, in cases where the time constraint is effective, any possible residual income will be used to purchase land and physical structure of the house because these commodities do not require time for consumption.

The time constraint of problem (10.5') directly imposes upper boundaries in S because of Assumption 10.11. An s on such a boundary corresponds to a situation where both income and time constraints are effective. Since the income constraint is always effective, $\tau'z - t = 0$ may actually correspond to a situation where time, rather than cost, is of essence. This is certainly possible, at least for higher income groups, in technologically advanced urban societies. Nevertheless, the analysis is considerably simplified if such cases are excluded.

ASSUMPTION 10.17: $\tau'z - t < 0.$

LEMMA 10.6:   Given y and s, z is a solution to problem (10.5') if and only if

$$u_{z_i} - \lambda_{p_i} \leq 0$$

that is, either

$$u_{z_i} - \lambda_{p_i} = 0 \quad \text{or} \quad z_i = \hat{z}_i \quad \text{or both} \qquad i = 1, \ldots, n+2$$

$$p'z - y = 0$$

Spatial Range

Definition 10.4:   The spatial range of a household, $\mathcal{P}$, is the set of all locations where this household attains a solution to problem (10.5').

Given that households have identical preference structures, $\mathcal{P}$ is a correspondence from Y to $\mathfrak{S}$. The representation of $\mathcal{P}$ in S is $\Phi\colon Y \to S$.

Lemma 10.7: $s \in \Phi[y]$ if and only if $p'[s]\hat{z} - y \leq 0$ and $E[s] - \hat{\mathcal{E}}[y] \geq 0$.

THEOREM 10.5:   If Φ is nonempty, it is compact.

CORROLARY: If $\mathcal{P}$ is nonempty, it is compact.

THEOREM 10.6:   If the Hessian matrix $(p'\hat{z})_{ss}$ is positive semidefinite on S, if Φ is nonempty, and if $E - \hat{\mathscr{E}} \geq 0$ for every s such that $\mathbf{p'\hat{z}} - y \leq 0$, then Φ is convex.

Theorem 10.6 points out the strong impact of the externality upon the form of spatial range representation. The spatial distribution of environmental quality may well prohibit convexity of Φ, at least to higher income households. Even if residential attractiveness is no problem, spatial range representation may not even be connected. This happens because the existing price structure affects the form of spatial range representation. If, for example, prices of composite goods are linearly increasing over their respective distances, if the price of the physical structure of the house is spatially invariant, and if land rent has the usual convex form on S, then, if residential attractiveness is no problem, Φ is convex. Of course, by Theorem 10.4, connectedness of Φ does not necessarily imply the same for $\mathscr{P}$. This plethora of assumptions emphasizes that, even under ideal conditions, the form of the spatial range can be very complicated indeed, and that, more often than not, the spatial range of a household is not a connected area.

THEOREM 10.7: If $E - \hat{\mathscr{E}} \geq 0$ for every s such that $\mathbf{p'\hat{z}} - y \leq 0$, and if $\Phi[y^1]$, $\Phi[y^2]$ are nonempty, then $\Phi[y^1] \supset \Phi[y^2]$ if and only if $y^1 > y^2$.

CORROLARY: If $\mathscr{E} - \hat{\mathscr{E}} \geq 0$ for every $\hat{\mathrm{s}}$ such that $(\mathbf{p} \cdot \mathscr{D} \cdot \delta)' \, \hat{z} - y \leq 0$ and if $\mathscr{P}[y^1]$, $\mathscr{P}[y^2]$ are nonempty, then $\mathscr{P}[y^1] \supset \mathscr{P}[y^2]$ if and only if $y^1 > y^2$.

Similarly to Theorem 10.6, Theorem 10.7 and its corrolary point out the strong impact of the externality upon spatial range. Spatial range increases with income provided that residential attractiveness is no problem. According to Assumption 10.13, the impact of residential attractiveness upon spatial range is opposite to that of income: the set of locations in $\mathfrak{S}$ such that $E - \hat{\mathscr{E}} \geq 0$ decreases as income increases. The interaction among spatial freedom and environmental restrictions induced by income determines spatial range.

THEOREM 10.8: If Φ is nonempty, it is upper semicontinuous on Y.

CORROLARY: If $\mathscr{P}$ is nonempty, it is upper semicontinuous on Y.

The correspondence Φ is not lower semicontinuous in general. An example where lower semicontinuity fails is shown on Figure 10-4. There is a single order hierarchy, so that $S \subset \mathscr{R}_+$ is represented along the vertical axis. The horizontal axis represents both Y and E. The graph of $p[s]\hat{z} - y = 0$, related to $S \times Y$, and the graph of $E[s]$, related to $S \times E$, have been

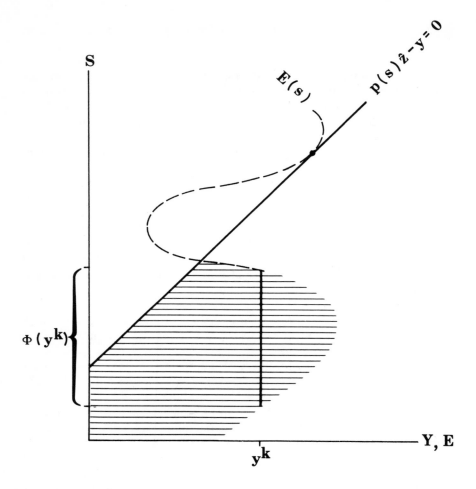

Figure 10-4. Φ Is Not Lower Semicontinuous

superimposed. Let $\hat{\mathscr{E}}[y^k] = y^k$. Then, it is easy to see that the shaded area and the dot satisfy both $p\hat{z} - y \leq 0$ and $E - \hat{\mathscr{E}} \geq 0$. Every other point does not satisfy both inequalities. In consequence, according to Lemma 10.7, the shaded area and the dot represent the graph of Φ on $S \times Y$. Clearly, Φ is not lower semicontinuous on Y.

THEOREM 10.9: If $E - \hat{\mathscr{E}} \geq 0$ for every s such that $\mathbf{p}'\hat{z} - y \leq 0$ and if Φ is nonempty, then Φ is continuous on Y.

CORROLARY: If $\mathscr{E} - \hat{\mathscr{E}} \geq 0$ for every $\mathfrak{z}$ such that $(\mathbf{p} \cdot \mathscr{D}^n \cdot \delta)' \hat{\mathbf{z}} - y \leq 0$ and if $\mathscr{P}$ is nonempty then $\mathscr{P}$ is continuous on Y.

Theorem 10.9 and its corrolary provide still another example of the strong impact of the externality upon spatial range. In general, it is concluded that spatial range is continuously increasing on Y provided that residential attractiveness is no problem. Otherwise, it is only upper semicontinuous and not necessarily increasing.

Income Range

Definition 10.5: The income range $\mathscr{Y}$ is the set with elements y such that $\mathscr{P}[y]$ is nonempty.

Clearly, only households with income in $\mathscr{Y}$ are relevant to the analysis.

ASSUMPTION 10.18: $Y \subset \mathscr{Y}$.

The form of Y has been imposed by Assumption 10.10. Are Assumptions 10.11 and 10.18 compatible? The following theorem answers this question in the affirmative.

THEOREM 10.10: If $\mathscr{Y}$ is nonempty, it is closed.

The remainder of this section demonstrates that, similarly to spatial range, income range is deeply affected by the externality. In fact, if residential attractiveness is no problem, income range attains a very simple structure.

THEOREM 10.11: If $E - \hat{\mathscr{E}} \geq 0$ for every s such that $\mathbf{p}' \hat{\mathbf{z}} - y \leq 0$ then a minimum (subsistence) income $\hat{y} \in \mathscr{Y}$ does exist.

It is important to understand that subsistence income cannot be determined independently of a known price system. In other words, subsistence is that necessary for survival under given economic conditions. For a known price system, Theorem 10.11 indicates that subsistence income exists; it is unique; and by Lemma 10.7 it represents the smallest possible income related to a potentially nonempty spatial range $\hat{\Phi}$. That this minimum income belongs in fact to $\mathscr{Y}$ depends upon the spatial distribution of residential attractiveness. If this is no problem then, by Theorem 10.7, $\hat{\Phi}$ is the smallest spatial range. Intuitively, given that most prices increase with distance because of transportation costs, $\hat{\Phi}$ must be related to locations of high accessibility. The emerging pattern suggests that subsistence income implies that there are households barely existing under conditions of maximum density in the vicinity of central areas within the urban system.

THEOREM 10.12:   If $E - \hat{\mathscr{E}} \geq 0$ for every s such that $\mathbf{p}'\hat{\mathbf{z}} - y \leq 0$, then $\mathscr{Y}$ is an interval.

It is easy to see that, in general, $\mathscr{Y}$ may or may not be an interval. In fact, even if it is an interval, $\hat{y}$ may or may not belong to it. Figures 10-5 and 10-6 provide examples where $\mathscr{Y}$ may or may not be an interval. The space is $\mathfrak{S}$. Three incomes are considered: $y^1 < y^2 < y^3$. The numbering of the contours is consistent with the income superscripts. The irregular contours define areas where the environmental constraint is satisfied. These areas decrease with income. The regular contours define areas where the budget constraint is satisfied. These areas increase with income. The intersection between the two types of areas corresponding to a particular income defines the spatial range for the households of this income. Spatial ranges have been shaded. In Figure 10-5, every income has a nonempty spatial range. In Figure 10-6, y^2 has an empty spatial range. In this case, $\mathscr{Y}$ is not an interval.

Clearly, these irregularities are a consequence of viewing $\mathscr{Y}$ as the outcome of both economic and behavioral constraints. Such a treatment implies that certain household types may not settle within a particular urban area because of purely environmental considerations. This is probably a rigid conclusion, one which may be attributed in part to the exogenous nature of $\mathscr{E}$. The world of the model does not allow for explicit interaction between man and the quality of his environment. Since, however, man creates his environment to a considerable extent, one may conclude that the impact of residential attractiveness is not as decisive as the model tends to suggest. It is probable that, although residential attractiveness influences the structure of spatial range, it does not influence the structure of income range: $\mathscr{Y}$ is in fact an interval due, for example, to the influence of the public sector on the externality.

Consumption Patterns

A $\mathbf{z}$ is called a consumption. The elements of a consumption may be either optimal or suboptimal.

Definition 10.6:   An optimal z_j satisfies $u_{z_j} - \lambda_{p_j} = 0$. Otherwise, it is called suboptimal.

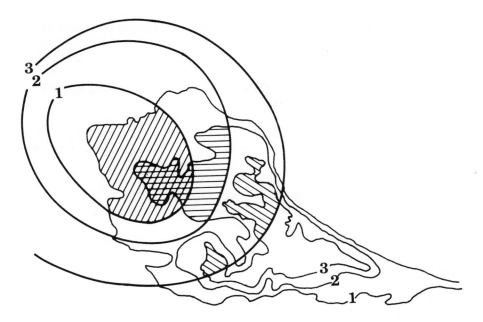

Figure 10-5. $\mathcal{Y}$ Is an Interval

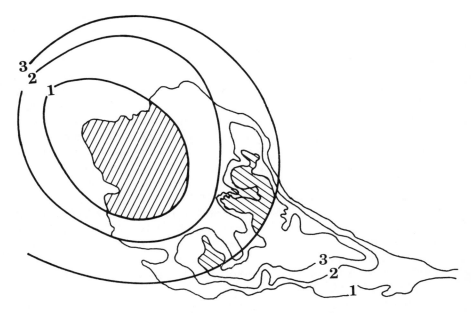

Figure 10-6. $\mathcal{Y}$ Is Not an Interval

Using Lemma 10.6, an optimal z_j implies $z_j \geq \hat{z}_j$, and a suboptimal z_k implies $z_k = \hat{z}_k$.

Consumptions may be classified in relation to optimality. Let I be the set of indices $\{1, 2, \ldots, n+2\}$. Consider an ordered partition of I, (J, K), such that the first set of the partition contains the indices of the optimal elements and the second set of the partition contains the indices of the suboptimal elements in a consumption. $J = \emptyset$ corresponds to $(\emptyset, I)$ and $K = \emptyset$ corresponds to $(I, \emptyset)$. J is called the optimal set of the consumption and K is called the suboptimal set. Then, consumptions may be characterized by this ordered partition.

Definition 10.7: (J, K) is called a consumption pattern. If $J = I$, the consumption pattern is optimal, otherwise it is suboptimal.

In order to determine λ unambiguously, there must be at least one optimal element in every consumption. In consequence, $(\emptyset, I)$ is impossible.

LEMMA 10.8:   If, at **s**, y^1 is related to J^1 and y^2 is related to J^2, $J \subseteq I$, then $y^1 > y^2$ implies $J^1 \supseteq J^2$, and $J^1 \supset J^2$ implies $y^1 > y^2$.

Lemma 10.8 relates consumptions of different households at the same location. It is also useful to study consumptions of the same household at different locations.

Consider a simple spatial economy with only two commodities and a single-order hierarchy. The first commodity represents the composite good of the first order. The second commodity may be taken to represent housing, a composite of structure and land. Residential attractiveness is not a problem. According to Assumption 10.7, both commodities are normal and, since there are only two commodities, they are substitutes. The price for the composite good of the first order is increasing with distance from the market, while the price for housing is invariant over S, as shown in Figure 10-7(a). Figure 10-7(b) shows the spatial structure of consumption. Since $\partial z_1 / \partial p_1 < 0$, $z_1[s]$ decreases away from the center and attains a subsistence level at A. Since $\partial z_2 / \partial p_1 > 0$, $z_2[s]$ increases away from the center and attains a maximum at A. Between A and B, $z_1[s] = \hat{z}_1$. The quantity $z_2[s]$ is determined by the portion of income available after the minimum necessary $\hat{z}_1$ has been purchased. Thus, $z_2[s]$ decreases and attains a subsistence level at B, the edge of $\Phi[y]$. The spatial allocation of income is shown in Figure 10-7(c) and the resulting consumption patterns are shown in Figure 10-7(d). The spatial transition from optimal to suboptimal is clearly indicated.

Thus, Φ can be partitioned into subsets that are homogeneous in respect to consumption behavior.

167

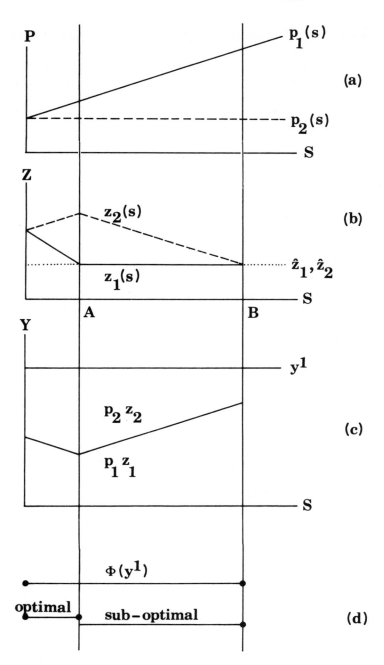

Figure 10-7. Consumption Patterns in a Two-Commodity Case

Definition 10.8: $\Phi_J[y]$, $J \subseteq I$, is the subset of $\Phi[y]$ related to $[J, K)$.

To say that the spatial structure of consumption patterns in the general case is far more complex than the simple example tends to suggest would be an understatement. Nevertheless, intuitively speaking, since most prices increase with distance, a core of abundance consumption is surrounded by areas of various mixed consumptions. As one moves away from central areas of the urban system, more elements enter the subsistence set K until subsistence consumption is reached at the boundary of the spatial range. These spatial transitions would appear to form patterns of generalized, irregular rings around the centers of the system. Of course, "islands" of a consumption behavior embedded within areas of different consumption behaviors, as well as "holes" representing spatial discontinuities of $\mathscr{P}$, may abound.

The two-commodity case can also be used to illustrate some of the main results concerning spatial range and income range. The spatial structure of consumption for $y^1 > y^2 > y^3 > \hat{y}$ is shown in Figure 10-8(a). The dot represents consumption of the subsistence income. The corresponding spatial allocations of income are shown in Figure 10-8(b). The line $\mathbf{p}'\hat{\mathbf{z}} - y = 0$ has been plotted on the same diagram. According to Lemma 10.7, this line defines the boundary of the correspondence $\Phi[y]$. In the figure, Φ has been shaded, and is shown to be compact, which agrees with theorem 10.5. Since $(\mathbf{p}'\hat{\mathbf{z}})_{ss} = 0$, $\mathbf{p}'\hat{\mathbf{z}}$ is convex so that Φ is convex, which agrees with theorem 10.6. Φ increases with income, which agrees with theorem 10.7. Finally, Φ is continuous, which agrees with theorem 10.9. The income range $\mathscr{Y}$ is shown on the y axis of Figure 10-8(b). Certainly $\mathscr{Y}$ is closed, which agrees with theorem 10.10; it contains the subsistence income, which agrees with theorem 10.11; and it is an interval, which agrees with theorem 10.12.

The idea of income groups is used in the following section. Income groups are determined by the inverse of Φ, $\Phi^{-1}: S \to Y$. For example, $\Phi_J^{-1}[\mathbf{s}]$ is the set of all $y \in Y$, $\mathbf{s} \in \Phi_J[y]$.

LEMMA 10.9: If $\Phi_J^{-1}[\mathbf{s}]$, $J \subseteq I$, is nonempty, then it is a closed-open interval.

Figure 10-9 emphasizes the relationship between spatial range and its inverse, income groups. The grouping agrees with Lemma 10.9.

Spatial Consumer Equilibrium

The foregoing sections of this chapter were developed around any price

169

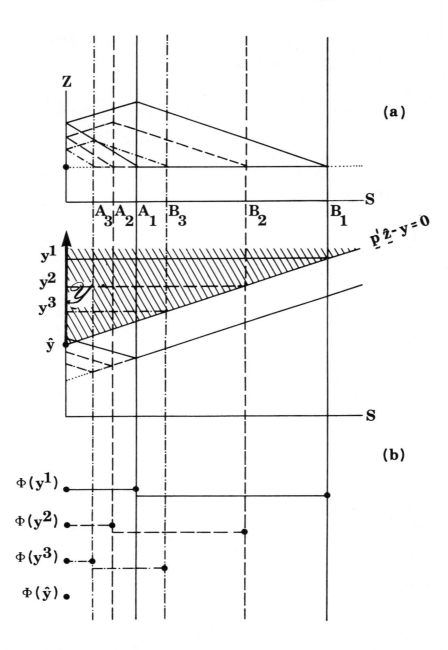

Figure 10-8. Spatial Range and Income Range in a Two-Commodity Case

170

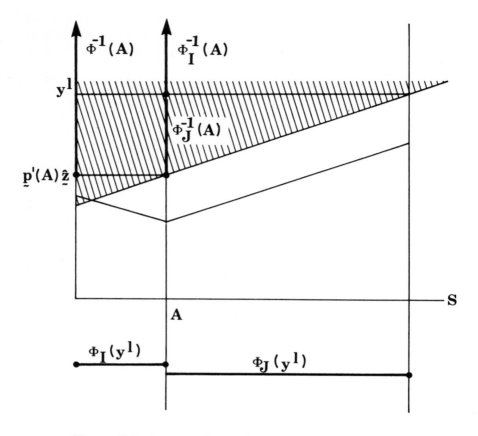

Figure 10-9. Income Groups in a Two-Commodity Case

system with prices continuous over S. Here, we will concentrate upon an important special case: a price system that leads to spatial consumer equilibrium. It will be seen that all the prices in this system are also continuous over S, so that the results of the previous sections hold.

Definition 10.9: A Casetti equilibrium for a household of income y is a price vector $(\mathbf{p}, \bar{r})$ and a consumption $(\bar{z}, \bar{q})$ such that $u = \bar{u}[y]$ for $\mathbf{s} \in \Phi[y]$.[h]

The new price system is constructed using problem (10.5) in conjunction with the spatial equilibrium condition (10.6). Therefore, Assumptions 10.12, 10.14, and 10.15 are replacing Assumptions 10.12′, 10.14′, and 10.15′

[h] Consumption $(\bar{z}, \bar{q})$ is by definition a solution to problem (10.5).

used in the previous sections. Given **p**, the unknown price $\bar{r}$ is determined through the spatial equilibrium condition. Thus, given **p**, $\bar{r}$ plays the role of a regulatory mechanism that forces the system to a state of spatial indifference.

Land Values

Different consumption patterns correspond to different structures of the equilibrium bid rent $\bar{r}$. Thus, $\bar{r}_I$ refers to optimal consumption and $\bar{r}_J$ refers to suboptimal (mixed) consumption. In this section, the behavior of bid rents for alternative consumption patterns is examined under conditions of spatial equilibrium. There is no reference to subsistence consumption. It is easy to see that, under conditions of a Casetti equilibrium, any income other than subsistence income cannot attain subsistence consumption. Also, the equilibrium bid rent that corresponds to subsistence income is not considered because subsistence income is defined only for a known price system.

The method of analysis is comparative statics. To ensure differentiality of the relevant Kuhn-Tucker conditions, the following assumption is introduced.

ASSUMPTION 10.19: $\Phi_J[y]$, $J \subseteq I$, has an interior.

This assumption is compatible with Theorem 10.5.

LEMMA 10.10: $\Phi_J^{-1}[s]$, $J \subseteq I$, has an interior.

The analysis is conducted on the interior of $\Phi_J \times \Phi_J^{-1}$.

LEMMA 10.11: $\bar{r}_J: \Phi_J \times \Phi_J^{-1} \to \mathcal{R}_+$, $J \subseteq I$, is differentiable on int $(\Phi_J \times \Phi_J^{-1})$.[1]

The bid rent functions of a household that correspond to different consumption patterns are combined to form a continuous surface:

LEMMA 10.12: $\bar{r}: \Phi \times Y \to \mathcal{R}_+$ is continuous on $\Phi \times Y$.

The next lemma provides the means for unambiguously constructing a spatial equilibrium composite rent surface $\bar{\bar{R}}$.

LEMMA 10.13: For every $y \in \mathcal{Y}$ there is a unique Casetti equilibrium.

[1] int A denotes the interior of A.

Definition 10.10: A state of spatial consumer equilibrium corresponds to Casetti equilibrium for all households.

At every location, the highest bidder captures the land. Thus, the spatial equilibrium composite rent surface is constructed at every **s** using the highest bid. Clearly, $\bar{\bar{R}}$ depends upon **s** but not upon y.

THEOREM 10.13: A spatial equilibrium composite rent function, $\bar{\bar{R}}$: $\cup_Y$ $\Phi \to \mathcal{R}_+$ exists.

Because of Lemma 10.13, $\bar{\bar{R}}$ is unique. $\bar{\bar{R}}$ may be related to a household through the idea of spatial equilibrium range representation $\bar{\bar{\Phi}}[y]$.

Definition 10.11: $\bar{\bar{\Phi}}[y] \subset \Phi[y]$; $\mathbf{s} \in \bar{\bar{\Phi}}[y]$ if and only if $\bar{r}[\mathbf{s}, y] = \bar{\bar{R}}[\mathbf{s}]$.

The spatial equilibrium range $\bar{\bar{\mathcal{P}}}[y]$ represents the only feasible spatial choice of the household under conditions of spatial consumer equilibrium. Any other location outside this range is irrelevant,

THEOREM 10.14: $\bar{\bar{R}}$: $\cup_Y \Phi \to \mathcal{R}_+$ is continuous on $\cup_Y \Phi$.

Theorem 10.14 is important because it indicates that the general results of the previous sections also hold in the case of spatial consumer equilibrium.

The distinction between $\Phi[y]$ and $\bar{\bar{\Phi}}[y]$ must remain clear. $\Phi[y]$ can be defined over any known price system that satisfies the continuity part of Assumption 10.9, but not necessarily over a spatial equilibrium price system. In the case of spatial equilibrium, however, only a subset of $\Phi[y]$ corresponds to $\bar{u}[y]$. Everything outside it clearly corresponds to less than, $\bar{u}[y]$ because, for **s** outside the spatial equilibrium range, $\bar{r}[\mathbf{s}, y] < \bar{\bar{R}}[\mathbf{s}]$. The subset of $\Phi[y]$ that corresponds to $\bar{u}[y]$ is precisely the spatial equilibrium range. It has already been stated that, if residential attractiveness is no problem, $\Phi[y]$ increases with income. The same does not necessarily apply to $\bar{\bar{\Phi}}[y]$.

Once the price system $[\mathbf{p}, \bar{\bar{R}})$ is determined, the Casetti equilibrium for a subsistence income household may be defined. By Theorem 10.11, $\hat{y}$ exists for the price system $(\mathbf{p}, \bar{\bar{R}})$ under reasonable conditions. By Theorem 10.5, the corresponding $\Phi[\hat{y}]$ is compact. Clearly, for subsistence consumption, $u: \Phi[\hat{y}] \to \mathcal{R}_+$. Since u is continuous, it attains a maximum by the Weirstrass theorem. The subset of $\Phi[\hat{y}]$ over which this maximum is attained can be defined as the spatial equilibrium range $\bar{\bar{\Phi}}[\hat{y}]$. Then, the utility maximum is $\bar{u}[\hat{y}]$.

Location Principles

THEOREM 10.15:   If u_y that corresponds to (J, K), $J \subseteq I$, is independent of s then $\partial \bar{r}_J / \partial y = 0$.

This theorem states conditions under which the bid rent function is independent of income. If there is an area A over which all households attain a particular consumption, then, under the conditions of Theorem 10.15, a state of locational indeterminacy results over A. Locational indeterminacy follows because the bid rent of any household coincides with the composite rent surface. This is in sharp contrast to the rings of identical income households found in other models. In fact, the surface cannot be described unless the spatial distribution of incomes is known a priori.

Experience dictates that spatial segregation by income does exist. However, it may not be always as strong as the income rings tend to suggest: at least in the case of locational indeterminacy, spatial segregation seems to be indirectly rather than directly dependent on income through indivisibilities in housing that prevent lower income households from entering higher income areas. To complete the picture, mechanisms that discourage higher income households from entering lower income areas should be proposed. The constraint on residential attractiveness is precisely such a mechanism.

THEOREM 10.16:   If $\partial \bar{r}_J / \partial y > 0$ and if $s \in \Phi[y^1]$, $\Phi[y^2]$, then $\bar{r}[s, y^1] > \bar{r}[s, y^2]$ if and only if $y^1 > y^2$.

Figure 10-10 shows how this theorem implies the emergence of generalized income rings. There is a single order hierarchy. The edge of the city is determined by the agricultural rent ρ. Y is a closed interval. Residential attractiveness is not a problem. Then, Φ_I is continuous and increasing on Y while Φ_I^{-1} is an interval decreasing on S. Locational indeterminacy has been assumed on Φ_I. The bid rent functions of $y^1 < y^2 < y^3$ have been noted.

Figure 10-10(a) relates to $\partial \bar{r}_J / \partial y > 0$. In this case, $\bar{r}_I[s]$ is the upper envelope. Beyond $\Phi_I[y]$, if $y < \max Y$, the household with income y is outbid. Thus, $\Phi_I[y] = \bar{\Phi}[y]$ which implies immediately that $\bar{\Phi}[y]$ is continuously increasing on the interior of Y. At $s = 0$, $\bar{\Phi}^{-1} = \Phi_I^{-1} = Y$; at $s = A$, $y \in \bar{\Phi}^{-1}$ if and only if $y \geq y^1$; and so on. Consequently, spatial choice increases with income in a definite manner: as distance from the center increases, the minimum income required for residence beyond this distance increases. It is interesting to note that, whereas the standard paradigm implies rings of identical income households, the new paradigm implies rings of households with income greater than or equal to a minimum. In the latter case, although

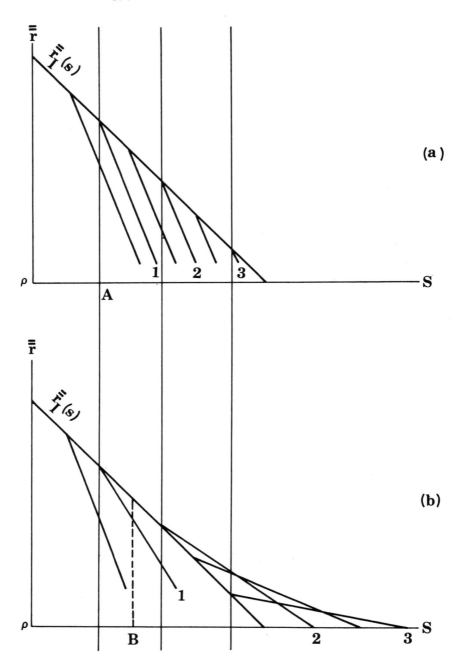

Figure 10-10. Spatial Patterns in a Single-Order Case

minimum income generally increases with distance, mixing is permitted. Moreover, phenomena such as high income neighborhoods in central areas appear to be quite natural.

The inequality $\partial \bar{F}_J / \partial y < 0$ is not possible in general. Cases where $\partial \bar{F}_J / \partial y > 0$ does not hold in general are also possible. Such a case is shown in Figure 10-10(b) where the standard paradigm emerges for locations $s > B$. For locations $s < B$, the emerging spatial pattern is identical with the pattern of Figure 10-10(a). In this case, the spatial choice of y^1 is continuous while the spatial choice of y^2 and y^3 is discontinuous.

Work with the Cobb-Douglas utility function has shown that $\partial \bar{F}_I / \partial y = 0$ and $\partial \bar{F}_J / \partial y > 0$. Thus, Figure 10-10(a) applies. In areas of pure locational indeterminacy, housing indivisibilities and residential attractiveness replace income as the determinants of location. Certainly, changes of the externality through time combined with the inevitable evolution of the hierarchical structure provide more intuitively satisfying explanations of the well-known urban migration patterns than the standard income rings. Generalized income zones are anticipated in the peripheral areas of the ideal urbanized region. In such areas, income increases away from the centers, provided that residential attractiveness is not a problem. Spatial range increases with income. The extreme, and in some respects realistic, example of the existing correspondence between socioeconomic status and spatial freedom is provided by the idea of a subsistence income group. Certainly, such regularities are deeply upset by the spatial distribution of $\mathscr{E}$: in reality, discontinuities of spatial choice abound.

Morphology

It is natural to assume that prices for the composite goods increase with distance. If it is also assumed that the price for the physical structure of the house is either spatially invariant or that it also increases with distance, then the following is true:

ASSUMPTION 10.20: $\mathbf{p}_s \geq \mathbf{0}$.[j]

LEMMA 10.14: If $E_s \leq \mathbf{0}$, then $\bar{F}$ is decreasing on Φ.[k]

THEOREM 10.17: If $E_s \leq \mathbf{0}$, then $\bar{\bar{R}}$ is decreasing on $\cup_Y \Phi$.

It can be seen that the shape of $\bar{F}$ and $\bar{\bar{R}}$ is affected by E_s. This gradient may well be positive. For example, the centers may exert a negative

[j]$(\mathbf{a_b}$ denotes the matrix with elements $\partial a_i / \partial b_j$.)

[k]$(a_b$ denotes the vector with elements $\partial a / \partial b_i$.)

influence upon residential attractiveness. More generally, E could have any continuous spatial distribution so that the gradient changes locally. A positive gradient may imply locally increasing $\bar{r}$ and $\bar{\bar{R}}$. In consequence, rents may not be monotonically decreasing away from the centers of the urban system.

THEOREM 10:18   If $E_s \leq 0$, then (i) $\bar{\bar{R}}$ attains a maximum at the location of the highest order centers; (ii) the values of $\bar{\bar{R}}$ that correspond to the locations of centers of a given order i decrease as the distances between these centers and higher than i order centers increase; (iii) local maxima correspond to the locations of centers (other than the highest order); (iv) there may be centers that do not correspond to local maxima; (v) maxima correspond only to the locations of centers.

This theorem indicates the morphological complexities of a land value surface unfolding over a multicenter environment. More intricate results related to environmental variations other than the ones adopted by this theorem are also available. The emerging pattern appears to be remarkably realistic. "Peaks" correspond to centers and "valleys" to relatively isolated areas. Higher "peaks" generally correspond to higher order centers, and the highest "peak" corresponds to the main center of the city.

Notes

1. W. Alonso, [1964].

2. M.J. Beckmann, [1969].

3. E. Casetti, [1971].

4. W. Christaller, 1933, *Die Zentralen Orte in Süddeutschland: eine Okonomisch-Geographische Untersuchung über die Gesetzmässgkeit der Verbreitung und Entwicklung der Siedlungen mit Städtischen Functionen.* Jena.

5. W.H. Long, [1971].

6. A. Lösch, 1943, *Die Räumliche Ordnung der Wirtscaft; eine Untersuchung über Sandort, Wirtschaftsgebiete und Internationalen Handel.* Jena.

7. R.F. Muth, [1969].

8. G.J. Papageorgiou, and E. Casetti [1971].

9. R.M. Solow, [1972].

11

Spatial Equilibrium with Local Public Goods: Urban Land Rent, Optimal City Size, and the Tiebout Hypothesis

Oscar Fisch

Almost two decades ago, Tiebout advanced the hypothesis that public expenditure theory simplifies itself at the local level, as people "vote with their feet" and move to homogeneous communities.[16] This homogeneity secures through the political process—collective action—that the urban dweller gets the tax-expenditure program that maximizes his and everybody's utility function.

In briefly examining Tiebout's hypothesis, Samuelson, after recognizing that this hypothesis "goes some way toward solving the problem," rejected the whole approach on three speculative grounds: (i) that existing urban communities are not homogeneous and, even given that a majority cannot get rid of a minority, the existing conflict is still unresolved; (ii) that population heterogeneity may also be a positive argument in the individual's utility function; and (iii) that there exists the disturbing ethical question "as to whether groups of like-minded individuals shall be free to run out on their social responsibilities."[14] The last argument is clearly a distributive problem that still disturbs many people. This argument has been used in support of some recent court decisions that have shaken the foundations of local governments. The distributive dimensions were formalized by—among others—Coleman[3] and Rawls;[13] an economic analysis was put forward by Arrow[1] in a set of sharply delineated propositions.

But it is Samuelson's first two arguments that question the workings of Tiebout's hypothesis in the real world. To his casual observation in 1958 that existing urban communities are not homogeneous, there was more than casual evidence to the contrary compiled, coincidentally., at the same time. Wood, in an exhaustive study of suburban communities, showed that a high degree of homogenization within communities was indeed the result of local politics due to jurisdictional fragmentation of metropolitan areas.[19] In a later study by Williams et al. the historical trend of Wood's findings was verified and it was contended further that community specialization, with respect to class or status, lifestyle, or wealth, is the main force behind the resistance to intercommunity cooperation in metropolitan areas.[18]

Oscar Fisch is a member of the Department of City and Regional Planning, The Ohio State University.

Granted that the process of homogenization within urban communities is taking place—due to a high degree of geographic mobility of the population—the existing conflict in the theory of public finance is reduced significantly at the local level, leaving the conflict unsolved only at higher jurisdictional levels of government, or equivalently, at broader spatial dimensions of public goods: metropolitan, state, and national.

After Samuelson's brief review, very little attention was paid, in theoretical terms, to Tiebout's hypothesis until two recent articles: one by Buchanan and Goetz[2] and the other by Ellickson.[6] Both formalize Tiebout's sixth assumption that:

For every pattern of community service set by, say, a city manager who follows the preferences of the older residents of the community, there is an optimal community size (p. 419).[16]

In trying to explain his sixth assumption, Tiebout argues that such a case "implies that some factor or resource is fixed. . . . " And, in order to support his case, he advances three different types of examples: (i) limited amount of residential land, i.e., fixed supply of a private good (land); (ii) institutional limits on land density, i.e., zoning ordinances constraining the consumption of land; and (iii) congestion or crowding of a "public good," i.e., limited capacity of the local beach (theory of clubs). We will show later that the first type of fixity is sufficient for this sixth assumption to hold.

Both analyses were carried out with the implicit or explicit thesis of the "congestion" of the public good: "crowding" of the local public good either in the consumption side (theory of clubs) or in the production side. Further, in the latter case, Ellickson stated that crowding in the production of local public goods is a required condition for the existence of optimal partitions of the population.

Oates advanced in an empirical study his capitalization assumption of local public expenditures and local taxes as a way of testing Tiebout's hypothesis:

If this is the case if (as the Tiebout model suggests) individuals consider the quality of local public services in making locational decisions, we would expect to find that, other things being equal (including tax rates) across communities, an increased expenditure per pupil would result in higher property values (p. 962).[11]

Oates used expenditure per pupil as a proxy for the output of educational services. Later research findings have shown that both are uncorrelated. Kiesling says:

. . . the relationship of performance to per pupil expenditure has been found to be, except in large urban school districts, disappointingly weak. This would imply, among other things, that the utilization of per capita cost figures for an index of public performance is a highly dangerous practice (p. 366).[9]

A full discussion of the Oates paper would carry us far beyond our subject, but since then, many writers have criticized Oates' findings on different grounds—mainly in the specification of the statistical model or in statistical procedures.[4,5,12] However, these criticisms are raised without taking issue with the theoretical problem of considering real estate values as an output indicator of the process of community homogenization—the core of Tiebout's hypothesis.

It is the purpose of this chapter to assess Tiebout's hypothesis in a more theoretical setting. First, we want to examine the spatial equilibrium conditions and urban land rents under the impact of local public services. Second, in order to clarify definitional aspects of local public goods, we want to examine the locational conditions of local public services and the spatial dimensions of exclusion or "appropriability" so important to the mode of economic organization and its relationship to such concepts as externalities or neighborhood effects (spillovers). Third, we want to show that adhering to Tiebout's original contention in explaining his sixth assumption can lead to a finite population as an optimal size. Fourth, we want to show that the political process leading to an optimal level of local public goods, simultaneously leads to an optimal size of local population, and thereby shows global conditions instead of merely marginal ones for such optimal solutions. Finally, we will show that property value is a very poor output indicator of Tiebout's hypothesis.

We will begin by deriving the spatial equilibrium conditions of a homogeneous population in a residential ring, reformulating a model by Solow in order to include a given spatial distribution of local public goods.[15] Embedded in the solution is the spatial pattern of consumption of the private good (residential land) and its rent function. Next, we will analyze the spatial characteristics of local public goods and their relation to concepts such as exclusion and spillover (neighborhood) effects. It is in this section also, that we show the simultaneous procedure used to arrive at an optimal level of public goods and of local population. Further, it is shown that the fixed supply of the private good (land) is a sufficient condition for a finite population. The third section of the chapter derives a direct measure of the total land market values of the community and the average market value of household's real estate holdings in that community; we also show the lack of correspondence between Tiebout's hypothesis and the capitalization assumption. The chapter concludes with a summary.

The Model: Spatial Equilibrium with Local Public Goods

The main thrust of Tiebout's hypothesis, in relation to his third assumption, is the homogenization of the local population as a result of "voting with their feet," a political process that rests on the assumption of high geographic mobility (Tiebout's first assumption). The final output of this process is that urban dwellers will choose the urban community that offers the tax-expenditure program that maximizes their welfare, thus providing the revelatory demand functions. This is in contrast with the higher jurisdictional public goods case where the individual has every reason not to provide such a function.

In theoretical terms, this homogenization process simplifies the analysis of public economics at the local level, because it allows, without making violence to the analysis, the introduction of the simplifying assumption that individuals have the same income and the same utility function. This allowance circumvents the definitional difficulties of interpersonally comparable utilities which permeate and block the theoretical analysis of public goods in general.

In the model we are developing here, it is considered that our city is a "city of equals:" equal tastes and equal income. The model is a reformulation of the standard model of urban spatial equilibrium—a reformulation that makes possible the explicit consideration of local public goods.

Physically, the city is circular with radius x_1. It has an inner ring with radius x_0 where land is used by the production functions of the CBD. The outer ring is composed of homogeneous residential land, and its total population N commutes to the CBD in order to deliver labor inputs.

Every individual, besides consuming the two private goods, urban land l and the composite consumption good c, consumes a public good g. The utility derived from the consumption of this public good may vary with distance $x \epsilon [x_0, x_1]$. The urban dweller's utility function is additive separable, with diminishing marginal utility in every argument:

$$u(c, l, g(x)) = \ln[c^\alpha l^\beta g(x)^\gamma] \tag{11.1}$$

The urban dweller's income y is assumed to be totally exhausted by the two private goods plus commuting transportation costs:

$$y = c + r(x)l + t(x) \tag{11.2}$$

where prices are in terms of the price of the composite good; land prices (rent) are given by $r(x)$, an unknown function; and transportation costs are given by $t(x)$, a known function. In maximizing (11.1) subject to (11.2), we have, from the usual first-order conditions,

$$\frac{\alpha}{c} = \frac{\beta}{r(x)l} \tag{11.3}$$

From (11.3) and making the corresponding substitution into (11.2), we see in (11.4) and (11.5) that every individual, in each location x, spends a fixed proportion of his income net of transportation in urban land, allocating the rest to the consumption of the composite good:

$$l(x)r(x) = \sigma(y - t(x)) \tag{11.4}$$

$$c(x) = (1 - \sigma)(y - t(x)) \tag{11.5}$$

where $\sigma = \beta/(\alpha + \beta)$. Replacing (11.4) and (11.5) into the utility function (11.1) we have

$$u(x) = \ln\left\{ (1 - \sigma)^\alpha \sigma^\beta (y - t(x))^{\alpha+\beta} \frac{g(x)^\gamma}{r(x)^\beta} \right\} \tag{11.6}$$

In our city of equals, and in equilibrium, no individual should have incentive to move. In other words, in equilibrium, as every urban dweller should be indifferent in relation to his final location, his utility must be constant over the geography of the city. Then it follows that

$$\frac{du(x)}{dx} = 0 = \frac{\alpha + \beta}{y - t(x)} \frac{dt(x)}{dx} + \frac{\beta}{r(x)} \frac{dr(x)}{dx} - \frac{\gamma}{g(x)} \frac{dg(x)}{dx} \tag{11.7}$$

from which we get, in separable form, the fundamental differential equation of the urban rent function:

$$\frac{dr(x)}{r(x)} = \frac{1}{\sigma} \frac{dt(x)}{y - t(x)} + \frac{\gamma}{\beta} \frac{dg(x)}{g(x)} \tag{11.8}$$

In solving (11.8), we have

$$\ln r(x) = \ln(y - t(x))^{1/\sigma} + \ln g(x)^{\gamma/\beta} + C \tag{11.9}$$

The constant of integration C is solved in terms of the values of the variables involved at the boundary x_0. At this initial point, $t(x_0) = 0$ in the simplifying assumption that there are no transportation costs within the CBD. It follows then that

$$C = \ln r(x_0) - \ln y^{1/\sigma} - \ln g(x_0)^{\gamma/\beta} \tag{11.10}$$

From (11.9) and (11.10), we have that the unit price (rent) of land is given by

$$r(x) = r(x_0) \left[\frac{y - t(x)}{y} \right]^{(\alpha+\beta)/\beta} \left(\frac{g(x)}{g(x_0)} \right)^{\gamma/\beta} \tag{11.11}$$

Substituting (11.11) into (11.4), the individual's consumption of land per household at distance x is given by

$$l(x) = \frac{\sigma y^{1/\sigma} g(x_0)^{\gamma/\beta}}{r(x_0)(y - t(x))^{\alpha/\beta} g(x)^{\gamma/\beta}} \tag{11.12}$$

The fixed supply of land at distance x, in an infinitesimal ring of width dx, is $s(x)$, $0 < s(x) \leqslant 2\pi x$. The demand for land at distance x is $l(x)n(x)\,dx$, where $n(x)$ is the number of urban dwellers living in the infinitesimal ring of width

dx. We assume that in equilibrium the market of urban land is cleared; then it follows that

$$s(x)\, dx = l(x)n(x)\, dx \qquad (11.13)$$

The total aggregate demand has the following integral constraint:

$$N = \int_{x_0}^{x_1} n(x)\, dx \qquad (11.14)$$

where N is the size of the urban population. From (11.12), (11.13), and (11.14), and making the corresponding substitution, the boundary condition $r(x_0)$ is computed by solving

$$\sigma g(x_0)^{\gamma/\beta} y^{1/\sigma} N - r(x_0) \int_{x_0}^{x_1} s(x)\, (y - t(x))^{\alpha/\beta} g(x)^{\gamma/\beta}\, dx = 0 \quad (11.15)$$

From the equilibrium condition (11.7), the individual's utility is invariant in relation to distance x. It follows that, in computing the utility of any one individual at any particular distance, we know everybody's level of utility u at any distance x. Using x_0 as that particular distance and from (11.6), we have

$$u = u(x_0) = \ln\left[\frac{(1 - \sigma)^{\alpha}\sigma^{\beta} y^{\alpha+\beta} g(x_0)^{\gamma}}{r(x_0)^{\beta}}\right] \qquad (11.16)$$

In this approach, the output of the system is the utility itself (11.16), allowing a direct measurement of benefits of public programs.

Equations (11.11), (11.12), (11.15), and (11.16) are the critical ones in analyzing in equilibrium the impact of any public program, which we will express in terms of $g(x)$, population size N, and distance x:

$$r(N, g(x), x) = r(N, g(x), x_0)\left[\frac{y - t(x)}{y}\right]^{(\alpha+\beta)/\beta} \left[\frac{g(x)}{g(x_0)}\right]^{\gamma/\beta} \qquad (11.17)$$

$$l(N, g(x), x) = \sigma y \div \left\{r(N, g(x), x_0)\left[\frac{y - t(x)}{y}\right]^{\alpha/\beta} \left[\frac{g(x)}{g(x_0)}\right]^{\gamma/\beta}\right\} \qquad (11.18)$$

$$r(N, g(x), x_0) = N\sigma y \div \left\{\left[\int_{x_0}^{x_1} s(x)\left[\frac{y - t(x)}{y}\right]^{\alpha/\beta} \left[\frac{g(x)}{g(x_0)}\right]^{\gamma/\beta}\, dx\right\} \quad (11.19)$$

$$u(N, g(x)) = \ln\left\{(1 - \sigma)^{\alpha}\left[\int_{x_0}^{x_1} s(x)(y - t(x))^{\alpha/\beta} g(x)^{\gamma/\beta}\, dx\right]^{\beta} \div N^{\beta}\right\} \quad (11.20)$$

From (11.20), we will define a new welfare function:

183

$$U(N, g(x)) = \left[\int_{x_0}^{x_1} s(x)(y - t(x))^{\alpha/\beta} g(x)^{\gamma/\beta} \, dx \right] \div N \qquad (11.21)$$

where

$$U(N, g(x)) = U[u(N, g(x))] = \left[\frac{\exp u(N, g(x))}{(1 - \sigma)^{\alpha}} \right]^{1/\beta}$$

is a monotonic transformation of the original utility function (11.1).

Equations (11.17), (11.18), and (11.19) give the spatial equilibrium conditions of the residential ring as functions of population size, the spatial distribution of local public goods and distance. Equation (11.21) gives the individual's and everybody's level of welfare in the community as a function of population size and the spatial distribution of public goods. We can turn our attention now to the political process—collective action—implicit in Tiebout's sixth assumption.

The Political Process: Local Public Goods and Optimal City Size

In order to differentiate between the level and the spatial distribution of the public physical output on the one hand, and on the other, the degree of spatial exclusiveness of the public physical output, let us define the following: $h(x)$ is the public physical output located in the infinitesimal ring of width dx at distance x. Then, the total public physical output G of the city is given by

$$G = \int_0^{x_1} h(z) \, dz \qquad (11.22)$$

Given (11.22), a public output density function can be defined as $p(z) = h(z)/G$. Also, a spillover function can be defined as $w(x, z)$, where $w(\cdot, z)$ weights the spillout effect of the public physical output h located at z, and $w(x, \cdot)$ weights the spillin effect to the household located at x.

In the specification of this spillover function rests the complex definitional aspect of the local public good. In one direction, it introduces the spatial dimensions of the concept of property rights, dimensions that are related to the mode of economic organization. In the other direction, it introduces the degree of "localness" of the public good: inspite of nonrivalriness of the public good, we have a loss in welfare due only to the locational fixities of both the physical output of the public program and of

184

the consumer of the public good, a loss that is a function of the physical distance separating production and consumption.[a]

Let us assume that

$$w(x, z) = 1 \quad \text{for all} \quad z = x; z, x \leq x_1 \tag{11.23}$$

$$w(x, z) = 0 \quad \text{for} \quad x > x_1 \tag{11.24}$$

$$w(x, z) = 0 \quad \text{for} \quad z > x_1 \tag{11.25}$$

Assumption (11.23) means that there are no spillouts from our community and (11.24) means that there are no spillins into our community; both assumptions are in strict correspondance with Tiebout's fifth assumption.[b]

If we assume further that

$$w(\cdot, z) = 0 \quad \text{for all} \quad x \neq z; x, z \leq x_1 \tag{11.26}$$

we have no spillovers among residential rings and the public physical output h is supplied at z exclusive of any other ring. Because of the continuous spatial distribution of population (11.13) and (11.18), only one household is located in an infinitesimal ring of width dx at distance z. Therefore, the degree of appropriability is optimal and perfectly subject to the pricing system. It follows that $g(x) = h(x)$ and $g(x)$ is a publicly supplied private good in this case, a case that does not need our attention here.

For a more general case, let us assume now that

$$w(\cdot, z) > 0 \quad \text{for some} \quad x \neq z; x, z \leq x_1 \tag{11.27}$$

Equation (11.26) means that there are spillovers (neighborhood effects) at least among some residential rings and that the public physical output h is supplied at z without any exclusivity in relation to at least one other ring. Equivalently, for the household located at z, the degree of appropriability is not optimal and therefore $h(z)$ is defined as a public good. It does not follow that every household located at $x \neq z$ is appropriating the total amount of $h(z)$. Because of the physical distance between the location of the public physical output at z and the location of the household at x, w can also be defined as a loss or distance dissipation function where

$$0 \leq w(x, \cdot) \leq 1 \quad \text{for all} \quad z \neq x; z, x \leq x_1 \tag{11.28}$$

---

[a] "Non-rivalness in consumption . . . does not mean that some subjective benefit must be derived, or even that precisely the same product quality is available to both. Consumer A who lives close to the police station has better protection than B who lives far away. Yet, the two consumption acts are non-rival, and we deal with a social good" (p. 126).[10]

[b] "The Public services supplied exhibit no external economies or diseconomies between communities" (p. 419).[16]

At every particular location $x \in [x_0, x_1]$, the total amount of public goods g is defined as

$$g(x) = \int_0^{x_1} w(x, z) h(z) \, dz \qquad x \in [x_0, x_1] \qquad (11.29)$$

And from (11.22), we have

$$g(x) = G \int_0^{x_1} w(x, z) p(z) \, dz = G v(x) \qquad (11.30)$$

where $v(x) = E[p(z) \mid w(x, z)]$ for $x \in [x_0, x_1]$, $0 < v(x) < 1$, E being the operator expected value of the function w. In the particular case where there are no dissipatory effects, then

$$w(x, \cdot) = 1 \quad \text{for all} \quad z \leqslant x_1 \qquad (11.31)$$

It follows from (11.30) that, in this case,

$$E[p(z) \mid w(x, z)] = 1 \rightarrow g(x) = G \qquad (11.32)$$

and there is no spatial impact of local expenditures on public goods in the residential ring.

If we relax (11.23) and (11.24), and define $w(x, \cdot) = 1$ for all z and $w(\cdot, z) = 1$ for all x, then the definitional boundaries between local public goods and higher jurisdictional levels of public goods (i.e., national defense) becomes blurred and a new conflicting situation arises. (See Williams[17].)

Given equation (11.30), let us redefine the results of the preceeding section as follows:

$$r(N, G, x) = r(N, G, x_0) \left[\frac{y - t(x)}{y} \right]^{(\alpha + \beta)/\beta} \left[\frac{v(x)}{v(x_0)} \right]^{\gamma/\beta} \qquad (11.33)$$

$$l(N, G, x) = \sigma y \div \left\{ r(N, G, x_0) \left[\frac{y - t(x)}{y} \right]^{\alpha/\beta} \left[\frac{v(x)}{v(x_0)} \right]^{\gamma/\beta} \right\} \qquad (11.34)$$

$$r(N, G, x_0) = \sigma N y \div \left\{ \int_{x_0}^{x_1} s(x) \left[\frac{y - t(x)}{y} \right]^{\alpha/\beta} \left[\frac{v(x)}{v(x_0)} \right]^{\gamma/\beta} dx \right\} \qquad (11.35)$$

Central to the collective action process, the welfare function is redefined as

$$U(N, G) = \left[G^{\gamma/\beta} \int_{x_0}^{x_1} s(x)(y - t(x))^{\alpha/\beta} v(x)^{\gamma/\beta} \, dx \right] \div N \qquad (11.36)$$

In (11.36), as in (11.2), the household's income is after-tax income, $y = \hat{y} - \Pi$, where $\hat{y}$ is pretax income and Π is local tax. This local tax is defined as a per capita load, $\Pi = C(G)/N$, where $C = C(G)$ is defined as a cost function of the local public sector,[e] with $C'(G) > 0$ and $C''(G) \geqslant 0$, the last as a simplifying assumption. It follows then that

$$y = \hat{y} - [C(G)/N] \tag{11.37}$$

Equations (11.36) and (11.37) give the required information to Tiebout's city manager to compute (simultaneously) the optimal level of local public goods and the optimal size of the local population.

From the first order condition of (11.36) and by making the corresponding substitution of disposable income given by (11.37), we have[d]

$$\frac{\partial U(N, G)}{\partial G} = 0 \rightarrow \gamma N \int_{x_0}^{x_1} s(x)(y - t(x))^{\alpha/\beta} v(x)^{\gamma/\beta} \, dx$$

$$- \alpha G C'(G) \int_{x_0}^{x_1} s(x)(y - t(x))^{(\alpha - \beta)/\beta} v(x)^{\gamma/\beta} \, dx = 0 \tag{11.38}$$

$$\frac{\partial U(N, G)}{\partial N} = 0 \rightarrow \beta N \int_{x_0}^{x_1} s(x)(y - t(x))^{\alpha/\beta} v(x)^{\gamma/\beta} \, dx$$

$$- \alpha C(G) \int_{x_0}^{x_1} s(x)(y - t(x))^{(\alpha - \beta)/\beta} v(x)^{\gamma/\beta} \, dx = 0 \tag{11.39}$$

For the second-order (necessary and sufficient) conditions for a maximum, the matrix

$$\begin{bmatrix} \dfrac{\partial^2 U(N, G)}{\partial N^2} & \dfrac{\partial^2 U(N, G)}{\partial N \partial G} \\[2ex] \dfrac{\partial^2 U(N, G)}{\partial N \partial G} & \dfrac{\partial^2 U(N, G)}{\partial G^2} \end{bmatrix} \tag{11.40}$$

must be negative semidefinite, i.e. the roots λ from the determinantal equation

$$\begin{bmatrix} \dfrac{\partial^2 U(N, G)}{\partial N^2} - \lambda & \dfrac{\partial^2 U(N, G)}{\partial N \partial G} \\[2ex] \dfrac{\partial^2 U(N, G)}{\partial N \partial G} & \dfrac{\partial^2 U(N, G)}{\partial G^2} - \lambda \end{bmatrix} = 0 \tag{11.41}$$

---

[e] In the specification of this cost function rests the critical theoretical difference with Ellickson.[5] In my case $C(G) = C(G, N)$, due to my assumption that $\partial C(G, N)/\partial N = 0$, and in order to show that without "crowding" in the production of public goods, Tiebout's sixth assumption still holds.

[d] For a discussion of x_1 free and endogeneously defined, and of why $(y - t(x_1))(dx_1/dN) = 0$ or equivalently $(y - t(x_1))(dx_1/dG) = 0$ holds, see Fisch.[7]

are zero or negative. It is shown in Appendix 11A that sufficient conditions hold.

From (11.38), (11.39), and Appendix 11A, and by defining the density function

$$f_0(x) = \left\{ s(x) \left[\frac{y^* - t(x)}{y^*} \right]^{(\alpha-\beta)/\beta} v(x)^{\gamma/\beta} \right\}$$

$$\div \left\{ \int_{x_0}^{x_1} s(x) \left[\frac{y^* - t(x)}{y^*} \right]^{(\alpha-\beta)/\beta} v(x)^{\gamma/\beta} dx \right\} \quad (11.42)$$

and by defining as the optimal disposable income

$$y^* = \hat{y} - \frac{C(G^*)}{N^*} \quad (11.43)$$

we can now state

Proposition 11.1: The optimal level of local public goods G^* and the optimal size of the local population N^* are given by the simultaneous solution of

$$\alpha C(G^*) - \beta N^* y^* E\left[f_0(x) \mid \frac{y^* - t(x)}{y^*} \right] = 0 \quad \text{and}$$

$$\alpha G^* C'(G^*) - \gamma N^* y^* E\left[f_0(x) \mid \frac{y^* - t(x)}{y^*} \right] = 0$$

Also, it follows from (11.38) and (11.39) that

$$\frac{[C(G^*)/G^*]}{C'(G^*)} = \frac{\beta}{\gamma} \quad (11.44)$$

from which we can now state

Proposition 11.2: At the optimal level of provision of local public goods, the ratio between average cost and marginal cost of the public good is equal to the ratio between the utility weight of residential land and the utility weight of the public good.

From the simultaneous solution of G^* and N^*, y^* is also defined. Then, from (11.33), (11.34), and (11.35), the spatial equilibrium in the city at the optimal level of local public goods and population size is given by

$$r(N^*, G^*, x) = r(N^*, G^*, x_0) \left[\frac{y^* - t(x)}{y^*} \right]^{(\alpha+\beta)/\beta} \left[\frac{v(x)}{v(x_0)} \right]^{\gamma/\beta} \quad (11.45)$$

$$l(N^*, G^*, x) = \sigma y^* \div \left\{ r(N^*, G^*, x_0) \left[\frac{y^* - t(x)}{y^*} \right]^{\alpha/\beta} \left[\frac{v(x)}{v(x_0)} \right]^{\gamma/\beta} \right\} \quad (11.46)$$

$$r(N^*, G^*, x_0) = \sigma N^* y^* \div \left\{ \int_{x_0}^{x_1} s(x) \left[\frac{y^* - t(x)}{y^*} \right]^{\alpha/\beta} \left[\frac{v(x)}{v(x_0)} \right]^{\gamma/\beta} dx \right\} \quad (11.47)$$

As local zoning ordinances have, as a main output, the physical regulation (lot size, type of structure, and land use) of urban land, then (11.46) gives the critical input for exclusion purposes in residential areas. We see then, as exclusion activities by zoning ordinances are possible at some finite cost (costs of enforcement and policing which are ignored here), property rights are reinforced through collective action. In a way, because the inability to exclude stops, the creation of a "market" *à la* Tiebout for local public goods is feasible, and possibly it is the expected output of the political process that is taking place in the fragmented jurisdictions of the metropolitan areas.

The Capitalization Assumption

Tiebout did not clarify, in his original formulation, whether the local tax is an income tax or a property tax. Nor did he clarify the legal arrangements of urban land ownership—land tenure—that he envisioned in the optimal supply of local public goods. And, as we will see immediately, land tenure should be introduced implicitly into our analysis in order to measure the impact of local taxes.

If the local tax is an income tax, we can see that the results of the preceeding sections apply to both cases of legal arrangements: tenants with absentee landlords and homeowners.

If the local tax is a property tax totally shiftable to land, then land tenure is an important input into our analysis and the results of the preceeding section should be reexamined.

In the extreme case of a city of tenants with absentee landlords, the tenants having the political power to tax and to distribute local public goods, and if the local tax is totally shiftable to land, the lower boundary of local public expenditures is at least the total value of urban land. This gives some support to the claim that property tax is a progressive tax under this legal arrangement and illuminates the historical and political controversy of property qualifications on voting that James Madison—among others—staunchly defended.[e]

---

[e] James Madison wrote: "In England, at this day, if elections were open to all classes of people, the property of landed proprietors would be unsure. . . . Landholders ought to have a share in the government, to support these invaluable interest. . . . They ought to be so constituted as to protect the minority of the opulent against the majority." (Cited in Gaffney[8] p. 408.)

But the degree of shiftability of property taxes is still an unsettled theoretical issue. Despite some grounds gained by the classical economists, the incidence of property taxes on urban land values remains an obscure area in the analysis of our economic organization.

It is in relation to this issue that Oates advanced his capitalization assumption of local public expenditures and taxes as a corroborative of Tiebout's hypothesis. It is the purpose of this section to show that property value is a poor output indicator of the optimal level of local public goods and taxes and of the optimal size of the population. In other words, we want to show that the capitalization assumption is alien to Tiebout's hypothesis and to its explicit homogenization process. In order to neutralize, in our analysis, the incidence of local taxes, we will transform our city of tenants of the second section into a city of homeowners, envisioning in our city of equals that the whole residential ring is owned by a corporation, with the residents as stockholders, receiving as dividends the economic rent of the urban residential land.

As the dividend of residential rent is reintroduced as personal income, we allow for continuous recontracting in the residential land market. We will show that there exists an equilibrium in that market and that the recontracting process is a stable system.

We define the total urban land rent of the initial round of the recontracting process as

$$R_0(G, N) = \int_{x_0}^{x_1^0} s(x) r(G, N, x) \, dx \tag{11.48}$$

and from (11.33), (11.35), and (11.48), and by making the corresponding substitutions, we have

$$R_0(G, N) = \sigma N y_0 E\left[\bar{f}_0(x) \mid \frac{y_0 - t(x)}{y_0}\right] \tag{11.49}$$

where the density function

$$\bar{f}_i(x) = \left\{ s(x) \left[\frac{y_i - t(x)}{y_i} \right]^{\alpha/\beta} v(x)^{\gamma/\beta} \right\} \div \left\{ \int_{x_0}^{x_1^i} s(x) \left[\frac{y_i - t(x)}{y_i} \right]^{\alpha/\beta} v(x)^{\gamma/\beta} \, dx \right\}$$

The dividend D accruing at the end of this initial round to every resident-stockholder is, from (11.49), given by

$$D_0 = \sigma y_0 \bar{E}_0 \tag{11.50}$$

where $E_i = E[\bar{f}_i(x) \mid (y_i - t(x))/y_i]$. The dividend given by (11.50) produces a first adjustment of personal income and a new estimate of land rent and dividend:

$$y_1 = y_0 + D_0 = y_0(1 + \sigma \bar{E}_0) \tag{11.51}$$

$$D_1 = \sigma y_1 \bar{E}_1 \tag{11.52}$$

$$y_2 = y_0 + D_1 = y_0(1 + \bar{E}_1 + \sigma^2 \bar{E}_1 \bar{E}_0) \tag{11.53}$$

In general, at the nth round of adjustment, we have that

$$D_{n-1} = \sigma y_{n-1} \bar{E}_{n-1} \tag{11.54}$$

$$y_n/y_0 = 1 + \sigma \bar{E}_{n-1} + \sigma^2 \bar{E}_{n-1} \bar{E}_{n-2} + \ldots + \sigma^n \bar{E}_{n-1} \bar{E}_{n-2} \ldots \bar{E}_1 \bar{E}_0 \tag{11.55}$$

In order to test if the terms of the series in (11.55) are monotonically decreasing, we compute the ratio between the nth and the $(n-1)$th term (ratio test):

$$\frac{\sigma^n \bar{E}_{n-1} \bar{E}_{n-2} \ldots \bar{E}_1 \bar{E}_0}{\sigma^{n-1} \bar{E}_{n-1} \bar{E}_{n-2} \ldots \bar{E}_1} = \sigma \bar{E}_0 < 1 \tag{11.56}$$

And it follows that

$$\lim_{n \to \infty} [\sigma^n \bar{E}_{n-1} \ldots \bar{E}_0] = 0$$

and that the series (11.55) is convergent. We can now state

Proposition 11.3: The recontracting process of the urban land market under the ownership arrangement is a stable system.

From (11.55) and (11.56), we can compute the equilibrium values of every resident's total income:

$$\lim_{n \to \infty} y_n = y = y_0 \left\{ 1 + \sigma E \left[f_0(x) \mid \frac{y - t(x)}{y} \right] \right\} \tag{11.57}$$

and the equilibrium values of (corporation assets) urban land (in rent flow):

$$\lim_{n \to \infty} R_n(G, N) = R(G, N) = \sigma N y E \left[f_0(x) \mid \frac{y - t(x)}{y} \right] \tag{11.58}$$

as well as the equilibrium values of every household's land holdings:

$$\lim_{n \to \infty} D_n(G, N) = D(G, N) = \sigma y E \left[f_0(x) \mid \frac{y - t(x)}{y} \right] \tag{11.59}$$

where y is after-tax income. In pretax income, (11.59) can be expressed as

$$D(G, N) = \sigma(\hat{y} - \Pi) E \left[f_0(x) \mid \frac{\hat{y} - \Pi - t(x)}{y - \Pi} \right] \tag{11.60}$$

It follows from (11.57) and (11.59) that the local tax can be treated indifferently, either as a property tax—independent of the degree of shifting—or as an income tax, and the results of this proceeding section can be applied without any change. The result in (11.60) has the following behavior (see Appendix 11A):

$$\frac{dD}{dG} = \frac{C'(G)}{N}\left\{\frac{\alpha}{\beta}\frac{E_0}{E_1} - \frac{\alpha + \beta}{\beta}\right\} < 0 \qquad (11.61)$$

$$\frac{dD}{dN} = \frac{C(G)}{N^2}\left\{\frac{\alpha + \beta}{\beta} - \frac{\alpha}{\beta}\frac{E_0}{E_1}\right\} > 0 \qquad (11.62)$$

From (11.61), (11.62), and from the assumption that $C(1) = 0$, it follows that

$$D^* = \underset{\substack{1 \leq G \leq \infty \\ 1 \leq N \leq \infty}}{\text{Max}}\{D(G, N)\} = \lim_{G \to 1} D(G, N) = \lim_{N \to \infty} D(G, N) \qquad (11.63)$$

Now we can state

Proposition 11.4:   The value of every household's land holdings attains a maximum when the local tax $\Pi = 0$, that is, when local public expenditure is nil or, equivalently, when local population size is infinite.

From the results in the preceding section, in the optimal solution, as $G^* > 1$ and $N^* \ll \infty$ it follows that

$$D(G^*, N^*) < D^* \qquad (11.64)$$

and we can state

Proposition 11.5:   At the optimal level of local public goods G^*, optimal local tax Π^*, and optimal population size N^*, the value of every household's land holdings is less than its maximum attainable value.

It follows from Propositions 11.4 and 11.5, that there is a total lack of correspondence between Tiebout's welfare conditions when the local political process reaches equilibrium (optimality) and local property values (land rent).

The results of Propositions 11.4 and 11.5 are graphically shown in Figures 11-1, 11-2, and 11-3. We can see that land value, as an output indicator of the workings of Tiebout's hypothesis, is totally unrelated to a maximum welfare granted by the homogenization process—implicit in that hypothesis—when it reaches its equilibrium size. Additionally, productivity differentials of the local tax as an incentive to move among communities also have a theoretical limitation. Let us assume that we have two cities A and B with identical geography, each having homogeneous populations with identical income, where

$$\beta_A = \beta_B \quad \text{and} \quad \gamma_A = \gamma_B$$

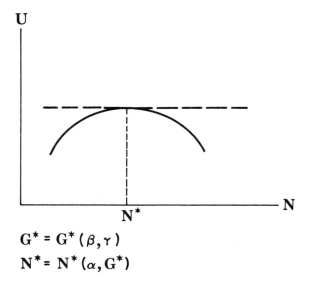

$$G^* = G^* (\beta, \gamma)$$
$$N^* = N^* (\alpha, G^*)$$

Figure 11-1. Welfare as a Function of Population Size

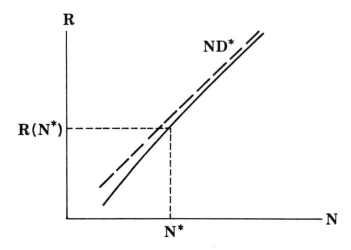

Figure 11-2. Total Land Rent as a Function of Population Size

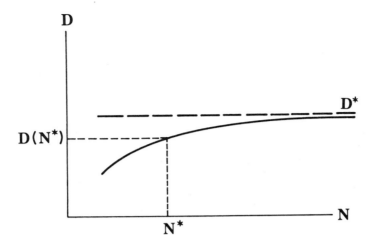

Figure 11-3. Value of Household Land Holdings as a Function of Population Size

Then, it follows from Proposition 11.2, in the assumption that there is high mobility of technological information in relation to the public sector,[f] that

$$G_A^* = G_B^* \quad \text{and} \quad C_A(G_A^*) = C_B(G_B^*)$$

Let us assume further that $\alpha_A \neq \alpha_B$ and that this inequality is sufficient to lead to

$$N_A^* \neq N_B^* \rightarrow \Pi_A^* \neq \Pi_B^* \rightarrow D_A(G_A^*, N_A^*) \neq D_B(G_B^*, N_B^*)$$

Therefore, in spite of different tax rates with the same public output, there is no incentive to shop elsewhere or to move out of any of these cities, because both are at the optimal level of welfare and any capitalization differential does not measure that particular optimal level.

Urban land rent is a poor indicator of the benefits of public programs in general, and in particular, of the workings of the Tiebout hypothesis: homogenization and optimal supply of local public goods. Differentials in productivity of local taxes are not always an incentive to move and we conclude that the capitalization assumption as a test is totally alien to Tiebout's hypothesis.

---

[f] Any assumption to the contrary in the public sector makes violence directly to Tiebout's assumption. It is very difficult to assume a high geographic mobility of the population with its implicit requirement of no cost and complete information, without assuming, at the same time, a complete flow of information (technological) in the public sector across jurisdictional boundaries.

Summary and Conclusions

It was shown that, granted the homogenization of the local population, the Tiebout hypothesis simplifies the analysis of local public finance. The required demand functions are revealed, a price (tax) is derived, and a "market" of local public goods is the warranted output. Implicit in the equilibrium conditions is the simultaneous derivation of an optimal (finite) population size, the fixed supply of land (private good) being a sufficient condition for that equilibrium.

It was shown that the spatial dimensions of public goods are an important factor in the degree of "localness" of the public good. Additionally, the spatial analysis strengthens the linkage between public goods and such concepts as externalities (neighborhood effects) and "appropriability." The spatial loss function clarifies the transformation of the public physical output into a local public good and a spatial measure of local public goods was defined for appropriate impact analysis on the land rent function.

It was shown that land rent is a poor output indicator of Tiebout's hypothesis. Granted that the homogenization process is taking place, the Tiebout hypothesis implicitly carries an efficient allocation. But there seems to exist a perceived conflict between efficiency and distributive aspects in the provision of local public goods. Recent court decisions in California (*Serrano vs. Priest*), in New Jersey (*Robinson vs. Cahill*), and court injunctions in Florida against a city council's instructions to the "excess" population to pack and move out—an implicit local police power required to implement Tiebout's sixth assumption—are all directly related to Samuelson's disturbing question as to "whether groups of like-minded individuals shall be free to run out on their social responsibilities and go off by themselves."[14]

It seems that the theoretical analysis of this perceived conflict is the most needed task in local public finance but it is totally independent of Tiebout's original formulation and concerns.

Appendix 11A

From equation (11.36), it follows that

$$\frac{\partial^2 U}{\partial G} = \frac{G^{(\gamma-2\beta)/\beta}}{N} y \left(\frac{E_0}{E_1}\right)\left(\frac{\gamma}{\beta}\right)^2$$

$$\left\{ \left(\frac{\alpha - \beta}{a}\right) E_0 - \left(\frac{\gamma + \beta}{\gamma} + \frac{\beta G C''(G) =}{\gamma C'(G)}\right) E_1 \right\} \qquad (11A.1)$$

$$\frac{\partial^2 U}{\partial N^2} = \frac{G^{(\gamma-2\beta)/\beta}}{N} y \left(\frac{E_0}{E_1}\right)\left(\frac{G}{N}\right)^2 \left\{ \left(\frac{\alpha - \beta}{\alpha}\right) E_0 - 2E_1 \right\} \qquad (11A.2)$$

$$\frac{\partial^2 U}{\partial G \partial N} = \frac{G^{(\gamma-2\beta)/\beta}}{N} y \left(\frac{E_0}{E_1}\right)\left(\frac{\gamma}{\beta}\right)\left(\frac{G}{N}\right) \left\{ 2E_1 - \left(\frac{\alpha - \beta}{\alpha}\right) E_0 \right\} (11A.3)$$

where $E_0 = E[f_0(x) \mid (y - t(x))/y]$ was defined in (11.42) and $E_1 = E[f_1(x) \mid (y - t(x))/y]$ and where the density function $f_1(x)$ is defined as

$$f_1(x) = \left\{ s(x) \left[\frac{y - t(x)}{y}\right]^{(\alpha-\beta)/\beta} v(x)^{\gamma/\beta} \right\}$$

$$\div \left\{ \int_{x_0}^{x_1} s(x) \left[\frac{y - t(x)}{y}\right]^{(\alpha-\beta)/\beta} v(x)^{\gamma/\beta} \right\}$$

From (11A.1), (11A.2), and (11A.3), the necessary and sufficient conditions for a relative maximum are that the roots λ of the determinantal equation

$$\begin{bmatrix} -\left(\frac{\gamma + \beta}{\gamma} + \frac{G C''(G)}{2C'(G)} + \lambda\right) & 1 \\ 1 & -(1 + \lambda) \end{bmatrix} = 0$$

be negative, is that $\beta > \gamma$ if $C''(G) = 0$ or $\beta(C'(G^*) + G^*C''(G^*)) > \gamma C'(G^*)$ if $C''(G) > 0$.

Notes

1. K.J. Arrow, 1971, "A Utilitarian Approach to the Concept of Equality in Public Expenditures," *Quarterly Journal of Economics,* vol. 85, 409-415.

2. J.M. Buchanan and Ch. J. Goetz, 1972, "Efficiency Limits of Fiscal Mobility: An Assessment of the Tiebout Model," *Journal of Public Economics,* vol. 1, 25-43.

3. J.S. Coleman, 1968, "The Concept of Equality of Educational Opportunity," *Harvard Educational Review,* vol. 38, 14-22.

4. M. Edel and E. Sclar, 1974, "Taxes, Spending and Property Values: Supply Adjustment in a Tiebout-Oates Model," *Journal of Political Economy,* vol. 82, 941-954.

5. B. Ellickson, 1971, "Jurisdictional Fragmentation and Residential Choice," *American Economic Review, Papers and Proceedings,* vol. 61, 334-339.

6. B. Ellickson, 1973, "A Generalization of the Pure Theory of Public Goods," *American Economic Review,* vol. 63, 417-432.

7. O. Fisch, [1975b].

8. M.M. Gaffney, 1972, "The Property Tax is a Progressive Tax," *Proceedings of 64th Annual Conference, National Tax Association,* Columbus, 408-426.

9. H.J. Kiesling, 1967, "Measuring a Local Government Service: A Study of School Districts in New York State," *The Review of Economics and Statistics,* vol. 49, 356-367.

10. R.A. Musgrave, 1969, "Provision for Social Goods," in J. Margolis and H. Guitton, (eds.), *Public Economics,* New York: St. Martin's Press.

11. W.E. Oates, 1969, "The Effects of Property Taxes and Local Public Spending on Property Values: An Empirical Study of Tax Capitalization and the Tiebout Hypothesis," *Journal of Political Economy,* vol. 77, 957-971.

12. H.O. Pollakowski, 1973, "The Effects of Property Taxes and Local Public Spending on Property Values: A Comment and Further Results," *Journal of Political Economy,* vol. 81, 994-1003.

13. J. Rawls, 1971, *A Theory of Justice.* Cambridge: Harvard University Press.

14. P. Samuelson, 1958, "Local Finance and the Mathematics of Marriage," Appendix to "Aspects of Public Expenditure Theories," *The Review of Economics and Statistics,* vol. 40, 332-338.

15. R.M. Solow, [1973a].

16. C.M. Tiebout, 1956, "A Pure Theory of Local Expenditures," *Journal of Political Economy,* vol. 64, 416-424.

17. A. Williams, 1967, "The Optimal Provision of Public Goods in a System of Local Government," *Journal of Political Economy,* vol. 74, 18-33.

18. O.P. Williams, H. Herman, C.S. Liebman, and T.R. Dye, 1965, *Suburban Differences and Metropolitan Policies.* Philadelphia: University of Pennsylvania Press.

19. R.C. Wood, 1958, *Suburbia: Its People and Their Politics.* Boston: Houghton Mifflin.

12

On Some Determinants of the Optimum Geography of an Urban Place

Nurudeen Alao

The term *optimum urban geographies* is perhaps one of the most felicitous among those that have appeared in urban literature in the last five years or so. Apparently first used by Solow[10] and Mirrlees,[7] it is meant to denote city distributions and urban land use structures that are in some well-defined sense or with respect to some well-defined optimal or efficient spatial criteria. The commonly invoked criteria include cost, cost-effectiveness, revenue, utility, welfare, and profits.

The use of these criteria has yet to reveal any intrinsically new focus for urban geographers. Rather it seems to indicate new possibilities for enriching and unifying the existing problem foci. An example is sufficient to underscore this last point. In urban and economic geography, there is, in existence, a body of concepts about the internal structure of cities which (concepts) are expressed in terms of three popular models—the concentric, the sector, and the multiple nuclei models—of urban land use. It has been possible to illuminate theoretical aspects of the concentric model via simple Von Thünian formulations, and we are beginning to explore the empirical meaning and validity of the underlying Von Thünian conditions. With respect to the sector and multinuclei models, we now realize the necessity for specifying the criteria which make them efficient forms of urban land uses. The criteria so far provided by factor analysis are too general and can hardly form the basis of rigorous analyses. The multinuclei model poses a further problem as yet scarcely articulated, much less solved: What is the optimum time-path of efficient urban land uses? One can only envision a new and richer synthesis emerging from the sharper foci provided by these questions.

The sharpening and unification of problem foci are also bound up with and sustained by a new tradition of analysis based on a common theme and methodology. The theme involves (i) the characterization, in their ideal form, of the processes, mechanisms, problems, and prospects of the urban type of spatial organization; (ii) mathematical descriptions of the structure of major urban land uses; (iii) analysis of the network of relationships among these land uses; and (iv) interpretation through mathematics of the

Nurudeen Alao is a member of the Department of Geography, University of Lagos, and Department of Geography, Northwestern University.

socioeconomic geography of these relationships and their welfare implications.

Control theory and its relatives have been the most important tools employed. Another important characteristic of the new tradition is the study of the similarities and differences between a centralized and a market approach to the location of the activities which define the internal geography of an urban place.

In this chapter, the expression *optimum geography* of an urban place simply means "optimum internal configuration of the specific land uses" in the urban place.

In view of its aim and methodology, this chapter may be regarded as a contribution to the emerging tradition. However, it goes further to argue that the emerging tradition so far succeeds in grapling with only one of the principal dimensions of the urban spatial organization, for there are other quite subtle dimensions that filter through the mesh of the present control theory approach.

Specifically, it studies two principal types of models. The first one is derived from, but elaborates on a basic formulation of Borukhov.[2] In this model, we focus upon the housing structure as well as the commuting cost to a punctiform CBD. A fundamental assumption involved here is that the social cost of maintaining the city is the sum of housing cost and transport cost, the latter of which is initially assumed to be constant per person per mile. The opportunity cost of land is assumed to be zero. We then ask two questions:

1. How does the market solution to our problem differ from the centrally determined solution? The former will be called an equilibrium solution and the latter an optimum solution.

2. What are the salient properties of the principal instruments by which land is allocated to housing and housing services are allocated to suburbanites?

In regard to the first question, we shall show that, under some plausible assumptions, the optimum and the equilibrium solutions are the same.

A second series of models then focuses upon the CBD to see how its spatial structure and texture are determined through the allocation of land to intra-CBD transport and the distribution of capital and labor intensity over space. The treatment of the CBD here differs considerably from the treatment given it by Solow,[10] Oron et al,[8] and Dixit.[3] Solow and Oron et al. assume that the circular CBD is already given and proceed to study the efficient structure of streets and residences. Important in the notion of efficiency is the concept of congestion cost. Dixit, on the other hand, constructs a model in which the efficient size of the CBD is endogenously determined; gross output depends continuously on the size of the CBD. An important point in Dixit's formulation is his assumption of increasing returns to scale in CBD production. However, he does not consider the internal texture of the CBD. Our second model will use production functions of constant returns to scale but justify the agglomeration of production in the CBD by the fact that "basic" outputs which sustain the city must be exported and "transportation economies" alone are enough to justify concentration around a centrally located port. Whereas, in some of the subsequent models we shall admit congestion cost in respect of commuter transport in the CBD, we will often assume a constant transport rate with respect to goods. This is not an unrealistic assumption quite apart from its intrinsic historical interest. We then indicate the source of divergence between the optimum solution and the equilibrium and point out major means that may be employed to attain efficiency through the market.

The final section discusses the achievements of the present approach and calls attention to other critical needs as yet scarcely probed. It must be emphasized here that the final section is important in that it is addressed to those phenomena by which the urban place ticks but to which we have as yet paid little attention.

Some Land Use Models

Model I: Residential Structure

Consider a uniform plain with a punctiform nucleus—the CBD centrally located. Locations in this plain are identified by the distance $s \geqslant 0$ from the CBD. Assume that in each belt ds of land s miles from the CBD, the total area of land available for housing purposes is $\theta s ds$.

Suppose that the city is to consist of N families in each of which there is exactly one person who must commute to the CBD each day, at a rate equal to ts for each person located at point s. Housing is produced with land l and capital k. Housing production function is assumed to be homogeneous of degree one and of the Cobb-Douglas form. Each family requires one unit of housing services, so that if at s there are $h(s)$ families, $h(s)$ housing services will be produced where

$$h(s) = l(s)^{1-\alpha} k(s)^{\alpha} \qquad 0 < \alpha < 1$$

$$l(s) = \theta \, s \qquad \theta > 0$$

$$k(s) = \text{quantity of capital employed in providing housing at } s \qquad (12.1)$$

Denote by ρ, the interest rate per annum on capital. Then the portion of the total cost of urban spatial organization expended at s is

$$C(s) = sth(s) + \rho(\theta s)^{(\alpha-1)/\alpha}h(s)^{1/\alpha}$$

The total cost of maintaining a city of radius $\bar{s}$ is

$$T(\bar{s}) = \int_0^{\bar{s}} (sth(s) + \rho(\theta s)^{(\alpha-1)/\alpha} h(s)^{1/\alpha})\, ds \qquad (12.2)$$

If $N(s)$ is the total number of families living within s miles of the CBD, we have

$$N(s) = \int_0^s h(s')\, ds' \qquad (12.3)$$

$$N'(s) = h(s) \qquad (12.4)$$

$$N(0) = 0 \quad \text{and} \quad N(\bar{s}) = N \qquad (12.5)$$

The central planner's problem is to find the urban boundary $\bar{s}$, and $h(s)$, which minimize (12.2) subject to (12.3), (12.4), and (12.5).
Define

$$H(s, h(s), \phi(s)) = -tsh(s) - \rho\,(\theta s)^{(\alpha-1)/\alpha}h(s)^{1/\alpha} + \phi(s)h(s) \qquad (12.6)$$

Pontryagin's maximum principle yields the following first-order conditions:

$$\frac{\partial H}{\partial N} = -\phi' = 0 \qquad (12.7)$$

$$0 = \frac{\partial H}{\partial h} \Rightarrow ts + \frac{1}{\alpha}\rho(\theta s)^{(\alpha-1)/\alpha}h(s)^{(1-\alpha)/\alpha} - \phi = 0 \qquad (12.8)$$

From (12.7), ϕ is a constant; and from (12.8), we obtain

$$h(s) = (\theta s)\left(\frac{\alpha}{\rho}\right)^{\alpha/(1-\alpha)} \{\phi - ts\}^{\alpha/(1-\alpha)} \qquad (12.9)$$

Invoking the transversality condition, we must have $H(\bar{s}, h(\bar{s}), \phi(\bar{s})) = 0$. Using (12.9), we see that this transversality condition implies that

$$\phi = t\bar{s} \qquad (12.10)$$

Using (12.5) and (12.10), we obtain

$$\bar{s} = \left(\frac{N}{\theta}\right)^{(1-\alpha)/(2-\alpha)} t^{1/(2-\alpha)}\left(\frac{\rho}{\alpha}\right)^{\alpha/(2-\alpha)} \left(\frac{2-\alpha}{(1-\alpha)^2}\right)^{(1-\alpha)/(2-\alpha)} \qquad (12.11)$$

A comment is in order at this juncture. Equations similar to (12.9) and (12.10) were obtained by Borukhov using the method of the calculus of variations together with some economic arguments which already seem to force in the operation of free enterprise into the model.² At any rate the costate variable described by (12.10) is obtained here far more transparently than it was by Borukhov and independently of any economic arguments. Equation (12.10) is extremely important for the subsequent discussions and interpretations.

Equation (12.9) yields the net housing (and hence population) density as a function of distance from the CBD. Thus,

$$(\theta s)^{-1} h(s) = f(s) = \left(\frac{\alpha}{\rho}\right)^{\alpha/(1-\alpha)} \{\phi - ts\}^{\alpha/(1-\alpha)}$$

So,

$$f'(s) = -\frac{\alpha t}{1 - \alpha} \left(\frac{\alpha}{\rho}\right)^{\alpha/(\alpha-1)} \{\phi - ts\}^{(2\alpha-1)/(1-\alpha)} < 0$$

and

$$f''(s) \gtreqless 0 \text{ according as } \alpha \gtreqless \tfrac{1}{2}$$

Consequently the net population density curve declines away from the core and may be convex or concave as the share of capital in housing is greater or less than the share of land. Using (12.7), we may interpret (12.9) as the marginal cost of locating an additional family in the city. This cost is constant in an efficient city.

Equation (12.11) is very iteresting in that it contains many (at least intuitively reasonable) facts about the comparative statics of the urban boundary $\bar{s}$. The boundary expands as population increases; $\bar{s}$ contracts as transport cost rises. However, $\bar{s}$ increases with capital cost since only in this way can more land be substituted for capital. The urban boundary $\bar{s}$ is inversely related to θ since the higher θ is, the greater will be the quantity of land available for structures at each location in space and hence the less the need for expansion. These conclusions hold under ceteris paribus qualifications which we have not bothered to state specifically.

Suppose the competitive market is the mechanism by which land is allocated to housing and by which families are located; will the housing density be different from (12.9) and will the radius of the city be different from (12.10)? Further, what are the spatial characteristics of the instruments of land allocation in the case of market mechanism?

Again the answers to these questions can be established in a fairly straightforward but interesting manner. To this end, we introduce the following assumptions about market mechanism.

Assumption 12.1:   Within every belt of width ds, s miles from the core, there is a uniform and competitive price of housing denoted $p(s)$.

Assumption 12.2: All land is publicly owned by the central authority, which rents parcels out to landlords at an annual competitive rental rate to be determined endogenously here. The total annual rental proceeds are then distributed equally among all urbanites. This is additional to the annual wage received for working in the CBD which is uniform for every urbanite. The rent to which we refer here is site rent or location rent.

Assumption 12.3: The goal of every landlord is to maximize profits where housing is produced only with land and capital and no labor, that is, according to equation (12.1).

Assumption 12.4: Transport rate t is a given uniform parameter.

Assumption 12.5: The cost of living borne by every urbanite must be equal at all locations.

The equilibrium solution may be worked out as follows: By Assumptions 12.1 and 12.3, $h(s)$ is determined to maximize, at each s, the expression

$$p(s)h(s) - \rho(\theta s)^{(\alpha-1)/\alpha} \{h(s)\}^{1/\alpha}$$

The first-order condition is that

$$h(s) = (\theta s) \left\{ \frac{\alpha p(s)}{\rho} \right\}^{\alpha/(1-\alpha)} \tag{12.12}$$

However, by Assumption 12.5, for every individual and at every location,

$$p(s) + ts = \phi \quad \text{(constant)} \tag{12.13}$$

And in particular, since $p(\bar{s}) = 0$ (rent at the margin is zero),

$$\phi = t\bar{s} \tag{12.14}$$

Substituting (12.13) for $p(s)$ in (12.12) we have

$$h(s) = \theta s \left\{ \frac{\alpha}{\rho}(\phi - ts) \right\}^{\alpha/(1-\alpha)} \tag{12.15}$$

Equation (12.9) is the same as (12.15), and (12.10) is the same as (12.14). Denote the location rent charged at s by $R(s)$; thus, $R(s)$ is the excess profit made per unit area; so,

$$\theta s \cdot R(s) = p(s)h(s) - \rho(\theta s)^{(\alpha-1)/\alpha}h(s)^{1/\alpha}$$

$$= (\theta s)\rho\left(\frac{1-\alpha}{\alpha}\right)\left\{\frac{\alpha}{\rho}(\phi - ts)\right\}^{1/(1-\alpha)} \tag{12.16}$$

So,

$$R(s) = (1 - \alpha)\left(\frac{\alpha}{\rho}\right)^{\alpha/(1-\alpha)} (\phi - ts)^{1/(1-\alpha)} \tag{12.17}$$

Clearly, from (12.17), we have

$$R'(s) < 0 \quad \text{and} \quad R''(s) > 0$$

Hence the competitive equilibrium rent profile declines away from the core and it is described by a convex curve. So we can conclude by saying that in respect of Model I, any equilibrium process satisfying Assumptions 12.1 through 12.5 is efficient and ensures equal distribution of income. The accomplishment of the latter is one of the prime functions of the local authority in the model.

We make two further remarks in concluding this section. First, although $R'(s)$ is defined at every s, $R''(s)$ may be infinitely large at the boundary $\bar{s}$. Second, if in Model I we insist that the opportunity cost of land is positive, the substantive conclusions—namely, equivalence of optimum and equilibrium solutions, negative gradient of housing density and of location rent, and constancy of marginal cost of location—remain valid although (12.9), (12.10), (12.15), and (12.16) become more complicated in form. Furthermore, when the opportunity cost of land is positive, $\bar{s}$ can no longer be solved in closed form in general.

We can complicate Model I to a considerable degree. We can introduce congestion costs and require land to be allocated to transportation in an efficient way. Such modifications have been carried out by Sheshinski.[9]

What we shall proceed to do now is to explore the spatial properties of an efficient CBD. An implicit assumption here is that the CBD's function is the production of basic (or export) goods which seek and are best established in central locations. Exploiting this assumption, we can regard the optimum geography of an urban place as determinable in two stages: the first stage establishes the structure and boundary of the CBD and the second stage determines optimal housing structure for the urban population using the boundary of the CBD as the "pole" to which all urban households are oriented.

Model IIa: Land Use in the CBD

The foregoing analysis in Model I can readily be extended to the investigation of the CBD in which only production takes place as defined in the last paragraph. Suppose as before that at every distance s, only θs units of land are available for production purposes, the remaining having been preempted for roads, etc. Denote by $x(s)$ the output of the basic urban good at s. We assume further that

$$x(s) = (\theta s)^\alpha n(s)^\beta k(s)^\gamma \qquad \alpha + \beta + \gamma = 1, \alpha > 0, \beta > 0, \gamma > 0, \quad (12.18)$$

where $n(s)$ is the number of workers employed at s and $k(s)$ is the quantity of capital used at s. We further assume that capital is employed to maintain the productivity of labor at a predetermined level λ.[a] Hence we have

$$k(s) = \lambda^\beta(\theta s)^{-\alpha/\gamma}x(s)^{(1-\beta)/\gamma} \qquad (12.19)$$

Total capital cost of urban output when the CBD extends to radius $\bar{s}$ is

$$\rho \int_0^{\bar{s}} \lambda^\beta(\theta s)^{-\alpha/\gamma}x(s)^{(1-\beta)/\gamma}\, ds$$

We assume constant unit transport rate t_1 on goods and t_2 per persons, so the total transport cost on goods—all of which are destined for the urban center for export—is

$$\int_0^{\bar{s}} t_1 s x(s)\, ds = \lambda \int_0^{\bar{s}} t_1 s n(s)\, ds$$

Similarly, the total commuting cost is

$$\lambda^{-1} \int_0^{\bar{s}} t_2 x(s)\, ds$$

We shall assume for simplicity that the opportunity cost of land is zero. We emphasize here that commuting cost is constant per person in the CBD. The total cost of production is given by

$$T(\bar{s},\ x(s)) = \int_0^{\bar{s}} \rho\lambda^\beta(\theta s)^{-\alpha/\gamma}x(s)^{(1-\beta)/\gamma} + (t_1 s + \lambda^{-1}t_2)x(s) \qquad (12.20)$$

The problem then is to find $x(s)$ and $\bar{s}$ which minimize (12.20) subject to

$$X'(s) = x(s) \qquad (12.21)$$

$$X(0) = 0 \qquad X(\bar{s}) = \lambda\bar{N} \qquad (12.22)$$

where $\bar{N}$ is the total number of urban workers and $X(s)$ is the total output produced within s miles of the core.

We have the following first-order conditions for the solution:

$$\phi' = 0 \quad \text{or} \quad \phi = \bar{\phi} \text{ (constant)} \qquad (12.23)$$

$$t_1 s + \lambda^{-1}t_2 + \left\{\frac{1-\beta}{\gamma}\rho\lambda^\beta\right\}\left\{\frac{x(s)}{\theta s}\right\}^{\alpha/\gamma} = \bar{\phi} \qquad (12.24)$$

The transversality condition $H(\bar{s}, x(\bar{s}), \bar{\phi}) = 0$ implies that

---

[a] A possible interpretation of this requirement is that land and capital are the basic inputs into basic production, and that labor is supportive and is required in direct proportion to output.

$$\bar{\phi} = t_1\bar{s} + \lambda^{-1}t_2 \qquad (12.25)$$

Substituting (12.25) back into (12.24), we have

$$\frac{x(s)}{\theta s} = K_1\{t_1(\bar{s} - s)\}^{\gamma/\alpha} \qquad (12.26)$$

where

$$K_1 = (\gamma(1 - \beta)^{-1}\rho^{-1}\lambda^{-\beta})^{\gamma/\alpha}$$

Substituting (12.26) into (12.21), integrating the result from 0 to $\bar{s}$ and equating to $\lambda\bar{N}$, we obtain

$$\bar{s} = \left(\frac{\lambda\bar{N}q}{K_2}\right)^r \qquad (12.27)$$

where

$$K_2 = \alpha^2\theta t_1^{\gamma/\alpha}K_1 \qquad q = (\alpha + \gamma)(2\alpha + \gamma) \qquad r = \alpha/2\alpha + \gamma$$

Thus we have obtained the values of $x(s)$ and $\bar{s}$ explicitly. From (12.26), we can easily see that land use intensity declines away from the center. Again, we can show that, under specific assumptions, the competitive market yields exactly the same solution. For, suppose that each producer at s chooses $x(s)$ at price $p(s)$ so as to maximize profits. Further, suppose we insist that zero profits are made at the margin $\bar{s}$. Finally there should be no inherent locational advantage for the export of $x(s)$. Each producer will in effect seek to maximize $\pi(s)$, given by

$$\pi(s) = p(s)x(s) - \rho\lambda^\beta(\theta s)^{-\alpha/\gamma}x(s)^{(1-\beta)/\gamma} - \lambda^{-1}t_2 x(s) \qquad (12.28)$$

where

$$p(s) + t_1 s = \bar{\phi} \text{ (constant)} \qquad (12.29)$$

The first-order condition requires that

$$\frac{x(s)}{\theta s} = K_1\{p(s) - \lambda^{-1}t_2\}^{\gamma/\alpha} \qquad (12.30)$$

and

$$\pi(\bar{s}) = 0 \Rightarrow \bar{\phi} = t_1\bar{s} + \lambda^{-1}t_2 \Rightarrow p(s) = \lambda^{-1}t_2 + t_1(\bar{s} - s) \qquad (12.31)$$

We have exactly the optimum solution given by (12.23), (12.24), and (12.25), if we substitute for $\bar{\phi}$ in (12.30). Equation (12.28) gives the total location rent at s as $\theta s R(s)$ where, after elementary manipulations,

$$\theta s R(s) = \theta s K_1 \frac{\alpha}{\alpha + \gamma}\{t_1(\bar{s} - s)\}^{(1-\beta)/\alpha} \qquad (12.32)$$

Thus,

$$R'(s) < 0 \quad \text{and} \quad R''(s) > 0$$

Hence, we may say that the equilibrium production and land use pattern is the same as the optimum and that the equilibrium rent profile is a convex declining function of distance.

Model IIb CBD Structure with Congestion Cost

There are many assumptions that may be considered unrealistic in the formulation of production in the CBD as outlined in Model IIb. The absence of congestion function in the transport is one of them. Furthermore, by fixing a priori the quantity of land used in transportation, we create a very specialized problem. There are, however, two principal difficulties in generalizing this formulation. First, if we must incorporate capital in the formulation, then, admitting a congestion function will often result in nonlinear differential equations which may be impossible to solve in closed form. Secondly, the sheer increase in the complexity of the formulation may make it extremely difficult to isolate the influence of the individual variables on the direction of solution. The price of complexity is often a restriction on insight.

A way out of this difficulty is to maintain two assumptions: (i) that capital is used mainly to maintain labor productivity at a predetermined uniform but presumably high level, λ_1 and (ii) that in the production of a basic good there is a fixed man/land ratio λ_2.

The upshot of these two assumptions is that if we postulate a production of the form (12.18), and denote by $L_1(s)$ the quantity of land devoted to the production of goods at s, we can define the quantity of capital used at s as

$$k(s) = \lambda_1^{1/\gamma} \lambda_2^{(1-\beta)/\gamma} L_1(s) \tag{12.33}$$

The congestion cost is defined after Vickrey to be[11]

$$W(s) = \alpha_1 \left[\frac{N(s)}{\theta s - L_1(s)} \right]^{\alpha_2} \quad \alpha_1 > 0 \quad \alpha_2 > 1$$

$$= \alpha_1 \psi(s)^{\alpha_2} \tag{12.34}$$

Here, $N(s)$ is the number of urbanites who work closer than s to the CBD. At every point s,

$$L_1(s) + L_2(s) = \theta s \tag{12.35}$$

where $L_2(s)$ is the quantity of land devoted to transportation. Recall that $N(s)$ is the number of persons who work less than s miles away from the urban center. Thus,

$$N(s) = \int_0^{\bar{s}} \lambda_2 L_1(s') \, ds'$$

or

$$N'(s) = \lambda_2(\theta s - L_2(s))$$

$$N(\bar{s}) = \bar{N} \tag{12.36}$$

Finally, we will assume for this formulation that output is evacuated at zero cost. The total social cost T of maintaining the CBD is

$$T(\bar{s}, \ L_2(s)) = \int_0^{\bar{s}} \{\rho \lambda_1^{1/\gamma} \lambda^{(1-\beta)/\gamma}(\theta s - L_2(s))$$

$$+ \ \alpha_1 \psi(s)^{\alpha_2} N(s) + R_A \theta s\} \, ds \tag{12.37}$$

where $R_A =$ the opportunity cost of land. The central planner's problem is to find $L_2(s)$ and $\bar{s}$ so that (12.37) is minimized subject to (12.36).

We define the Hamiltonian H as

$$H(s, L_2(s), \phi(s)) = -\rho \lambda^{1/\gamma} \lambda_2^{(1-\beta)/\gamma}(\theta s - L_2(s))$$

$$- \ \alpha_1 \psi(s)^{\alpha_2} N(s) - R_A \theta s + \lambda_2 \phi\{\theta s - L_2(s)\} \tag{12.38}$$

and obtain (first-order conditions)

$$\phi' = \alpha_1 \psi(s)^{\alpha_2} + \alpha_1 \alpha_2 \psi(s)^{\alpha_2} = \alpha_1 (1 + \alpha_2) \ \psi(s)^{\alpha_2} \tag{12.39}$$

$$\rho \lambda_1^{1/\gamma} \lambda_2^{(1-\beta)/\gamma} + \alpha_1 \alpha_2 \psi(s)^{\alpha_2+1} - \lambda_2 \phi = 0 \tag{12.40}$$

So, using (12.39) and (12.40), we obtain

$$\psi(s) = \omega_1 s + K \tag{12.41}$$

where $\omega_1 = \lambda_2/\alpha_2 > 0$

$$K = \psi(\bar{s}) - \omega_1 \bar{s} \geqslant 0$$

Combining (12.39), (12.40), and (12.41), we obtain the following differential equation:

$$L_2'(s) = - \frac{\omega_1 + \lambda_2}{\omega_1 s + K} L_2(s) + \frac{\lambda_2 \theta s}{\omega_1 s + K}$$

which yields

$$L_2(s) = \frac{\lambda_2 \theta s}{\omega_1 + \lambda_2} - \frac{\lambda_2 \theta}{(\omega_1 + \lambda_2)(2\omega_1 + \lambda_2)}(\omega_1 s + K)$$

$$+ M^*(\omega_1 s + K)^{-\epsilon_1} \qquad (12.42)$$

where $\qquad \epsilon_1 = \omega_1^{-1}(\omega_1 + \lambda_2) \qquad M^* = \dfrac{\lambda_2 \theta K^{\epsilon_1}}{(\omega_1 + \lambda_2)(2\omega_1 + \lambda_2)}$

$$\epsilon_2 = \omega_1^{-1}(2\omega_1 + \lambda_2)$$

From (12.42), we have

$$L_2'(s) = \frac{\lambda_2 \theta}{\omega_1 + \lambda_2} - \frac{\omega_1 \lambda_2 \theta}{(\omega_1 + \lambda_2)(2\omega_1 + \lambda_2)}$$

$$- \frac{\lambda_2 \theta(\omega_1 + \lambda_2)}{(\omega_1 + \lambda_2)(2\omega_1 + \lambda_2)}\left\{\frac{K}{\omega_1 s + K}\right\}^{\epsilon_2}$$

$$> \frac{\lambda_2 \theta}{\omega_1 + \lambda_2} - \frac{\omega_1 \lambda_2 \theta}{(\omega_1 + \lambda_2)(2\omega_1 + \lambda_2)} - \frac{\lambda_2 \theta(\omega_1 + \lambda_2)}{(\omega_1 + \lambda_2)(2\omega_1 + \lambda_2)}$$

$$= 0$$

Also,

$$L_2''(s) > 0 \qquad (12.43)$$

To obtain the boundary $\bar{s}$ explicitly we evaluate H at $\phi(\bar{s})$, $L_2(\bar{s})$, and $\bar{s}$ and equate the result to zero. However, this transversality condition can no longer be solved for $\bar{s}$ in closed form; and, hence, we cannot ascertain in general the sensitivity of the CBD boundary to variation in the parameters which define congestion, labor productivity, and opportunity cost of land. Nevertheless, this model yields precise information about the quantity of land that should be devoted to transportation to cope with congestion at various points in the CBD and the efficient land use intensity at every point in the CBD as well.

Model IIc: Further Generalization for the CBD

The second of the two assumptions introduced in Model IIb has the effect of linearizing the capital requirement function. Actually, we can remove that assumption of fixed land: labor ratio. The result of such removal is a further difficulty in obtaining a closed-form solution for some variables, but we can still obtain some valuable information as to the properties of the solution. As in Model IIb, write capital requirement as

$$k(s) = \lambda^{-\beta/\gamma} x(s)^{(1-\beta)/\gamma} L(s)^{-\alpha/\gamma}$$

Now, congestion cost may simply be related to cumulative output, since this is proportionate to the number of workers. Thus, in this model:

$$\bar{\alpha}_1 \psi(s)^{\alpha_2} = \bar{\alpha}_1 \left\{ \frac{X(s)}{s - L_1(s)} \right\}^{\alpha_2}$$

where $X(s)$ is the total output at least s miles away from the center. Thus,

$$X'(s) = -x(s) \qquad X(0) = \lambda_1 \bar{N} \qquad X(\bar{s}) = 0 \qquad (12.44)$$

Hence, the total social cost of production in and maintaining the CBD up to a distance of $\bar{s}$ is

$$T = \int_0^{\bar{s}} \left\{ \rho\lambda^{-\beta/\gamma} x(s)^{(1-\beta)/\gamma} L_1(s)^{-\alpha/\gamma} + \bar{\alpha}_1 \psi(s)^{\alpha_2} X(s) + R_A \theta s \right\} ds \qquad (12.45)$$

Again, the planner's objective is to find $\bar{s}$, $x(s)$, and $L_1(s)$ which minimize (12.45) subject to (12.44).

The necessary conditions are as follows (where ϕ is the costate variable):

$$-\phi' = \bar{\alpha}_1(1 + \alpha_2)\psi(s)^{\alpha_2} \qquad (12.46)$$

$$\phi = \rho\lambda^{-\beta} \frac{1 - \beta}{\gamma} x(s)^{\alpha/\gamma} L_1(s)^{-\alpha/\gamma} \qquad (12.47)$$

$$-\frac{\alpha\rho}{\gamma} \lambda^{-\beta/\gamma} x(s)^{(1-\beta)/\gamma} L_1(s)^{-(1-\beta)/\gamma} + \bar{\alpha}_1\alpha_2\psi(s)^{\alpha_2+1} = 0 \qquad (12.48)$$

The equations can be solved explicitly for x/L_1 in terms of $\psi(s)$. Instead of undertaking the solution exercise, we shall proceed with some qualitative interpretations. Here, ϕ' may be interpreted as the optimum rent gradient since ϕ measures the marginal location cost for an additional output. The competitive rent gradient will, on the other hand, be equal to $-\alpha_1\psi(s)^{\alpha_2}$. Thus, competitive process rent $R(s)$ will in general be lower than $\phi(s)$, and the consequent disparity in allocation can be worked out using our previous method. The imposition of toll—(measured as $R(s) - \phi(s)$)—provides at least one means of bringing the equilibrium and the optimum into coincidence.

To summarize, the sequence of models in this section has yielded answers to many critical questions about the characteristics of the efficient disposition of land uses in the urban place. Under fairly stringent conditions, we can describe the efficient spatial structure of housing where capital intensity is allowed to vary over space. We found out, in respect to housing, that the market mechanism yields the same solution where land is publicly owned and the government redistributes revenue from land rent so that urbanites are equally well off. We have provided three CBD models of varying complexity. We have obtained efficient land use intensity as a function of distance with and without congestion effect. In the absence of congestion cost, land use intensity definitely declines away from the core. It is particularly noteworthy that we obtain this result even when the production function has no inherent scale economies. In the absence of congestion cost, the equilibrium and optimum solutions are the same, and, furthermore, the higher the urban population, ceteris paribus, the larger is the CBD. In the presence of congestion, a toll will be required to make the equilibrium solution equal to the optimum.

Critical Remarks and Conclusions

The analysis in the preceding section has revealed some of the important questions that can thoroughly be answered through the new methodology. The approach is normative and many of the locational adjustment processes are often transparently depicted. The major determinants of land use structure that we have studied are accessibility and factor substitutability. There are many good historical reasons that justify this focus.[5] There is also an important empirical reason behind the treatment of labor in the foregoing models. It has often been observed that the productive services offered by the city have the special feature that they involve a relatively high labor input in proportion to output.[1] Further, this high proportion has remained in spite of technological progress. This fact is, in the view of this writer, a strong evidence of the service and the supportive roles of labor in urban output. Such are precisely the roles played by labor in our models. These, then are some of the key virtues of our analysis. It has, however, many shortcomings which are in themselves quite instructive to analyze.

First, the optimum geography discussed here is a "relative optimum" because the framework of the analysis is the partial equilibrium one in which some (otherwise crucial) variables are held constant, and in which attention is restricted to only one urban place.

Secondly, although there is a sense in which one can extract cost-benefit information regarding CBD expansion from the analysis, the whole focus of discussion has been on the cost aspect of land use and production in the CBD. It is in this focus that the major limitation of our attempt lies, for we have not sought the real benefits of the urban form of spatial organization, and it is these benefits that, in comparison to costs, are subtle and elusive and that quite often justify the size and structure of urban spatial organization. It is also the subtlety of the benefits that makes the urban place a very easy target for criticism in terms of "excessive" size, "excessive" congestion, and "excessive" pollution. The key question then is how do these urban benefits arise and how can we ultimately measure them? In the remainder of this section, we shall attempt (from an eclectic view point) to sketch answers to this intriguing question as well as provide some caveats.

The answers to this question call for an understanding of the nature of these benefits. In the view of this writer, the benefits have two components—economic and cultural. Urban places constitute spatial modes for economically effecting the production as well as the exchange of secondary, tertiary, and quarternary outputs. These outputs include industrial goods, tertiary goods, services, and information. In these activities, scale as well as external economies are of importance. The technology of transport and communication influences the degree of concentration and of spatial intensity of the activities. In fact, some recent theoretical studies indicate that even when there are visible negative externalities present in the urban place, taxing the source of such negative externalities would only cause substitution away from the source and towards other inputs without decreasing the size of the city.[4] On the cultural side there are certain public services and facilities that demand large population concentration for support. It has also been claimed that urban structure provides the atmosphere needed for the fast growth and diffusion of innovations.[5]

With regard to the problems analyzed in this chapter, the benefits so far identified are important only to the extent that their magnitude and quality are affected by the internal texture of the land uses in the CBD. We are ignorant about the sensitivity of the benefits to the variations in internal structure. Our analysis is structured on the assumption that commercial and residential land uses must be segregated. In particular, it will be interesting to know conditions under which urban benefits are higher with integrated land uses than with segregated land uses. Mills has considered such a problem, but, again, only from the transport cost side and with very simple production functions.[6] It will also be interesting to know the way in which urban benefits are enhanced through the emergence of multiple activity centers. It is appropriate here to remark that many of the more recent efforts in the direction of constructing multipolar urban models have not provided the needed insight as to the rationale for these centers. What we need in this regard are evolutionary models that depict the optimal growth path of city land uses in such a way that the emergence of multiple centers becomes visible as part of the process of locational adjustment towards optimum or equilibrium. This is probably a very complex idea that may initially be worked out at a verbal level and the various components of which may later be rigorously formulated. One should also point out that a utility formulation cannot, at this stage, provide the answers that we are seeking, since the more fundamental interrelationships existing among the benefit items have yet to be studied.

Two critical notes may then be struck in conclusion. First, future efforts at constructing multicenter models are not likely to be very productive until the nature of benefits generated by unipolar urban structures is clearly understood. Secondly, such an understanding requires the synthesis of various theoretical and empirical findings in urban history, sociology, economics, economic history, political science, and geography. Thus, this is an area in which virtually every social sience must be involved if a deep understanding is to be achieved. And a deep understanding is a prerequisite for valid comprehensive urban policy statements.

Notes

1. K.J. Arrow, 1970, "The Effects of the Price System and Market on Urban Economic Development," in K.J. Arrow, et al. (eds.), *Urban Processes: As Viewed by the Social Sciences*. Washington, D.C.: The Urban Institute.

2. E. Borukhov [1973].

3. A. Dixit [1973].

4. J.V. Henderson [1974a].

5. E. Lampard, 1954, "The History of Cities in the Economically Advanced Areas," *Economic Development and Cultural Change,* vol. 3, 81-136.

6. E.S. Mills [1972b].

7. J.A. Mirrlees [1972].

8. Y. Oron, et al. [1973].

9. E. Sheshinski [1973].

10. R.M. Solow [1973a].

11. W. Vickrey [1965].

13 Optimum and Market Land Rents in the CBD City

David A. Livesey

This paper examines the optimum and market allocations of land within the CBD. It concentrates particularly upon an urban model in which the city consists only of a CBD. The structure and problems of the suburbs are entirely ignored. This is because the work is intended eventually to link up with the work of other authors who have concentrated exclusively upon suburban problems. The object is to construct and solve a realistic model of a CBD in which the profits from an increasing returns industry are maximized, subject to the costs of congestion that arise from the workers' journeys to and from work.

The CBD City

Most of the recent articles on mathematical theories of optimal city size have concentrated upon those aspects of the urban economy that determine the land use pattern in the suburbs. Suburban problems have been studied with the almost total exclusion of those economic activities that take place in the CBD. It is almost as though the new urban economists' believed that urban problems can conveniently be compartmentalized into suburban problems and city-center problems which are individually solvable. The suburban planner, who subscribes to this view, would only consider the CBD insomuch as it determines the inner boundary of the suburbs and dictates the number of people who commute toward the city center through the suburbs. Armed with these few parameters the planner would confidently draw up the socially desirable suburban land use pattern. It is analogous to the economist who believes that economic policy can be divided into short-run and long-run aspects. The optimal short-term economic policy, in this view, is to return the economy to the long-run equilibrium path as quickly as is consistent with short-term constraints. In order to consider the validity of this compartmentalization, it is necessary to consider both the suburbs and the city center before determining the extent to which urban problems can be decomposed.

David A. Livesey is a member of the Department of Applied Economics, University of Cambridge.

Livesey[2] and Sheshinski[6] both used this approach to test the validity of the suburban land use pattern derived by Mills and de Ferranti.[5] A necessary step in their solution was to consider CBD land use when suburban costs are neglected: a complementary problem to that considered by Mills and de Ferranti, which we shall here call the CBD city. The CBD city is considered to be made up entirely of a CBD with all the workers living outside the city limits. Land must be allocated between transportation and business uses so that for a given number of workers, N, social costs are minimized and an optimum radius for the city, ϵ, is determined. All the workers are assumed to travel to and from the city boundary along the radius passing through their place of work.

The CBD city is assumed to be circular with only θ ($\leq 2\pi$) radians of land suitable for either business or transportation purposes. Every point in the city is identified by its distance from the city center, u. This implicitly assumes that one is indifferent between points equidistant from the city center. The number of travelers at a point is denoted by $T(u)$; the amount of land used for transportation by $L_2(u)$; and $L_1(u)$ denotes the land used for business purposes. Since the land on which the city is to be built is assumed to have a social rental value of R_A when used for some other economic activity such as agriculture, we can argue on efficiency grounds that all available land at any radius θu is allocated for either business or transportation purposes. Hence,

$$L_1(u) + L_2(u) = \theta u \tag{13.1}$$

Equally, it is impossible to allocate more than all the available land to a single use. This physical constraint is implied by (13.1) and the following constraints:

$$L_1(u) \geq 0 \quad \text{and} \quad L_2(u) \geq 0 \tag{13.2}$$

Since all the N workers in the CBD live in the suburbs, it follows that

$$T(0) = 0 \quad \text{and} \quad T(\epsilon) = N \tag{13.3}$$

The density of workers on business land in the CBD, $a_c(u)$, is initially assumed to be a constant value, a_c. We will reconsider this assumption later, and consider an economic model that explains the density of workers in the CBD. Armed with this assumption, we can derive an expression for the number of people working in the CBD at a radius u from the city center.

$$N_c(u) = a_c L_1(u) = a_c(\theta u - L_2(u)) \tag{13.4}$$

From our earlier assumption about people's route to work, we can derive the integral equation

$$T(u) = \int_0^u N_c(v) \, dv \tag{13.5}$$

When (13.4) is incorporated, differentiation yields

$$T'(u) = a_c \theta u - a_c L_2(u) \tag{13.6}$$

This completes our description of the CBD city.

Quite obviously, we have greatly simplified the functions of a central business district but the aim has been to capture the key features that will allow us to discuss the problem of traffic congestion. Congestion reduces the speed of traffic flow and increases journey times and operating costs. The costs of congestion are a common feature of many recent papers on urban economics. Most of these have used a formula linking the travel cost, the number of travelers, and the capacity of the road, which was originally suggested by Vickrey[7].

$$p(u) = \bar{p} + \rho_1 \left[\frac{T(u)}{L_2(u)} \right]^{\rho_2} \tag{13.7}$$

where we have assumed that the capacity of a road is solely determined by the amount of land it uses; $\bar{p}$ represents the cost of operating a car plus the time cost of uncongested travel; and the second term reflects the view that congestion costs rise rapidly as road use increases beyond its designed capacity. In most recent work, authors have assumed, for the sake of mathematical simplicity, that $\bar{p} = 0$.

The Optimum CBD City

Before we embark upon market solutions for the CBD city, it is as well to summarize the key features of the socially optimum solution. In the CBD, social costs arise from congestion and from the alternative use value of the land. Hence, total social costs are given by the integral

$$\int_0^\epsilon \left[\rho_1 T(u) C(u)^{\rho_2} + R_A \theta u \right] du \tag{13.8}$$

where $C(u) = T(u)/L_2(u)$. The problem is to choose a city size, ϵ, that will minimize (13.8) but still employ N workers. Full details of the solution are given in an earlier publication (pp. 151-156).[2] Here we only sketch their principal conclusions, since we shall solve a similar but more complex model in a later section.

One can establish that at no point in the CBD city, whatever the value of N and R_A, are the constraints of (13.2) binding. In other words, land is always used for both industrial and transportation purposes. There is, for a given working population N, a minimum city size ϵ_{min}, given by

$$a_c \theta \epsilon_{min}^2 / 2 = N \tag{13.9}$$

and a maximum city size, ϵ_{max}, given by

$$a_c \theta \epsilon_{max}^2 = (\rho_2 + 2)N \tag{13.10}$$

Both of these city sizes are independent of the alternative land rental value R_A.

The allocation of land to transportation purposes is

$$L_2(u) = \frac{\rho_2 \theta u}{\rho_2 + 2} - \frac{\rho_2 \theta (G - \epsilon)}{(\rho_2 + 1)(\rho_2 + 2)} \left[1 - \left(\frac{G - \epsilon}{G - \epsilon + u} \right)^{\rho_2 + 1} \right] \tag{13.11}$$

where G and ϵ are given by

$$R_A \theta \epsilon = \rho_1 \rho_2 \left(\frac{a_c G}{\rho_2} \right)^{\rho_2 + 1} \left[\theta \epsilon - \frac{(\rho_2 + 1)N}{a_c G} \right] \tag{13.12}$$

and (13.11) evaluated at s, since $L_2(\epsilon) = \rho_2 N / a_c G$. We can also show that

$$L_2(u) \leq \frac{\rho_2 \theta u}{\rho_2 + 2} \tag{13.13}$$

because the second term on the right side of (13.11) is always negative.

The implication of these results is that if, as is often assumed, $\rho_2 = 2$, then the ratio of maximum city size to minimum city size is $\sqrt{2}$ to 1. Also the land devoted to transportation is, at every point in the city, less than one-half the total land available.

Mills' Market Model of the CBD

In our search for a satisfactory market model of the CBD city, we begin with the model, outlined by Mills, in which the city exists because there are increasing returns arising from production on a contiguous site.[3] Hence, like Dixit,[1] Mills assumes that the CBD consists mainly of one factory that can be described by the Cobb-Douglass production function:

$$X_1 = A L^\alpha N^\beta K^\gamma \tag{13.14}$$

where $\alpha + \beta + \gamma = H$, the returns to scale. Unless the quality and quantities of the services provided by land are dependent upon its location, we need increasing returns to scale for our CBD city to exist.[a] X_1 is the total output of goods in the CBD and L, N, and K are the total inputs of land, labor, and capital goods used in the production process. All these variables refer, as does the production function itself, to the total inputs and outputs. It follows from our earlier definitions that

$$L = \int_0^\epsilon L_1(u) \, du \tag{13.15}$$

---

[a] A short and lucid account of the reasons for the existence of cities is given by Mills (pp. 5-9).[4]

The second economic activity in our CBD city is transportation which, as Mills recognized, is a sector where a great deal of factor substitution is possible. Clearly, the output of transportation services X_2 could be made to be dependent upon the number of people employed in that sector and the capital investment in transportation equipment. Instead, it is assumed that there is a constant ratio between the amount of land devoted to transportation and the output, measured in the number of passenger miles, that is,

$$L_2(u) = bX_2(u) \tag{13.16}$$

Next, we need to consider the market conditions. Since the city's size is endogenous to our analysis, it is reasonable to assume that workers and investment have to be bid away from alternative uses represented by the exogenously given wage rate w and the rental rate on capital, r. The demand for the output X_1 must depend upon its price, p_1, since it is produced under conditions of increasing returns to scale. We therefore assume that

$$X_1 = a_1 p_1^{-\lambda_1} \tag{13.17}$$

where $\lambda_1 > 1$. Hence, the profit arising from production in the CBD is

$$p_1 X_1 - R_A L - wN - rK \tag{13.18}$$

where the rental value of the land used by the CBD is the exogenously given rate R_A. If we assume that our urban entrepreneur is a profit maximizer, then the marginal productivity conditions imply that

$$\frac{\alpha_1(1 - 1/\lambda_1)}{R_A L} = \frac{\beta(1 - 1/\lambda_1)}{wN} = \frac{\gamma(1 - 1/\lambda_1)}{rK} = \frac{1}{p_1 X_1} \tag{13.19}$$

The total profit, (13.18), becomes

$$p_1 X_1 [1 - (1 - 1/\lambda_1)H] \tag{13.20}$$

which is only nonnegative if

$$H \le \frac{\lambda_1}{\lambda_1 - 1} \tag{13.21}$$

We shall proceed as though (13.21) holds true, which means that the demand for a good produced under conditions of large increasing returns to scale has a low price elasticity.

To solve this market model of the CBD, we begin with the relationship between the amount of land and the number of people employed, given in (13.19) which can be written as

$$\alpha w \int_0^\epsilon N(v) \, dv = \beta R_A \int_0^\epsilon L_1(v) \, dv \tag{13.22}$$

The transportation sector services the total number of workers passing a point, hence (13.16) is

$$L_2(u) = bX_2(u) = b \int_0^u N(v) \, dv \qquad (13.23)$$

which Mills then takes to be

$$L_2(u) = b \frac{\beta R_A}{\alpha w} \int_0^u L_1(v) \, dv \qquad (13.24)$$

Substituting for $L_2(u)$, from (13.24), into equation (13.1) and differentiating with respect to u yields

$$L_1'(u) + \frac{b\beta R_A}{\alpha w} L_1(u) = \theta \qquad (13.25)$$

At the city center there is no land, that is, $L_1(0) = 0$, so the solution of (13.25) may be expressed as

$$L_1(u) = \frac{\theta \alpha w}{b\beta R_A} \left[1 - \exp\left(\frac{-b\beta R_A u}{\alpha w} \right) \right] \qquad (13.26)$$

From these results, Mills (pp. 206-207)[3] draws some fairly strong conclusions about CBD traffic congestion. Before we examine these in any detail, we need to compare the results with those obtained earlier for the optimum CBD.

Some Reservations

We will now critically contrast the results of the previous two sections and find them both to be unsatisfactory in some aspects. It would not normally be unusual to find some descrepancies between socially optimum and market solutions, since we might reasonably hope to reconcile the differences through a system of taxes and subsidies. But here we shall discover that the two models have a few fundamental differences that stem from their specifications. These differences are fairly obvious. In considering the optimum CBD city, we did not discuss the productive side of the CBD at all and, instead, concentrated exclusively upon the choice of transportation land use pattern that minimized social costs. The market model, on the other hand, assumed a fixed land-to-travelers ratio in transportation and concentrated upon the economics of production.

As far as the market model of transportation is concerned, the key assumption is (13.16). When we identify the output of the transportation system as the number of travelers, we see that it implies that

$$C(u) = \frac{T(u)}{L_2(u)} = \frac{1}{b} \qquad (13.27)$$

The effect of this assumption is to reduce our social costs function, (13.8), to

$$\int_0^\epsilon \left[\rho_1 L_2(u) b^{-(\rho_2+1)} + R_A \theta u \right] du \qquad (13.28)$$

subject to (13.3) and (13.6). We have no choice about the level of congestion at different points in the city; we are effectively assuming that it is a constant:

$$T'(u) + a_c b T(u) = a_c \theta u \qquad (13.29)$$

determines $T(u)$ to be

$$T(u) = \frac{\theta}{b} \left[u - \frac{1 - e^{-a_c bu}}{a_c b} \right] \qquad (13.30)$$

assuming that $T(0) = 0$. Given that $T(\epsilon)$ must equal N, (13.30) will determine ϵ, the size of the CBD city. We also now know the land use pattern since (13.27) and (13.30) yield an expression for $L_2(u)$, which in its turn dictates, using assumption (13.1), that

$$L_1(u) = \frac{\theta}{a_c b}(1 - e^{-a_c bu}) \qquad (13.31)$$

Even though we have yet to say anything about production, except that it employs N workers, we have derived an equation that is identical to (13.26) when

$$a_c = \beta R_A / \alpha w \qquad (13.32)$$

We have, however, reduced the problems to their lowest common denominator and, thereby, dictated the level of social costs, as we shall now show.

From the marginal productivity conditions we can derive N, L, and K, while using (13.30), the social costs, (13.28), become

$$\int_0^\epsilon \{ \rho_1 b^{-(\rho_2+1)} b T(u) + R_A \theta u \} du$$

$$= \frac{1}{2} \{ R_A + \rho_1 b^{-(\rho_2+1)} \} \theta \epsilon^2 - \rho_1 N / a_c b^{\rho_2+1} \qquad (13.33)$$

Since, as we have previously established, ϵ is solely a function of N determined by (13.30), the social costs in this version of the CBD city are solely a function of the fixed linear relations between the outputs of production and transportation and their relative inputs of land.

The time has come to take stock of our progress so far. It is obvious from the foregoing discussion that both the optimum and the market models make restrictive assumptions which rob their subsequent analysis of more general conclusions. To assume, as we do for the market model that congestion (the ratio of travelers to land devoted to transportation) is a constant means that our plans for the optimum CBD city are so constrained that the level of total social costs cannot be varied. On the other hand, the assumption for the optimum model, that the land-labor ratio is constant in the production sector regardless of its location, is also restrictive, even though it appears to follow from our market analysis. Some of these difficulties stem from the specification of the production function (13.14) in terms of *total* land devoted to production and the *total* number of workers employed. This yields marginal productivity conditions relating the exogenously given wage rate and land rental rate to the total number of people employed and the total amount of land used in production. A certain amount of hand waving is required to get from equation (13.23) to equation (13.24). It does not necessarily follow, as is there implicitly assumed, that the land-labor ratio is constant throughout the CBD and equal to the aggregate value.

The market analysis neglected to discuss the costs of congestion in the CBD. Even if it is argued that a separate calculation has been done for the transport sector, which has resulted in the fixed congestion parameter approach of equation (13.16), it is not explained who bears these costs. If they are paid by the workers, then the labor force will not be indifferent between the various locations possible for their employment in the CBD. Effectively, each man is paid less the nearer the city center he works. This is of course inconsistent with the assumption of an exogenously determined wage rate. That assumption can only be sustained if the firm pays for each worker's congestion costs. Any payments made by the firm will reduce profits and should appear in the definition of profits, (13.18). We have now arrived at a situation in which the wage rate depends upon the location and hence, since it is cheaper to produce near the edge of the city, land rents will also depend upon location. It is by no means certain therefore that the labor-land ratio will be constant throughout the CBD.

The optimum analysis failed to consider the social profit of production, and concentrated instead upon the social costs of congestion. We will therefore now extend the earlier analysis to include the production sector; and, in particular, the land-labor ratio will be allowed to vary.

Optimum Solution with Production

Here, we wish to consider the allocation of land within the CBD of what Dixit[1] has called the optimum factory town. There is one firm producing a single commodity under increasing returns to scale with the production function specified in (13.14). The problem is to maximize the social benefits of production when weighed against the social costs of congestion. We therefore wish to minimize

$$\int_0^\epsilon \left[\rho_1 T(u) C(u)^{\rho_2} + R_A \theta u + wN + rK - \rho_1 X_1 \right] du \qquad (13.34)$$

subject to the constraints (13.1) and (13.2) on the allocation of land, the definition (13.3) of N, and the demand function (13.17). In (13.34), we have effectively combined the social function (13.8) with the profit function (13.18), except that we have omitted the $R_A L$ term. The social cost of land is now covered by the $R_A \theta u$ term, which costs not only land used for production but also the land used for transportation. It was yet another unsatisfactory feature of the market model that no one paid for the transportation system's use of land.

For every point in the CBD we must choose the amount of land to devote to transportation, $L_2(u)$, and this will determine the amount of land available for productive uses. We also need to decide how many men will work at a particular location—or, to put it another way, the optimum land-labor ratio, $a_c(u)$, where

$$N_c(u) = a_c(u) L_1(u) \qquad (13.35)$$

At the edge of the CBD city, we have to have accumulated sufficient land and labor for the aggregate marginal social efficiency conditions to hold. We say "the edge of the city" because we have only specified an aggregate production function. This has rather drastic consequences without further assumptions.

Consider the following solution, which is optimal for the problem set out above. The CBD is entirely devoted to productive activity, there is no land used for transportation, and so

$$L = \int_0^\epsilon L_1(u) = \tfrac{1}{2} \theta \epsilon^2 \qquad (13.36)$$

At every point, except the edge of the city ($u = \epsilon$), no workers are employed and hence

$$a_c(u) = 0 \quad \text{for all} \quad u \, \varepsilon \, [0, \epsilon] \qquad (13.37)$$

But at the edge of the city,

$$a_c(\epsilon) = N/\theta\epsilon \qquad (13.38)$$

so that

$$T(\epsilon) = \int_0^\epsilon a_c(u) L_1(u) \, du = N \qquad (13.39)$$

No one travels within the CBD; but, at the edge, the factory town employs N workers. This may be the optimum solution but it is a very limiting world. It implies that N men working on the periphery of a large plant are just as efficient as the same number of people spread around the site. If we are interested in the distribution of workers throughout the CBD, then there are two alternatives open to us.

The first approach is to assume an aggregate technology which determines the input ratios and these land-labor, and land-capital relations must hold at every point in the city. This is very like our earlier analysis. Once again, a_c is a constant, but it is no longer defined as in equation (13.32)—the formula takes into account the costs of congestion. We shall now formally specify the problem as:

$$\text{minimize} \quad wN + rK - p_1X_1 + \int_0^\epsilon \left[p_1T(u)C(u)^{p_2} + R_A\theta u \right] du \quad (13.40)$$

subject to

$$T'(u) = a_c(\theta u - L_2(u)) \qquad (13.41)$$

$$N = T(\epsilon) \qquad (13.42)$$

$$X_1 = a_1p_1^{-\lambda_1} = AL^\alpha N^\beta K^\gamma \qquad (13.43)$$

$$L = \int_0^\epsilon L_1(u) \, du = \frac{N}{a_c} \qquad (13.44)$$

$$0 \leq L_2(u) \leq \theta u \qquad (13.45)$$

$$C(u) = T(u)/L_2(u) \qquad (13.46)$$

Since $C(u)$ becomes infinite when $L_2(u) = 0$, and $T(u) \neq 0$, no part of the optimally planned CBD city can have zero land allocated for transportation since it would imply infinite social costs. The Hamiltonian, H, for the problem is

$$H = p_1T(u)C(u)^{p_2} + R_A\theta u + [a_c\lambda(u) + \mu(u)][\theta u - L_2(u)]$$

where $\mu(u)$ is the multiplier applying to the remaining part of constraint (13.45), and $\lambda(u)$ is the Lagrangian multiplier for the differential equation (13.41). Given the close similarity with Livesey[2] we can safely assume that $\mu(u) = 0$ for all u.

In fact the whole problem, defined by equations (13.40) to (13.46), can be solved by using the results of the optimum-city model. The principal difference is that the working population of the CBD is endogenous. It can be derived by substituting for K in equation (13.43) the marginal productivity of capital condition, which is identical to the appropriate part of

(13.19). The other marginal conditions are however different since at the CBD boundary the shadow price of land, $\lambda(\epsilon)$, reflecting as it does the decrease in social costs that would arise from devoting extra land to the city, must be equal to the extra rental, $R_A\theta\epsilon$. This is the same transversality condition as equation (13.12). The extra degree of freedom introduced by the condition that

$$\lambda(\epsilon) = w - \frac{\beta(1 - 1/\lambda_1)p_1X_1}{T(\epsilon)} \tag{13.47}$$

in other words the marginal productivity of an extra man must equal his wage rate and the cost of the land needed to employ and transport him.

We thus have a model of the CBD city such that it can be solved completely and the results contrasted with those of Mills market model. One conclusion Mills draws from equation (13.26) is that "in a sufficiently large city, transportation will require nearly all the land near the edge of the CBD." This result is not true for our model since, from equation (13.13), we have an upper bound on the land used for transportation. We note that this result arises in a model in which there is a constant land-labor ratio throughout the CBD, in order to examine the implications of relaxing this assumption we need to take a more disaggregated approach.

A Disaggregated Approach

The second approach to the optimum CBD city problem is to disaggregate the technology so that the production function is location specific, that is,

$$X_1(u) = AL_1(u)^\alpha N_c(u)^\beta K(u)^\gamma \tag{13.48}$$

but price is still determined by total production

$$\int_0^\epsilon X_1(u) \, du = a_1 p_1^{-\lambda_1} \tag{13.49}$$

Our problem is now to

$$\text{minimize} \quad -a_1^{1/\lambda_1} Y(\epsilon)^{1 - 1/\lambda_1} + wT(\epsilon) + rZ + \int_0^\epsilon [p_1 T(u)C(u)^{\rho_2} + R_A\theta u] \, du$$

by choosing $L_2(u)$, $N_c(u)$ and $K(u)$. We have the following differential equations as constraints.

$$T'(u) = N_c(u) \qquad Y'(u) = X_1(u) \qquad Z'(u) = K(u)$$

The Hamiltonian is

$$H = p_1 T(u)C(u)^{\rho_2} + R_A\theta u + \lambda(u)N_c(u) + \phi(u)X_1(u) + \psi(u)K(u)$$

Hence, in the optimal CBD, the following marginal conditions must hold:

$$\frac{\partial H}{\partial L_1(u)} = \rho_1\rho_2 C(u)^{\rho_2+1} + \frac{\phi(u)\alpha X_1(u)}{L_1(u)} = 0 \qquad (13.50)$$

$$\frac{\partial H}{\partial N_c(u)} = \lambda(u) + \frac{\phi(u)\beta X_1(u)}{N_c(u)} = 0 \qquad (13.51)$$

$$\frac{\partial H}{\partial K(u)} = \frac{\phi(u)\gamma X_1(u)}{K(u)} + \psi(u) = 0 \qquad (13.52)$$

$$-\lambda'(u) = \frac{\partial H}{\partial T} = \rho_1(\rho_2 + 1)C^{\rho_2} \qquad (13.53)$$

$$-\phi'(u) = \frac{\partial H}{\partial Y} = 0 \qquad (13.54)$$

$$-\psi'(u) = \frac{\partial H}{\partial K} = 0 \qquad (13.55)$$

We also know from the terminal costs that

$$\lambda(\epsilon) = w, \quad -\phi(\epsilon) = \left(1 - \frac{1}{\lambda_1}\right)\left(\frac{Y(\epsilon)}{a_1}\right)^{1/\lambda_1} \quad \text{and} \quad \psi(u) = r$$

Our marginal productivity conditions are therefore

$$-\phi(u)X_1(u) = \frac{rK(u)}{\gamma} = \frac{\lambda(u)N_c(u)}{\beta} = \frac{\rho_1\rho_2 C(u)^{\rho_2+1}L_1(u)}{\alpha} \qquad (13.56)$$

which can be contrasted with those given in (13.19). The Hamiltonian along the optimal path is

$$H = \rho_1 C(u)^{\rho_2} T(u) + R_A\theta u + \phi(u)X_1(u)[1 - \beta - \gamma]$$

and must be zero when $u = \epsilon$. Hence

$$-R_A\theta\epsilon = \phi(\epsilon)X_1(\epsilon)\left[1 - \beta - \gamma - \frac{\alpha}{\rho_2}\frac{L_2(\epsilon)}{L_1(\epsilon)}\right] \qquad (13.57)$$

which like (13.12) is a transversality condition. It implies that

$$L_2(\epsilon) < \frac{\rho_2\theta\epsilon}{\rho_2 + \alpha/(1 - \beta - \gamma)} \qquad (13.58)$$

for a positive solution to exist.

It is convenient to examine these conditions by first considering how they relate to the chapter by Alao in this volume. He works with constant returns to scale in the production sector and does not consider the revenue from the sales of the product. Instead he assumes that capital is used to maintain labor productivity at a predetermined rate. He is thus able to eliminate a factor of production from the model. If we use the marginal condition relating to capital in equation (13.56) we can rewrite (13.48) as

$$x_1(u) = BL_1(u)^{\alpha/(1-\gamma)}N_c(u)^{\beta/(1-\gamma)} \qquad (13.59)$$

where B depends not only on the constants of the model but also on $Y(\epsilon)$. There is therefore a constant capital-output ratio in the CBD City. It is the one possibility which Alao does not discuss although it arises naturally in our problem. If we also assume a constant land-labor ratio then we have the problem which is identical to Alao's section II(b). Indeed his results correspond to those given in the previous section. The marginal condition for land becomes

$$\frac{-\phi(u)X_1(u)}{L_1(u)} = \frac{\rho_1\rho_2 C^{\rho_2+1} + a_c\lambda(u)}{\alpha + \beta} \qquad (13.60)$$

which when there are constant returns to scale conveniently makes the left side a constant. We can then proceed by differentiating (13.50) with respect to u and the results of the foregoing section then reemerge.

The most general solution to the problem posed by this disaggregated approach appears to be too difficult to derive by analytical techniques. But we have established that the land-labor ratio is only constant throughout the CBD under certain conditions.

Little has been said in the later sections of this chapter about the divergence between the optimum and the market solutions. This is because when we are dealing, as we have been, with a single producer who pays the commuting costs of his workers within the CBD there is no difference between the two solutions. By adopting an increasing returns approach we have explained why the city exists but have not completely captured other important aspects of the CBD. There are still many important unanswered questions to tackle.

Notes

1. A. Dixit, [1973].
2. D.A. Livesey, [1973].
3. E.S. Mills, [1967].
4. E.S. Mills, [1972b].
5. E.S. Mills, and D.M. deFerranti [1971].
6. E. Sheshinski, [1973].
7. W. Vickrey, [1965].

14 Dynamic Aspects of Land Use Pattern in a Growing City

David Pines

Most analytical models of urban structure refer to one-stage allocation problems. Although the recent interesting statistical analysis of Harrison and Kain[4] showed statistically that the existing land use pattern can be explained by a cumulative process, they do not suggest any coherent theoretical framework. Thus, the effect of the pattern of population growth on the structure of resource allocation within the city is entirely disregarded. Existing models implicitly assume either that the resource allocation takes place at one point in time, or that there are no adjustment costs. This approach may be quite satisfactory within the context of positive economics, as Muth[11] (pp. 94-95) argues against Turvey. Within the context of normative economics, however, it may be misleading, as will be demonstrated in this paper.

The main reason why the literature overlooks the time dimension is perhaps the difficulty involved in including both time and space in a continuous optimization model. This requires simultaneous integration over both space and time. One way to overcome this difficulty is to give up the elegancy of analytical models and to define space and/or time discretely. Consider, for instance, the linear programming model of Mills.[8] It can further be extended to include more than one stage without introducing unmanageable difficulties. (See for instance Ben-Shahar el al.[1,2] and Ripper and Varaiya.[15]) Indeed, giving up the analytical approach, which requires continuity, the scope for a priori theorems is very limited. Such models can be used only for simulations based on specific data and sensitivity analysis. However, they are useful at least in demonstrating that some of the conclusions implied by the static models are not necessarily valid in the more realistic planning problems in which time is accounted for.

First, we will propose, for instance, that when the development takes place in stages, the optimal land use pattern need not be continuous. "Leap-frog sprawl" can sometimes be the most efficient pattern. Moreover, in a multistage development plan, "irregular" density gradients

David Pines is a member of the Department of Economics and Center for Urban and Regional Studies, Tel-Aviv University.

The author is indebted to Elhanan Helpman for his very helpful suggestions, and to Jacob Shaya for the numerical calculations.

may be optimal. The density can decrease with accessibility, rather than increase as implied in one-stage optimal allocation problems (see, for example, Pines[14] and Ripper and Varaiya[15]). The evolving structure of the city can be shown to depend on its pattern of growth and the cost of capital.

The role of these two factors is discussed next, with reference to a circular city which is developed in two stages. A criterion for the effect of the pattern of growth and the cost of capital is suggested. It is applied to a simplified two-stage model. This application indicates that the city tends to become more suburbanized as the rate of its growth increases and the cost of capital decreases.

In order to examine the quantitative importance of the rate of growth on the evolving structure of the city, a simplified two-stage model is solved up to algebraic equations. Using the parameters of Mills[9] (pp. 109-115), it comes out that the quantitative effect of introducing the time dimension is negligible. The area of the inner city (that part of the city that is developed during the first stage) decreases by only 1.4 percent, and the area of the city as a whole by only 1.0 percent, if half of the population is located in the second stage while future expenditures are extremely discounted. The author cannot yet report whether this exterme insensitivity results from the specific model or the parameters used in the numeric calculations.

The assumption underlying the models in this chapter is that adjustment costs are infinite. The need for a more general dynamic model with positive but less than infinite adjustment costs is discussed in the concluding remarks of the chapter.

Trade-Off Between Space and Accessibility Through Time

The dilemma of space versus accessibility is one of the main issues in optimal resource allocation within an urban setting. When more space is allocated to a household for residential use, it is possible either to increase the consumption of housing per household with a given amount of nonland resources, or to save nonland resources, given the per capita consumption of housing. However, these benefits are offset by a reduction in accessibility, resulting from the increase in the demand for transportation or the decrease in the supply of transportation.

In a one-period model, the optimal solution of this dilemma implies that the density necessarily declines with distance (if distance is not an argument in the utility function) and that the urban land is continuously developed. But this must not be true in a multiperiod optimal allocation of land, in which case, the trade-off is not only between space and accessibility in one period, but between space in the present versus space in the future and space in the present versus accessibility in the future. In

Table 14-1
Alternative Programs

	Stage 1				Stage 2			
Program	Zone 1	Zone 2	Zone 3	Zones 1 + 2 + 3	Zone 1	Zone 2	Zone 3	Zones 1 + 2 + 3
1	x	x		$2x$	x	x	y	$2x + y$
2	x		x	$2x$	x	y	x	$2x + y$
3		x	x		y	x	x	$2x + y$
4	y			y	y	x	x	$2x + y$
5	y			y	y	y		$2y$
6	y			y	y		y	$2y$
7		y		y	x	y	x	$2x + y$
8		y		y	y	y		$2y$
9		y		y		y	y	$2y$
10			y	y		y	y	$2y$
11			y	y	y		y	$2y$
12			y	y	x	x	y	$2x + y$

order to illustrate the more complex dilemma, consider the following simple allocation problem discussed by Pines[14] and Ohls and Pines.[12]

1. $2x$ housing units are to be allocated in stage 1, and an additional $2x$ housing units are to be allocated in stage 2.

2. There are three zones of equal size, differing in their accessibility to the destinations of trips. The first is the most accessible, the third is the least accessible.

3. Each of the subareas can be developed in either low or high density. Low density means x units per zone. High density means $y = 2x$ units per zone. The lower density (x units per zone) is assumed to be associated with higher welfare and/or lower costs.

4. The following criteria are to be used by the planner:

   (a) It is better when transportation costs at stage 1 are lower.

   (b) It is better when transportation costs at stage 2 are lower.

   (c) It is better when the level of housing welfare at stage 1 is higher.

   (d) It is better when the level of housing welfare at stage 2 is higher.

The set of alternatives is described in Table 14-1.

   According to the above criteria, programs 6 through 12 are inefficient, since each of these is inferior with respect to *all the criteria* relative to at least one of the programs 1 through 5. Consider, for instance, program 7. It implies, on one hand, higher transportation costs than program 4 in both stages; that is, it is inferior to 4 with respect to criteria (a) and (b). On the other hand, the density distribution is the same in 7 and 4 in both stages; therefore, the housing welfare is the same; that is, program 7 is equal to 4

Table 14-2
Advantages (+) and Disadvantages (−) of Program 3

	Criteria			
Relative to Program	(a)	(b)	(c)	(d)
1	−	+	0	0
2	−	+	0	0
4	−	0	+	0
5	−	−	+	+

with respect to criteria (c) and (d). Therefore, program 7 is inferior to program 4.

Programs 1 through 5 are efficient. Each member of any possible pair is better than the other with respect to at least one of the above criteria. Consider, for example, program 3, the relative advantages and disadvantages of which are summarized in Table 14.2.

Within the list of efficient programs, 2 and 3 involve discontinuous development. It can be shown by further analysis that under the above assumptions alternative 2 can never be simultaneously superior to 3 and 4. But 3—the remaining alternative involving discontinuous sprawl—can be the most preferable. It dominates the other four alternatives if the disadvantages associated with higher density are substantial relative to the transportation costs, and if the discount factor is neither extremely high nor extremely low.[12] The discount factor depends on the rate of interest and the time interval between the stages, that is, on the rate of growth.[a]

To sum up, in optimization through time, the optimal shape of the density gradient is affected by the interest rate and the expected pattern of growth of the city. There exist combinations of interest rates and city growth rates which imply irregular shapes of density gradients, which cannot be efficient in one stage planning problems.

Optimal Allocation of Resources Within a Concentric City That Is Developed in Stages

The subject of this section is the effect of a city's rate of growth on its size. To begin with, a fairly general model is elaborated and the effect of the cost of capital and the rate of growth on the resulting size of the city is examined. Unfortunately the effects are too complicated for deriving specific conclu-

---

[a]The above problem can easily be formulated in linear programming terms. There exists a weighting system which will imply not only discontinuous development, but also a nondecreasing density gradient within some portion of the city.[14,15]

sions in the general case. Thus, more restrictive assumptions are introduced and for these restricted cases more conclusive results are derived.

Consider first the problem of Mills and de Ferranti,[10] with the extension of Legey, Ripper, and Varaiya,[6] but assume that the planner takes into account the growth of population in determining the optimal resource allocation. In order to simplify the analysis, the growth is represented by two stages of development. During the first stage, the population of the city is n_1 and during the second stage $n_1 + n_2$.

As in the problem of Mills and de Ferranti, the concentric city is composed of a Central Business District (CBD) where people work surrounded by a suburb where people live. In the present problem, however, the suburb itself is composed of two rings, inner ring and outer ring. The inner ring is developed during the first stage and it accommodates n_1 households. The allocation of resources within it cannot be adjusted during the second stage (that is, the investment in the inner ring is irreversible). The outer ring of the suburb is developed during the second stage and it accommodates n_2 households.

The planner determines the resource allocation within the suburb; the size of the CBD is predetermined. More specifically, the planner determines the allocation of land and a composite factor of production to housing and transportation. Allocating more resources to transportation enables a higher velocity of traffic for a given volume. Allocating more resources to housing enables more households to live closer to the center, thus reducing the average volume of traffic.

The object of the planner is to minimize a weighted sum of the composite factor of production, the quantity of urban land deprived from alternative uses, and the time spent in trips during the two stages of development. The weights depend on the rate of discount, the time lengths of the two stages, and the value of time spent in transportation. Assuming that land is purchased rather than rented, the following weighting system (in which i = discount rate and r = time interval between the two stages) can be defined:

$w^1(i, r)$ inputs of land and capital in the first stage

1   inputs of land and capital in the second stage

$w^2(i, r)$ transportation costs during the first stage

$w^3(i)$ transportation costs during the second stage

By assumption:

$$w_i^1, w_r^1 > 0 \qquad w_i^2, w_r^2 > 0 \qquad w_i^3 < 0$$

This weighting system evaluates each cost item at the beginning of the second stage.

Assume that the value of time spent in trips per unit of distance is $\tau(T(u), N(u))$ where $T(u)$ is the production of transportation capacity u miles from the center and $N(u)$ is the number of households living between u and the boundary of the city. It is assumed that

$$\tau_T < 0, \quad \tau_{TT} > 0, \quad \tau_N > 0, \quad \text{and} \quad T_{NN} > 0$$

where a subscript denotes the variable with respect to which $\tau(\cdot)$ is differentiated.

For the first stage we have

$$\tau(T_1(u), N_1(u)) \quad \text{for} \quad \varepsilon \leq u \leq \bar{u}$$

where $N_i(u)$ = number of households living between u and the boundary of the city during the first stage

ε = radius of the CBD

$\bar{u}$ = radius of the city during the first stage.

For the second stage we have

$$\tau(T_1(u), N_1(u)+n_2) \quad \varepsilon \leq u \leq \bar{u}$$

$$\tau(T_2(u), N_2(u)) \quad \bar{u} \leq u \leq \bar{\bar{u}}$$

where $\bar{\bar{u}}$ is the radius of the city during the second stage.

The production function of transportation is assumed to be homogeneous of the first degree with respect to land and a composite factor of production. One can write:

$$T(u) = t(u)l(u)$$

where $t(u)$ = average product of land in transportation at u

$l(u)$ = land used in the production of transportation at u

By virtue of linear homogeneity, the quantity of the composite factor of production used in producing transportation can be expressed as $f(t(u))l(u)$.

By assumption, each household is supplied by a predetermined quantity of housing and housing is produced by a homogeneous funtion of the first degree in land and a composite factor of production. One can write:

$$N_i(u) = h(u)(l(u) - \theta(u)) \tag{14.1}$$

where $h(u)$ = average density (households per unit of land) at u

$\theta(u)$ = urban land available for development at u

and a dot denotes differentiation with respect to distance.

By virtue of linear homogeneity the composite factor of production used in housing can be expressed as $g(h(u))(\theta(u) - l(u))$.

Total costs incurred during the first stage and the second stage are, respectively,

$$\int_{\varepsilon}^{\bar{u}} \{w^2(i, r)\tau(t_1(u)l_1(u), N_1(u)) + w^1(i, r)[f(t_1(u))l_1(u)$$

$$+ g(h_1(u))(\theta(u) - l_1(u)) + \theta(u)R_A]\}\,du$$

and

$$\int_{\varepsilon}^{\bar{u}} [w^3(i)\tau(t_1(u)l_1(u), N_1(u)) + n_2]\,du + \int_{\varepsilon}^{\bar{u}} [w^3(i)\tau(t_2(u)l_2(u), N_2(u))$$

$$+ f(t_2(u))l_2(u) + g(h_2(u))(\theta(u) - l_2(u)) + \theta(u)R_A]\,du$$

where R_A, the opportunity costs of a unit of land, are assumed to be constant.

Minimization of these two expressions provides the objective function. Thus:

Subject to (14.1) and the boundary conditions[b]

$$N_1(\varepsilon) = n_1 \tag{14.2}$$

$$N_1(\bar{u}) = 0 \tag{14.3}$$

$$N_2(\bar{u}) = n_2 \tag{14.4}$$

$$N_2(\bar{\bar{u}}) = 0 \tag{14.5}$$

we define the Hamiltonian functions in (abbreviated notation) as

$$\mathcal{H} = w^2\tau(t_1l_1, N_1) + w^1[f(t)l_1 + g(h_1)(\theta - l_1) + \theta R_A]$$

$$+ w^3\tau(t_1l_1, N_1+n_2) + \Pi_1(u)h_1(l - \theta) \qquad \varepsilon \leq u \leq \bar{u} \tag{14.6}$$

where $\Pi_1(u)$ is the costate variable associated with $N_1(u)$; and

$$\bar{\mathcal{H}} = w^3\tau(t_2l_2, N_2) + f(t_2)l_2 + g(h_2)(\theta - l_2)$$

$$+ \theta R_A + \Pi_2(u)h_2(l_2 - \theta) \qquad \bar{u} \leq u \leq \bar{\bar{u}} \tag{14.7}$$

where $\Pi_2(u)$ is the costate variable associated with $N_2(u)$.

Given $\bar{u}$, the necessary conditions for optimum allocation are

$$\frac{\partial \bar{\mathcal{H}}}{\partial t_1} = (w^2\tau_T + w^1 f')l_1 + w^3\tau_T l_1 = 0 \tag{14.8}$$

---

[b]This is an extended model of Mills and de Ferranti applied to two stages. Some of the extensions are included in Legey, Ripper and Varaiya.[6] But under the present formulation the functions are not fully specified.

$$\frac{\partial \bar{\mathcal{H}}}{\partial l_1} = w^2 \tau_T t_1 + w^1(f - g) + w^3 \tau_T t_2 + \Pi_1 h_1 = 0 \tag{14.9}$$

$$\frac{\partial \bar{\mathcal{H}}}{\partial h_1} = (w^1 g' - \Pi_1)(\theta - l_1) = 0 \tag{14.10}$$

$$\frac{\partial \bar{\mathcal{H}}}{\partial N_1} = w^2 \tau_N(t_1 l_1, N_1) + w^3 \tau_N(t_1 l_1, N_1 + n_2) = -\dot{\Pi}_1 \tag{14.11}$$

$$\frac{\partial \bar{\mathcal{H}}}{\partial t_2} = (w^3 \tau_T + f')l_2 = 0 \tag{14.12}$$

$$\frac{\partial \bar{\mathcal{H}}}{\partial l_2} = w^3 \tau_T t_2 + f - g + \Pi_2 h_2 \tag{14.13}$$

$$\frac{\partial \bar{\mathcal{H}}}{\partial h_2} = (g' - \Pi_2)(\theta - l_2) = 0 \tag{14.14}$$

$$\frac{\partial \bar{\mathcal{H}}}{\partial N_2} = w^3 \tau_N = -\dot{\Pi}_2 \tag{14.15}$$

and the transversality condition

$$\bar{\mathcal{H}}(\bar{u}) = 0 \tag{14.16}$$

Using equations (14.8) through (14.16) to solve for the optimal t_j, h_j, l_j, and Π_j $(j = 1, 2)$, the first three can be substituted into the objective function to obtain an indirect cost function in $\bar{u}$.

$$F(\bar{u}, i, r) + G(\bar{u}, i, r)$$

The minimization problem can thus be reduced to

$$\min_{\bar{u}} (F + G)$$

The first-order condition of this reduced minimization problem is

$$F_{\bar{u}} + G_{\bar{u}} = 0 \tag{14.17}$$

and the second-order condition is

$$F_{\bar{u}\bar{u}} + G_{\bar{u}\bar{u}} > 0 \tag{14.18}$$

Since by displacement of equilibrium, condition (14.17) does not change, it follows that, for, $K = i, r$,

$$\frac{d\bar{u}}{dK} = \frac{-(F_{\bar{u}K} + G_{\bar{u}K})}{F_{\bar{u}\bar{u}} + G_{\bar{u}\bar{u}}}$$

By the second-order condition, the denominator is positive. Hence, for $K = i, r$,

$$\text{sign } \frac{du}{dK} = - \text{ sign } (F_{\bar{u}K} + G_{\bar{u}K})$$

and it can be verified that

$$F_{\bar{u}} = \mathcal{H}(\bar{u}) \quad \text{and} \quad G_{\bar{u}} - \bar{\bar{\mathcal{H}}}(\bar{u}) \tag{14.19}$$

Hence, for $K = i, r$,

$$\text{sign } \frac{du}{dK} = - \text{ sign } (\bar{\mathcal{H}}_K(\bar{u}) - \bar{\bar{\mathcal{H}}}_K(\bar{u})) \tag{14.20}$$

where $\bar{\mathcal{H}}_K(\bar{u})$ and $\bar{\bar{\mathcal{H}}}_K(\bar{u})$ denote the variations of $\bar{\mathcal{H}}(\bar{u})$ and $\bar{\bar{\mathcal{H}}}(\bar{u})$ with K, where l_j, t_j, h_j, and $\Pi_j (j = 1, 2)$ are at their optimal level. It follows from the boundary conditions (14.3) and (14.4) and from the first-order conditions (14.8) through (14.10) and (14.12) through (14.14) that at $\bar{u}$

$$\bar{\mathcal{H}}_K(\bar{u}) = w_K^2 \tau + w_K^1 [f(t_1)l_1 + g(h_1)(\theta - l_1) + \theta R_A]$$
$$+ w_K^3 \tau + h_1(l_1 - \theta)(\partial \Pi_1/\partial K) \qquad K = i, r$$
$$\bar{\bar{\mathcal{H}}}_K(\bar{u}) = -[w_K^3 \tau + h_2(l_2 - \theta)(\partial \Pi_2/\partial_K)]$$

In order to derive, from the above criterion, unambiguous implications, more restrictive assumptions are required. For instance, assume that there exist fixed proportions between the maximum volume of traffic and the transportation capacity, that is,

$$\frac{N_1 + n_2}{t_1 l_1} = \text{constant} \qquad \frac{N_2}{t_2 l_2} = \text{constant}$$

and if, in addition, $\tau, \tau_T, \tau_N \equiv 0$, the sign of du/dK is unambiguous. This case corresponds to the positive model of Mills.[7]

Under the above restrictive specifications and by virtue of linear homogeneity, one can write

$$f(t) = \psi\left(\frac{N}{l}\right) \qquad \Psi' > 0 \tag{14.21}$$

The Hamiltonian $\bar{\mathcal{H}}$ now becomes

$$\bar{\mathcal{H}} = w^1 \left[\Psi\left(\frac{N_1 + n}{l}\right) l + g(h_1)(\theta - l_1) + \theta R_A \right] + \Pi_1(u)h_1(l - \theta)$$

It follows from the first-order conditions that in this case, for $K = i, r$,

$$\bar{\mathcal{H}}_K(\bar{u}) = \frac{w_K^1 \mathcal{H}(\bar{u})}{w^1} \tag{14.22}$$

One can verify that, under this specification, $\bar{\mathcal{H}}(\bar{u}) > 0.$[c] Since w^1 is the coefficient of future value, $w_K^1 > 0$ for $K = i, r$. Equations (14.20) and (14.22) imply, therefore, that $d\bar{u}/dK < 0$ for $K = i, r$.

To sum up, under the above specification which corresponds to Mills[7] with the modifications of Pines,[13] the city becomes more suburbanized as its rate of growth increases and the cost of capital decreases.

The intuitive explanation of the above result is straightforward. $\bar{\mathcal{H}}(u) > 0$ implies that the boundary of the inner ring is extended beyond its optimal location, where $\bar{\mathcal{H}}(\bar{u}) = 0$. This results in some loss in resource allocation from the point of view of the inner ring. However, as the boundary is extended further away, total costs in the outer ring decline (as long as $\dot{\theta} > 0$; if $\dot{\theta} < 0$, then the costs of the outer ring increase with $\bar{u}$ rather than decrease). The planner extends the boundary $\bar{u}$ as long as the saving in the outer ring is just offset by the loss in the inner ring. However, in carrying this cost benefit analysis, the relative weight of the costs of the inner city increases with i and r. Therefore, as i and r increase, the boundary $\bar{u}$ approaches its optimal location, where $\bar{\mathcal{H}} = 0$, from the point of view of the inner city (that is, $\bar{u}$ tends to decline).

A rapid rate of growth is represented by a small value of r. Thus, a city of a given size of population is likely to be more compact the slower the rate of its growth. The empirical evidence on the relation between density and the rate of growth in the last fifty years is consistent with this result (see, for example Duncan et al.[3]; and Wingo[16] (pp. 23-25). This empirical relation is explained, however, by the introduction of motoric transportation and the increase in car ownership during that period (see, for example, Muth,[11] p. 147; and Wingo[16] pp. 23-25. In terms of the model presented here, this relation must hold even if the rate of motorization does not change. Thus, if the effect of i and r is considerable, such a relation should not be a result of the short sightedness of the planners in the past, but can be justified rationally. Of course, one should be careful in using the model presented here to explain empirical evidence. It is a normative model rather than a positive one.

In order to examine the quantitative importance of the effect of i and r, numeric calculations are carried out for a simplified two-stage model, in which the net residential density h is also predetermined.

Assume that

$$\theta(u) = \bar{\theta}u \qquad \text{and} \qquad T(u) = \gamma l^\alpha(u)K(u)^\beta \qquad \alpha + \beta = 1$$

---

[c] Differentiating the Hamiltonian $\bar{\mathcal{H}}$ with respect to distance and substituting the appropriate first-order conditions into the result yield $\dot{\bar{\mathcal{H}}} = \dot{\theta}[R_A + \Psi - \Psi'(N_2/l)]$. Substituting the first-order conditions into the Hamiltonian $\bar{\mathcal{H}}(u)$ it follows that if $\bar{\mathcal{H}} = 0$ the expression in parentheses is negative and therefore $\dot{\bar{\mathcal{H}}} < 0$ for $\dot{\theta} > 0$. These relations and the transversality condition $\bar{\mathcal{H}}(\bar{u}) = 0$ imply that $\bar{\mathcal{H}}(\bar{u}) > 0$. It follows, therefore, from equations (14.17), (14.18), and (14.19) that $\bar{\mathcal{H}}(\bar{u}) > 0$.

where $T(u)$ = transportation capacity produced

$l(u)$ = land input in the production of transportation capacity

$K(u)$ = quantity of the composite factor of production used in the production of transportation

The quantity of the composite factor of production in a given distance is $[K(u)/l(u)]l(u)$; accordingly, the cost of the composite input in a given distance is

$$r \frac{K(u)}{l(u)} l(u) = \rho_0 \left[\frac{N(u)}{l(u)} \right]^{\rho_1} N(u)$$

where $\rho_0 =$ $(1/b)^{1/\beta} r$

$b =$ per household capacity of transportation

$r =$ price of the composite factor of production

$\rho_1 =$ α/β

Corresponding to this specification, we define

$$w^1(i, r) f(t_1(u)) = w(i, r) \rho_0 \left[\frac{N_1(u) + n_2}{l(u)} \right]^{\rho_1} (N_1(u) + n_2) \quad \varepsilon \leq u \leq \bar{u}$$

and

$$f(t_2(u)) = \rho_0 \left[\frac{N_2(u)}{l_2(u)} \right]^{\rho_1} N_2(u) \quad \bar{u} \leq u \leq \bar{\bar{u}}$$

where $w_i, w_r > 0$. It can be shown that under this specification

$$\text{sign} \, d\bar{u}/di = \text{sign} \, d\bar{u}/dt < 0$$

The first-order conditions imply in this case that

$$\frac{N_2(u)}{l_2(u)} = \frac{\alpha\beta}{\alpha} Q \qquad (14.23)$$

where $Q = H + \bar{\bar{u}} - u$

$$H = \frac{\alpha}{\alpha\beta} \left(\frac{\beta R_A}{\rho_0} \right)^{\beta}$$

Solving the appropriate linear differential equations (see Mills and deFerranti[10]) one obtains

$$N_2(u) = \beta a \bar{\theta} \left[\frac{\beta}{1+a} (Q^{(1+\beta)/\beta} - H^{(1+\beta)/\beta}) + u Q^{1/\beta} - \bar{u} H^{1/\beta} \right] (14.24)$$

Using the boundary conditions for $\bar{u}$, $N_2(\bar{u}) = n_2$, the above function becomes an algebric equation in $\bar{u}$ and $\bar{\bar{u}}$.

Similar relations hold for the inner city:

$$\frac{N_1(u) + n_2}{l_1(u)} = \frac{a\beta}{\alpha} P(u) \tag{14.25}$$

where

$$N_1(u) + n_2 = \quad P(u)^{-\alpha/\beta} \left\{ n_2 P(\bar{u})^{\alpha/\beta} + \frac{\beta^2 a\bar{\theta}}{1+\beta} [P(u)^{(1+\beta)/\beta} - P(\bar{u})^{(1+\beta)/\beta}] \right.$$
$$\left. + \beta a\bar{\theta}[uP(u)^{1/\beta} - \bar{u}P(\bar{u})^{1/\beta}] \right\} \tag{14.26}$$

Using the boundary condition for ε, $N_1(\varepsilon) = n_1$, the above function is reduced to an algebric equation in $\bar{u}$ and K.

Finally, the transversality condition (14.17) is applied to this specific case which, together with the boundary conditions (14.3) through (14.5), implies that

$$w(i, r) \left\{ \frac{\alpha\rho_0}{\beta} \left[\frac{a\beta}{\alpha}(K - \bar{u}) \right]^{1/\beta} \left[\frac{n_2}{a\beta(K - \bar{u})} - \bar{\theta}\bar{u} \right] + \bar{\theta}\bar{u}R_A \right\}$$
$$- \left\{ \frac{\alpha\rho_0}{\beta} \left[\frac{a\beta}{\alpha}(H + \bar{\bar{u}} - \bar{u}) \right]^{1/\beta} \left[\frac{n_2}{a\beta(H + \bar{\bar{u}} - \bar{u})} - \bar{\theta}\bar{u} \right] + \bar{\theta}\bar{u}R_A \right\}$$
$$= 0 \tag{14.27}$$

which results in an equation in $\bar{u}$, $\bar{\bar{u}}$ and K. Thus, we have three algebric equations, (14.24), (14.26), and (14.27), in $\bar{u}$, $\bar{\bar{u}}$ and K.

In order to examine the sensitivity of the city size to the rate of interest, the above system was solved with the parameters of Mills[9] (pp. 114-115). It was verified, however, that for these parameters, $l_2(u)$ reaches its constrained value of θu, that is, there exists a saturated region near the CBD (see Legey, Ripper, and Varaiya[6]). Therefore, an additional equation for ε

$$l_1(\varepsilon) - \theta\varepsilon = 0 \tag{14.28}$$

was introduced.

The result of the sensitivity analysis with respect to $w(i, r)$ is summarized in Table 14.3, where $w = 1$ means either zero time interval between the two stages or zero cost of capital. Hence, the entries for ε, $\bar{u}$, and $\bar{\bar{u}}$ for $w = 1$ correspond to the conventional one-stage planning procedure. $w = \infty$ represents infinite time interval or cost of capital.

As expected a priori, the sizes of both the inner city and the city as a whole decline continuously with the cost of capital and the length of the time interval between the stages, but both are extremely insensitive. The range of change of the area of the inner city is about 1.4 percent and that of the city as a whole is within 1.0 percent.

Table 14-3
Sensitivity Analysis with Respect to $w(i, r)$

$w(i, r)$	ε	$\bar{u}$ (miles)	$\bar{\bar{u}}$ (miles)
1	2.582	6.044	7.077
2	2.566	6.022	7.057
10	2.555	6.005	7.044
∞	2.555	6.001	7.040

A sensitivity analysis is carried out now to verify whether this rigidity results from the specific parameters used in the calculations.

Concluding Remarks

We have argued in this chapter that the pattern of growth of the city affects its optimal land use pattern. Moreover, some implications of the static approach to optimal resource allocation within an urban setting need not be valid in a dynamic context. For instance, optimal resource allocation through time does not necessarily imply that discontinuous development is inefficient. Nor does it imply any specific regular density gradient. But as a matter of fact, it is not the introduction of time per se which makes the difference; what makes the problem dynamic is the dependence of future optimal decision on present resource allocation.

In the two illustrations presented here, this dependence results from the absolute irreversibility of the allocation determined in the first stage. Thus, in the first illustration, the density cannot be changed once a subarea is built up. In the second illustration, the production of transportation and housing cannot be modified in the second stage. However, the dependence of future outcomes on current allocation is not only a result of absolute irreversibility, like the one embodied in the above two illustrations. Such dependence is implied whenever there are positive adjustment costs. Irreversibility is just an extreme case of prohibitively high adjustment costs. The existence of adjustment costs rather than the inclusion of the time dimension per se is what makes the difference between static and dynamic analysis—for if there are no costs of adjustment, any stage of development can be handled independently of future needs.

A more realistic approach must allow for adjustments at less than prohibitively high costs. The model should allow for demolition and renewal, the construction of highways and subways, etc. Introducing "reasonable" adjustment costs in analytical models seems to involve some difficulties, although it is not difficult to incorporate demolition and renewal in a model where both location and time are discretely defined.[1,2,15] Demolition and renewal are associated with fixed cost elements, and therefore with decreasing average costs as a function of the adjustment.

Elsewhere[5] we have tried to characterize the dynamic pattern of optimal resource allocation within an urban setting. We minimized transportation and housing costs through time. Time was defined continuously, and space was defined discretely. Thus we minimized a sum (over all subareas) of integrals (over time) of housing and transportation costs. Cost of housing was represented by $g(H_i h_i)$, where H denoted the housing stock in subarea i and $h_i = \dot{H}_i$. Increasing marginal costs of adjustment were represented by $g_{h_i h_i} > 0$. Decreasing marginal adjustment costs were represented by $g_{h_i h_i} < 0$. Assuming increasing marginal costs of adjustment, we succeeded in characterizing the growth pattern, and showed that the evolving land use pattern depends crucially on the pattern of growth of the population. Moreover, the dynamic pattern of land use changes through time is definitely different from what is implied in a comparative static analysis. But the assumption of increasing marginal costs of adjustment is somewhat unrealistic in view of the fixed cost element involved in demolition. Assuming decreasing marginal costs of adjustment, we failed to fully characterize the evolving land use pattern. This area, I believe, calls for additional research.

Notes

1. H. Ben-Shahar et al. [1969].

2. H. Ben-Shahar et al. [1971].

3. B. Duncan, G. Sabagh, and D. van Arsdol, Jr., 1962, "Patterns of City Growth," *The American Journal of Sociology*, vol. 67, 418-429.

4. D. Harrison, Jr. and J.F. Kain, 1974, "Cumulative Urban Growth and Urban Density Function," *Journal of Urban Economics*, vol. 1, 61-98.

5. O. Hochman and D. Pines [1973].

6. L. Legey, M. Ripper, and P. Varaiya [1973].

7. E.S. Mills [1967].

8. E.S. Mills [1972a].

9. E.S. Mills [1972b].

10. E.S. Mills and D.M. deFerranti [1971].

11. R.F. Muth [1969].

12. J.C. Ohls and D. Pines [1975].

13. D. Pines [1970a].

14. D. Pines [1970b].
15. M. Ripper and P. Varaiya [1974].
16. L. Wingo, Jr. [1961b].

15

A Vintage Model with Housing Production

Richard F. Muth

One of the most frequently heard criticisms of economic models of urban residential land use is that they neglect the durability of residential real estate. Such criticism is motivated in part, perhaps, by a misguided desire for descriptive realism of assumptions rather than by limitations in the conformity of the implications of urban economic models to real world phenomena. By and large, current spatial models of urban residential land use which treat housing as nondurable agree rather well with patterns of urban population distribution in U.S. cities. Their principal defect, in this author's judgement, is that they rather substantially underestimate the land area occupied by cities and thus overestimate average population densities.[7] Regardless of their spatial aspects, however, urban housing markets exhibit interesting regularities associated with the age of dwellings. Understanding such regularities would be greatly facilitated by an explicit theory of the durability of residential structures.

One such theory has been proposed in an earlier paper,[6] and the author is currently engaged in some empirical testing of it. There, particular attention was paid to the effects of in-migration of a lower relative income group on urban housing markets. At the same time, attention was concentrated on the characteristics of dwellings as they age, and little explicit attention was given to the production of housing services when residential structures are durable. This paper is an elaboration of our earlier one, and gives much more attention to housing production. Doing so yields interesting new implications regarding the effect of age of dwellings upon the intensity of urban residential land use. However, here, as earlier, explicit consideration of spatial aspects of urban housing markets is neglected. For analytic simplicity we make certain drastic assumptions, namely that production functions are Cobb-Douglas and that the market is in a steady state characterized by constant growth rates of all variables. Indeed, explicit analytic solutions would be impossible without such simplifications.

Most of our earlier conclusions regarding the characteristics of dwelling units associated with their age at any moment and their changes over time apply in this extended version of the model. These are developed below and

Richard F. Muth is a member of the Department of Economics, Stanford University.

The author is grateful for the financial support of the Domestic Studies Program of the Hoover Institution.

245

summarized in the section following, where some new implications regarding rent-to-value ratios for dwellings and their depreciation rates over time are discussed as well. Some implications of durability for the intensity of urban residential land use are also derived. As in nondurable models, dwelling unit density varies inversely with income and directly with land rentals, but the output of housing services per unit of land depends only upon the level of land rentals in relation to nonland costs of producing housing services. Dwelling unit density increases or decreases with age depending upon whether the rate of growth of housing demand resulting from income growth exceeds the rate of growth of land rentals. So long as the latter exceeds the growth rate of construction costs, however, the output of housing services per unit of land is likely to decline with age of dwelling.

We will next consider conditions of equilibrium in the local urban land market and solve for the level of urban land rentals and their rate of growth over time. The same section will also consider the level of aggregate population density and its relation to population density in newly built units, and show that the former may either be greater or smaller than the latter depending upon the relative values of certain given conditions. Finally, the levels of urban land rentals and population densities implied by the durable model of housing relative to those implied by the corresponding nondurable model are compared. In principle, the nondurable model may either over- or underpredict these relative to the durable model. The calculations presented in the final section of the chapter are based upon what seem empirically sensible values for the typical U.S. city, and imply that the durable model predicts aggregate population densities which are about one-fifth greater than the nondurable model.

An Extended Model of Durable Housing

The earlier version of our model paid little attention to the production of housing, assuming merely that durable assets were purchased at a given unit price. Here, explicit consideration is given to the inputs of nonland capital per dwelling, k_τ, and land per dwelling, l_τ, at time τ when the structure is built. Housing producers also make current expenditures for maintenance and other purposes, $m(t)$, over the life of the dwelling. In addition to incurring unit costs for nonland capital, $N(\tau)$, at the time of construction, producers pay unit land rentals, $r(t)$; unit prices for current inputs, $s(t)$; and property taxes at the rate θ on the value of the dwelling over its life $\tau \le t \le \tau + T$, where T is the age at which the dwelling is removed from the housing stock. In its most general formulation, the problem considered would be extremely complex analytically, which gives rise to two simplifying assumptions. The first is that the flow of housing services from a dwelling, $q_\tau(t)$, is given by the Cobb-Douglas function, with constant returns to scale. Also, current nonland capital inputs, $k_\tau(t)$, are assumed to decline at a constant relative rate in physical terms per unit time, δ, so

$$q_\tau(t) = e^{-a\delta(t-\tau)} k_\tau^a l_\tau^b m(t)^c \tag{15.1}$$

with $a + b + c = 1$. Secondly, we assume a dynamic steady-state equilibrium where all variables grow at constant relative rates over time.

The value of a dwelling to its developer at the time of its construction is given by

$$V(\tau) = W_\tau(\tau) - k_\tau N(\tau) - l_\tau \int_\tau^{\tau+T} r(t) e^{-i(t-\tau)}\,dt + e^{-iT} V(\tau + T) \tag{15.2}$$

And $W_\tau(t)$, the present value of discounted income from the dwelling, is given recursively by

$$W_\tau(t) = \int_t^{\tau+T} R_\tau(v) e^{-i(v-t)}\,dv - \theta \int_t^{\tau+T} W_\tau(v) e^{-i(v-t)}\,dv \tag{15.3}$$

Here,

$R_\tau(t) =$ the rental value of the dwelling net of current expenditure but gross of property taxes

$i =$ the rate of future payments and receipts discounted by the developer.

As formulated in (15.2) and (15.3), the developer, in essence, leases the land upon which the dwelling is built and is responsible for the property taxes on the dwelling during the period of his lease. At the end of his lease, the land is redeveloped, and the subsequent developer pays the property taxes on the land. Land rentals, $r(t)$, are thus net of taxes.

Differentiating (15.2) gives us

$$W_\tau(t) = -R_\tau(t) + (i + \theta)W_\tau(t)$$

so

$$W_\tau(t) = e^{(i+\theta)t}\left[C - \int_{t_0}^t R_\tau(v) e^{-(i+\theta)v}\,dv \right]$$

When replaced, $W_\tau(\tau + T) = 0$, which implies that

$$W_\tau(t) = \int_t^{\tau+T} R_\tau(v) \exp[-(i + \theta)(v - t)]\,dv \tag{15.4}$$

Rentals net of current expenditures are gross rentals, $G_\tau(t)$, less current expenditures, $M(t) = s(t)m(t)$. As shown earlier[6] (pp. 142-145), a unit substitution elasticity of housing for other consumption implies

$$G_\tau(t) = \alpha y(t)^\beta \left\{ 1 + \ln \left[\frac{q_\tau(t)}{\hat{q}(t)} \right] \right\}$$

$$= \alpha y(\tau)^\beta \left\{ 1 + \ln \left[\frac{q_\tau(t)}{\hat{q}(t)} \right] \right\} e^{\beta \omega (t - \tau)} \qquad (15.5)$$

where $y =$ income per household

$\beta =$ the income elasticity of housing demand

$\omega =$ the growth rate of income

$\hat{q}(t) =$ the size of dwelling which yields the maximum unit rental

Maximizing $R_\tau(t)$ implies that

$$\frac{\partial R_\tau(t)}{\partial m(t)} = G_q(q_m - s) = 0 \quad \text{or} \quad m(t) = c\alpha y(t)^\beta s(t)^{-1} \qquad (15.6)$$

Thus,

$$R_\tau(t) = \alpha y(t)^\beta \left\{ (1 - c) + \ln \left[\frac{q_\tau(t)}{\hat{q}(t)} \right] \right\} \qquad (15.7)$$

Substituting (15.4) into (15.2), and assuming stationarity, or $V(\tau) = V(\tau + T) = V$, we have

$$V = \left(\frac{1}{1 - e^{-iT}} \right) \left\{ \int_\tau^{\tau+T} R_\tau(v) \exp[- (i + \theta)(t - \tau)] dt \right.$$

$$\left. - k_\tau N(\tau) - l_\tau \int_\tau^{\tau+T} r(t) \exp[- i(t - \tau)] dt \right\}$$

with $R_\tau(t)$ given by (15.7). The producer chooses k_τ, l_τ, and T so as to maximize V. It is further assumed that competition among producers implies $V_{max} = 0$. Differentiating V with respect to k_τ, equating to zero, and solving, yields

$$k_\tau = a\alpha y(\tau)^\beta [d_N N(\tau)]^{-1}$$

where

$$d_N = \frac{(i + \theta - \beta\omega)}{1 - \exp[-(i + \theta - \beta\omega)T]} \qquad (15.9)$$

Similarly,

$$l_\tau = b\alpha y(\tau)^\beta \left[\frac{d_N r(\tau)}{d_r}\right]^{-1}$$

where

$$d_r = \frac{(i - \rho)}{1 - e^{-(i-\rho)T}} \tag{15.10}$$

assuming that rentals per unit of land grow at a constant relative rate ρ. Since the discounted present value of future land rentals equals $r(\tau)/(i - \rho)$, the land cost variable in (15.10) may be interpreted as that fraction of this discounted present value attributed to the life of the dwelling (with an exponential weight) multiplied by the same discount rate which converts nonland capital expenditure to its annual rent cost.

The rate of flow of housing services per dwelling may now be determined by substituting (15.6), (15.9), and (15.10) into (15.1), yielding

$$q_\tau(t) = q_\tau(\tau) \exp\{[c(\beta\omega - \sigma) - a\delta](t - \tau)\} \tag{15.11}$$

where σ is the annual rate of increase in the unit price of current inputs, and

$$q_\tau(\tau) = \alpha y(\tau)^\beta p_\tau(\tau)^{-1} \tag{15.12}$$

Here the unit price of housing services of newly built dwellings has a familiar Cobb-Douglas form,

$$p_\tau(\tau) = \left[\frac{d_N^{a+b}}{a^a b^b c^c d_r^b}\right] N(\tau)^a r(\tau)^b s(\tau)^c = p_0(0)e^{\lambda\tau} \tag{15.13}$$

where $\lambda = a\nu + b\rho + c\sigma$, with ν being the annual rate of growth in the unit price of nonland capital inputs or construction costs. Thus, the rental value per unit of services from newly built dwellings is proportional to the weighted geometric mean of the implicit rental rates of nonland capital and land and of the price of current inputs, the weights being the exponents of the production function for housing services. Similarly, the growth rate of this new rental value is an arithmetically weighted average of the growth rates of input prices.

The third decision of the producer is the length of life of dwellings. Differentiating (15.8) with respect to T gives

$$\frac{\partial V}{\partial T} = \frac{-ie^{-iT}V}{(1 - e^{-iT})} + \left(\frac{1}{1 - e^{-iT}}\right)\{R_\tau(\tau + T)e^{-(i+\theta)T} - l_\tau r(\tau + T)e^{-iT}\}$$

$$= 0 \tag{15.14}$$

When evaluated at $V = 0$, postponing replacement costs nothing, so replacement occurs once the net rental of the dwelling discounted for property tax payments equals the opportunity cost of the land on which it is built. Substituting (15.11) and $y(t) = y(\tau) \exp[\omega(t - \tau)]$ into (15.7), then the resulting expression and $r(t) = r(\tau) \exp[\rho(t - \tau)]$ into (15.14) yields

$$\ln\left[\frac{q_\tau(\tau)}{\hat{q}(\tau + T)}\right] = -(1 - c) - [c(\beta\omega - \sigma) - a\delta]T$$

$$+ \frac{bd_r}{d_N} \exp[-(\beta\omega - \theta - \rho)T] \qquad (15.15)$$

Now, where $\hat{p}(t)$ is the maximum price per unit of housing services or the price per unit of the optimal size dwelling, from (15.5) and (15.12) we get

$$\hat{p}(\tau + T)\hat{q}(\tau + T) = \alpha y(\tau + T)^\beta = p_\tau(\tau)q_\tau(\tau)e^{\beta\omega T}$$

so, using (15.15),

$$\hat{p}(\tau + T) = p_{\tau+T}(\tau + T)\exp\left[-(1 - c) + \psi T + \frac{bd_r}{d_N}e^{-(\beta\omega - \theta - \rho)T}\right]$$

where $\psi = a(\delta + \beta\omega - v) + b(\beta\omega - \rho)$. Hence, $\hat{p}(t) = \hat{p}_0\, e^{\lambda t}$ for constant T, and

$$\hat{q}(t) = \alpha y(t)^\beta p(t)^{-1} = \hat{q}_0 e^{(\beta\omega - \lambda)t} \qquad (15.16)$$

Using (15.11), (15.12), (15.16),

$$\frac{q_\tau(t)}{\hat{q}(t)} = \left[\frac{\hat{p}(\tau)}{p_\tau(\tau)}\right]e^{-\psi(t-\tau)} \qquad (15.17)$$

and from (15.7), where $u = t - \tau$,

$$R_\tau(t) = \alpha y(t)^\beta\left[\psi(T - u) + \frac{bd_r}{d_N}\exp\langle-(\beta\omega - \theta - \rho)T\rangle\right] \qquad (15.18)$$

The rest of the solution is easily obtained, though with some rather tedious manipulation which we supress. Substituting (15.18) into (15.4), gives us

$$W_\tau(t) = \frac{\alpha y(t)^\beta}{i + \theta - \beta\omega}\left\{\psi(T - u) - \left[\frac{1 - \exp\langle-(i + \theta - \beta\omega)(T - u)\rangle}{i + \theta - \beta\omega}\right]\right.$$

$$\cdot\left.\left[\psi - b(i - \rho)\left(\frac{1 - \exp\langle-(i + \theta - \beta\omega)T\rangle}{\exp\langle\beta\omega - \theta - \rho)T\rangle - \exp\langle-(i + \theta - \beta\omega)T\rangle}\right)\right]\right\} \qquad (15.19)$$

Substituting (15.19) with $u = 0$ into (15.2) then gives

$$V = \frac{\alpha y(t)^\beta F(T)}{(1 - e^{-iT})(i + \theta - \beta\omega)}$$

where

$$F(T) = \psi T - \left(\frac{1 - \exp\langle-(i + \theta - \beta\omega)T\rangle}{i + \theta - \beta\omega}\right) \times$$

$$\left[\chi - b(i - \rho)\left(\frac{1 - \exp\langle-(i + \theta - \beta\omega)T\rangle}{\exp\langle(\beta\omega - \theta - \rho)T\rangle - \exp\langle-(i + \theta - \beta\omega)T\rangle}\right)\right] \quad (15.20)$$

where $\chi = \alpha(i + \theta + \delta - \nu) + b(i + \theta - \rho)$. Thus, $V = 0$ implies $F(T) = 0$. As in the simpler version of the vintage model, the root of $F(T)$ can be determined by iterative calculation. This root is, of course, a constant for given parameters of the production function and constant growth, discount, and tax rates.

Relation of Dwelling Unit Characteristics to Age

The model and solution derived in the foregoing section differ in detail and analytic complexity from the early version but yield essentially similar results. In particular, the demand function for new dwellings and the demand functions for the various inputs are of essentially the same form as the demand function for housing services. Furthermore, under the assumption of constant growth rates of income and prices of inputs into the production of housing, the size of new dwellings, the size of dwelling bringing the maximum rental rate per unit, and this maximum price all grow at constant relative rates over time. This section will analyze the variation of certain characteristics of the housing stock and residential land use with age of dwelling. The following section will consider characteristics of housing market equilibrium and compare these with a model of the housing market which neglects durability.

From $G_t(u) = R_t(u) + M(t)$ and (15.6) and (15.18), the gross rental value of (housing expenditure on) dwellings of different ages is

$$G_t(u) = \alpha y(t)^\beta \left\{\psi(T - u) + \frac{bd_r}{d_N} \exp[-(\beta\omega - \theta - \rho)T] + c\right\} \quad (15.21)$$

This also resembles our earlier result, the principal difference being that rentals do not decline to zero as a dwelling approaches its replacement time. Rather they approach a positive amount sufficient to cover current expenditure on the dwelling plus an amount to cover a pro rata share of land value. Gross rentals still decline at a constant rate with age, however, in the more complicated model here. The present value of discounted future net rentals, or a dwelling's value, $W_t(u)$, is, of course, given by (15.19). From it, the rate of decline in value at a given time is readily calculated. Thus, rent-to-value ratios and depreciation rates in value terms may be readily calculated. Examples of such ratios implied by the model will be shown in the final section of the chapter. Finally, that age of dwelling, $\hat{u}$, at which it is of the optimal current size is determined by setting (15.17) equal to one; doing so, we obtain

$$\hat{u} = T - \frac{\left\{(1 - c) - \dfrac{bd_r}{d_N}\exp[-(\beta\omega - \theta - \rho)T]\right\}}{\psi} \tag{15.22}$$

Unlike the simpler version of my model, the more complicated version here has certain implications for residential land use in relation to the age of dwellings built upon it. Substituting $y(t) = y(\tau)\exp[\omega(t - \tau)]$ and $r(t) = r(\tau)\exp[\rho(t - \tau)]$ into (14.10), dwelling unit density is

$$l_t(u)^{-1} = \frac{d_N}{b\alpha d_r}y(t)^{-\beta}r(t)e^{(\beta\omega - \rho)u} \tag{15.23}$$

Not surprisingly, dwelling unit density varies inversely with income and directly with land rentals. Whether older dwellings are more densely built or not depends upon the rate of growth of land rentals in relation to the growth in housing demand resulting from increases in income. Where the former is small, as it may be in areas closer to the city center, land would indeed be more densely built upon the older the dwelling. However, in suburban areas where land rentals are growing more rapidly the reverse may well be true.

The intensity of residential land use may also be characterized by the rate of flow of housing services per unit of land. From (15.11) and (15.12),

$$q_t(u) = \alpha_y(t)^{\beta}p_t(t)^{-1}e^{-\psi u}$$

so multiplying by (15.23),[a]

$$(q/l)_t\,(u) = (q/l)_t\,(0)e^{-\phi u} \tag{15.24}$$

where

$$\left(\frac{q}{l}\right)_t(0) = \frac{a^ac^cd_N^cN(t)^{-a}s(t)^{-c}r(t)^{1-b}}{b^{1-b}d_r^{1-b}}$$

and

$$\phi = a(\delta + \rho - \nu) - c(\beta\omega - \rho)$$

If, as seems likely, current expenditures are a small fraction of the total associated with housing, the variation of (15.24) with age of dwelling depends upon the rates of physical deterioration of nonland capital with age

---

[a] The value of housing output per unit of land, of course, is obtained by multiplying (15.21) by (15.23).

and the growth rates of land rentals and unit construction costs. Since $\delta \geq 0$, if land rentals grow more rapidly than construction costs over time, newer dwellings would give off a larger flow of housing services per acre per unit time than older ones.

Market Equilibrium

To this point, the level and growth rates of factor prices have been considered as given. It seems perfectly reasonable to take the rate of income growth as well as the growth rate of unit construction costs and current input prices as given by the larger economy in which a local housing market is embedded. Surely, though, land as an input is specific to this market—that is, is in less than infinitely elastic supply to it. In addition, the rate of population growth may well depend upon the growth of housing prices there. This section, then, will inquire into how the rental value of land and its rate of growth are determined in the local market. We will, however, abstract from the much more difficult problem of the spatial structure of this market.

Let the aggregate quantity of land supplied to the market, $\bar{L}(t)$, grow exogenously at the rate ζ per unit time and depend as well on the level of residential land rentals:

$$\bar{L}(t) = \bar{L}_0 e^{\zeta t} \left[r(t)/r_0 \right]^\gamma = \bar{L}_0 e^{(\zeta + \gamma \rho)t} \tag{15.25}$$

The quantity of land built upon at any moment of time is $L_t = L_0 e^{\xi t}$; so,

$$\bar{L}(t) = \int_{t-T}^{t} L_\tau \, d\tau = \frac{L_0(1 - e^{-\xi T})}{\xi} e^{\xi t} \tag{15.26}$$

Thus, $\xi = \zeta + \gamma \rho$ and $L_t / \bar{L}(t) = \xi/(1 - e^{-\xi T}) = d_l$. Under conditions of constant growth rates of residential land supply and rentals, then, the amount of land being built upon at any moment grows at the same rate as the aggregate stock of residential land. The situation is quite similar with regard to population. Let $\bar{H}(t)$, the aggregate number of households living in the local housing market, grow at an exogenous rate μ. In addition, let it be proportional to the price per unit of housing services, or

$$\bar{H}(t) = \bar{H}_0 e^{\mu t} \left[\frac{\hat{p}(t)}{\hat{p}(0)} \right]^\eta = \bar{H}_0 e^{(\mu + \eta \lambda)t} \tag{15.27}$$

Let the number of households housed in newly built dwellings at any moment be $H_t = H_0 e^{\pi t}$. Integrating as above,

$$\frac{H_t}{\bar{H}(t)} = \frac{\pi}{1 - e^{-\pi T}} = d_\pi \tag{15.28}$$

and $\pi = \mu + \eta\lambda$.

Equilibrium in the local land market requires that the quantity of land demanded for new housing equal the quantity supplied at each point in time, or $H_t l_t = L_t$. Substituting (15.23) and the definitions above,

$$H_0 e^{\pi t} \times \frac{\alpha b d_r}{d_N} y_0^\beta e^{\beta \omega t} r_0^{-1} e^{-\rho t} = L_0 e^{\xi t}$$

or

$$r_0 e^{\rho t} = \frac{\alpha b d_r d_\pi}{d_N d_l} \frac{\bar{H}_0}{\bar{L}_0} y_0^\beta \exp[(\pi + \beta\omega - \xi)t] \qquad (15.29)$$

Therefore,

$$r_0 = \frac{b\alpha d_r d_\pi}{d_N d_l} \frac{\bar{H}_0}{\bar{L}_0} y_0^\beta \qquad (15.30)$$

substituting from (15.13), (15.26), and (15.28) and solving, we have

$$\rho = \frac{\mu + (a\nu + c\sigma)\eta + \beta\omega - \zeta}{1 + \gamma - b\eta} \qquad (15.31)$$

Knowing r_0 from (15.30) one thus determines $p_0(0)$ and so $\hat{p}(0)$. In like manner, knowing ρ from (15.31) one then knows λ, ξ, and π.

At this point one readily derives the aggregate population density for the local housing market. From (15.29),

$$\frac{\bar{H}(t)}{\bar{L}(t)} = \frac{d_N d_l}{b\alpha d_r d_\pi} y(t)^{-\beta} r(t)$$

$$= \frac{d_l}{d_\pi} l_t(0)^{-1} \qquad (15.32)$$

where, of course, $l_t^{-1} = H_t / L_t$. Aggregate population density may be either greater than or less than density on land just built upon. It is easily shown that

$$\frac{\partial}{\partial a}\left[\frac{a}{1 - e^{-aT}}\right] > 0$$

so $\bar{H}(t)/\bar{L}(t) \gtreqless H_t / L_t$ as $\xi \gtreqless \pi$, or as

$$\zeta + (\gamma - b\eta)\beta\omega \gtreqless \mu + (a\nu + c\,\sigma)\eta \qquad (15.33)$$

It is far from clear, then, that new dwellings will always be built to greater than average densities.

In exploring some of the model's properties it is instructive to consider for a moment the implications of the analytically simpler model in which housing is nondurable but where everything else is essentially the same as in the durable model. Let the demand function per household be $q(t) = \alpha y(t)^\beta p(t)^{-1}$, and the production function for housing services be $q(t) = k(t)^a l(t)^b m(t)^c$. Equating the value of the marginal product of land to its rental value gives

$$l(t)^{-1} = \frac{1}{b\alpha} y(t)^{-\beta} r(t) \tag{15.34}$$

Equating, in turn the demand for land to its supply,

$$H(t)l(t) = b\alpha H(t)y(t)^\beta r(t)^{-1} = \Gamma(t)r(t)^\gamma$$

so

$$r(t) = \left[\frac{b\alpha H(t)}{\Gamma(t)} y(t)^\beta \right]^{1/(1+\gamma)} \tag{15.35}$$

Substituting in (15.34), we have

$$\frac{H(t)}{L(t)} = [b\alpha y(t)^\beta]^{-\gamma/(1+\gamma)} \Gamma(t)^{-1/(1+\gamma)} H(t)^{1/(1+\gamma)} \tag{15.36}$$

Where housing is nondurable, all housing is new and there is no distinction between average population densities and those in newly built housing.

Comparing constant terms in (15.23) and (15.34), population densities in new housing predicted by the durable model are greater, equal to, or less than those predicted by the nondurable model depending upon whether $d_N \gtreqless d_r$ or, from (15.9) and (15.10), $\rho \gtreqless \beta\omega - \theta$. The latter, as we argue in the next section, is typically about zero in U.S. cities; so long as land rents are growing then, the durable model will predict higher newly built densities than the corresponding nondurable model.

Substituting $\bar{L}(t) = \Gamma(t)r(t)^\gamma$ into (15.30) gives

$$r(t) = \left[\frac{b\alpha d_r d_\pi}{d_N d_l} \frac{\bar{H}(t)}{\Gamma(t)} y(t)^\beta \right]^{1/(1+\gamma)} \tag{15.37}$$

Equation (15.37), when substituted into (15.32), then yields

$$\frac{\bar{H}(t)}{\bar{L}(t)} = \left[\frac{b\alpha d_r d_\pi}{d_N d_l} y(t)^\beta \right]^{-\gamma/(1+\gamma)} \Gamma(t)^{-1/(1+\gamma)} \bar{H}(t)^{1/(1+\gamma)} \tag{15.38}$$

Comparing (15.37) and (15.38) with (15.35) and (15.36), the only differences are the discount factors in the former pair. As just noted, d_N will typically exceed d_r, so on this account the durable model predicts lower land rent and higher aggregate population densities than the nondurable model. However, if d_π exceeds d_l by enough, as determined by inequality (15.33), the result may go the other way.

A Numerical Illustration

The calculations in this section are presented primarily to illustrate the nature of the solution to our durable housing model. However, since the numerical values of the parameters used are, in general, appropriate for the typical U.S. city today, these calculations do say something about the model's applicability even though they are in no sense an empirical test of it. Before getting in to the calculations themselves, we will discuss the parameter values used and their rationale.

The data relating to new, FHA insured houses in 1966 reveal that land accounts for roughly 10 percent of their value (see Muth[4]). Thus, we use $a = 0.9(1 - c)$ and $b = 0.1(1 - c)$. Another study[5] found current expenditures to be one-third of capital expenditures on housing, which would imply that $c = 0.25$. Current expenditures in these data, however, included expenditures for utilities and amortization of heating and cooking equipment in addition to those for maintenance and repair. Defining housing to exclude household operation, $c = 0.15$ is probably a better value. Over the first half of this century, real construction costs increased at an annual rate of about 1 percent per year (Muth,[3] p. 74). Since maintenance and repair of dwellings employs much the same class of inputs used in their construction, it seems sensible to the $\sigma = 0.01$, as well. Cross-section evidence suggests $\beta \cong 1.25$,[1] and per capita income historically has grown at about 2 percent per year. Since these calculations are meant to refer to whole cities, it seems appropriate to take $\eta = 0$; the average growth rate for U.S cities in this century then implies $\mu = \pi = 0.02$. Producers of housing are largely unincorporated, so it seems reasonable to take $i = 0.07$, about half the rate earned on capital in manufacturing.[10] Finally, in the past, property tax rates have averaged about 2.5 percent per year in the U.S. (Muth,[3] pp. 91-92).

Throughout this chapter, spatial considerations have been neglected; but understanding the supply of land to urban areas requires brief consideration of space. Urban residential land rentals tend to decline at a roughly constant relative rate, $g = 0.2$, with distance from the city center.[12] The rental of land in nonurban uses, $\bar{r}$, is largely independent of the amount of land used for urban purposes. Thus, where r_0 is the rental of land at the city center and $\bar{x}$ the distance from the center to the city's edge

$$r_0 = \bar{r}e^{g\bar{x}} \quad \text{and} \quad L = \frac{f}{2}\bar{x}^2,$$

where $0 < f \le 2\pi$ describes the fraction of land surrounding the center available for urban uses. Land rentals at any distance from the center, of course, will vary proportionally with those at the center so long as g is fixed. Differentiating,

$$dr_0 = e^{g\bar{x}} d\bar{r} + gr_0 d\bar{x} \quad \text{and} \quad dL = \frac{2L}{\bar{x}} d\bar{x},$$

so

$$\frac{dL}{L} = \frac{2}{g\bar{x}} \left(\frac{dr_0}{r_0} - \frac{d\bar{r}}{\bar{r}} \right).$$

Consequently, $\gamma = 2/g\bar{x}$ and $\zeta = -\gamma d\bar{r}/\bar{r}$. Now, in 1970 census data indicate that U.S. urban areas averaged 141.5 sq. mi. of land area ([11], Table 20, p. 74), or for $f = 2\pi$, $\bar{x} = 6.7$ mi. and $\gamma = 1.5$. Furthermore, since 1940 the average value of land and buildings per acre in agriculture has grown at an annual rate of almost exactly 3 percent per year. This implies $\zeta = -.045$.

Dwelling unit values as usually measured, $W_t^*(u)$, include the present value of the reversion of the land at the end of the unit's life, $Z_t(u)$, in addition to the present value of future quasi-rents, $W_t(u)$ as given by (15.19). To compare the model's implications with real-world data, it is appropriate to calculate property values inclusive of the present value of the reversion. The value of the land at time $\tau + T$, when it reverts to its owner is $r(\tau + T)/(i - \rho)$, since taxes on the land are paid by subsequent developers. Hence, using (15.10),

$$Z_t(u) = l_\tau x \frac{r(\tau)e^{\rho T}}{i - \rho} x e^{-i(T-u)}$$

$$= \frac{b\alpha y(t)^\beta}{i + \theta - \beta\omega} \left[\frac{e^{-(i-\rho)t}}{1 - e^{-(i-\rho)T}} \right]$$

$$\times [1 - \exp\langle -(i + \theta - \beta\omega)T \rangle] e^{(i-\beta\omega)u} \quad (15.39)$$

Adding (15.39) to (15.19) then gives $W_t^*(u)$.

To highlight the effects of durability of residential structures, it is interesting first to consider the case of extreme durability where $\delta = c = 0$. Here dwellings do not deteriorate at all physically and no current expenditures are made on them. The parameter values described earlier imply $\rho = 0.036$ using (15.31), hence using (15.20) to solve for T implies the latter is approximately 57.9 years. Using (15.21) and W^*, one can then calculate the first and third columns of Table 15.1. The values of depreciation rates shown there agree quite closely with the estimate of about 2 percent per year derived by Grebler, Blank, and Winnick.[2] The rent-to-value ratios shown in the first column, though, are somewhat smaller than the 11 percent based on 1940 census data cited by Reid.[9] Taking $c = 0.15$ doesn't affect the rate of growth of land rentals so long as $\eta = 0$ (indeed, ρ is independent of δ as well), and merely multiplies $F(T)$ and W^* by a constant. Hence, T and $-W^{*'}/W^*$ are likewise unchanged. The rent-to-value ratios

Table 15-1
Rent-to-Value Ratios and Rates of Depreciation in Value by Age of Dwelling

	$\delta = 0$			$\delta = .02$	
	G/W^*		$-W^{*\prime}/W^*$	C/W^*	$-W^{*\prime}/W^*$
Age	$c = 0$	$c = .15$		$c = 0$	
0	.082	.094	.012	.098	.029
10	.083	.097	.014	.10	.037
20	.084	.10	.016	.11	.048
30	.087	.11	.019	.11	.056
40	.092	.12	.026	—	—
50	.10	.14	.045	—	—

for $c = 0.15$ shown in the second column of Table 15-1 agree much more closely with the 1940 census data.

The values in the last two columns of Table 15-1 were calculated for $\delta = 0.02$ and $c = 0$. As noted above, ρ is unchanged, but T falls to about 36.4 years. The implied depreciation rates shown in Table 15-1 for $\delta = 0.02$ seem too high. Likewise, the implied coefficient for G/y^β on u in (15.21) is approximately -0.0042 for $\delta = 0.02$, $c = 0$, while for $\delta = 0$, $c = 0$ (0.02) it is -0.0017 (-0.0015). The latter agree much more closely with our recent empirical estimates.[3] We are therefore inclined to conclude that dwellings do not necessarily deteriorate at all physically as they age. Rather, their decline in value and eventual replacement result from the fact that, being fixed in size, they ultimately become too small relative to market demand to yield a quasi rent in excess of the opportunity cost of the land on which they are built.

Finally, what do the above values imply about the predictions concerning population densities of the durable model as compared with the corresponding nondurable model? For $\delta = 0$, the ratio $d_r/d_N \cong 0.55$. For $\rho = 0.036$, $\xi = 0.009$ and $d_\pi/d_l \cong 1.32$, indeed greater than one but not enough so to offset the value of the former. (Actually, the land area of U.S. cities has grown considerably faster than 1 percent per year, indeed at about 4 percent per year from 1950 to 1970, or faster than population.) Thus the durable model predicts land rentals which are about 12 percent smaller and population densities which are about 21 percent greater than the nondurable model. (Though it is seemingly counter intuitive that lower land rents are associated with larger population densities, recall that the appropriate land cost measure for the durable model from (15.10) is $d_N r/d_r$; land cost is indeed higher for the durable model.) The model of housing durability presented here may indeed be useful for understanding certain phenomena associated with age of dwellings. But it is by no means clear that it would improve the empirical conformity of models of urban spatial structure which assume housing is nondurable. For, the greatest limitation of the latter is that they predict average population densities that are too large, not too small.

Notes

1. F. De Leeuw, 1971, "The Demand for Housing: A Review of Cross-Section Evidence," *Review of Economics and Statistics*, Vol. 53, 1-10.

2. L. Grebler, D.M. Blank, and L. Winnick, 1956, *Capital Formation in Residential Real Estate*. Princeton: Princeton University Press, pp. 377-382.

3. R.F. Muth, [1960].

4. R.F. Muth, [1971], pp. 246, 251.

5. R.F. Muth, [1973a], pp. 74-75.

6. R.F. Muth, [1973b].

7. R.F. Muth, [1975a].

8. R.F. Muth, "The Influence of Age of Dwellings on the Location of Households by Income and on Housing Expenditures," manuscript.

9. M.G. Reid, 1962, *Housing and Income*. Chicago: The University of Chicago Press, p. 43.

10. G.J. Stigler, 1963, *Capital and Rates of Return in Manufacturing Industries*. Princeton: Princeton University Press.

11. U.S. Bureau of the Census, 1973, *1970 Census of Population*, Vol. I, Pt. 1. Washington, D.C.: U.S. Government Printing Office.

12. K. Wieand, Jr. and R.F. Muth, 1972, "A Note on the Variation of Land Values with Distance from the CBD in St. Louis," *Journal of Regional Science*, Vol. 12, 469-473.

16 Short-Run Dynamics in the Spatial Housing Market

Alex Anas

Despite numerous contributions since the early papers of Alonso,[1] Muth,[7] Beckmann,[3] and Mills,[5] models of urban spatial structure have relied on long-run equilibrium analyses. Here, we depart from this trend.

A dynamic model of urban form would have to account for at least two observations about urban growth and change. Firstly, capital put into streets and housing is extremely durable and once put into place can be converted only very slowly and at substantial cost. Secondly, both urban households and suppliers of housing will base present decisions on their expectations about the future. These considerations play a major role in this paper.

Several authors have made the closed-city, open-city distinction, though the terminology was coined by Wheaton.[8] He argues that cities in developing countries where a subsistence rural welfare level persists are "open," as there is always a large number of migrants that can move into a city and damp out welfare effects of local advantages. In contrast modern industrialized cities can be viewed as "closed" to the extent that they are isolated from the rest of the economy. This chapter will first review the standard static model for "open" and "closed" monocentric cities. A dynamic model will then be developed by assuming myopic market behavior and strictly peripheral housing construction. A loglinear utility function is assumed and recursive equations are derived by performing a two-time-period analysis. The effects of income and price changes and of population growth on the structure of rents, welfare, and urban densities is examined and it is shown that the rentals profile need not be downward sloping, that housing can become abandoned as rents in parts of the city can become negative. It is also shown that with continuously occurring extension of the city, residential densities will decline with distance only under certain special behavior over time of income, prices, and transport costs. We will examine housing conversion decisions within the open and closed

Alex Anas is a member of the Department of Civil Engineering, The Technological Institute, Northwestern University.

This chapter is based on the author's doctoral dissertation.[2] The author would like to thank his dissertation advisors, Professors Britton Harris, James Barr, and Tony Smith for their helpful comments and criticisms.

261

contexts, first while retaining the myopia assumption and then with the myopia assumption relaxed. The speculative release of farmland and the supply of housing are analyzed in the presence of expectations and foresight into the future. The chapter will close with a brief discussion of the policy implications of the analysis.

The Static City: Long-Run Equilibrium

Consider the circular monocentric city. It is concentric with a circular work center of small radius. Households in the city are identical in tastes and incomes and locate within the residential belt around the center. One worker from each household is employed in the center and commutes to work daily. Travel within the center is assumed to be costless while travel within the residential belt is congestion free and an increasing function of distance from the work center.

The typical household has a loglinear utility function:

$$u(x) = \alpha \ln z(x) + \beta \ln k(x) + \gamma \ln q(x) \qquad \alpha + \beta + \gamma = 1 \quad (16.1)$$

where z, k, and q are the amounts of composite good, housing capital, and land consumed by the household. A household's distance from the center is denoted by x. The budget constraint is:

$$w = pz(x) + \rho k(x) + r(x)q(x) + c(x - g) \qquad (16.2)$$

where
$w =$ household income

$p =$ the price of the composite good

$\rho =$ the price of capital

$r(x) =$ the price of land at x

$c(x - g) =$ the costs of commuting to the edge of the center which has radius g

Of the 2π radians of land available at every distance x from the center, θ radians ($0 < \theta \le 2\pi$) are allocated to housing, while the remaining $2\pi - \theta$ radians are used in roads. Each household located within the thin ring of width dx at distance x consumes $q(x)$ units of land. City population in households is then expressed as

$$N = \theta \int_{g}^{\bar{x}} q(x)^{-1} x \, dx \qquad (16.3)$$

If the city is open, then, given p, w, ρ, $\bar{r}$, g, $c(x - g)$, and the utility level $\bar{u}$, the model can be solved for N, the city size. If the city is closed, then, given p, w, ρ, $\bar{r}$, g, $c(x - g)$, and $\bar{N}$, the model can be solved for u^*, the equilibrium utility level. The prices p and ρ are determined through trade within the national interurban market, and thus they will be exogenously given for both a closed and an open city.

For a closed city we maximize (16.1) subject to (16.2) and derive the following demand functions:

$$z(x) = \alpha[w - c(x - g)]p^{-1} \tag{16.4}$$

$$k(x) = \beta[w - c(x - g)]\rho^{-1} \tag{16.5}$$

$$q(x) = \gamma[w - c(x - g)]r(x)^{-1} \tag{16.6}$$

The equilibrium condition assuring uniform utility over the urban space is:

$$r'(x)q(x) + c'(x - g) = 0 \tag{16.7}$$

Solving this differential equation by substituting for $q(x)$ and integrating, one gets the rent gradient for the city.

$$r(x) = r_0\left(1 - \frac{c(x - g)}{w}\right)^{1/\gamma} \tag{16.8}$$

Here, $r_0 = r(g)$ is the rent at the edge of the center and is related to the constant of integration C, such that $r_0 = Cw^{1/\gamma}$. We ought to have for equilibrium that $r(\bar{x}) = \bar{r}$, that is, the urban border rent matches the exogenous rural rent $\bar{r}$. Thus, from (16.8),

$$r_0 = \bar{r}\left(1 - \frac{c(\bar{x} - g)}{w}\right)^{-1/\gamma} \tag{16.9}$$

By substituting into (16.1) the equilibrium utility level is found to be:

$$u^* = \ln(\alpha^\alpha\beta^\beta\gamma^\gamma) + \ln[w - c(\bar{x} - g)] - \alpha \ln p - \beta \ln \rho - \gamma \ln \bar{r} \tag{16.10}$$

For an open city (16.1) can be solved for $z(x)$ yielding:

$$z(x) = \exp(\bar{u}/\alpha)k(x)^{-\beta/\alpha} q(x)^{-\gamma/\alpha} \tag{16.11}$$

Rent per unit of land is then expressed as

$$r(x) = [w - c(x - g) - \rho k(x) - \exp(\bar{u}/\alpha)k(x)^{-\beta/\alpha} q(x)^{-\gamma/\alpha}] \div q(x) \tag{16.12}$$

The owner of land will choose $k(x)$ and $q(x)$ so as to maximize the value of (16.12). It will be found that:

$$q(x) = \{\alpha^{-\alpha} \beta^{-\beta} \exp(\bar{u}) \rho^\beta[w - c(x - g)]^{-(\alpha+\beta)}\}^{1/\gamma} \tag{16.13}$$

and that the demand for z and k is as in (16.4) and (16.5).

The crucial difference between the open and closed cities is that in the former income increases lead to density and rent increases throughout the city, whereas in the closed city this effect occurs in an outer part of the city with the opposite effect occurring in the inner part. This and other comparative static effects are proved formally by Wheaton[8] for a general utility function with z and q as arguments.

It is crucial to note that the "standard" static model recapitulated here describes a Pareto efficient equilibrium outcome for the simple case in which unchanging parameter values are accurately anticipated, future gains are not discounted, and all decisions are simultaneously made under conditions of perfect information.[a] With these assumptions, the problem reduces to that of the maximization of current utility by households and of current profits by investors. If it is postulated that the static equilibrium is the outcome of a series of adjustments (that is, decisions are not simultaneous), it then becomes necessary to assume that adjustment and conversion costs are nonexistent and that households are perfectly mobile. If any of these assumptions is removed, the validity of the standard static model as a description of the market process collapses. A meaningful model of urban growth will have to be cognizant of the durability of urban capital and the costs, speed, and sequential nature of urban density adjustments. In the following sections several steps will be taken in this direction.

Myopic Behavior and Short-Run Peripheral Growth

Basic Assumptions

Let us conceive of the urban area's history as a sequence of brief time periods, say "years." Every year a number of new households arrive at the city. These are identical in preferences to older households and are similarly employed at the city center for the same income. Preferences do not change over time. Each household spends all of its annual income on housing, land, and the composite good. The composite good is perishable and is consumed within the year. Nothing is saved for future consumption.

Households and entrepreneurs investing in housing, as well as landowners and farmers, are shortsighted. In each period, both sets of agents behave as if they expected no additional growth and price or income changes to occur in the future. Thus, households maximize current utility while investors maximize current profits. Although households are "myopic in time" they are not "myopic in space." Within each year a household is sensitive to the level of its welfare relative to that of all other

---

[a] All exogenous quantities are here referred to as parameters.

households within the urban space and will move at negligible cost if it has to.

In addition we initially assume that housing once built is not converted. Thus, the city's growth is accommodated by new construction at the periphery.

Equilibrium at the Urban Fringe

Let us add $\Delta N(t)$ households to a closed city of $\bar{N}(t)$ households in competitive equilibrium at time t. We will then have $\bar{N}(t + 1) = \bar{N}(t) + \Delta N(t)$. These households will attempt to locate at the city fringe. Competitive bidding for land and the provision of housing under the stated myopia assumptions will determine a new distribution of land plots and housing beyond the city limit $\bar{x}(t)$. Each household attempts to maximize its utility subject to its budget constraint. These are written as[b]

$$u(x, t+1) = \alpha \ln z(x, t+1) + \beta \ln k(x, t+1) + \gamma \ln q(x, t+1)$$

$$\alpha + \beta + \gamma = 1 \qquad x \geq \bar{x}(t) \qquad (16.14)$$

$$\bar{w}(t + 1) = (1)z(x, t+1) + p(t + 1)k(x, t+1) + r(x, t+1)q(x, t+1) + \bar{c}(x - g)$$

$$x \geq \bar{x}(t) \qquad (16.15)$$

where $\bar{w}(t + 1) = w(t + 1) - c(\bar{x}(t) - g)$

$\bar{c}(x - g) = c(x - g) - c(\bar{x}(t) - g)$

Maximizing (16.14) subject to (16.15), we obtain

$$z(x, t+1) = \alpha[\bar{w}(t + 1) - \bar{c}(x - g)] \qquad (16.16)$$

$$k(x, t+1) = \beta[\bar{w}(t + 1) - \bar{c}(x - g)]\rho(t + 1)^{-1} \qquad (16.17)$$

$$q(x, t+1) = \gamma[\bar{w}(t + 1) - \bar{c}(x - g)]r(x, t+1)^{-1} \qquad (16.18)$$

For equilibrium at the urban fringe we ought to have

$$r'(x, t+1)q(x, t+1) + \bar{c}'(x - g) = 0 \qquad x \geq \bar{x}(t) \qquad (16.19)$$

Solving this in the familiar way gives us

$$r(x, t+1) = r(\bar{x}(t), t+1)\left[1 - \frac{\bar{c}(x - g)}{\bar{w}(t + 1)}\right]^{1/\gamma} \qquad x \geq \bar{x}(t) \quad (16.20a)$$

and with $r(\bar{x}(t+1), t+1) = \bar{r}(t + 1)$, we can write

$$r(\bar{x}(t), t+1) = \bar{r}(t + 1)\left[1 - \frac{\bar{c}(\bar{x}(t + 1) - g)}{\bar{w}(t + 1)}\right]^{-1/\gamma} \qquad (16.20b)$$

---

[b] We assume, for simplicity, that the transport cost structure $c(x - g)$ is not a function of time, and that "$p = 1$ and constant" is the numeraire price.

The fringe rent gradient is fully determined once $\bar{x}(t + 1)$, the new city border, is known. This is obtained by integrating and solving iteratively the following equation:

$$\bar{N}(t + 1) - \bar{N}(t) = \theta \int_{x(t)}^{\bar{x}(t+1)} q(x, t+1)^{-1} x \, dx \qquad (16.21)$$

The maximized fringe utility level is

$$u^*(x \geq \bar{x}(t), t+1) = \ln(\alpha^\alpha \beta^\beta \gamma^\gamma) + \ln[w(t + 1) - c(\bar{x}(t) - g)]$$
$$- \beta \ln \rho(t + 1) - \gamma \ln r(\bar{x}(t), t+1) \qquad (16.22)$$

Suppose that rents within the older residential belt have not yet responded to fringe developments, by subtracting (16.22) from (16.10) for time t, and simplifying:

$$u^*(t) - u^*(x \geq \bar{x}(t), t+1) = \ln\left[\frac{w(t) - c(\bar{x}(t) - g)}{w(t + 1) - c(\bar{x}(t + 1) - g)}\right]$$
$$+ \ln\left[\frac{\bar{r}(t + 1)}{\bar{r}(t)}\right]^\gamma + \ln\left[\frac{\rho(t + 1)}{\rho(t)}\right]^\beta \qquad (16.23)$$

If the left side of (16.23) is equal to zero, fringe utility will be equal to the inner belt utility level of the previous period. Transforming (16.23) we see that:

$u(t + 1) \gtreqless u(t)$ as

$$\left[\frac{w(t + 1) - c(\bar{x}(t + 1) - g)}{w(t) - c(\bar{x}(t) - g)}\right]\left[\frac{\bar{r}(t)}{\bar{r}(t + 1)}\right]^\gamma \left[\frac{\rho(t)}{\rho(t + 1)}\right]^\beta \gtreqless 1 \qquad (16.24)$$

To assure $u^*(t) = u^*(x \geq \bar{x}(t), t+1)$, if income were to stay unchanged, then the opportunity cost of land and/or the price of capital would have to drop. If the latter were to stay constant, income would have to be

$$w(t + 1) = w(t) + [c(\bar{x}(t + 1) - g) - c(\bar{x}(t) - g)] \qquad (16.25)$$

where the term in brackets is the rise needed to just cover travel costs across the newly developed fringe. If the fringe welfare is lower than $u^*(t)$, fringe households would be willing to pay higher rents for inner locations, and owners of inner housing will raise rents willingly until the fringe and inner belt utility levels are equalized. Conversely, if the fringe utility level is higher than the preceding inner belt utility, inner belt households will show willingness to move out to the fringe. This will force owners of inner housing to lower rents until the fringe and inner utility levels are equalized. We will have

$$u^*(x \geq \bar{x}(t), t+1) = u^*(g \leq x < \bar{x}(t), t+1) \qquad (16.26a)$$

To summarize, the Pareto inefficient short-run equilibrium described above is the solution to a simultaneous equations system, namely (16.16), (16.17), (16.18), (16.19), (16.21), and (16.26), subject to $r(\bar{x}(t+1), t+1) = \bar{r}(t+1)$. These are solved for $\bar{x}(t+1)$, $z(x, t+1)$, $k(x, t+1)$, $q(x, t+1)$, and $r(x, t+1)$ where $x \geq \bar{x}(t)$ and also for $z(x, t+1)$ where $g \leq x < \bar{x}(t)$. For an open city $u(t+1)$, is exogenously given and $\Delta N(t)$ is solved for. For this case, the equivalent of (16.26a) is

$$u(t + 1) = u(x \geq \bar{x}(t), t+1) = u(g \leq x < \bar{x}(t), t+1) \qquad (16.26b)$$

If we disturb a static closed city by adding an increment of population, at the end of the second period the short-run welfare will be lower than the welfare of the corresponding static city and the short-run city will have a larger radius. If we disturb an open static city, say by decreasing in income, fewer households will be accommodated in the short-run city than in its long-run equivalent.

Inner-Belt Equilibrium and the Rentals Profile

The rent paid at time $t + 1$ for a house built at time t will be denoted as $R(x, t+1)_t$. (Hereafter, a subscript t will denote the date of construction.) This rent cannot be decomposed into land and capital expenditures. Since housing capital and land parcels are fixed within the inner belt, utility is maximized by allocating all income after locational expenditures to the purchases of the composite good. Rearranging the budget constraint

$$z(x, t+1) = w(t + 1) - R(x, t+1)_t = c(x - g) \qquad g \leq x < \bar{x}(t) \qquad (16.27)$$

We can find, from (16.26) that for uniform utility in a closed city we ought to have

$$z(x, t+1) =$$

$$\left[\frac{w(t + 1) - c(\bar{x}(t + 1) - g)}{w(t) - c(\bar{x}(t) - g)} \right]^{1/\alpha} \left[\frac{\bar{r}(t)}{\bar{r}(t + 1)} \right]^{\gamma/\alpha} \left[\frac{\rho(t)}{\rho(t + 1)} \right]^{\beta/\alpha} z(x, t)$$

$$g \leq x < \bar{x}(t) \qquad (16.28a)$$

For an open city, the equivalent equation is

$$z(x, t+1) = \exp[\bar{u}(t + 1)/\alpha]k(x)_t^{-\beta/\alpha}q(x)^{-\gamma/\alpha} \qquad (16.28b)$$

If we abbreviate (16.28a) as:

$$z(x, t+1) = K_t(t + 1)z(x, t) = \alpha K_t(t + 1)[w(t) - c(x - g)] \qquad (16.28c)$$

and substitute this into (16.27), solving the latter for $R(x, t+1)_t$ thus,

$$R(x, t+1)_t = w(t + 1) - \alpha K_t(t + 1)w(t)$$

$$+ [\alpha K_t(t + 1) - 1]c(x - g) \qquad (16.28d)$$

we note that

$$R'(x, t+1)_t = [\alpha K_t(t + 1) - 1]c'(x - g) \gtreqless 0 \text{ as } K_t(t + 1) \gtreqless 1/\alpha \quad (16.29)$$

Thus, inner-belt house rents can be decreasing, invariant, or increasing with distance. This ambiguity does not exist for the long-run equilibrium configuration for which house rents will decrease with distance. For the fringe, where housing and land rents can be separated at time $t + 1$,

$$R(x, t+1) = (1 - \alpha)[w(t + 1) - c(x - g)] \qquad g \le x < \bar{x}(t) \quad (16.30)$$

and house rent is always a declining function of distance. From (16.29), we can also state that

$$R'(x, t+1)_t \gtreqless 0 \quad \text{as} \quad u(t + 1) \gtreqless (1/\alpha)^\alpha u(t) \quad (16.31)$$

Since $1/\alpha > 1$, an increasing profile occurs when utilities are sufficiently rising over time.

At $x = \bar{x}(t)$, the city's rental profile at time $t + 1$ will be discontinuous. The size and sign of this jump for the simple case of w, $\bar{r}$, and ρ invariant over time, is easily derived. Let us define the jump at $\bar{x}(t)$ at time $t + 1$ as $_{t+1}\delta_{\bar{x}(t)}$. We then have:

$$_{t+1}\delta_{\bar{x}(t)} = \lim_{\varepsilon \to 0} [R(\bar{x}(t) - \varepsilon, t+1) - R(\bar{x}(t), t+1)] \quad (16.32)$$

Utilizing (16.28d) and remembering that we have kept w, ρ, and $\bar{r}$ constant,

$$_{t+1}\delta_{\bar{x}(t)} = \alpha\left\{ 1 - \left[\frac{w - c(\bar{x}(t + 1) - g)}{w - c(\bar{x}(t) - g)}\right]^{1/\alpha} \right\}[w - c(\bar{x}(t) - g)] \quad (16.33)$$

Since $c(\bar{x}(t + 1) - g) > c(\bar{x}(t) - g)$, the jump is positive, that is, there is a sudden decline as one moves through $x = \bar{x}(t)$ and away from the center.

It is of interest to look at the model by imposing an arbitrary subdivision of inner-belt rents into capital and land payments. An institutional arrangement under which such a subdivision may arise is that of the public taxation of one of the factors. If the government is to collect land rents, for example, it might determine $r(x, t+1)$, collect $r(x, t+1)q(x)_t$ leaving the residual to the owners of housing. Alternatively, the government may collect an amount per unit of housing capital owned, in which case owners of land collect what would be rentals to land. Possibly, all capital old and new might be priced at its current opportunity cost, that is, $\rho(g \le x < \bar{x}(t), t+1) = \rho(t + 1)$. The land rent profile is then derived to be

$$r(x, t+1)_t = [w(t + 1) - \rho(t + 1)k(x)_t - c(x - g) - z(x, t+1)] \div q(x)_t$$

$$g \le x < \bar{x}(t) \quad (16.34)$$

Substituting and simplifying gives us

$$r(x, t+1)_t = \frac{1}{\gamma} \left\{ \left[\frac{w(t+1) - c(x-g)}{w(t) - c(x-g)} \right] - \frac{\alpha z(x, t+1)}{z(x, t)} \right.$$

$$\left. - \frac{\beta \rho(t+1)}{\rho(t)} \right\} r(x, t)_t \qquad g \leq x < \bar{x}(t) \qquad (16.35)$$

where $z(x, t+1)$ is given in (16.28). The jump in this profile is defined as

$$_{t+1}\delta_{\bar{x}(t)} = \lim_{\varepsilon \to 0} [r(\bar{x}(t) - \varepsilon, t+1) - r(\bar{x}(t), t+1)] \qquad (16.36)$$

For the case of $w, \rho, \bar{r}$ invariant we find that

$$_{t+1}\delta_{\bar{x}(t)} \gtreqqless 0 \quad \text{as} \quad \alpha + \gamma \gtreqqless \alpha H_t^{1/\alpha} + \gamma(1/H_t)^{1/\gamma} \qquad (16.37)$$

where

$$H_t = \left[\frac{w - c(\bar{x}(t+1) - g)}{w - c(\bar{x}(t) - g)} \right]$$

Generalization for n Time Periods

According to the model, a city that has lived through $i = 1 \ldots n$ periods will consist of n annular bands provided that some growth has occurred during every time period. For an n-year-old closed city it will be required for equilibrium that $u^*(x \geq \bar{x}(n-1), n) = u^*(\bar{x}(i-1) \leq x < \bar{x}(i), n)$ for all $i = 1 \ldots n - 1$ and $r(\bar{x}(n), n) = \bar{r}(n)$. Setting the utility in the ith band of the city equal to the freely maximized fringe utility results in the analogue of (16.28) gives us

$$z(x, n) = \left[\frac{w(n) - c(\bar{x}(n) - g)}{w(i) - c(\bar{x}(i) - g)} \right]^{1/\alpha} \left[\frac{\bar{r}(i)}{\bar{r}(n)} \right]^{\gamma/\alpha} \left[\frac{\rho(i)}{\rho(n)} \right]^{\beta/\alpha} z(x, i)$$

$$\bar{x}(i-1) \leq x < \bar{x}(i) \qquad (16.38a)$$

Other equations are similarly generalized. For an open city, we may simply write

$$z(x, n) = e^{u(n)/\alpha} k(x)_i^{-\beta/\alpha} q(x)_i^{-\gamma/\alpha} \qquad \bar{x}(i-1) \leq x < \bar{x}(i) \qquad (16.38b)$$

Continuous Growth and the Structure of Urban Densities

We have created a picture of urban growth as a lumpy occurrence. The process of simultaneous decisions at the fringe is better approximated when time intervals are very brief and the urban border moves out only at infinitesimal increments at a time. With all parameters smoothly changing,[e] residential density at the fringe of a closed city will be

$$D(\bar{x}(t)) = \frac{\bar{r}(t)}{\gamma}[w(t) - c(\bar{x}(t)-g, t)]^{-1} \qquad (16.39a)$$

This implies that if $\dot{r}(t) = 0$, $\dot{w}(t) = 0$, and $\dot{c}(x(t)-e, t) = 0$, then densities throughout the urban area increase with distance. This is precisely what one would expect intuitively: At large distances from the center the household has less disposable income to spend on land and thus tends to economize on land consumption. Each incremental addition to the housing stock is a higher-density development than that of the previous period. Residential densities are in reality observed to be declining with distance. Assuming that the myopia assumptions are approximately correct, that is, farmland is released at its current opportunity cost and not speculatively, then the short-run closed model can predict declining densities if it is only recognized that over the past eight to ten decades incomes have increased while transport costs have declined due to transport improvements.

The open model presents a different picture.

$$D(\bar{x}(t)) = \{\alpha^\alpha\beta^\beta[w(t)-c(\bar{x}(t)-g, t)]^{\alpha+\beta} e^{-\bar{u}(t)}\rho(t)^{-\beta}\}^{1/\gamma} \qquad (16.39b)$$

Simplifying further gives us

$$D(\bar{x}(t)) = (\alpha\beta)^{(\gamma-1)/\gamma}\gamma^{(\gamma-1)} e^{-\bar{u}(t)}\rho(t)^{-\beta}\bar{r}(t)^{(1-\gamma)} \qquad (16.39c)$$

Densities are independent of disposable income, and thus invariant with distance if $\dot{u}(t) = 0$, $\dot{\rho}(t) = 0$ and $\dot{r}(t) = 0$. Densities will increase with distance as $\dot{u}(t) < 0$, $\dot{\rho}(t) < 0$ or $\dot{r}(t) > 0$ and immigrants flock into the city.

Surprising insight is thus gained into the structure of urban densities in contrast to the long-run model which cannot explain densities with reference to parameter changes.

Housing Obsolescence and Abandonment

Rents within an inner band of the city can become negative. From (16.28d) it can be seen that for a closed city this will occur when

$$\frac{w(n) - c(x - g)}{w(i) - c(x - g)} < \alpha K_i(n) \qquad (16.40a)$$

A rising rentals profile implies $\alpha K_i(n) > 1$. Thus, if (16.40) holds, then rents

[e] With continuously occurring extension of the city and smoothly changing parameters, discontinuities in the rentals profile will vanish [see (16.33) and (16.37)], and the profile can have any shape depending on the time profiles of income, of prices, and—for the open city—of welfare.

within the ith band and within radius $x < x(i)$ will be negative. This occurs when welfare is rising and is compatible with increases in income and/or drops in $\bar{r}$ or ρ or both. Another case arises when $\alpha K_i(n) < 1$. Then, the left side of (16.40) will be less than $\alpha K_i(n)$ only if $w(n)$ is sufficiently smaller than $w(i)$. This will occur when utilities are rising despite falling incomes due to sufficiently falling $\bar{r}$ and/or ρ. Rents will be negative outside a radius $x < \bar{x}(i)$ and within the ith band.

For an open city, the equivalent of (16.40) is

$$w(n) - c(x - g) < e^{u(n)/\alpha} k(x)_i^{-\beta/\alpha} q(x)_i^{-\gamma/\alpha} \qquad (16.40b)$$

Rents can become negative independently of $\bar{r}(n)$ and $\rho(n)$ depending on sufficient drops in income and/or sufficient rises in welfare.

Negative rents simply mean that houses built in the past are now obsolete given the current price and welfare circumstances. Typically, as welfare rises, old housing, though technically sound, is found to be obsolete. Households will abandon these units unless they are subsidized by an amount equal to the absolute value of the negative rent. If the city is closed, abandoning households will seek to locate at the fringe. If the city is open, they will outmigrate to other cities where income is higher or transportation is less expensive.

Myopic Behavior and Housing Conversion

The assumption that housing once built is not converted may seem like a serious limitation, yet the model as it is has significant explanatory power. Harrison and Kain[4] have performed an empirical study of urban densities in which the peripheral growth assumption held, although their study was not based on a theoretical model such as the one developed here. They reported that the results were at least as good as those of empirical studies of urban densities based on long-run assumptions (see, e.g., Mills[6]).

In this section, the infinite housing durability assumption will be relaxed. Figure 16-1 shows the budget line of a household at distance x from the center of an open city. The welfare level $\bar{u}$ is exogenously given and constant. In the $z - q$ plane, $(w - \rho k - c)$ is the available income; and r, rent per unit of land, is the absolute value of the slope of the budget line of a household at distance x from the center of an open city. If the household is presently consuming (z_1, q_1), the tangency point was once at A_1. The current position OE implies that $(w - \rho k - c)$ has decreased and that land rents have fallen. If (z_2, q_2) is consumed, then the tangency was once at A_2 meaning that $(w - \rho k - c)$ has increased and land rents have risen. Assuming that the conversion involves a change in q (lot size) alone, after conversion profits per unit of land are maximized by a shift from OE to

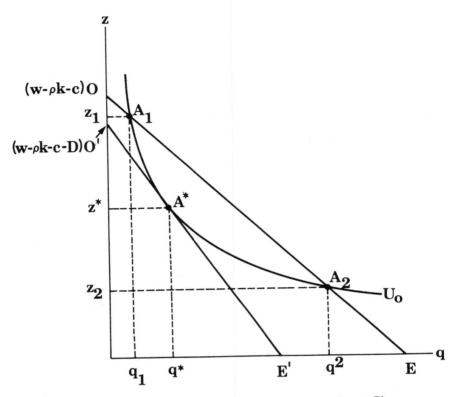

Figure 16-1. Housing Conversion in an Open City

$O'E'$, where D represents the cost of demolishing the unit at A_1 or at A_2 and $D[k_1, q_1] \neq D[k_2, q_2]$. If demolition costs are so large that $O'E'$ is parallel to OE, then the developer will be indifferent between converting and not converting. If the slope of $O'E'$ is smaller than that of OE, the conversion will not be attempted.

The more general conversion problem in which both capital and lot size are variable can be expressed as follows.

$$\max_{k(x)_t, q(x)_t} \left\{ \frac{R(x, t)_t}{q(x)_t} - \frac{D[q(x)_i, k(x)_i]}{q(x)_i} - \frac{\rho(t)k(x)_t}{q(x)_t} \right\} \qquad t > i \qquad (16.41a)$$

where

$$R(x, t)_t = w(t) - c(x - g) - e^{\bar{u}(t)/\alpha} k(x)_t^{-\beta/\alpha} q(x)_t^{-\gamma/\alpha}. \qquad (16.41b)$$

If the value of (16.41a) is larger than

$$[R(x, t)_i - \rho(t)k(x)_i] \div q(x)_i \qquad (16.42a)$$

where

$$R(x,t)_i = w(t) - c(x - g) - e^{\bar{u}(t)/\alpha}k(x)_i^{-\beta/\alpha}q(x)_i^{-\gamma/\alpha} \qquad (16.42b)$$

then conversion will be attempted and the myopic landowner's profits per unit of land will be maximized. It is worthwhile to note that if the value of (16.41a) is larger than that of (16.42a) and both are negative, then abandoned units will remain undemolished.

In a closed city conversion, decisions are more complex because they depend on the maximized fringe welfare, which in turn depends on the number of families locating at the fringe, which in turn depends on the number of newly available units in the inner city. Thus, in a closed city, the decisions of one developer are thoroughly dependent on the decisions of every other developer; while in an open city, each developer can expect to realize the gains resulting from his contemplated action regardless of the decisions of other developers. The elements of risk and uncertainty involved in closed-city conversions are thus much more severe than they would be in open-city conversion decisions. When many developers in a closed city attempt conversions simultaneously, each might and can expect to gain from such individual action, although the resulting change in densities might be such that the expectations of all or most landowners are disappointed.

Speculation, Foresight, and Expectations in the Open City

The assumption that will be relaxed in this section is that of myopic decision making on the part of developers. In doing so we will still view households as perfectly and costlessly mobile and myopic.

Consider first the intertemporal calculus underlying a farmer's decision to release his land. Land will be released at time i, if and only if

$$\max_{k(x)_i, q(x)_i} \int_i^\infty \left[\frac{\hat{R}(x,t)_i - \hat{\rho}(t)k(x)_i}{q(x)_i} \right] dt \geq \int_i^\infty \bar{F}(t)\, dt \qquad x \geq \bar{x}(i-1) (16.43a)$$

where the symbol $\hat{}$ denotes an expected quantity; the symbol $\bar{}$ denotes an expected quantity at the urban border, (the farmer does not consider future conversions that might follow his decision at time i); and

$$\hat{R}(x,t)_i = \hat{w}(t) - \hat{c}(x-g, t) - \exp[\bar{a}(t)/\alpha]\, k(x)_i^{-\beta/\alpha}\, q(x)_i^{-\gamma/\alpha} \qquad (16.43b)$$

If all farmers have uniform expectations, fringe land will be released in a continuous manner; but if expectation structures differ, a leapfrogging effect may result leading to a discontinuous distribution of housing of the same vintage. We assume uniform expectations in what follows.

If fringe land is being released, the owner of land must choose $q(x)_i$ and

$k(x)_i$. Maximizing expected profits, that is, the left side of (16.43a), one gets

$$k(x)_i = \beta \frac{\int_i^\infty [\hat{w}(t) - \hat{c}(x-g, t)]\,dt}{\int_i^\infty \hat{\rho}(t)\,dt} \qquad x \geq \bar{x}(i-1) \qquad (16.44)$$

$$q(x)_i = \frac{\left\{\int_i^\infty \exp[\bar{\bar{u}}(t)/\alpha]\,dt\right\}^{\alpha/\gamma} \left[\int_i^\infty \hat{\rho}(t)\,dt\right]^{\beta/\gamma}}{\alpha^{\alpha/\gamma}\beta^{\beta/\gamma}\left\{\int_i^\infty [\hat{w}(t) - \hat{c}(x-g, t)]\,dt\right\}^{(\alpha+\beta)/\gamma}} \qquad x \geq x(i-1) \qquad (16.45)$$

As the time horizon shrinks to the current time period, (16.44) and (16.45) reduce to (16.5) and (16.13), respectively. The city will expand until a point is reached where a farmer right at the boundary can expect to make just as much per unit of land if he converts, as he would if he didn't convert. The new population increment and city boundary will be thus determined.

The owner of a unit that was built at time j will demolish and replace it at time $i(i > j)$ if

$$\max_{q(x)_i, k(x)_i} \int_i^\infty \left[\frac{\hat{R}(x,t)_i - \hat{\rho}(t)k(x)_i}{q(x)_i}\right] dt - \frac{D[k(x)_j, q(x)_j, i]}{q(x)_j}$$

$$> \int_i^\infty \left[\frac{\hat{R}(x,t)_j - \hat{\rho}(t)k(x)_j}{q(x)_j}\right] dt \qquad (16.46)$$

A more complex view of housing can be achieved by introducing maintenance and depreciation. This hinges on replacing $k(x)$, housing capital, with $h(x, t)$, housing services, where $h(x, t)_i = k(x)_i^a \exp[-a\eta(t-i)] \times m(x, t)^b$ where a and b are coefficients, η is the rate of depreciation, and $m(x, t)$ denotes variable maintenance inputs. The above problems would then involve maximization with respect to $k(x)_i$, $q(x)_i$, and $\hat{m}(x, t)_i$.

Policy Implications

Within the confines of positive analysis alone one cannot go far toward deriving precise policy conclusions. This task would require a normative model of urban growth in which an optimum housing expansion-conversion process is derived and its market decentralization is examined. Yet positive analysis is sufficient in pinpointing the policy issues that would have to be resolved by normative analyses. The main issue at hand is the extent to which optimum urban growth plans which recognize the durability of housing and the presence of expectations are inferior to long-run static configurations and the extent to which short-run configurations can approach over time the Pareto efficient static configuration, through public intervention.

The major source of short-run inefficiency is myopic investment decisions in durable capital stock. Public policy could therefore be designed so as to make accurate foresight into the future possible. This outlook will involve stimulating or regulating land speculation so that the long-run value of land is better approximated at the time of its release. The optimum extent of speculative activity could be derived within an optimum growth analysis. A normative approach would also tell us the extent to which urban renewal (housing replacement) activity ought to absorb our energies, and the extent to which housing abandonment is a symptom of healthy growth rather than a serious malady. Finally, it might tell us whether efficient land use patterns can be realized as a market process by influencing agents' expectations as opposed to by employing direct controls such as zoning.

Notes

1. W. Alonso [1964].
2. A. Anas [1975a].
3. M.J. Beckmann [1969].
4. D. Harrison, Jr., and J.F. Kain, 1974, "Cumulative Urban Growth and Urban Density Functions," *Journal of Urban Economics*, vol. 1, 68-69.
5. E.S. Mills [1967].
6. E.S. Mills, 1970, "Urban Density Functions," *Urban Studies*, vol. 7, 5-20.
7. R.F. Muth [1969].
8. W.C. Wheaton [1974a].

17 The Meaning of Entropy Maximizing Models

Michael J. Webber

Some land use phenomena occur more frequently in nature than do others. A pricing mechanism for land apparently exists only in some human societies, while a negative exponential decay of land occupation rates, away from some central peak, is observed in some nonhuman societies as well as in urban areas: see, for example, the map in Altman and Altman[1] and the table and discussion in Webber.[22] Such variations in the frequency with which phenomena occur indicate that very widespread regularities should be explainable by elementary and general models which are made more specialized when particular societies are to be examined.

Most writing in this area involves attributes, such as price of land, that are found only in a subset of human societies. By contrast, this chapter will discuss a class of models, based on the entropy maximizing principle, that can be applied to a wider set of societies. (The price paid for this generality is a loss of richness, for entropy maximizing models embody a smaller set of concepts than do "economic" models; thus, land price is not examined.)

Unfortunately, the philosophic basis of entropy maximizing models seems to be widely misunderstood. It is therefore the aim here to dispel some of these misunderstandings about the meaning of entropy maximizing models of urban structure. Such misunderstandings are primarily associated with the view that these models are merely analogies drawn from statistical mechanics, that they are based on the assumption of random behaviour, and that they only describe systems at equilibrium. This chapter will also demonstrate the falsity of the notions that entropy maximizing models are predicated on equal a priori probabilities and can encompass only independent events. We begin by briefly outlining a standard model in order to illustrate how these misunderstandings may have arisen; make a short incursion into information theory; state the paradigm in general terms; explain and justify the paradigm; and, finally, show how unreasonable are the misconceptions.

A Standard Model

A given city comprises a set, $\mathscr{L}$ of discrete regions. Within this city there

Michael J. Webber is a member of the Department of Geography, McMaster University.

The author gratefully acknowledges that preparation of this chapter benefitted from his discussion with Tony Smith.

277

are N people making decisions to locate (that is, choosing one region). N_i of them choose to locate in a region or cell $L_i(L_i \in \mathcal{L})$, which is located at a generalized cost c_i from the origin: c_i, $N_i \in \mathcal{R}^+$, the set of nonnegative real numbers. It is given that

$$\sum_{L_i} N_i = N \qquad L_i \in \mathcal{L} \qquad (17.1)$$

because everyone must make a location decision; it is also known, as a matter of observation perhaps, that

$$\sum_{L_i} N_i c_i = \bar{c} \qquad L_i \in \mathcal{L} \qquad (17.2)$$

Each cell is equally likely a priori to be chosen, and individuals use a randomizing device to choose their actual region, subject to (17.1) and (17.2).

The most likely distribution of people among regions is that which can occur in the maximum number of ways. This distribution is the one maximizing

$$W = \frac{N!}{\prod_{L_i} N_i!} \qquad L_i \in \mathcal{L}$$

which, for large values of N_i, has the same solution as the values of Np_i obtained from

$$\max S = - \sum_{L_i} p_i \ln p_i \qquad L_i \in \mathcal{L} \qquad (17.3)$$

where $N_i = Np_i$. It is well known that the solution of (17.3) with (17.2) and (17.1) is

$$p_i = p(0)e^{-\alpha c_i} \qquad (17.4)$$

where α is a Lagrangian multiplier to be evaluated (see Wilson[26] and Eastin and Shapiro[6]).

It is necessary that (17.4) satisfy the constraints (17.1) and (17.2). Thus, substitute (17.4) in (17.1):

$$\sum_{L_i} p_i = \sum_{L_i} p(0)e^{-\alpha c_i} = 1 \qquad L_i \in \mathcal{L}$$

whence

$$p(0) = \left[\sum_{L_i} e^{-\alpha c_i} \right]^{-1} \qquad L_i \in \mathcal{L}$$

Equally, from (17.2)

$$\sum_{L_i} p_i c_i = \frac{\bar{c}}{N} = \frac{\sum_{L_i} c_i e^{-\alpha c_i}}{\sum_{L_i} e^{-\alpha c_i}} \qquad L_i \in \mathscr{L}$$

determines α. By substituting (17.4) in (17.3), we see that

$$S = -\ln p(0) + \alpha \frac{\bar{c}}{N}$$

Explicit solutions of this form are extensively discussed by Tribus[19] and Webber.[24]

The model has several pleasing properties as a device for estimating the location of people. The form of (17.4) is gratifying in view of Clark[5] and many later writers. The model can easily be extended to a city in which there are several types of people: if the locations of these types are not independent, a density hollow may arise at the core of the city.[21] Other extensions are possible, in the same manner that Wilson[27] has extended his basic transport flow model. Notice also that if probabilities are not equal a priori, the maximand (17.3) may be replaced by

$$S^1 = -\sum_{L_i} p_i \ln \frac{p_i}{q_i} \qquad L_i \in \mathscr{L} \qquad (17.5)$$

where q_i is the a priori probability of an individual choosing to locate in cell L_i. See Batty[2] for urban applications of (17.5).

Such a model has several characteristics which distinguish it from the model to be advanced later in the chapter. Firstly, probabilities are objective: p_i is the relative frequency with which L_i is chosen by the population of the city. Secondly, a physical process of choice is envisaged, in which individuals choose regions at random (each region being equally likely to be chosen a priori, in the simplest model). It is, perhaps, unfair to label this a "Wilson" model, because Wilson[26] does refer to other interpretations of (17.3); nevertheless, this model is the interpretation which he stresses earlier,[25] and because of his pioneering and dominating position as an entropy maximizing model builder for urban systems, this objective model has become standard.

The line of thought which concludes with (17.4) derives from a statistical mechanical investigation by Boltzmann which concerned the likelihood of finding a system in a given state. It continues to be important in statistical physics. One can readily sympathize with the view that the standard model is merely a statistical mechanical analogy of a sophisticated kind (the processes are regarded as similar). Equally, acceptance of the standard model in urban studies should be tempered by the realization that the conceptual bases of Boltzmann's work are far from sound (see, for example, the critical discussions in Jaynes[13] and Georgescu-Roegan[7]).

Two other important consequences follow from the standard model. These are, first, that in the long run the system is most likely to be found in the state which has maximum entropy; and, secondly, that if a system is evolving, its most likely direction of evolution is toward the state of maximum entropy. These consequences are results of Liouville's theorem, for a proof of which see Tolman.[17] In turn, the results imply that entropy is most likely to be increasing if it is not at a maximum and that when entropy is at a maximum it is most likely that the system state is not changing: that is, the state with maximum entropy is a time-independent or equilibrium state. In such an objective analysis, maximum entropy and equilibrium are inextricably linked. But this standard model is not the only interpretation of the entropy maximizing formalism.

Information and Uncertainty

Consider now the problem of locating a single individual in one of the regions of the city. Let p_i be the probability that the individual locates in region $L_i \in \mathcal{L}$; $p_i \geq 0$, and

$$\sum_{L_i} p_i = 1 \qquad L_i \in \mathcal{L}$$

An observer is uncertain about the actual outcome of the location process: the actual choice cannot be predicted. Denote this uncertainty by $S(p_1, p_2, \ldots, p_M)$ if there are M regions in the city. If $p_1 = p_2 = \ldots = p_M$, the uncertainty is denoted by $S(M)$.

Shannon[16] and Khinchin[14] prove the following:

THEOREM 17.1   Let $S(p_1, \ldots, p_M)$ be a function defined for any integer M and for all values of $p_1, p_2, \ldots, p_M$ such that $p_i \geq 0$ $(i = 1, \ldots M)$ and

$$\sum_{i=1}^{M} p_i = 1$$

If, for any M, this function has the following properties:

a. $S(M) = S(1/M, \ldots, 1/M)$ is a monotonically increasing function of M $(M = 1, 2, \ldots)$;

b. $S(ML) = S(M) + S(L)$ $(M, L = 1, 2, \ldots)$;

c.　$S(p_i, \ldots, p_M) = S(p_x, 1-p_x) +$

$$P_x \cdot S\left(\frac{p_1}{p_x}, \frac{p_2}{p_x}, \ldots, \frac{p_j}{p_x}\right) + (1 - p_x) \cdot S\left(\frac{p_{j+1}}{1-p_x}, \frac{p_{j+2}}{1-p_x}, \ldots, \frac{p_M}{1-p_x}\right)$$

where

$$p_x = \sum_{i=1}^{j} p_i; \quad \text{and}$$

d.　$S(p, 1-p)$ is a continuous function of p,

then

$$S(p_1, \ldots, p_M) = -C \sum_{i=1}^{M} p_i \log p_i$$

where C is an arbitrary positive constant and the base of logarithms is any number greater than unity. We shall let $C = 1$, and the base of logarithms be e.

This is a fundamental theorem of information theory. Observe that in the standard model the function S is an approximation to $(\ln W - \ln N!)N$. By contrast, the value of S derived from Theorem 17.1 is not an approximation, it is an exact equation. Other sets of axioms have been proposed which also generate S. Equally, other axioms for an uncertainty measure have been proposed which yield other definitions of uncertainty. The key axiom in this set is (b), for this is common to all sets of axioms which generate S as a measure of uncertainty.

It is a natural extension of the notion of entropy to suppose that if knowledge about the outcome of a process B causes uncertainty about the outcome of the process A to fall, then knowledge of B imparts information about A. In particular, the information conveyed about the outcome of one process A by another process B is defined to be

$$I(A \mid B) = S(A) - S(A \mid B)$$

where $S(A \mid B)$ is the conditional entropy (average uncertainty about A given that an outcome of B has occurred). If the message is definite (informs the observer that one possible outcome of A has occurred) then $S(A \mid B) = 0$, from which we have

$$I^1(A \mid B) = S(A).$$

The Paradigm: Formalism

Actually, urban modelers are not concerned solely with the location of a particular individual. They also need to know that individual's occupational status, income group, education level, race, house quality, and the changes in all of these variables over time. As a matter of choice, we shall suppose here that all these variables are discrete, including time.

There exist, therefore, v possible types of individual where, by "type," is mean an individual with a distinguishable location in phase space. If, for example, there is a two-fold classification of occupational status (S_1 and S_2), a two-fold classification of race (R_1 and R_2), and three time periods (T_1, T_2, and T_3), the phase space in six dimensional—$S(T_1)$, $S(T_2)$, $S(T_3)$, $R(T_1)$, $R(T_2)$, $R(T_3)$—and the individual can take on one of two values in each dimension, assuming that race can change over time.

Consider a single individual. There is a probability $w^{(\alpha)}$ ($\alpha = 1, \ldots, v$) that this individual is of type α:

$$w^{(\alpha)} \geq 0 \quad (\alpha = 1, \ldots, v) \qquad \text{and} \qquad \sum_{\alpha=1}^{v} w^{(\alpha)} = 1$$

The individual's characteristics are represented by an n-component vector $X^{(\alpha)} = (x_1^{(\alpha)}, x_2^{(\alpha)}, \ldots, x_n^{(\alpha)})$, where $x_i^{(\alpha)}$ is the ith component of the vector $X^{(\alpha)}$ in the coordinate system $\{\psi_1\}$, which has n dimensions. Vectors are normalized:

$$\sum_{i=1}^{n} [x_i^{(\alpha)}]^2 = 1 \tag{17.6}$$

There may be defined a function G, with two arguments, i and j:

$$g_{ij} = \sum_{\alpha=1}^{v} w^{(\alpha)} x_i^{(\alpha)} x_j^{(\alpha)} \tag{17.7}$$

known as the autocorrelation between dimensions i and j. The matrix

$$G = (g_{11}, g_{12}, \ldots, g_{1n}, \ldots, g_{nn})$$

is the autocorrelation matrix. And, clearly, from (17.7), G is symmetrical, that is, $g_{ij} = g_{ji}$.

The diagonal elements of G are

$$P = (\rho_1, \rho_2, \ldots, \rho_n)$$

where

$$\rho_i = \sum_j g_{ij} \, \delta_{ij} \quad \text{(Kronecker's delta)}$$

By (17.6), it is apparent that

$$\rho_i \geq 0 \quad (i = 1,\ldots,n) \qquad \text{and} \qquad \sum_{i=1}^{n} \rho_i = 1$$

Therefore it is possible to define an entropy function

$$S^1 = - \sum_{i=1}^{n} \rho_i \ln \rho_i \qquad (17.8)$$

This definition of entropy suffers from two defects: first, the values of ρ_i and S^1 depend on the choice of coordinate system $\{\psi_i\}$, which arises because, secondly, the vectors $X^{(\alpha)}$ are not necessarily orthogonal—the events of being type $\alpha = 1$ and type $\alpha = 2$ are not necessarily independent. The following theorem indicates how to remove these difficulties.

THEOREM 17.2   Obtain from G its eigenvalues λ_k and eigenvectors ϕ_k. Then

a.   in the coordinate system $\{\phi_k\}$, $g_{ij} = \lambda_i \delta_{ij}$;

b. $\lambda_i \geq 0$ all i and $\Sigma_i \lambda_i = 1$;

c.   the eigenvectors are mutually orthogonal;

d.   a given matrix G can be represented in only one way as a mixture of orthogonal states, if the eigenvectors are nondegenerate; and

e.   for given $\{w^{(\alpha)}\}$ and $\{X^{(\alpha)}\}$,

$$- \sum_i \lambda_i \ln \lambda_i \leq - \sum_j \rho_j \ln \rho_j$$

There exist matrices $F^{(1)}, F^{(2)},\ldots, F^{(m)}$; the elements of $F^{(h)}$ are denoted $(F_{ij}^{(h)}, i,j=1,\ldots,n)$ and are measured in the $\{\psi_i\}$ coordinate system. For a given type of individual α, the expected value of F^h is

$$\langle F^{(h)} \rangle_\alpha = \sum_{i=1}^{n} \sum_{j=1}^{n} x_i^{(\alpha)} x_j^{(\alpha)} F_{ij}^{(h)})$$

and its average over all types, $\alpha = 1,\ldots, v$, is

$$\langle F^{(h)} \rangle = \sum_{\alpha=1}^{v} w^{(\alpha)} \langle F^{(h)} \rangle_\alpha$$

$$= \sum_i \sum_j \lambda_i \delta_{ij} f_{ij}^{(h)}$$

where $f^{(h)}$ is the representation of $F^{(h)}$ in the new coordinate system $\{\phi_i\}$.

Now, suppose that probabilities are to be assigned to the event that the individual shall be of type α, $\alpha = 1, \ldots, v$. It is known that m expected values, $\langle F^{(1)} \rangle, \ldots, \langle F^{(m)} \rangle$, are given. The general entropy-maximizing paradigm is: choose $\{\lambda_i\}$ to maximize

$$S = - \sum_i \lambda_i \ln \lambda_i \qquad (17.9)$$

subject to

$$\langle F^{(1)} \rangle = \sum_{\alpha=1}^{v} w^{(\alpha)} \langle F^{(1)} \rangle_\alpha$$

$$\vdots \qquad\qquad\qquad (17.10)$$

$$\langle F^{(m)} \rangle = \sum_{\alpha=1}^{v} w^{(\alpha)} \langle F^{(m)} \rangle_\alpha$$

$$\Sigma \lambda_i = 1 \qquad (17.11)$$

S is a concave function of the $\{\lambda_i\}$. Therefore if the matrix of second order partial derivatives of the Lagrangian with respect to the $\{\lambda_i\}$ is negative definite or negative semidefinite when evaluated at a local maximum point, there exists a unique maximum of S. The conditions on this maximum are that

$$- \ln \lambda_k^* - 1 - \beta^{(0)} - \sum_{h=1}^{m} \beta^{(h)} \sum_i \sum_j \left(\delta_{ij} f_{ij}^{(h)} + \lambda_k^* \delta_{ij} \frac{\partial f_{ij}^{(h)}}{\partial \lambda_k} \right)$$

$$= 0 \quad \text{all } k \qquad (17.12)$$

and that

$$\langle F^{(h)} \rangle = \sum_i \sum_j \lambda_i^* \delta_{ij} f_{ij}^{(h)}, \qquad h = 1, 2, \ldots, m$$

At this maximum,

$$S^* = 1 + \beta^{(0)} + \sum_{h=1}^{m} \beta^{(h)} \langle F^{(h)} \rangle$$

and $\partial S^* / \partial \langle F^{(h)} \rangle = \beta^{(h)}$. The $\beta^{(h)}$ and $\beta^{(0)}$ are Lagrangian multipliers to be evaluated; and, as this last relation makes clear, they are to be interpreted as measuring the marginal entropy of a change in the value of a constraint.

In the particular case in which the constraints are linear, that is in which $\partial f_{ij}^{(h)} / \partial \lambda_k = 0$, equation (17.12) reduces to the simple form

$$\lambda_i^* = \exp \left[-\beta^{(0)} - 1 - \sum_{h=1}^{m} \beta^{(h)} f_{ij}^{(h)} \right] \qquad \text{all } i.$$

Again, in the one-dimensional case, this reduces to the formalism of the standard model.

This paradigm is derived from Jaynes,[11,12] who followed von Neumann[20] in the use of (17.9) as a definition of entropy. The statement of the constraints is obviously tailored to the needs of thermodynamicists. Two generalizations may be useful in the urban context. First, the constraints may embody relationships among the variables other than observations of the form (17.10) about some averages: for example, a model of the evolution of part of the urban system may be embodied in these constraints. Secondly, some of the constraints (such as those on community spending of its income) may be expressed as inequalities. The necessary change of mathematical structure is immediately evident.

The Paradigm: Justification I

Once the set of values of $\{\lambda_i^*\}$ are known, the probability $w^{(\alpha)*}$ of the individual being in state α may also be found. This method thus enables the modeler to assign probabilities $w^{(\alpha)*}$ to the event of an individual being in state α. Thus the assignment (17.12) is that assignment of probabilities to states which leaves the modeler maximally uncertain about the actual state of the individual, uncertainty being defined as (17.9).

Were there no constraints (17.10) and no information about the interdependence of dimensions, we would have

$$w^{(\alpha)} = \frac{1}{v} \qquad \alpha = 1, \ldots, v$$

and the uncertainty would be

$$S_2^* = -\sum_\alpha \frac{1}{v} \ln \frac{1}{v} = \ln v$$

which is the maximum possible. Because of the constraints, the maximum value of S falls to S^*, given by (17.9), with (17.12). Therefore, from the definition of information,

$$I(A \mid C) = S^*(A) - S^*(A \mid C)$$
$$= \ln v - \left(-\sum_i \lambda_i^* \ln \lambda_i^* \right) \qquad (17.13)$$

where A is identified as the problem without constraints, and C is the problem as defined under Formalism. Any other assignment of probabilities than (17.12) which is consistent with the constraints—$\{\lambda_i\}$, generated by a process C^1, for example—has lower entropy: that is, $S^*(A \mid C) > S(A \mid C^1)$, from which we get

$$I(A \mid C) < I(A \mid C^1) \qquad (17.14)$$

The inequality (17.14) indicates that the constraints (17.10) must contain an amount of information equal to $I(A\,|\,C)$. Equally, the assignment of probabilities (17.12) is that assignment which assumes that the amount of information in the constraints is at a minimum, $I(A\,|\,C)$. Any other assignment of probabilities, such as $\{\lambda_i^!\}$, assumes that the constraints contain more information than this minimum, that the outcome of the trial is less uncertain than it might be. Since by hypothesis, the modeler's knowledge is completely summarized in (17.10), there is no reason to justify the assumption that the constraints contain more information than (17.13) or that the outcome is less uncertain than (17.12). There is therefore a sense in which the modeler who passes from (17.10) to $\{\lambda_i^!\}$, has added some of his own "private" information or bias to the solution of the problem. This gives some feeling for the logical principle advanced by Jaynes:[10] given the observer's knowledge about the system, the minimally biased probability assignment is that which maximizes (17.9) subject to (17.10) and (17.11). The maximum entropy distribution is uniquely determined as the one which is maximally noncommittal with regard to missing information.

This justification for maximizing (17.9) bears no relation at all to the argument leading to a standard model. Whereas in a standard model the assigned probabilities represent a distribution that is more likely to occur than any other, an information approach to assigning $\{\lambda_i^*\}$ cannot predict the likelihood that the assigned $\{\lambda_i^*\}$ are "correct," that is, that the $\{\lambda_i^*\}$ would describe the outcome of a long sequence of trials. An entropy-maximizing modeler has no knowledge of the likelihood that the $\{\lambda_i^*\}$ describe the observed distribution of choices over a long period, because such a likelihood depends at least on the likelihood that the observed data are sufficient to characterize $\{\lambda_i^*\}$. Equally, there is no sense in which the $\{\lambda_i^*\}$ of (17.12) are least likely to be wrong or to minimax the errors of prediction. This characteristic of Jaynes' interpretation of the paradigm arises because the model contains no process which determines the outcome of a trial, in contrast to a standard model, which explicitly relies on the assumption of random choice. Jaynes' interpretation thus relies solely on a logical principle, not on a model of society. A standard model purports to predict the state of society, given a process and some constraints; a Jaynes' model determines what the modeler is legitimately entitled to conclude from the constraints, "legitimate" being defined by the logical principle.

A second point of difference exists between the two interpretations. In the standard model, the probabilities are the relative frequencies with which the individuals choose a particular location, and Np_i is therefore the density of population of cell L_i. In Jaynes' interpretation, $\{\lambda_i^*\}$ yields the probability that a given individual will be found in state α. It may be possible to interpret such probabilities in an objective or relative-frequency sense (the given individual makes many trials), but it is also possible to interpret λ_i^* subjectively without the notion of an infinite series of trials. This is an important generalization accomplished by Jaynes' interpretation, bought by considering only a single individual. Thus, λ_i is not a relative population density, because the means and variances of population density in a given cell can only be calculated by sampling from the $\{\lambda_i^*\}$ for the N individuals.

The information model only yields probabilities. Once these probabilities have been estimated, a statistical model of society may be built which describes how a series of individuals make location choices, each with an initial probability of being in state α given by $w^{(\alpha)}$. Such is a sampling process, which may be based on independent or interdependent trials: there is no limitation to the case of independent trials. The entropy maximizing model then yields information not given by an "economic" model, namely the variance of population density in given states.

The Paradigm: Justification II

In the previous section, we have established that the use of the entropy maximizing formalism can be justified by a logical principle, due to Jaynes. The formalism solves the problem of finding a distribution of probabilities which is consistent with a given set of constraints: given the constraints find $\{\lambda_i^*\}$. The amount of information contained in the constraints can be measured as $I(A\,|\,C)$, in equation (17.13), and for a given set of constraints, there is a unique probability distribution which is consistent both with the constraints and their information content. This is the only use of the formalism that Jaynes apparently envisages; it is also the only manner in which the formalism has been employed in research into the structure of urban areas.

Yet scientific problems do not always have this form. Indeed, it seems that, so far, urban research has largely evolved in a different manner, namely by finding a set of constraints that would produce a given observed result. Thus, typically, the $\{p_i\}$ or $\{\lambda_i\}$ are known, and some constraints must be imposed on behavior to generate these distributions: for example, this is how knowledge about population densities evolved. This is an inversion of the problem solved by Jaynes.

We can prove that any probability distribution over the states $\alpha = 1, \ldots, v$ that can be expressed as the exponent of functions of these states (such as the geometric, normal, lognormal), is uniquely associated by the entropy maximizing formalism with a set of constraints on the moments of those functions of state. Thus, given a probability distribution $\{\lambda_i\}$ that can be expressed in exponential form, a set of constraints C on the moments can be found such that $\{\lambda_i\}$ is a maximum entropy distribution subject to those constraints. If a smaller set of constraints, $C^1 \subset C$, is constructed, the modeler must add information to obtain $\{\lambda_i\}$ from C^1. If a larger set of constraints, $C'' \supset C$, is assumed, more than $\{\lambda_i\}$ could be inferred from C''; and $\{\lambda_i\}$ may not be consistent with those constraints. The modeler is attempting to discover a set of constraints which contain just sufficient information to reduce uncertainty from $\ln m$ to $S(\lambda_1 \lambda_2, \ldots)$.

The constraints must now receive an interpretation different from that employed in the previous section or in standard models. In the two earlier interpretations of the formalism, the constraints are usually regarded as representing given data, on for example, the expected cost of trips by the individual; alternatively, they may represent known relations between variables, particularly in the multidimensional cases. The constraints thus represent observations that "happen to be." But in this additional role of the formalism, the constraints are not observations; rather, they are effective constraints that actually limit potential behavior, just as income limits choice in a utility maximizing model. Thus, what requires explanation is not why population densities in a city are distributed as the negative exponential but rather why the expected distance of an individual from the city center is constrained in some fashion. In this case, the entropy maximizing formalism is a device that identifies the constraints that must be explained if some observation is to be regarded as natural.

Misconceptions Again

In the opening paragraph of this chapter, several misconceptions about the notion of entropy and the formalism of maximizing entropy were identified. In the first section, these conceptions were briefly raised in relation to the standard interpretation of the formalism. These errors include the ideas that entropy must increase over time, that a maximum entropy distribution describes a system in equilibrium, and that the formalism is employed in urban geography merely by analogy with statistical mechanics.

It is common, particularly among economists, to regard entropy as a physical concept, the use of which in urban geography represents yet another borrowing from physics (see Beckmann and Golob[4] and Hansen[9]). This is particularly easy to understand since the standard model is a Boltzmann model and the first substantial use of the method in geography was to derive the interaction equation or gravity model, which had itself been borrowed directly from Newtonian mechanics.[25] Thus, Beckmann and Golob regard entropy maximization as a "metaphysical method" and feel that

Presumably entropy is a measure of diversity, but its operational meaning in connection with travel decisions is obscure. The derivation usually given is a non-critical adaptation of an argument from Kinetic Gas Theory to an economic situation. (Beckmann and Golob,[4] p. 3)

Now this is clearly not true of the use of Jaynes' formalism, for that formalism simply does not have any physical content. The use of this method has been justified by some purely mathematical reasoning, which has no substantive content, and by a logical principle. Indeed, Jaynes regards statistical mechanics as one particular example of the use of his principle, and raises the

. . . possibility that we have now reached a state where statistical mechanics is no longer dependent on physical hypotheses, but may become merely an example of statistical inference. (Jaynes,[10] p. 621)

Of course, the formalism was discovered and first used by physicists; but the differential calculus was discovered and first employed by physicists, a fact which hardly implies that urban growth theorists are using an analogy from mechanics.

Similarly, in social science, it is common to investigate the notion of increasing entropy[28] and to suppose that entropy-maximizing models assume an equilibrium.[18] As we have seen in the first part of this chapter, the standard model can relate entropy and equilibrium, though this must be carefully handled (see Wilson,[26] pp. 122-124). However, the purely mathematical and subjective definition of entropy advanced in this paper bears no relation to the notion of equilibrium: entropy is used merely to define the legitimacy of inference. In particular, the general formalism we have described can be dynamic, without any alteration of structure.

One final, but important, misconception must be dispelled. Consider the standard location model initially described. This is derived from an urn model and interpreted as defining the most likely pattern of population in a region if it is assumed that behavior is independently random, that there are no preferences at the individual scale for particular locations and that behavior is not necessarily cost minimizing. These behavior patterns are regarded as assumptions which justify the use of entropy-maximizing models.[8,15,25] Since the assumptions, particularly the first two, are regarded as intuitively implausible, the entropy-maximizing procedure is itself cast in doubt. But in Jaynes' interpretation, such a view is wrong, for the subjective entropy-maximizing procedure does not rely on these assumptions. Rather, the subjectivist would observe that the formal equivalence of the subjective and standard models implies that the available information is consistent with the hypotheses that behavior is independently random, exhibits no individual preferences, and need not minimize costs. No such hypotheses are necessary, but if some process must be invented as a psychological prop for urban scholars, then those at least have the advantage of being consistent with such data as are observed.

Conclusions

There can be little doubt that the paradigm described here is immensely powerful, and yet that its potential has been little realized by urban modelers. There exist three major areas in which progress must be made. First, the general paradigm must be investigated theoretically, perhaps on the basis of hypothesized constraints. Secondly, and this is essentially an empirical question, the equal a priori event must be defined: this issue is raised by Webber.[24] Thirdly, it has been supposed that knowledge is available to be encoded in the constraints, or that constraints are identified which are consistent with given observations. But when theoretical issues are addressed, the constraints must be derived and the numerical values of particular statistics must be established by reference to prior theory. Unless the constraints can be justified by such a derivation, the theoretical use of the formalism (as opposed to its planning uses) remains open to the charge that

. . . its proponents have become skilled virtuosos in subjecting every problem to this approach and inventing ad hoc constraints to make entropy fit the case (Beckmann,[3] p. 2).

Notes

1. S.A. Altman and J. Altman, 1970, *Baboon Ecology*. Basel: Karger A. G., p. 118.

2. M. Batty, 1974, "Spatial Entropy," *Geographical Analysis*, vol. 6, 1-32.

3. M.J. Beckmann, 1973, "Entropy, Gravity, Utility and All That," manuscript.

4. M.J. Beckmann and T.F. Golob, 1971, "On the Metaphysical Foundations of Traffic Theory: Entropy Revisited," Paper presented at the Fifth International Symposium on the Theory of Traffic Flow and Transportation, Berkeley, California.

5. C. Clark, 1951, "Urban Population Densities," *Journal, Royal Statistical Society*, ser. A, vol. 114, 490-496.

6. R.V. Eastin and P. Shapiro, 1973, "The Design of a Location Experiment," *Transportation Research*, vol. 7, 17-22.

7. N. Georgescu-Roegen, 1971, *The Entropy Law and the Economic Process*. Cambridge: Harvard, pp. 141-169.

8. P. Gould, 1972, "Pedagogic Review," *Annals, Association of American Geographers*, vol. 62, 689-700.

9. S. Hansen, 1972, "Utility, Accessibility and Entropy in Spatial Modelling," *Swedish Journal of Economics*, vol. 74, 35-44.

10. E.T. Jaynes, 1957, "Information Theory and Statistical Mechanics I," *Physical Review*, vol. 106, 620-630.

11. E.T. Jaynes, 1957, "Information Theory and Statistical Mechanics. II," *Physical Review*, vol. 108, 171-190.

12. E.T. Jyanes, 1963, "Information Theory," in K.W. Ford (ed.), *Statistical Physics*, vol. 3, New York: Benjamin, pp. 182-218.

13. E.T. Jaynes, 1967, "Foundations of Probability Theory and Statistical Mechanics," in M. Bunge (ed.), *Delaware Symposium in the Foundations of Physics*, New York: Springer-Verlag, pp. 77-101.

14. A.I. Khinchin, 1957, "The Entropy Concept in Probability Theory," in A.I. Khinchin, *Mathematical Foundations of Information Theory*. New York: Dover, pp. 1-28.

15. R. Lee, 1974, *Entropy Models in Spatial Analysis*. Discussion Paper 15, Department of Geography, University of Toronto, pp. 26-29.

16. C.E. Shannon, 1948, "A Mathematical Theory of Communication," *Bell System Technical Journal*, vol. 27, 379-423 and 623-656.

17. R.C. Tolman, 1938, *The Principles of Statistical Mechanics*. Oxford: Oxford University, chs. 3 and 9.

18. S.G. Tomlin, 1969, *A Kinetic Theory of Traffic Distributions and Similar Problems*. Working Paper 46, Center for Environmental Studies.

19. M. Tribus, 1969, *Rational Descriptions, Decisions and Designs*. Oxford: Pergamon, pp. 124-127.

20. J. von Neumann, 1943, *Mathematische Grundlagen des Quantenmechanik*. New York: Dover.

21. M.J. Webber, 1975a, "Entropy Maximizing Models for Nonindependent Events," *Environment and Planning A*, vol. 7, 99-108.

22. M.J. Webber, 1975b, *Analysis of Land Use and Density Surfaces*. Discussion Paper No. 2, Department of Geography, McMaster University, pp. 66-69.

23. M.J. Webber, "Elementary Entropy Maximising Probability Distributions: Analysis and Interpretation," *Economic Geography* (forthcoming).

24. M.J. Webber, ''Entropy Maximising Models for the Distribution of 'Expenditures','' manuscript.

25. A.G. Wilson, 1967, ''A Statistical Theory of Spatial Trip Distribution Models,'' *Transportation Research*, vol. 1, 253-269.

26. A.G. Wilson, 1970, *Entropy in Urban and Regional Modelling*. London: Pion.

27. A.G. Wilson, 1972, *Further Developments of Entropy Maximising Transport Models*. Working Paper 20, Department of Geography, University of Leeds.

28. M.J. Woldenberg and B.J.L. Berry, 1967, ''Rivers and Central Places: Analogous Systems,'' *Journal of Regional Science*, vol. 7, 129-139.

A Coded Bibliography of the New Urban Economics

This bibliography was compiled by A. Anas and D.S. Dendrinos in conjunction with their survey of the new urban economics (Chapter 3 of this volume). References with an asterisk are additions to the original bibliography. Those without an asterisk are followed by an identification string of nine numbers. The coding of the identification is as follows:

A. Type of publication:
   1. Book
   2. Article in journal or book
   3. Note or comment in journal
   4. Unpublished manuscript or mimeo
   5. Doctoral dissertation
   6. Forthcoming

B. Type of contents:
   1. Review and/or discussion
   2. Discussion of general issues without a particular model
   3. A model with a generalized form of key equations such as production and utility functions
   4. A model with a specific form of key equations such as production and utility functions
   5. A specific model as in (4) above, solved and tested through numerical simulation
   6. A specific model as in (4) tested empirically

C. Year of publication:
   1. 1960-1970
   2. 1971
   3. 1972
   4. 1973
   5. 1974
   6. 1975

D. Type of analysis:
   1. Market equilibrium
   2. Equilibrium versus optimum
   3. Mixed economy

4. Social cost minimum
5. Social welfare maximum
6. Nonapplicable

E. Presence or absence of externalities:
1. One or more externalities, such as congestion, pollution, or environmental density, are analyzed.
2. Externalities are not discussed or analyzed
3. Nonapplicable

F. Sectors jointly modeled, such that at least some results in one sector depend on the presence of at least one of the other sectors:
1. Residential, employment, transportation
2. Residential, transportation
3. Employment, transportation
4. Employment, residential
5. Residential
6. Employment
7. Transportation
8. Nonapplicable

G. Type of residential market discussed or modeled:
1. Land market only
2. Housing market only
3. Both land and housing market
4. Nonapplicable

H. Method of mathematical analysis and representation of space:
1. Linear programming, nonlinear programming, or other discrete methods; discrete space.
2. Calculus or calculus of variations; continuous space
3. Nonapplicable

I. Static versus dynamic analysis:
1. Static model; space only
2. Dynamic model; time only
3. Dynamic model; space and time
4. Nonapplicable

Alao, N., 1974. "An Approach to Intraurban Location Theory," *Economic Geography*, vol. 50, 59-69.   245124121

*Alao, N., 1975. "On Some Determinants of the Optimum Geography of An Urban Place," ch. 12 of this volume.

*Alonso, W., 1960a. *A Model of the Urban Land Market: Location and Densities of Dwellings and Businesses*. Ph.D. dissertation. Philadelphia: University of Pennsylvania.

Alonso, W., 1960b. "A Theory of the Urban Land Market," *Papers and Proceedings of the Regional Science Association*, vol. 6, 149-157.
231124121

Alonso, W., 1964. *Location and Land Use—Toward a General Theory of Land Rent*. Cambridge: Harvard University Press.   131124121

*Amson, J.C., 1972. "The Dependence of Population Distribution on Location Costs," *Environment and Planning*, vol. 4, 163-181.

*Anas, A., 1975a. *Spatial Growth and Dynamics in the Urban Housing Market*. Ph.D. dissertation. Philadelphia: University of Pennsylvania.

*Anas, A., 1975b. "Short-Run Dynamics in the Spatial Housing Market," Ch. 16 of this volume.

Anas, A., and D.S. Dendrinos, 1975. "The New Urban Economis: A Brief Survey." Ch. 3 of this volume.   415638434

Artle, R.A., 1971. "Discussion of Market Choices and Optimum City Size," *American Economic Review*, vol. 61, 354-355.   312411321

*Artle, R., 1973. *Cities as Public Goods*. Memo No. ERL-M417, Electronics Research Laboratory, University of California, Berkeley.

*Artle, R., and P. Varaiya, 1974. *On the Existence of Positive Rent Gradients in Thünen Models*. Memo No. ERL-M459, Electronics Research Laboratory, University of California, Berkeley.

Averous, C.P., and D.B. Lee, 1973. "Land Allocation and Transportation Pricing in a Mixed Urban Economy," *Journal of Regional Science*, vol. 13, 173-185.   244323121

Barr, J.L., 1972. "City Size, Land Rent and the Supply of Public Goods," *Regional and Urban Economics*, vol. 2, 67-103.   233125321

Barr, J.L., 1973. "Tiebout Models of Community Structure," *Papers and Proceedings of the Regional Science Association*, vol. 30, 113-139.
234125121

Beckmann, M.J., 1957. "On the Distribution of Rent and Residential Density in Cities." Paper presented at the Inter-Departmental Seminar on Mathematical Applications in the Social Sciences, Yale University.
440125121

Beckmann, M.J., 1969. "On the Distribution of Urban Rent and Residential Density," *Journal of Economic Theory*, vol. 1, 60-68.   241125121

Beckmann, M.J., 1970. "Equilibrium vs. Optimum: Spacing of Firms and Patterns of Market Areas." Manuscript.   441226121

Beckmann, M.J., 1972. "Von Thünen Revisited: A Neoclassical Land Use Model," *The Swedish Journal of Economics*, vol. 74, 1-7. 243128121

*Beckmann, M.J., 1973. "Equilibrium Models of Residential Land Use," *Regional and Urban Economics*, vol. 3, 361-368.

Beckmann, M.J., 1974. "Spatial Equilibrium in the Housing Market," *Journal of Urban Economics*, vol. 1, 99-107.   245125321

*Beckmann, M.J., 1975. "Spatial Equilibrium in the Dispersed City." Ch. 8 of this volume.

*Ben-Shahar, H.; A. Mazor; and D. Pines, 1969. "Town Planning and Welfare Maximization: A Methodological Approach," *Regional Studies*, vol. 3, 105-113.

*Ben-Shahar, H.; A. Mazor; and D. Pines, 1971. *A Linear Programming Model for Optimizing Land Use*. Working Paper No. 5, Center for Urban and Regional Studies, Tel Aviv University.

Bollobas, B., and N. Stern, 1972. "The Optimal Structure of Market Areas," *Journal of Economic Theory,* vol. 4, 174-179.   233236421

*Blackburn, A.J., 1971. "Equilibrium in the Market for Land: Obtaining Spatial Distributions by Change of Variable," *Econometrica*, vol. 39, 641-644.

*Borukhov, E., 1971. "Diseconomies of Scale in Urban Transportation," *Southern Economic Journal*, vol. 38, 79-82.

Borukhov, E., 1973. "City Size and Transportation Costs," *Journal of Political Economy*, vol. 81, 1205-1215.   244422121

Capozza, D.R., 1973. "Subways and Land Use," *Environment and Planning*, vol. 5, 555-577.   244121321

*Capozza, D.R., 1975. "Employment/Population Ratios in Urban Areas: A Model of the Urban Land, Labor, and Goods Markets." Ch. 9 of this volume.

*Casetti, E., 1967. "Urban Population Density Patterns: An Alternate Explanation," *Canadian Geographer*, vol. 11, 96-100.

*Casetti, E., 1969. "Alternative Urban Population Density Models: An Analytical Comparison of Their Validity Range." In J. Scott (ed.), *London Papers in Regional Science*, vol. 1, Studies in Regional Science. London: Pion. pp. 105-113.

Casetti, E., 1970a. *Spatial Equilibrium Distribution of 'Rich' and 'Poor' Households in an Idealized Urban Setting*. Discussion Paper 13, Department of Geography, The Ohio State University.   441125121

*Casetti, E., 1970b. *On the Derivation of Spatial Equilibrium Urban Land Value Functions*. Discussion Paper 14, Department of Geography, The Ohio State University.

Casetti, E., 1971. "Equilibrium Land Values and Population Density in an Urban Setting," *Economic Geography*, vol. 47, 16-20.   242125121

Casetti, E., 1972. "Spatial Equilibrium in an Ideal Urban Setting with Pareto Distributed Incomes." In E. Cripps (ed.), *Proceedings of the Annals of Regional Science*. London: Pion.   243125121

Casetti, E., 1973. "Urban Land Value Functions. Equilibrium vs. Optimality," *Economic Geography*, vol. 49, 357-365.   244215121

*Casetti, E., 1974. "Optimum Urban Population Densities." In M. Yeates (ed.), *Proceedings of the International Geographical Union Commission on Quantitative Geography*. Montreal: McGill-Queen's University Press. pp. 113-120.

Casetti, E., and G.J. Papageorgiou, 1971. "A Spatial Equilibrium Model of Urban Structure," *Canadian Geographer*, vol. 15, 30-37.   242125121

Delson, J.K., 1970. "Correction on the Boundary Conditions in Beckmann's Model on Urban Rent and Residential Density," *Journal of Economic Theory*, vol. 2, 314-318.   311125121

Dendrinos, D.S., 1975. *A Dynamic General Market Equilibrium Model of Urban Form*. Ph.D. dissertation. Philadelphia: University of Pennsylvania.   556124123

Dixit, A., 1971. "Route Choice and Congestion in Urban Transport." Manuscript.   442411121

Dixit, A., 1973. "The Optimum Factory Town," *Bell Journal of Economics and Management Science*, vol. 4, 637-651.   254211121

*Evans, A.W., 1974. *Rent and Housing in the Theory of Urban Growth*. WN 381, Center for Environmental Studies, London.

*Fahri, A., 1973. "Urban Economic Growth and Conflicts: A Theoretical Approach," *Papers and Proceedings of the Regional Science Association*, vol. 31, 95-124.

Fales, R., and L. Moses, 1972. "Land Use Theory and the Spatial Structure of the Nineteenth-Century City," *Papers and Proceedings of the Regional Science Association*, vol. 28, 49-80.

Fisch, O., 1974. "Impact Analysis on Optimal Urban Densities and Optimal City Size," *Journal of Regional Science*, vol. 14, 233-246.
                 245211121

*Fisch, O., 1975a. "Externalities, the Urban Rent and Population Density Functions: The Case of Air Pollution," *Journal of Environmental Economics and Management*, vol. 2.

*Fisch, O., 1975b. "Optimal City Size, Land Tenure and the Economic Theory of Clubs," *Journal of Regional and Urban Economics*, forthcoming.

*Fisch, O., 1975c. "Spatial Equilibrium with Local Public Goods: Urban Land Rent, Optimal City Size, and the Tiebout Hypothesis." Ch. 11 of this volume.

298

Forsund, F.R., 1972. "Allocation in Space and Environmental Pollution," *The Swedish Journal of Economics*, vol. 74, 19-35.   243114311

*Gannon, C.A., 1973. "Intraurban Industrial Location and Interestablishment Linkages," *Geographical Analysis*, vol. 5, 214-244.

*Goldberg, V.P., and K.M. Krtesel, 1971. *Urban Form and the Allocation of Land to Streets*. Research Report 22, Institute of Governmental Affairs, University of California, Davis.

Goldstein, G.S., and L.N. Moses, 1973. "A Survey of Urban Economics," *Journal of Economic Literature*, vol. 11, 471-495.   214638434

*Goldstein, G.S., and L.N. Moses, 1975. "Interdependence and the Location of Economic Activities," *Journal of Urban Economics*, vol. 2, 63-84.

*Harris, B., 1975. "Notes on the Relation Between Mathematical Land Use Theory and Public Policy Applications." Ch. 1 of this volume.

Harris B., et al., 1966. *Research on an Equilibrium Model of Metropolitan Housing and Locational Choice*. Interim report, University of Pennsylvania, Philadelphia.   461125311

Hartwick, J.M., 1974. "Price Sustainability of Location Assignments," *Journal of Urban Economics*, vol. 2, 147-161.   255228411

*Hartwick, J.M.; U. Schweizer; and P. Varaiya, 1975. "Comparative Statics of a Residential Economy with Several Classes," Ch. 4 of this volume.

Hartwick, P.G., and J.M. Hartwick, 1974. "Efficient Resource Allocation in a Multinucleated City with Intermediate Goods," *Quarterly Journal of Economics*, vol. 88, 340-352.   255224311

*Henderson, J.V., 1974a. "Optimum City Size: The External Diseconomy Question," *Journal of Political Economy*, vol. 82, 373-388.

*Henderson, J.V., 1974b. "The Sizes and Types of Cities," *American Economic Review*, vol. 64, 640-656.

*Henderson, J.V., 1975. "Congestion and the Optimum City Size," *Journal of Urban Economics*, vol. 2, 48-62.

Herbert, J., and B. Stevens, 1960. "A Model for the Distribution of Residential Activity in Urban Areas," *Journal of Regional Science*, vol. 2, 21-36.   241125311

Hochman, O., and D. Pines, 1971. "Competitive Equilibrium of Transportation and Housing in the Residential Ring of an Urban Area," *Environment and Planning*, vol. 3, 51-62.   313413421

Hochman, O., and D. Pines, 1972. "Note on Land Use in a Long Narrow City," *Journal of Economic Theory*, vol. 5, 540-541.   213113421

*Hochman, O., and D. Pines, 1973. *Dynamic Aspects of Land Use Pattern in a Growing City*. Working Paper No. 17, Center for Urban and Regional Studies, Tel Aviv University.

*Kanemoto, Y., 1973. "Congestion and Cost-Benefit Analysis in Cities." Manuscript.

*Kanemoto, Y., 1974a. "A Note on a Concealed Nonconvexity in Urban Residential Models." Manuscript.

*Kanemoto, Y., 1974b. "Optimum, Market and Second Best Land Use Patterns in a von Thünen City with Congestion." Manuscript.

*Kirwan, R.S., and M.J. Ball, 1974. "The Microeconomic Analysis of a Local Housing Market," *Papers from the Urban Economics Conference, 1973*, vol. 1. London: CES CP9. Pp. 113-199.

Kraus, M., 1974. "Land Use in a Circular City," *Journal of Economic Theory*, vol. 8, 440-457.   245213421

Lave, L., 1970. "Congestion and Urban Location," *Papers and Proceedings of the Regional Science Association*, vol. 25, 133-150. 241112121

*Lave, L., 1974. "Urban Externalities," *Papers from the Urban Economics Conference 1973*, vol. 1. London: CES CP9. Pp. 37-95.

Lee, D.B., and C.P. Averous, 1973. "Land Use and Transportation: Basic Theory," *Environment and Planning*, vol. 5, 491-502.   244122121

Legey, L; M. Ripper; and P. Varaiya, 1973. "Effects of Congestion on the Shape of a City," *Journal of Economic Theory*, vol. 6, 162-179.
                                                                          244212221

Levhari, D.; Y. Oron; and D. Pines, 1972. *In Favor of Lottery in Cases of Non-Convexities*. Working Paper 10, Center for Urban Studies, Tel Aviv University.   423218424

Lind, R.C., 1973. "Spatial Equilibrium, the Theory of Rents and Public Program Benefits," *Quarterly Journal of Economics*, vol. 87, 188-207.
                                                                          234132111

Livesey, D.A., 1973. "Optimum City Size: A Minimum Congestion Cost Approach," *Journal of Economic Theory*, vol. 6, 144-161. 244411121

*Livesey, D.A., 1975. "Optimum and Market Land Rents in the CBD City." Ch. 13 of this volume.

*Long, W.H., 1971. "Demand in Space: Some Neglected Aspects," *Papers and Proceedings of the Regional Science Association*, vol. 2, 54-60.

Mackinnon, J., 1974. Urban General Equilibrium Models and Simplicial Search Algorithms," *Journal of Urban Economics*, vol. 1, 161-184.
                                                                          255112111

*Mieszkowski, P., 1972. "The Property Tax: An Excise Tax or a Profits Tax?" *Journal of Public Economics*, vol. 1, 73-96.

Mills, E.S., 1967. "An Aggregative Model of Resource Allocation in a Metropolitan Area," *American Economic Review*, vol. 57, 197-210.
241121321

Mills, E.S., 1969. "The Value of Urban Land." In H.S. Perloff (ed.), *The Quality of the Urban Environment*. Baltimore: Johns Hopkins. Pp. 231-253.
221128434

Mills, E.S., 1970. "The Efficiency of Spatial Competition," *Papers and Proceedings of the Regional Science Association*, vol. 25, 71-82.
241224121

Mills, E.S., 1972a. "Markets and Efficient Resource Allocation in Urban Areas." *The Swedish Journal of Economics*, vol. 74, 100-113.
243211311

Mills, E.S., 1972b. *Studies in the Structure of the Urban Economy*. Baltimore: Johns Hopkins.
153111321

Mills, E.S., 1972c. *Urban Economics*. Oakland: Scott, Foresman.
123611321

Mills, E.S., 1974. "Mathematical Models for Urban Planning." Manuscript.
455211311

Mills, E.S., and D.M. deFerranti, 1971. "Market Choices and Optimum City Size," *American Economic Review, Papers and Proceedings*, vol. 61, 340-345.
242412121

Mills, E.S., and J. Mackinnon, 1973. "Notes on the New Urban Economics," *Bell Journal of Economics and Management Science*, vol. 4, 593-601.
214638434

*Miron, J.R., 1975. "City Size and Land Rents in a Closed Model of Urban Spatial Structure." Ch. 5 of this volume.

Mirrlees, J.A., 1972. "The Optimum Town," *The Swedish Journal of Economics*, vol. 74, 114-135.
233212121

Mirrlees, J.A., 1973. "Rejoinder to Richardson—2," *Urban Studies*, vol. 10, 271.
300000000

*Miyao, T., 1974. *Dynamic and Comparative Statics in the Theory of Residential Location*. Working Paper 7411, Institute for the Quantitative Analysis of Social and Economic Policy, University of Toronto.

*Mogridge, M.J.H., 1974. "Some Thoughts on the Economics of Intraurban Spatial Location of Homes, Worker-Residences and Workplaces," *Papers from the Urban Economics Conference, 1973*, vol. 1. London: CES CP9. Pp. 247-301.

Mohring, H., and M. Harwitz, 1962. *Highway Benefits: An Analytical Framework*. Evanston: Northwestern University Press.
121111121

Montesano, A., 1972. "A Restatement of Beckmann's Model of Urban Rent and Residential Density," *Journal of Economic Theory*, vol. 4, 329-354.
241125121

*Moses, L.N., 1962. "Towards a Theory of Intra-Urban Wage Differentials and Their Influence on Travel Patterns," *Papers and Proceedings of the Regional Science Association*, vol. 9, 53-63.

*Moses, L.N., and H.F. Williamson, Jr., 1967. "The Location of Economic Activity in Cities," *American Economic Review*, vol. 57, 211-238.

*Mullally, H., 1975. *General Equilibrium in a Spatial Economy*. Ph.D. dissertation. Hamilton: McMaster University.

*Mullally, H., and G.J. Papageorgiou, 1975. "Consumer Preferences and Urban Spatial Structure." Paper presented at the Annual Meeting of the Association of American Geographers, Milwaukee.

Muth, R.F., 1960. "The Demand for Nonfarm Housing." In Harberger (ed.), *Demand for Durable Goods*. Chicago: University of Chicago Press. Pp. 29-96.   221335331

Muth, R.F., 1961a. "Economic Change and Urban Rural Land Conversions," *Econometrica*, vol. 29, 1-23.   311125321

Muth, R.F., 1961b. "The Spatial Structure of the Housing Market," *Papers and Proceedings of the Regional Science Association*, vol. 7, 207-220.   221125321

Muth, R.F., 1967. "Comment on Moses and Williamson," *American Economic Review*, vol. 57, 239-241.   311338434

Muth, R.F., 1968. "Urban Residential Land and Housing Markets." In H.S. Perloff and L. Wingo (eds.), *Issues in Urban Economics*. Baltimore: Johns Hopkins. Pp. 285-333.   211135321

Muth, R.F., 1969. *Cities and Housing*. Chicago: University of Chicago Press.   131125221

*Muth, R.F., 1971. "The Derived Demand for Urban Residential Land," *Urban Studies*, vol. 8, 243-254.

*Muth, R.F., 1973a. "Capital and Current Expenditures in the Production of Housing." In C.L. Harris (ed.), *Government Spending and Land Values*. Madison: The University of Wisconsin Press. Pp. 65-78.

*Muth, R.F., 1973b. "A Vintage Model of the Housing Stock," *Papers and Proceedings of the Regional Science Association*, vol. 30, 141-156.

Muth, R.F., 1974. "Moving Costs and Housing Expenditires," *Journal of Urban Economics*, vol. 1, 108-125.   235215222

*Muth, R.F., 1975a. "The Numerical Solution of Urban Residential Land-Use Models," *Journal of Urban Economics*, forthcoming.

*Muth, R.F., 1975b. "A Vintage Model with Housing Production." Ch. 15 of this volume.

Nelson, R.H., 1971. *The Theory of Residential Location*. Ph.D. dissertation. Princeton: Princeton University.   532125121

*Nelson, R.H., 1972. "Housing Facilities, Site Advantages and Rent," *Journal of Regional Science*, vol. 12, 249-259.

Nelson, R.H., 1973. "Accessibility and Rent: Applying Becker's 'Time Price' Concept to the Theory of Residential Location," *Urban Studies*, vol. 10, 83-86.   234125121

*Niedercorn, J.H., 1971. "A Negative Exponential Model of Urban Land Use Densities and Its Implications for Metropolitan Development," *Journal of Regional Science*, vol. 11, 317-326.

*Oates, W.E.; E.P. Howrey; and W.J. Baumol, 1971. "The Analysis of Public Policy in Dynamic Urban Models," *Journal of Political Economy*, vol. 79, 142-153.

*Ohls, J.C., 1974. "Filtering in Housing Markets." Manuscript.

*Ohls, J.C., and D. Pines, 1975. "Discontinuous Urban Development and Economic Efficiency," *Land Economics*, forthcoming.

*Ohls, J.C.; R.C. Weisberg; and M.J. White, 1974. "The Effects of Zoning and Land Value," *Journal of Urban Economics*, vol. 1, 428-444.

*Olsen, E.O., 1969. "A Competitive Theory of the Housing Market," *American Economic Review*, vol. 54, 612-621.

*Oron, Y., 1972. *Optimal Resource Allocation Versus Competitive Resource Allocations in a Mono-Center Urban Form*. Ph.D. dissertation. Tel Aviv: Tel Aviv University.

*Oron, Y., and D. Pines, 1972. "The Effect of Efficient Pricing of Air Pollution on Intra-Urban Land Use Pattern." Manuscript.

Oron, Y.; D. Pines; and E. Sheshinski, 1973. "Optimum vs. Equilibrium Land Use Pattern and Congestion Toll," *Bell Journal of Economics and Management Science*, vol. 4, 619-707.   254211321

Oron, Y.; D. Pines; and E. Sheshinski, 1974. "The Effect of Nuisances Associated with Urban Traffic on Suburbanization and Land Values," *Journal of Urban Economics*, vol. 1, 382-394.   245212121

Papageorgiou, G.J., 1971a. "A Generalization of the Density Gradient Concept," *Geographical Analysis*, vol. 3, 121-127.   242125121

Papageorgiou, G.J., 1971b. "The Population Density and Rent Distribution Model within a Multicentre Framework," *Environment and Planning*, vol. 3, 267-282.   242125121

Papageorgiou, G.J., 1971c. "A Theoretical Evaluation of the Existing Population Density Gradient Functions," *Economic Geography*, vol. 47, 21-26.   222125121

*Papageorgiou, G.J., 1972. "Population Density and Quality of the Environment," *Papers of the 22nd International Geographical Congress*, Montreal. Pp. 921-922.

Papageorgiou, G.J., 1973a. "The Impact of the Environment Upon the Spatial Distribution of Population and Land Values," *Economic Geography*, vol. 49, 251-256.   444125121

*Papageorgiou, G.J., 1973b. "Spatial Equilibrium within a Hierarchy of Centers with Distributed Incomes." Papers presented at the Thirteenth European Congress of the Regional Science Association, Vienna.

*Papageorgiou, G.J., 1975. "Spatial Consumer Equilibrium." Ch. 10 of this volume.

Papageorgiou, G.J., and E. Casetti, 1971. "Spatial Equilibrium Residential Land Values in a Multicentre Setting," *Journal of Regional Science*, vol. 11, 385-389.   242125121

*Papageorgiou, G.J., and H. Mullally, 1975. *Urban Residential Structure*. Discussion Paper 3, Department of Geography, McMaster University.

Pines, D., 1970a. "The Exponential Density Function. A Comment," *Journal of Regional Science*, vol. 10, 107-110.   241125121

*Pines, D., 1970b. *Urban Sprawl and Resource Allocation: An Additional Case for Scatteration*. Working Paper No. 2, Center for Urban and Regional Studies, Tel Aviv University.

Pines, D., 1972. "The Equilibrium Utility Level and City Size: A Comment," *Economic Geography*, vol. 48, 439-443.   242125121

Pines, D., 1974. "A Note on the Relationship Between Public Programs Benefits and Its Effects on Equilibrium Rent." Manuscript.

444122121

*Pines, D., 1975a. "Dynamic Aspects of Land Use Patterns in a Growing City." Ch. 14 of this volume.

Pines, D., 1975b. "On the Spatial Distribution of Households According to Income," *Economic Geography*, vol. 51, 142-149.   435125221

Pines, D., and Y. Weiss, 1975. "Land Improvement Projects and Land Values." Manuscript.   436115121

*Polinski, A.M., and D. Rubinfeld, 1974. "The Long-Run Incidence of a Residential Property Tax and Local Public Services." Manuscript.

*Polinski, A.M., and S. Shavell, 1972. *Air Pollution and Property Values in a General Equilibrium Model of an Urban Area*. Working Paper No. 1207-5, The Urban Institute, Washington, D.C.

*Ratford, B.E., 1973. "A Note on Niedercorn's Negative Exponential Model of Urban Land Use," *Journal of Regional Science*, vol. 13, 135-138.

Richardson, H.W., 1973. "A Comment on Some Uses of Mathematical Models in Urban Economics," *Urban Studies*, vol. 10, 259-270.

214611121

*Richardson, H.W., 1975a. "On the Possibility of Positive Rent Gradients," *Journal of Urban Economics*, forthcoming.

*Richardson, H.W., 1975b. "Relevance of Mathematical Land Use Theory to Applications." Ch. 2 of this volume.

*Richardson, H.W.; M.J. Vipond; and R.A. Furbey, 1974. "The Determinants of Urban House Prices," *Urban Studies*, vol. 11, 190-199.

*Ridker, R.G., and J.A. Henning, 1967. "The Determinants of Residential Property Values with Special Reference to Air Pollution," *Review of Economics and Statistics*, vol. 49, 246-257.

Riley, J.G., 1972. *Optimal Towns*. Ph.D. dissertation. Cambridge: Massachusetts Institute of Technology.   543511121

Riley, J.G., 1973. "Gammaville. An Optimum Town," *Journal of Economic Theory*, vol. 6, 471-482.   244524121

Riley, J.G., 1974. "Optimal Residential Density and Road Transportation," *Journal of Urban Economics*, vol. 1, 230-250.   235511121

*Ripper, M., and P. Varaiya, 1974. "An Optimizing Model of Urban Development," *Environment and Planning*, vol. 6, 149-168.

*Rose-Ackerman, S., 1974. "On the Use of Urban Economics in CostBenefit Analysis." Manuscript.

*Rose-Ackerman, S., 1975. "Racism and Urban Structure," *Journal of Urban Economics*, vol. 2, 85-103.

Rothenberg, J., 1973. "Discussion on 'Congestion and the Optimum City Size'," *American Economics Review, Papers and Proceedings*, vol. 63, 67-70.   214638434

*Schuler, R.E., 1974a. "The Interaction Between Local Government and Urban Residential Location," *American Economic Review*, vol. 64, 682-696.

*Schuler, R.E., 1974b. *Spatial Equilibrium Models of Urban Residential Location—Varying Household Tastes and Model Misspecification*. Working Paper 77, Department of Economics, Cornell University.

*Senior, M.L., 1974. "Approaches to Residential Location Modelling 2: Urban Economic Models and Some Recent Developments (A Review)," *Environment and Planning*, vol. 6, 369-409.

Sheshinski, E., 1973. "Congestion and Optimum City Size," *American Economic Review, Papers and Proceedings*, vol. 63, 61-66.
                                    244111210

Solow, R.M., 1972. "Congestion, Density and the Use of Land in Transportation," *The Swedish Journal of Economics*, vol. 74, 161-173.
                                    243112121

Solow, R.M., 1973a. "Congestion Cost and the Use of Land for Streets,"

Bell Journal of Economics and Management Science, vol. 4, 602-618.
244112121

Solow, R.M., 1973b. "On Equilibrium Models of Urban Locations." In J.M. Parkin (ed.), *Essays in Modern Economics*. London: Longmans. Pp. 2-16.
244121121

Solow, R.M., 1973c. "Rejoinder to Richardson—1," *Urban Studies*, vol. 10, 271.
314638434

Solow, R.M., and W.S. Vickrey, 1971. "Land Use in a Long Narrow City," *Journal of Economic Theory*, vol. 3, 430-447.

Starrett, D.A., 1972. *On the Optimal Degree of Increasing Returns*. Discussion Paper 230, Institute of Economic Research, Harvard University.
433211121

Starrett, D.A., 1974. "Principles of Optimal Location in a Large Homogeneous Area," *Journal of Economic Theory*, vol. 9, 418-448.
434211121

Stern, N.H., 1972. "The Optimal Size of Market Areas," *Journal of Economic Theory*, vol. 4, 154-173.
233236421

Stern, N.H., 1973. "Homogeneous Utility Functions and Equality in 'The Optimum Town'," *The Swedish Journal of Economics*, vol. 75, 204-207.
234515121

Strotz, R.H., 1965. "Urban Transportation Parables." In J. Margolis (ed.), *The Public Economy of Urban Communities*. Baltimore: Johns Hopkins. Pp. 127-169.
231511121

*Strotz, R.H., 1968. "The Use of Land Rent Changes to Measure the Welfare Benefits of Land Improvements." In Haring (ed.), *The New Economics of Regulated Industries*. Los Angeles: Economic Research Center, Occidental College.

Stucker, J.P., 1973. *Transport Improvements, Commuting Costs, and Residential Location*. Santa Monica: RAND Corporation. 434122121

*Stull, W., 1972. *An Essay on Externalities, Property Values, and Urban Zoning*. Ph.D. dissertation. Cambridge: Massachusetts Institute of Technology.

Stull, W., 1973. "A Note on Residential Bid Price Curves," *Journal of Regional Science*, vol. 13, 107-113.
244125121

Stull, W., 1974. "Land Use and Zoning in an Urban Economy," *American Economic Review*, vol. 64, 337-347.
235134121

*Southey, C., 1974. "Spatial Rents, Spatial Competition, and Efficiency," *Canadian Journal of Economics*, vol. 7, 260-272.

*Sweeney, J.L., 1971. *A Dynamic Theory of the Housing Market*. Ph.D. dissertation. Stanford: Stanford University.

Sweeney, J.L., 1974. "A Commodity Hierarchy Model of the Rental Housing Market," *Journal of Urban Economics*, vol. 1, 288-234.
225132511

*Sweeney, J.L., 1975. "Quality, Commodity Hierarchies, and Housing Markets," *Econometrica*, forthcoming.

Tolley, G.S., 1974. "The Welfare Economics of City Bigness," *Journal of Urban Economics*, vol. 1, 324-346.
245124821

Varaiya, P., and R. Artle, 1972. "Locational Implications of Transaction Costs," *The Swedish Journal of Economics*, vol. 74, 174-183.
243125121

*Vickrey, W., 1965. "Pricing as a Tool in Coordination of Local Transportation." In J. Meyer (ed.), *Transportation Economics*. New York: National Bureau of Economic Research.

*Wabe, J.S., 1971. "A Study of House Prices as a Means of Establishing the Value of Journey Time, the Rate of Time Preference and the Valuation of Some Aspects of Environment in the London Metropolitan Region," *Applied Economics*, vol. 3, 247-256.

Webber, M.J., 1973. "Equilibrium of Location in an Isolated State," *Environment and Planning*, vol. 5, 751-759.
244121121

Wheaton, W.C., 1972. *Income and Urban Location*. Ph.D. dissertation. Philadelphia: University of Pennsylvania.
563125311

Wheaton, W.C., 1974a. "A Comparative Static Analysis of Urban Spatial Structure," *Journal of Economic Theory*, vol. 9, 223-237. 235125121

Wheaton, W.C., 1974b. "Linear Programming and Locational Equilibrium: The Herbert-Stevens Model Revisited," *Journal of Urban Economics*, vol. 1, 278-288.
245125311

*White, L.J. and M.J. White, 1974. "The Tax Subsidy to Owner-Occupied Housing: Who Really Benefits?" Manuscript.

*White, M.J., 1975. "The Effects of Zoning on the Size of Metropolitan Areas." Manuscript.

*Wilkinson, R.K., 1972. *The Determinants of Relative House Prices*. London: CES CP, Center for Environmental Studies.

Wingo, L., Jr., 1961a. "An Economic Model of the Utilization of Urban Land for Residential Purposes," *Papers and Proceedings of the Regional Science Association*, vol. 7, 191-205.
231122121

Wingo, L., Jr., 1961b. *Transportation and Urban Land*. Washington, D.C.: Resources for the Future.
141122121

Wright, C., 1971. "Residential Location in a Three Dimensional City," *Journal of Political Economy*, vol. 79, 1378-1387.
242125121

Yamada, H., 1972. "On the Theory of Residential Location: Accessibility, Space, Leisure and Environmental Quality," *Papers and Proceedings of the Regional Science Association*, vol. 29, 125-135.   233121521

Yellin, J., 1974. "Urban Population Distribution, Family Income and Social Prejudice," *Journal of Urban Economics*, vol. 1, 21-48.

235116321

About the Editor

George J. Papageorgiou received his diploma in Architecture from the National Technical University of Athens, Greece, in 1959. After a brief period of private practice, he studied Ekistics at the Athens Technological Organization between 1963-1965. His work gradually shifted from the small scale to the large, from the concrete to the abstract, and from application to analysis. In 1966, he came to the Ohio State University where he received the M.C.P. in 1967 and the Ph.D. in Geography in 1970.

Related Lexington Books

Conroy, Michael E., *The Challenge of Urban Economic Development: Alternative Goals for the Economic Structure of Cities*, 144 pp., 1975

Grieson, Ronald E., editor, *Urban Economics and Public Finance: Essays in Honor of William S. Vickery*, In Press

Harris, Curtis, C., Jr., *Locational Analysis: An Interregional Econometric Model*, 320 pp., 1972

Richardson, Harry W., *Housing and Urban Spatial Structure: A Case Study*, In Press

Rust, Edgar, *No Growth: Impact on Metropolitan Areas*, In Press

Struyk, Raymond, J., *Urban Home Ownership: The Economic Determinants*, In Press

Wheat, Leonard F., *Regional Growth and Industrial Location*, 240 pp., 1973